MW00809754

Many red devils ran from my heart
And out upon the page.
They were so tiny
The pen could mash them.
And many struggled in the ink.
It was strange
To write in this red muck
Of things from my heart.

– Stephen Crane

GHOSTS AND BALLYHOO
MEMOIRS OF A FAILED L.A. MUSIC JOURNALIST

THOMAS WICTOR

4880 Lower Valley Road • Atglen, PA 19310

All photos from the author's collection unless otherwise credited.
All poetry by Stephen Crane unless otherwise credited.

Permissions

Excerpts of "Interviewing Bassist Stories" on Talkbass.com, copyright © 2012. Talk Music Group Inc. All rights reserved. Reprinted with permission.

Lyrics of "God Only Guards the Tool Shed" by Stephen Jay, copyright © 2012. Ayarou Music (BMI). All rights reserved. Reprinted with permission.

Lyrics of "Trouble" by Stephen Jay, copyright © 1997. Ayarou Music (BMI). All rights reserved. Reprinted with permission.

Photo of Anne Kadrovich by Al Seib, copyright © 1997. Los Angeles Times. Reprinted with permission.

Review of *In Cold Sweat: Interviews with Really Scary Musicians* by Ben Watson, copyright © 2001. *The Wire* Magazine. All rights reserved. Reprinted with permission.

Acknowledgements

Without direct help or inspiration from the following, this book would not have been possible. I owe them all a debt I can't repay, except to try and be the best person I can.

Daniel Barrett; Bryan Beller; Bob Biondi; Joe Cady; Karl Coryat; Stephen Crane; Paul Determan; Leslie Ditto; Steiv Dixon; Brian Fox; David Fuerst, M.D.; Carmen; Carrie Gonzales; Ventsilav Gramatki; Stephen Jay; Anne Kadrovich; Mike Keneally; Chris Maury; Róisín Murphy; Bac Nguyen, M.D.; Matt Resnicoff; Martin Richardson; Jim Roberts; Alfredo Saddun, M.D.; Dr. Rolf Schamberger; Pete Schiffer; Gene Simmons; Ray Shulman; Jason S. Sitzes; Curt Smith; Syd the Second; Mikhail Vasilyevich Supotnitskiy, M.D.; Talkbass.com; John Taylor; Georgia Thunes; Scott Thunes; Kenneth Tye, M.D.; Suzanne Vega; Ben Watson; Andy West; Tim Wictor; Mel Zerman; and Neil Zlozower.

And thanks to Tracy Brett, Jeff Consntantine, Dan Garneau, Martin Gallagher, Eric Jones, Mike Kocik, Mark McCann, Tom Pickel, David Rae, Brittany Rich, and David Sierra for their good eyes.

For Carmen and Scott.

Cover design by Tim Wictor.
Book design by Robert Biondi.

Copyright © 2013 by Thomas Wictor.
Library of Congress Catalog Number: 2012954931.

All rights reserved. No part of this work may be reproduced or used in any forms or by any means – graphic, electronic or mechanical, including photocopying or information storage and retrieval systems – without written permission from the publisher.

The scanning, uploading and distribution of this book or any part thereof via the Internet or via any other means without the permission of the publisher is illegal and punishable by law. Please purchase only authorized editions and do not participate in or encourage the electronic piracy of copyrighted materials.

"Schiffer," "Schiffer Publishing Ltd. & Design," and the "Design of pen and ink well" are registered trademarks of Schiffer Publishing, Ltd.

Printed in the United States of America.
ISBN: 978-0-7643-4338-4

We are always looking for people to write books on new and related subjects. If you have an idea for a book, please contact us at the address below.

Published by Schiffer Publishing Ltd.
4880 Lower Valley Road
Atglen, PA 19310
Phone: (610) 593-1777
FAX: (610) 593-2002
E-mail: Info@schifferbooks.com.
Visit our web site at: www.schifferbooks.com
Please write for a free catalog.
This book may be purchased from the publisher.
Please include $5.00 postage.
Try your bookstore first.

In Europe, Schiffer books are distributed by:
Bushwood Books
6 Marksbury Ave.
Kew Gardens, Surrey TW9 4JF
England
Phone: 44 (0)20 8392-8585
FAX: 44 (0)20 8392-9876
E-mail: info@bushwoodbooks.co.uk
www.bushwoodbooks.co.uk
Free postage in the UK. Europe: air mail at cost.
Try your bookstore first.

Contents

Introduction

I was the most haunted person you could ever meet. Places, books, movies, animals, occurrences, sounds, and smells left me shivering, sometimes for years. Mostly, though, people and music haunted me. I've recently come to realize the inevitability of my becoming a music journalist despite my stutter, my lack of musical training, and my difficulties interacting with people. My lifelong pattern has been to pursue that which has haunted me. I say "has been" because I may – *may* – have finally changed my ways. Time will tell.

This memoir is about my ten years as a music journalist in Los Angeles, my obsessive quest to "help" one of the finest musicians I've ever met, and my inability to move beyond a failed relationship with a woman I'll call Carmen, a musician herself. The remarkable way in which this memoir came about has determined the form it takes, which is seven anthologies of short stories by me, and six interludes of words spoken by former Frank Zappa bassist Scott Thunes (pronounced TOO-niss), my central musical ghost. I first interviewed him in 1996 and wrote an article about him for *Bass Player*, titled "Requiem for a Heavyweight?" It was this article and the interview I conducted with bassist Gene Simmons of Kiss, published in *Bass Player* as "Call Him Doctor Love," that convinced me I had a permanent place in the world of music journalism. As you will see, those two interviews actually signed my death warrant in the field.

Since I've already written extensively about Thunes and Simmons in my first book *In Cold Sweat: Interviews with Really Scary Musicians* [Limelight Editions, 2001], this memoir will touch only peripherally on the experience of sitting down with them in 1996. Simmons haunted me almost as much as Scott Thunes, but as with virtually all of the musicians I interviewed in my career, there was no question of further engagement with him after our initial interaction. It was just business. A few were different. John Taylor of Duran Duran, Stephen Jay of the "Weird Al" Yankovic band, and Bryan Beller of far too many projects to mention (This is *my* memoir, Bryan! *Mine!* Write your own!) come to mind. But for some reason Scott Thunes and I had a much longer, much more personal relationship until I ended it in 2003, when I resigned from music journalism and cut off all contact with people connected to the decade-long debacle I'd engineered for myself.

What haunted me most about Scott Thunes was that *he'd* resigned from music years before I did, an absolute tragedy in my mind. Bass was my chosen instrument; when listening to music, I always heard the bass first and foremost. There is no bassist like Scott Thunes. His is an entirely original voice that relies on no obvious influences. He is unique in his ability to express emotion on his instrument, particularly when performing live with other musicians. Rather than play bass lines, Scott *accompanies* his band mates in the traditional sense, improvising flourishes and ornamentation that propel the players into a much higher, much more passionate level of musicianship. It's a remarkable skill, and it tore out my heart that he had given it up.

Despite my genuine liking of Thunes and my admiration for his talent, perceptive readers will probably be able to work out for themselves another reason I was obsessed with helping him. There's no need for me to spell it out. Instead, I'll let everything just sort of unfold. Since Thunes haunted me almost as much as my long-departed Carmen, I've decided to include long passages of his own words, the majority of which are taken from an unpublished interview I conducted with him in 1997. Thunes's story is central to mine, but not for the reasons I originally thought.

It was extremely difficult for me to reconstruct the timeline of my stint at *Bass Player* because I'd deleted all my e-mails from the magazine and Miller Freeman had canceled my free subscription in 2002. I haven't read the magazine in over ten years. Some of the dates I give of events may not be completely accurate. Who cares, though?

This is a strange book, the strangeness of which is as inevitable as both my career in music journalism and its demise. I'm a strange person, and the way the book came to be is one of the strangest episodes I've ever witnessed. I happen to be a believer in both destiny and free will. Maybe I'll write about that someday. For now, I present these anthologies and interludes of hauntings, of what to do and not to do, and of how to be and not to be.

One of my favorite painters is Otto Dix, a veteran of World War I. His images are truly the most disgusting, horrific, unflinching portrayals of war ever created. Critics couldn't understand why he produced such art. Dix's answer has stuck with me ever since I read it over twenty years ago: "Painting is an act of banishment." I *had* to write this book. Readers should know I wrote it entirely without malice, except for a handful of sentences that are very malicious toward two people. Since I earned the right to be momentarily malicious, I don't apologize. On the whole, this memoir was written so that I could come to terms, bear witness, and entertain you, but mostly it was a way for me to banish.

Thomas Wictor
August 2012
Los Angeles

Anthology One
Prelude to Essence
1962-1985

If there is witness to my little life,
To my tiny throes and struggles,
He sees a fool;
And it is not fine for gods to menace fools.

The Future Tastes like Soap

I have five brothers and one sister. My oldest brother Tim was a singer; my younger brother Pat is a professional singer-songwriter-guitarist who plays on the folk circuit; and my youngest brother Eric was a bassist. Dad was forced to play clarinet in school, and Mom was something of a music prodigy on the piano, although she gave it up early. My older brother Paul and my sister Carrie are music fans who never played instruments themselves. Paul bought an electric guitar in college, but mostly it just leaned against the wall.

My siblings and I were born in Venezuela. Our father – an executive at Creole Petroleum Corporation – owned the only record player in our house. He used it for his collection of Mitch Miller albums, Viennese waltzes, British parlor music, Sousa marches, ragtime, Irving Berlin, and operettas such as *The Red Mill*. That's what most music was to me. Because I spent my first ten years in Venezuela, I missed the sixties' rock culture. By the time I was about seven, I was vaguely aware of older kids getting into trouble when they were shipped off to the States after eighth grade, which was what happened in our oil camp. You finished eighth grade, went to the States to attend high school, and came back with "drug problems" and long hair. We all had crew cuts in my family. Except for my sister and mother.

To me, drugs meant medicine. The older kids with their scary long hair talked to each other about music and drugs, and I imagined them playing ragtime with banjos and tinkling pianos while drinking cherry-flavored cough syrup and taking aspirin. I didn't want to ever move to the States. It seemed like a terrifying place where inexplicable things happened to you. We'd visit my sweet maternal grandmother in Los Angeles and go to Miami every now and then on summer vacation, but I wanted to live out my life in Campo Verde, Tia Juana, safe from long hair and drugs.

Aside from Dad's music, I was inundated with gaita, Venezuelan folk music from the state of Zulia. Most gaitas originated in Maracaibo. They're churning, percussive carnival rides that have a characteristic *one-two-three, one-two-three, one-two-three, one-two-three* beat weaving through them. The instruments used – some descended from African imports – include the furro (a friction drum), the tambora (a two-headed drum tuned with ropes), maracas, the charrasca (a steel tube with slots cut in it and scraped with a metal rod), and the ubiquitous four-stringed cuatro. Joselo and Simón Díaz recorded comic gaitas by Venezuela's most famous pop composer, Hugo Blanco, whose "Moliendo Café" was played everywhere we went. I found Simón Díaz's nasal cretin-voice embarrassing and his humor incomprehensible, but I laughed at his gaitas because all the adults around me did. I figured they knew something I didn't.

Another song I remember was "Gaita y Trompetas," by Trío Venezuela, which may have contributed to my lifelong love of the trumpet. Gaita was usually in the background at our house, issuing from the TV, occasionally the record player, and usually the radio. Our Venezuelan maids lived for it. We also had a copy of Herb Alpert and the Tijuana Brass's *Whipped Cream and Other Delights,* with the naked lady on the cover blanketed in foamy, white goodness. "A Taste of Honey" was my favorite track. I listened to it countless times when Dad was at work. It took me places in my mind; somehow it was the sound of travel, adulthood, and a wonderful future hopefully filled with naked ladies giving me inviting looks. About the only other pop song that has stayed with me from my Venezuelan period is Miriam Makeba's "Pata Pata," a smash hit. I mimicked the lyrics, which were in the Bantu language of Xhosa. In Spanish, *pata* means either foot or female duck, so as I sang along I pictured a duck with false eyelashes, lipstick, and giant webbed feet, stomping around in a snit.

If "Gaita y Trompetas" and Herb Alpert actuated in me a nascent affinity for the trumpet, haircuts are responsible for my indestructible horror of the accordion. My father took my three brothers and me to a barber shop run by Italians who used what we called a "mouse" to buzz our heads flat. We had to sit on a board laid across the arms of the chair, a humiliating strip of toilet paper wrapped around our necks before the cape was draped over us. After the sixty-second shearing, they brought out the straight razor, grinningly sharpened it on the leather strop that they somehow conveyed they wanted to whip across our rear ends just for fun, roughly forced down our heads with rock-hard hands, and scraped our napes, sometimes drawing blood. Then the talcum powder, applied to our razored flesh with a brush that produced a choking cloud of baby-smell. Off came the cape, and before they let us down they gave us a brutal, twisting cheek pinch that we could feel like a face slap for hours afterward. The whole time, accordion music was excreted from the sound system. "Guaglione." "Santa Lucia." And the mother of all accordion atrocities, "Tarantella Napoletana."

It was older, music-loving kids who were responsible for getting my brother Paul in terrible trouble. Though to me these impossibly mature people were indistinguishable from grownups, in reality they were only twelve or thirteen. They liked to wreak havoc with elementary schoolers; in our oil camp everyone knew each other, and parents would often call you inside to offer you a freshly baked cookie or brownie if they saw you walking by. When I was about six I was invited into somebody's home for a peanut-butter cookie, my favorite. For some reason the fork marks really comforted me. Cookie in hand, I went to the son's room, where he lay sprawled on his bed talking to three or four friends. He was in eighth grade.

There was a big, red, freaky, plastic potato with a demented, bug-eyed leer lying on the floor. It looked childlike, a hideous Dr. Moreau boy-tuber hybrid. *Spudsie* was written on it in white letters.

"What's *that?*" I asked.

"That's the Hot Potato," the eighth grader said.

"What's it for?"

"It's a game. You wind it up and toss it around to each other before the timer goes off."

"What happens when the timer goes off?"

"It blows up the whole house. Here, let's give it a try."

He leaned over to pick it up.

"*No!*" I screamed and ran home as fast as I could. I've always believed what people tell me. It made perfect sense for parents to give their kids toys that would explode and kill everybody in the family. In our oil camp, Mr. Gordy had elves living in his barbecue, and if you caught one it'd say, "Okay, what do you want?" and build whatever toy you described; there was a giant, bipedal, child-eating monster in the jungle surrounding us; and Mrs. Der Garry told me that every weekend Venezuelans went out to the golf course, stood in a big circle, and shot each other with pistols until everybody was dead.

The eighth grader with the deadly Hot Potato taught Paul a song that I didn't understand. Paul – who was seven – came into the playroom and sang it to us in front of our mother. Her lips pressed into the fierce line that terrified us, Mom wordlessly dragged him by the wrist into the kitchen and washed out his mouth with a bar of soap. I'd never seen that happen before, except in cartoons. Later I got to experience it myself. For those of you who haven't had the pleasure, the soap is crammed into your gob and furiously swiped in and out. The roof of your mouth functions as a washboard, producing generous amounts of lather. Mom was partial to Dial; it has a very distinct flavor, like a flowery, peppery, zesty cheese.

After Paul had his mouth washed out, Tim explained to us in our room what the song meant. His words were inconceivable. I genuinely had no idea what he meant in terms of mechanics, ballistics, and logical outgrowth of his description as it pertained to what I was expected to do when I grew up. Suddenly, the beautiful naked lady on the cover of *Whipped Cream and Other Delights* was too awful to contemplate. It was as though Tim had lost his mind and from now on would blabber nothing but vileness that had no place in my world. Here's the song the eighth grader taught Paul that resulted in my mother introducing him to the taste of Dial.

> *It is luck*
> *To fuck*
> *With a duck*

Bad-tempered Gloria to the Village

Every Friday at school we all had to assemble in the courtyard and sing the American and Venezuelan national anthems as we faced both flags. Though I grew up speaking Spanish, nobody ever taught me the words to "Gloria al Bravo Pueblo" ("Glory to the Brave People"), so I just sang what I heard.

> *Gloria bravo al pueblo* (Bad-tempered Gloria to the village)
> *Que jugo lanzó* (That threw juice)
> *La ley esperando* (The law is waiting)
> *Labia studio no* (Not a labia studio)
> (Repeat)
>
> *Abrazo cadenas* (Hug chains)
> *Gritar al señor* (Yell to the mister)
> *Gritar al señor* (Yell to the mister)
>
> *El pobre sucho sal* (The poor crippled salt)
> *Libertad pidió* (Asked for liberty)
> *En este santo hombre* (In this holy man)
> *Ejemplo de sabor* (Example of flavor)
> *Eh, vi egoísmo* (Hey, I saw selfishness)
> *¿Qué otra de Truffaut?* (What other of Truffaut?)

And so on.

I'd heard of Truffaut, but I didn't know what he did or why we had to sing about him. Adults said that he was a genius. I wondered if he might be a scientist in a white lab coat, a guy who worked on the space program everybody talked about.

When we sang "The Star-Spangled Banner," I thought the line was "the bums bursting in air." I pictured whiskered hobos in the sky exploding and raining blood and guts down on us. Nobody told us what "spangled" meant, either. I thought it was the same as "scrambled," my favorite way to have eggs.

For years, whenever I sang the American national anthem I saw the flag covered with scrambled eggs while tramps – cigar butts jutting from their mouths and handkerchief bundles on sticks clutched in their hands – floated overhead, popping like balloons.

It *Does* Make Me Want to Do Something with my Feet: Run

Inevitably, what I'd feared for most of my childhood happened in 1972 and Creole's parent company Exxon transferred Dad to the States. Tyler, Texas, would be our new home. I left our oil camp with dread, convinced that we were on our way to a crumbling, adobe hacienda in the desert, surrounded by steers and cacti. Instead, we got to live in a giant ranch house on seven acres of land, with hundred-foot pine trees as far as the eye could see. We were taught to watch out for scorpions, cottonmouths, and tornados; I learned on my own to beware of many Texans. Within one minute of meeting me, the neighbor kids – a delegation from two families – asked if I believed in evolution. I didn't understand the question.

"Do you believe in evolution or the Bible?"

At the time I was a coerced Catholic. The only Bible I'd read was one I'd found in my parents' closet. It disturbed me greatly because it had medieval-style illustrations of chain-mailed knights in battle. They used broadswords and double-bladed axes to chop off heads and hack huge, black, ovoid gashes with folded-back red lips into their enemies' arms, faces, and abdomens, but everybody looked serene and dreamy, even the severed heads lying on the ground. Some of the wounded had satisfied expressions, as though they liked having gaping slices in their bodies. The pages of that Bible were made of some weird paper that was crispy and tissue thin. It had a musky, vinegary, intimate odor, in my imagination the fragrance emitted by those fleshy, black-and-red sword cuts. I neither believed nor disbelieved in the Bible. When I thought about it at all, I just wondered why the knights in the illustrations were so untroubled or pleased by their horrendous injuries.

But since I was a fan of Louis Leakey and was fascinated by protohumans, hominids, archaic Homo sapiens, and Cro-Magnons, I said, "Well, we're descended from creatures that evolved into us." I had no clue where this was going. The topic had never come up in my life.

My new neighbors were outraged. "Bull-*shyit!* The Bible doesn't say we're descended from 'creatures'! It says on the sixth day God created man in His own image!"

We had a huge fight, and that was the end of that. For the three years we lived in Tyler, I had maybe twenty conversations with the neighbor kids. Their hostility made it easy for my brother Tim and me to do what we called "spying," which was to go out late at night and steal the heads from their sprinkler systems. Tim collected them for some reason. When the neighbors' automatic timers went off, jets of water spewed from the lawn thirty feet into the air while Tim and I laughed.

In Texas, music made even less of an impact on me than it had in Venezuela. Dad continued his ownership of the family record player, and none of us kids had radios. I remember somehow hearing Tanya Tucker's "Delta Dawn" what seemed like every single day we lived in Tyler, along with "I am Woman" by Helen Reddy. Both songs made me sick. We watched *The Sonny and Cher Comedy Hour* on TV and got to know the song "I Got You Babe," which also made me sick.

The music I liked was TV theme songs. A piece that gave me goose pimples was composer Gil Mellé's opening theme for *Kolchak: The Night Stalker.* The change that occurs thirty seconds into the piece is still one of the most phenomenal works of musical genius I've ever heard, and the ending is spectacular. I was shocked to learn decades later that Mellé wrote that composition in twenty minutes. Another favorite was the theme to *Barnaby Jones,* by the legendary composer Jerry Goldsmith. I'd watch the show just to hear that music, which struck me as poignant and heroic like the old detective, Jones, himself.

Generally, I felt music was something to be avoided unless it was part of a TV show or movie. I've always been a film fanatic, experiencing movies instead of watching them. Ray Anthony and His Orchestra's recording of the theme from *The Incredible Shrinking Man* had a trumpet that made my hair stand on end, while Shirley Bassey belting out "Goldfinger" was as good as music got. Tim would do a killer impression of Bassey, down to holding the song's impossible final note. He'd been clandestinely listening to my mother's Sinatra, Ella Fitzgerald, and Paul Smith Trio albums in the den when Dad was at work.

The only record I listened to was a Disney album full of perverted songs. There was some German-accented doggerel about the "Three Little Pigs" that I learned phonetically, like the Venezuelan national anthem.

> *Eestas neek tine sausage meat?*
> *Adas peestas sausage meat.*
> *Eestas neek tine picksen feet?*
> *Adas peestas picksen feet.*
> *Eestas gootfa schvainas, too?*
> *Daddy's goostas schvainas, too.*
> *Eestas neek tine curlicue?*
> *Adas peestas curlicue.*
> *Horken cork*
> *Gassav shnaap*
> *Hammen cake*
> *Porken chop*
> *Picksen feet*
> *Sausage meat*
> *Leedle pixies*
> *Gootoo yeet.*

As with all things German except for some art, Tim loathed that song. He'd curl his lip and sneer, "Chermany, laand ov *myoozeek.*" To this day, all you have to do to make him crazy is play any kind of German folk music, especially if it has clarinets or violins. Or yodeling. Hell for Tim would be eternity in Bavaria.

The best part of the Disney album was the "Jack and the Beanstalk" section, when the giant fell to his death from the castle in the clouds, with a hideous scream of "*Eeeeeeeeee-hyaaaaa-hyaaaaaa-hyaaaaa-haaaaaaaaaaaaaa!*" as tympani thundered and an orchestra shrieked out a swirling, descending cacophony in a minor key. It always made my skin crawl and every hair on my body stand up – just the sort of record for little kids. Tim could imitate the giant's scream perfectly. He'd chase us around at night doing it. Even though we knew it was just our brother, it was terrifying.

When Dad came home after work, he'd pull shut the accordion doors of the den and turn on his Mitch Miller or waltzes. Once I went in to ask him for help on my homework. A frenetic ragtime piece blared from the speakers of the Zenith cabinet record player.

Over the noise Dad shouted, "Doesn't that make you wanna do something with your feet?"

To my utter horror, he began dancing a wild jig, the first time I'd ever witnessed him do such a thing, his fists clenched in front of him and going up and down as though he were pumping up a bicycle tire, his long legs kicking out sideways in rhythm to the banjo strumming, his keys and coins jingling crazily in his pockets.

That image went smashing into my hippocampus, which instantly fired it through my neural pathways into my cortex, where it remains unchanged to this day, fresh and pristine as a newly minted penny.

Led Zeppelin and the First Ghost

In 1975 Exxon transferred Dad to the Netherlands. He went on ahead, and the rest of us followed in a KLM Boeing 747. The flight was long, ten or eleven hours. I've always been terrified of flying, almost to the point of becoming comatose. To survive, I kept myself distracted by listening to music. The flight attendants gave us cheap plastic headphones that we plugged into little sockets in our seats, and there was a dial we turned to choose from several programs that repeated every hour. I caught the Captain and Tennille's "Love will Keep us Together," which was bouncy but actually pretty gross, as well as Neil Sedaka's "Laughter in the Rain." While I really liked the sinister title, the song itself didn't do anything for me.

And then something hit me like a fist to the jaw, a brutal, pounding, thrusting, filthy, exceptionally exciting tune that was like nothing I'd ever heard. The vocalist was somehow screaming at a low volume; the drums made my feet tap; the guitars were like a chorus of banshees; and there was some low-frequency instrument in there that matched my heartbeat. The song was "Trampled Underfoot," by Led Zeppelin. Since the lyrics were about cars, I pictured the musicians as muscular garage mechanics, their faces twisted with belligerence. I listened to that song every time it was repeated, trying to absorb it into my bloodstream. It had the same effect on my brothers Paul and Pat. Tim liked it well enough, but he was already devoted to jazz vocalists by that time.

In Rijswijk, our new home, we all bought transistor radios and listened incessantly to Radio Caroline, a pirate station on a ship anchored offshore to avoid the limitations placed on the state-run broadcasters of Europe. Radio Caroline was a lifesaver because the Dutch music scene was a nightmare. Smash hits included André van Duin's *"Willempie,"* about a retarded man singing in a retarded voice about his retarded life; Corrie van Gorp's rousing oompah-march *"Zo Slank zijn als je Dochter"* ("As Slim as Your Daughter"), the chorus punctuated by the *boing* of a Jew's harp; and Nico Haak's Dutch version of "Put Another Nickel in the Nickelodeon." Music that could drive you immediately out of your skull.

Occasionally, we'd see someone like Kate Bush, who sang "Wuthering Heights" on *Top Pop*. She was the first in a long line of small, intense, dark-haired musicians who had a profound effect on me. Boney M, Bonnie Tyler, and Patricia Paay made less of an impression, even though they were on *Top Pop* every four seconds, along with French *artiste* Carlos singing "Big Bisous." Tim preferred BBC jazz shows on the radio and was the first of us to start buying records, rereleased albums long out of print in the U.S. He'd listen to them on headphones while the rest of us suffered through "Daddy Cool."

It was in Holland that I met my first ghost. I'll call her Brigitte. She was a blonde, blue-eyed dual national of the U.S. and another country, the most beautiful girl I'd ever seen. Her family lived a few doors down from us and we were in the same grade, but she was popular while I was – to be blunt – a disaster. Photos of me from that era are indescribably embarrassing. I looked exactly like an unmarried, forty-year-old Eastern European woman, with shoulder-length hair and big, ugly glasses. My siblings and I had transferred into the school in the middle of the year, making me the newly arrived weirdo as out of place as an octopus in a pine tree. Brigitte was polite to me, but we didn't have much to do with each other at first.

Brigitte's brother and sister became good friends of my family. One or the other would always be over at our house, to the point that my mother began referring to them as her two extra children. Brigitte gradually warmed to me. It turned out she had quite a good sense of humor; on the bus to school one morning, she told me a silly, literate, Dadaist joke that made me laugh because it was so unexpected coming from someone as removed as she generally was.

Q: What was Beethoven's favorite fruit?
A: *Ba*-na-na-naaaah!

When her family came back from a vacation in Kenya, she was so tan that she literally looked like a black person. She came over to our house wearing a button-up shirt with the hem tied under her breasts to show her mahogany stomach. "I *broiled* myself," she said. "Like a steak. God knows what it's going to do to me in thirty years."

Her aura of sadness was extremely attractive. I wanted to help her and make her happy. Of course, I was also madly in love with her. I wrote, "I love Brigitte Cardei" on a tiny slip of paper, rolled it up, and tucked it into the clear plastic body of a ballpoint pen so I could always have it close to me. One day at school a guy sitting behind me asked to borrow a pen. He was a Dutch kid whose parents sent him to the American school to perfect his English. Although I hated him because his English was so fluent that he was able to bully me with stupendous effectiveness every single day, I went into what Tim calls the "rabbit trance" and handed over my Brigitte pen without thinking.

A few seconds later, I felt a tap on my shoulder. I turned around and saw this Dutch degenerate with his Moe Howard soup-bowl haircut holding my little love note, unrolled. Grinning from ear to ear, he went into a demented, chanting ecstasy like someone speaking in tongues, jerking his head violently back and forth and thrusting his chin at the ceiling: "I'm gonna tell *Brigitte* and she's gonna find *out* and you're gonna be *so embarrassed* and everyone's gonna *laugh* at you and the whole *school* is gonna know and you're gonna wanna *kill yourself* and we're all gonna *laugh* our *asses* off! Uh-huh-uh-huh-uh-huh-uh-*huhhhh!*"

And he *did* tell her. And he *did* tell the whole school. And they *did* laugh. And I *did* want to kill myself. But the funny thing is, the person who saved me from total mental collapse was Brigitte. She became my friend, whether out of pity or because she was just naturally a kind person, I'll never know. Regardless, she and I became inseparable for a few months. She was really very nice. What I interpreted as aloofness was shyness. Despite her astonishing beauty, she was unsure of herself. We took walks almost every evening and rode the street car into the Hague to see movies. We even went all the way to the beach at Scheveningen and crawled around the abandoned German coastal bunkers from World War II. When I found out that her father had been transferred and they had to move to the U.S., I was devastated.

The last night I saw her, we went to a nearby park and sat on the swings, talking as the fog rolled in. She said she hoped she'd see me again someday, but we both knew the odds were against it. The children of men who worked in the oil business were nomads. We got used to coming and going, meeting new people and then leaving them. Lasting friendships were rare. At about ten o'clock, she said, "Well, I have to go."

"Would you mind if I don't walk you home?" I asked. She lived only a block away, and I was afraid I'd burst into tears. I still hadn't recovered from the humiliation of having my secret love note shown to the whole school.

"No, it's okay. Just stay here. I'll see you later, Tom. Goodbye."

And she turned and disappeared into the fog.

The Land of the Midnight Sun and the Second Ghost

In 1978 Exxon transferred Dad to Norway. Since we arrived in Stavanger at the beginning of the school year, this time I thought I might be able to fit in more easily than I had in the Netherlands, but it wasn't to be. Most of the kids at the American school were the children of diplomats or southern oil workers. There were rigidly defined cliques, and if you couldn't slot yourself into any of them, you were out of luck.

I was amazed at the amount of drugs available. Hash, pot, meth, mushrooms, and LSD were yours for the asking, despite the risks. European social democracies only pay lip service to liberalism and openness. The Dutch and Norwegian cops were absolutely brutal. Dutch cops wore steel-toed boots – the better to kick your shins – and Norwegian cops hit you in the kidneys with phone books so it wouldn't leave a mark. I was so afraid of the police in Stavanger that I didn't try drugs until I was eighteen. Instead, I drank myself into oblivion, like everyone else. Norwegians have a tradition of emptying all bottles opened at a party. They also drink aquavit that can be up to 50 percent alcohol by volume. Until I went to Japan, I never saw so many drunks in my life. For a long time I was one of them.

Easily the stupidest thing I did was to accept a matchbox full of peyote buttons from one of those share-the-wealth-type druggies who live to turn on others, especially clueless rubes like me. He told me to eat all of them, which I did at home that night because my family was out of the country. After about an hour I started throwing up, and with each heave I went further out of my mind. No visions or hallucinations, just complete mental chaos. I remember babbling incoherently to myself about Catholicism, saints, and demons; I took a long walk at three in the morning, describing all my actions and thoughts out loud. The havoc in my head lasted two full days. To try and keep from being slung into outer space forever, I lay in bed and read a novel over and over: *Paradise Alley,* by Sylvester Stallone. I still associate the book with terrifying psychosis I thought would never end. Later I discovered that the thirty or so peyote buttons I ate constituted a mammoth, horrendously dangerous dose. It wasn't the last practical joke played on me in my life.

In Norway my music education took off. My siblings and I built up record collections after we found out that the biggest shop in Stavanger let prospective customers listen to the LPs. The old man who ran the store was such a heavy smoker that his fingers were dark brown. He rolled his own with the delicious, fragrant Norwegian shag. One time he squatted to lift a pile of LPs and released such a howling, phlegmy grunt as he straightened that people covered their ears and ran out of the building. It sounded like someone being disemboweled.

The band that had the biggest influence on me at this time was the Police. I decided I had to learn to play guitar like Andy Summers. My younger brother Pat helped me pick out an acoustic guitar that the shop clerk converted to left handed by taking a huge file, gouging out the three narrowest slots on the nut, and switching over the strings. It took him about forty-five seconds. I tried for months to learn how to play the thing, but it was boring and tedious, and I actually hated the sound of it. After a long struggle, I gave it to Pat.

When I graduated from high school I had no idea what to do. Dad found me work at a shore-support base that reloaded supply ships for oil platforms in the North Sea. It was a ludicrously dangerous job. My boss once told me to take a crowbar and jiggle a giant section of steel pipe into place because it was sitting slightly crooked on the pile where the crane had placed it. What they didn't tell me is that if you move something that weighs several tons using a crowbar and that object falls onto the crowbar, the crowbar will instantly weigh several tons. It was ripped out of my hands, dislocating my thumbs, and then it hit me in the chest and pinned me against the railing of the supply ship. There was just enough room for my body between the railing and the end of the crowbar. Another inch and it would've pierced my sternum and gone into my heart.

We had a family friend I'll call Lola, a phenomenal musician. She played percussion, guitar, bass, keyboards, and sang. At her suggestion I decided to take up the electric bass. I was eighteen, late to be starting, but I wanted to play like Sting. "Message in a Bottle" was my all-time favorite song, and being able to play that bass line would be amazing. Lola and Pat said they'd help me pick out a bass; I went on ahead to the guitar store and waited an hour, which was typical, because Lola was chronically late. Irate and clueless about instruments, I eventually bought a black Fender Musicmaster, a short-scale bass. As soon as the clerk rang up my sale and handed me my purchase, Pat and Lola skidded around the corner and exploded into the store. They berated me for buying such a small, dopey instrument. It would be cripplingly neck heavy once I flipped it over to play it left handed, they said, because the strap would have to be attached to the short horn. I would also be unable to play the highest frets.

That made me so angry I defiantly vowed to keep it. And I did for two years, thus preventing myself from learning how to properly play the bass until I bought my first left-handed model when I was twenty. Lola made up for it by becoming the first girl to let me touch her pubic hair. That same night, in the middle of a frozen lake far from shore and prying eyes, she took my hands and put them into her heavy coat and under her bra. What felt like two thumbs popped out against my palms. I was amazed at how hard they were and how fast they snapped to attention, as though they were spring loaded.

Lola shrugged and said, "Nipples are weird things."

My shiny new Fender made me hunger for a more varied musical diet. In listening to as many different records as I could, I discovered the Norwegian New Wave band De Press. For some reason, I responded to singer-bassist Andrej Nebb on a gut level. He showed me the mystery of great art and the importance of developing a style. Though I tried to copy what he played, his tone, note choices, and exuberance made it impossible. De Press songs such as "Block to Block," "Kic Me Rusia," and "Bo Jo Cie Kochom" skillfully conveyed elation, sadness, humor, and anger all at once. I couldn't figure out how so much conflicting emotion could be packed into short, simple pop tunes. When I first saw De Press perform live, I was flabbergasted. Nebb was missing the thumb, middle, and ring fingers of his left hand; he fretted those fast, bouncy bass lines with only his index finger and pinkie. Andrej Nebb is the musician who gave me my inaugural lessons in artistry and overcoming loss.

The year I worked in Stavanger, I became very close to a girl I'll call Jennifer. I'd known her family since we moved to Norway, but she was two grades behind me. Somehow we became pals. She was an ice skater, a tremendous pianist, and bore an eerie resemblance to the young Shirley MacLaine. I was a friend of her brother; when he went off to college I continued going over to her house to gossip with her loud, drunken mother, the two of us knocking back endless slugs of scotch in the kitchen. One evening Jennifer played me John Barry's "Midnight Cowboy Theme" on the piano. It was the first piece of music I ever heard that moved me almost to tears. Though from that point on I was deeply in love with her, I never told her. She liked athletes and good-looking guys who blow dried their hair. I wanted to tell her that they'd never appreciate her the way I did, but I already knew that when someone isn't attracted to you, it doesn't matter how much you appreciate them. She wanted us to just be friends.

Another reason I loved her was her wacky sense of humor. We made each other berserk with laughter. She was utterly cracked up by that Brooke Shields TV commercial in which she says, "You wanna know what comes between me and my Calvins? Nothing." She'd mimic Brooke in a ditzy, squeaky, little-girl voice, then she'd change over to a slow, deep, draggy devil-voice, distorting her mouth, making one corner go down so she looked brain damaged. I'd laugh until I couldn't breathe. Her smile was exactly like Barbra Streisand's. It indicated lethal vulnerability.

Jennifer was an only daughter; her three brothers were brutish dullards, while she was immensely intelligent and sensitive. She had terrible fights with her parents for no reason I could perceive. One night they called and asked me to come over and take her out of the house. I drove Jennifer up to a radio tower on the top of a hill and sat there while she sobbed that her father had called her a whore and said he wished she'd never been born.

Her father was a raging drunk like her mother. He smoked cigars, sang opera, and hawked without spitting. He'd do an aria, pause to make a guttural *hhrrrrrrrrechhhhhh* noise, and go on singing, glass of scotch in one hand and cigar in the other.

I knew Jennifer was a virgin, because she'd confided in me that the kids in her grade were all screwing each other and they made fun of her for not joining in. She once asked me what sex was like, and when I started to tell her, she immediately said, "Okay, stop. Stop. I don't want to talk about it anymore. It's too weird."

In the car, I had no clue how to handle such a situation. I was eighteen years old, trying to comfort someone in total psychological meltdown after the people who'd done it to her had fobbed her off on me. She cried for about five hours straight while I sat there helplessly. When she was exhausted and nearly asleep, she said she wanted to go home. Back at her house, we found her parents waiting in the open front doorway to greet her. They embraced her as though all were forgiven and closed the door in my face. I drove home and got seriously drunk with a bottle of rum I'd hidden under my bed. Jennifer and I never spoke about that night.

I turned Jennifer on to hashish about four months later. She instantly loved it and fell in with the stoners at school. That was the end of her ice skating and piano playing. She's spent the majority of her life drunk and addicted to drugs. Her parents told Pat her fate when he ran into them at one of his shows a few years ago. "She's completely lost in drugs," her mother said. I can believe it. By the time I left for college, she smoked, snorted, swallowed, and drank everything, in the most titanic amounts she could ingest into her petite frame. In the last photo I saw of her, she was bloated and slitty eyed, with an expression of utter misery and hate. She was only twenty-eight but looked sixty.

We make our own choices. From the time I was seventeen until I was thirty I probably experienced a total of fourteen days of sobriety. I know full well that Jennifer would have discovered drugs and alcohol on her own. Even so, the fact remains that I'm the one who introduced them to her.

I'm sorry, Jennifer. I have no excuses.

In my filing cabinet I still have the last note she gave me. It says, "I owe you one performance of 'Midnight Cowboy Theme.' Jennifer." She used to give me those notes every time I went to her house as a way of making sure I'd come back to see her again. That was silly of her; I loved every second I spent with her and would've given anything for more time. I'd also give anything to take back the night I introduced her to hash. After the first big lungful, she smiled her fragile Barbra Streisand smile and said, "*God,* this feels good!"

She wore Love's Baby Soft perfume, a scent I can't bear to this day.

The Punk who Set Me on My Course

In 1981 I enrolled as a freshman at Lewis and Clark College in Portland, Oregon. My dorm roommate was a skinny little guy with black bondage pants, a torn black T-shirt, black Keds high tops, and spiked black hair. Great, I thought. He's going to puke on me and smile as he does it, like Paul Cook in the poster for *The Great Rock 'n' Roll Swindle.* Though he'd arrived in our room only a few minutes before I did, he'd already taped up two incredible charcoal studies, his own original art. One showed a panicked man in a chair, his mouth being violated by a pop-eyed, gloating, sweating, slobbering dentist with a drill the size of a cruise missile suspended from the ceiling. The other depicted a finger-snapping hipster in a zoot suit standing under a streetlamp at night; instead of a head, all he had from the neck up was a gigantic, toothy grin. They were astonishing works, hilarious and utterly disturbing in their oral themes.

My roommate's name was Joe Cady. He reminded me of a theory I'd read somewhere that maybe rocks are alive, but we just can't tell because their movements take millions of years and are imperceptible to us. Talking to Joe sometimes made me wish for a fast-forward button. He answered when he was ready, often spending endless seconds going "Hmmmmmmmmmmmm" before he produced actual words. The first breakfast we shared together in the cafeteria, he ordered bacon, fried eggs, hash browns, and toast, which he proceeded to eat with his hands. Then he picked up and licked the plate.

"There," he said when he was finished. "I just broke every single one of my mother's rules about eating, and now I don't ever have to do it again." After that he always ate with a knife and fork like a nice young man.

That was his terrible secret. He was incredibly... *nice*. He had a MusicMan Sting Ray guitar and a fretless electric guitar he'd made himself. Since all I had was my ridiculous, upside-down Fender Musicmaster bass that I could barely play, we couldn't jam, but he turned me on to music I never knew existed: Gang of Four. Massacre. The Slits. The Stranglers. King Crimson. The Descendants. The Dead Kennedys. Public Image Limited. The Specials. Wall of Voodoo. Oingo Boingo. Devo. X. Joy Division. Siouxsie and the Banshees. The Au Pairs. The Waitresses. Romeo Void. Yes. The Clash.

And most importantly, Gentle Giant. I was utterly unfamiliar with progressive rock, but when Joe put on "Free Hand" from *Playing the Fool: the Official Live Gentle Giant,* I couldn't believe that a human being could play bass like that. The bassist's name was Ray Shulman, and he instantly became my hero. Hearing that version of the song for the first time was like having a portal opened on an incomprehensibly beautiful land I could enter if I were worthy, and the only way to become worthy was to practice. Soon after learning about Gentle Giant, I parted with my poor Fender Musicmaster, but not before ruining it by having the frets pulled out at great expense. I also wanted a whammy bar put on it, since Joe had introduced me to Stanley Clarke, but the guitar-store clerks finally took mercy on me and told me I'd be wasting my money.

To replace the Fender Musicmaster, I bought a proper left-handed Carvin bass and an amplifier. Now Joe and I could play together. We tried all sorts of things, but I was just never any good. One of our dorm mates had John Entwistle's solo album *Too Late the Hero,* which had a great song called "Talk Dirty." It centered on a fast, jangly, macho bass riff that was impossible. One night on a floor party I was introduced to a bassist visiting a friend in the dorm, and he asked me if I'd learned the bass part for "Talk Dirty."

"Sure," I said.

"Cool! Show me."

I picked up my bass, plugged it in, and after a moment of fumbling said, "Oh, wait. 'Talk Dirty'? No, I don't know that one. I was thinking of a different song." Since I always turned beet red when I drank, maybe nobody noticed my shame at being caught in a lie. The guy then asked me for my left-handed bass, took my pick, and played the part flawlessly on what was for him a bass strung upside down.

Joe was present when I learned another lesson. We went to see a well-known Portland fusion band I liked because the bassist used a MusicMan Sting Ray, the same series as Joe's guitar. This bass wasn't available in left-handed models at the time, and previously made left-handed specimens were impossible to find. I envied any bass player who had a Sting Ray; it's famous for the deep treble sound it gets when you use the thumb-slapping technique. After a few songs, the band invited a well-known bassist up from the audience to play. He plugged in his own bass, an expensive custom job with an amazing tone. His solo was astonishing not for its speed – because it wasn't fast – but for its melodic sense and the sheer logic of the note choices. The only way I can explain it is that as each note was played, you'd think, "Of *course!*" He was a master.

When the band's bassist got back on stage, Joe whispered to me, "How the hell is he going to follow *that?*" Well, what he did during his own solo was pull every single trick out of his hat. Slapping, two-handed tapping, flamenco strumming, chords, Pete Townsend windmills – the works. It was ghastly. He was like some jealous schmuck trying to show off for his girlfriend after they'd watched a musclehead do forty pull-ups. It went on forever, and the sound was atrocious. People actually got up and left.

"This is really horrible," Joe said. "His whole life he's never going to get over that solo."

I can still see that desperate Sting Ray player, getting more and more ridiculous by the second, when all he had to do was applaud the other bassist and then go back to what he did best. It relieved me of most of my self-imposed pressure to play like Ray Shulman. I knew I'd probably never get there, and after watching a perfectly fine bassist self-immolate in public because someone else was much better, I stopped feeling so bad about my inability to progress beyond a certain point.

The first song Joe and I learned to play together all the way through was "London Calling," by the Clash. It's a deceptively hard bass line full of subtle glissandos, skillful variations, and individual notes that somehow swell in volume. The unique mushy-but-woody tone of the bass is pretty much impossible to duplicate and obscures Paul Simonon's sophisticated rhythms and fingerings. "London Calling" taught me how fun and rewarding it is to perform actual compositions in their entirety. The song has a timeless, genreless quality that makes it an eternal classic. Thirty years after I first heard it, I still love "London Calling," primarily because of the masterful bass.

There were jazzers at my college who'd come into the practice rooms and sit there smirking and rolling their eyes as they watched Joe and me jam. Once a pianist asked me for my left-handed bass and started slapping it, saying, "Hey, look at *me!* Look at *me!* I'm Jameel Washington Jones! I'm a *muthafucka!*" He banged away on it as unmusically as he could while his own bassist laughed. When he handed it back to me, he said, "You guys done yet? Can we play now?"

Of course we cleared out for them because they were great musicians. Though they were just a couple of years older than me, they all looked like they were in their late forties. I was amazed at their dissolution. Joe and I drank beer or smoked pot almost every day, yet we were nowhere near as ravaged. I couldn't imagine the titanic amount of booze needed to erode a twenty-three-year-old into late middle age. The pianist had a receding hairline that he pretended didn't exist by teasing his tresses upward in a kind of hipster bird's nest. It gave him a freakishly tall science-fiction forehead, as though he'd been partially stretched in an accident with a black hole.

Joe transferred to U.C. Santa Cruz in 1983. I missed him terribly. It's too bad he didn't get to see what I did to the 1970s Hohner hollow-bodied fretless bass I bought at a flea market. Someone had replaced the bridge with one made out of cast iron, like frying-pan material, and the finish was worn off half the fingerboard. The action was almost an inch high; I found out later there was nothing I could do about it because the end of the truss rod had somehow been broken off. I removed the finish with a deadly toxic paint-stripper gel and a scraper, and then I spray-painted the whole thing black with cans of Krylon lacquer. Everyone on my dorm floor called it the Bat Bass.

Since it was a right-handed bass and I played it left handed, my wrist kept turning down the volume knobs. The only way to avoid that was to wear it on my chest, but that forced me to position my picking hand with a ninety-degree bend at the wrist. Playing for more than five minutes was too painful; I could feel tendons giving way. The action was still an inch high, which hurt the fingers on my fret hand, and the black spray paint on the fingerboard was immediately abraded away by the strings. It came off in little shavings, like crinkly black inchworms.

After a few fruitless months of noodling with it, I hooked together every guitar cord I could find in the college, plugged the Bat Bass into my amp, and pitched it off the top of the six-story dorm. It made a humming, booming sound on the way down and smashed into fragments in the parking lot, producing the most incredible noise, an explosion set to music: a crash and about a hundred different notes played at once. I should've filmed it.

Joe isn't a ghost; he's the only person from college with whom I've stayed in contact. He lives in Paris now, with his wife Violette, and he works in communication and marketing for a French online-services startup. Not only is he remarkable for having kept in touch, Joe is also – as he reminded me when I asked him if I could write about him in my memoir – the one person on earth who's urinated on me. We'd stayed up all night drinking and then crashed. Hours later I clawed my way back to consciousness due to a growing sensation of heat on my chest. There was Joe standing next to my bed, peeing on me.

"Joe!" I screamed. *"What the fuck are you doing?"*

He gazed down at me, mumbled, "Oh. Sorry," and went back to bed. After I stripped off my wet clothes and took a boiling-hot shower, I slept on the couch in the lounge. The next day, when I told Joe what he'd done, he didn't believe me. He was mortified. Always pale, he went nearly translucent and produced a strange, shuddering giggle. Maybe I was the reason he changed colleges. I didn't even remember the incident until he brought it up, so no harm done.

After Joe triggered the right synapses, though, I did recollect something noteworthy: It burns when you're peed on, in case anyone is curious. My chest radiated heat for hours, as though I'd swallowed a tiny nuclear reactor.

I Don't Wanna be Like Any of These Guys

Joe being out of the picture, I now played more with tapes than people. I also had two consecutive private bass teachers I hired through the college. The first was a fat jazzer. He was a great bassist, but our lessons were at eight in the morning, about five hours after he got home from the previous night's gig. Sometimes he was still drunk or high. Mostly what he did was talk about his excesses or how much he hated successful musicians. I once asked him if he could show me how to play the bass solo in the Who's "My Generation."

"Fuck!" he yelled. "Goddammit! Shit! You too? Fine. Here!" And he whipped it out in about four seconds, his pudgy hands and caterpillar fingers flying. "There! Happy? That's all you guys wanna learn! 'My Fuckin' Generation'! Don't you understand how simple and stupid it is?"

He told me proudly about the night he played with a legendary jazz pianist. To prepare for the gig, they sat around drinking wine, about a bottle apiece. Then they did a whole ounce of coke and smoked joints the size of "elephant dicks." Right before they went onstage, the pianist took an eyedropper full of heroin and snorted it, one sniff per nostril.

"He was so fucked up he couldn't even speak! He was like, '*Thih neh tha wuh rih'n buh Koh Puhtuh.*' And he played flawlessly!"

My second bass teacher was much nicer, but he had the totally flat eyes I'd learned to recognize as a sign of long-term, heavy drug use. Sure enough, he soon began regaling me with stories of his fifteen years as a junkie. I tried to get him to teach me the bass line for Massacre's "Legs," but he said after playing the tape I'd given him dozens of times, his wife was ready to murder him. He never even came close.

I was part of a cover band for a while. We were popular at school or fraternity parties because we had a repertoire of about eighty songs. One night our drummer got bombed and tried to drive home. I ended up taking his car keys, and we got into a fist fight. He never forgave me for embarrassing him in front of everybody. For some reason he wasn't embarrassed that he could barely stand, and the fight consisted of him swinging haymakers at me that I didn't even have to dodge. He punched at the empty air three feet in front of my face. I knew in my bones that he was going to kill somebody that night; it was the strongest premonition I've ever had. Hopefully, the person I saved went on to great happiness and fulfillment. Maybe it was someone who's reading this memoir. Even though it ruined my relationship with my drummer, I'd do it again, so don't feel bad. I don't even remember his name. Brad? Chad? One or the other.

The only other bassist I knew was a kid who had a fretless Fender Precision with a maple neck, like the one Sting used. This guy always wore a bayonet in a scabbard strapped to his wrist, and his friend ate his food with drumsticks he used as chopsticks. I was embarrassed to be even remotely connected to almost every musician associated in any way with my college. They were all drunks, druggies, and crazed attention whores. I did my share of boozing, drugging, and seeking attention, but these people devoted their entire existences to it. By the time I graduated I knew there had to be more to life than acting like a complete bozo in public or sitting around talking about 'shrooms and cannabis for hours at a time. It was amazing how dull these people were, even though they styled themselves great artists. I recognized that I wasn't an artist, but at least I wasn't a tedious assemblage that said and did the exact same things night after night. They were already locked into 100 percent conformity and they weren't even out of college yet.

It scared me to death that people could be so generic. How in the world would I live among them?

Music Used for Mass Murder

In 1982 my father was transferred to London. He, my mother, and my brother Pat rented a house at Tobin Close, near Primrose Hill. In the summer my brother Paul and I went to visit, since we loved London. Everything about it was beautiful: the history, the architecture, the museums, the smell, and the incredible subway system. I even loved British food, especially the strangely dense, tall slices of sandwich bread; the peanut butter; the Cadbury's chocolate bars; and the Wimpy's hamburgers and fries – I mean "chips." There were also millions of tiny shops that sold long out-of-production model kits unavailable in the U.S.

A little before noon on July 20, 1982, Paul and I left the house to wander. We decided to walk through Regent's Park, since we're big fans of greenery and topiary. Our destination was Hamleys Toy Shop, but we were in no hurry to get there. We took the Primrose Hill Bridge over Regent's Canal and entered the park. The path through the sports pitches went across Longbridge toward Queen Mary's Gardens. When we got to the Inner Circle we arbitrarily turned left. If we'd turned right, we would've encountered the path that led to the bandstand. The entrance to the path was about 300 feet from the bandstand, where at that moment a military band played songs from *Oliver!* to a crowd of about 120 sitting in lawn chairs. We would've heard the band, and since I was a musician and military buff, I would've wanted to go over and listen.

A few minutes after we turned left on the Inner Circle, there was a massive explosion behind us. I knew instantly it was a terrorist bomb, even though I'd never heard even a tape of a real device going off. Unlike a Hollywood explosion, this was unbelievably short and violent, mostly the sound of breakage, like a million glass china cases being smashed with a million sledgehammers. It lasted less than a second but created a huge shock wave.

This was actually the second bomb of the day in London. The first had been detonated by remote control as tourists watched soldiers of the Household Cavalry ride to Buckingham Palace for the Changing of the Guards ceremony. Four men of the Blues and Royals – Roy Bright, 36; Anthony Daly, 23; Simon Tipper, 19; and Jeffrey Young, 19 – were killed or later died of their injuries. The bomb consisted of ten pounds of explosives wrapped in six-inch nails, which scythed into the crowd of onlookers. Paul and I didn't know about this attack because we hadn't listened to or watched the news before we went out.

The bomb under the bandstand was even larger than the first one. It, too, contained six-inch nails, but it was detonated with a timer, having been put there weeks earlier. It killed seven bandsmen of the Royal Green Jackets: Graham Barker, 36; John Heritage, 29; Robert Livingston, 31; John McKnight, 30; George Mesure, 19; Keith Powell, 24; and Laurence Smith, 19. Dozens of tourists – including children and the elderly – were injured. If Paul and I had taken the path to the bandstand, we would've come within fifty feet of the explosion. The dead and wounded were dismembered. Nails and body parts were found well over 150 feet away.

Both bombs were the handiwork of the Provisional Irish Republican Army, which proudly took the credit but expressed surprise that powerful explosives set off in crowds of civilians would injure civilians. The experience of narrowly escaping a terrorist attack by sheer, dumb luck left me in a state of depression, hypervigilance, and post-traumatic stress that lasted years. Loud noises still scare me, and I can't stand fireworks shows. I also instantly developed a visceral hatred for the Irish that took me over two decades to shake off. The sound of an Irish voice often made me leave the room. When drunk I'd pick fights with Irish people and make fun of their accents, calling them names like "Seamus O'Fiddle-faddle-dee-biddle-dee-bum" and telling them, "Oh, 'tis a foine shillelagh for me to lather ye with, isn't it, Paddy? Saints preserve us, but yer oies are as brown and lovely as a freshly poured Guiness, are they not, me lad? May I offer ye a foine poteeto and an abortion?"

Prior to July 20, 1982, I'd been vaguely sympathetic to the goal of a reunited Ireland, but after the bombing I rooted for the British to exterminate as many IRA terrorists as they could. I began obsessively studying terrorism and counterterrorism; I researched the British Special Air Service and MI-6, the Dutch *Bijzondere Bijstands Eenheid,* the German *Grenzschutzgruppe 9,* the French *Groupe d'Intervention de la Gendarmerie Nationale,* the Spanish *Grupo Especial de Operaciones,* the Israeli *Shayetet 13,* and the American Delta Force.

For twenty years I memorized details of operations in which terrorists were ruthlessly killed without being given a chance to surrender. Those were my favorite missions. They were made even better when it was reported that the terrorist pled for mercy or screamed in fear or pain. The GSG-9 rescue of the passengers of Lufthansa Flight 181 at Mogadishu, on October 18, 1977, code named Operation Fire Magic *(Unternehmen Feuerzauber),* filled me with savage glee because the Germans first had Somali soldiers create a diversion by lighting a big fire that drew three of the terrorists into the cockpit to gawp and gesticulate like apes. Then the GSG-9 assault team – led personally by Colonel Ulrich K. Wegener, the forty-eight-year-old founder of the unit – threw flash-bang grenades at the windows, used ladders to storm the plane through three doors simultaneously, and shot all four idiotic hijackers, including one cowering in the toilet like a shithouse rat. It was a near-perfect rescue, marred only by the fact that they didn't finish off the single simian that survived.

My years of hate accomplished nothing. They certainly didn't prevent the people I hated from committing their terrorism. Eventually, I was able to stop blaming the entire nation of Ireland for what happened on July 20, 1982, but the Regent's Park bombing was the reason I didn't listen to U2 unless I had no choice. My college cover band played "New Year's Day" and "Pride (In the Name of Love)"; I rationalized it because the bassist, Adam Clayton, is British.

Thirty years later I no longer hate, and I don't celebrate the killing of terrorists. Instead, I view it the way Tim does, as taking out the garbage: an unpleasant but necessary chore. Those who take out the garbage remain my heroes. However, I'm sure they wouldn't have liked to know me during the period I drooled over their exploits and demanded they descend to the level of the creatures they were forced to relieve of their existence. The truth is that special operators wouldn't like to know me today either, which is all right. I'm still too close to the subject, so the best thing for me to do is stay out of it and let the dispassionate professionals do their jobs.

Currently, one of my favorite singers is Róisín Murphy, who's as Irish as a selkie. She has as much to do with July 20, 1982, as I have with Pancho Villa's murder of sixteen American businessmen on January 11, 1916. The only thing I care about is her music, which awes me with its artistry, makes me laugh, and always improves my mood.

I've also discovered the beauty of traditional Irish blessings. This one is appropriate.

May you have the hindsight to know where you've been,
The foresight to know where you're going,
And the insight to know when you're going too far.

I'm sorry, Ireland. It was wrong to hold all of you responsible for the actions of a few. Please forgive me.

Small Drunks who Love the Bass

During the winter of 1983-84, I spent six months on an exchange program in Sapporo, Japan. Even though I planned on getting a Bachelor of Arts degree in history, I had a vague notion that if I learned to speak Japanese I could somehow be involved in the country's emerging and unstoppable superpower status. I stayed with a host family that had three children: a sixteen-year-old boy, a fourteen-year-old-boy, and a nine-year-old girl. During the six months I lived with them, the older boy spoke to me twice; the younger boy spoke to me once; and the girl never spoke to me. Not once. The family said they'd signed up as a host family so I could teach their kids English.

My classmates and I studied a lot, but mostly we drank. The Japanese have a unique approach to higher education: All that matters is being accepted into a college or university. The entrance exams consist of everything you'd learn pursuing a bachelor's degree. You basically get your entire college education out of the way at the beginning, and then you drink for four years. The Americans were the only people in the school actually studying.

The Japanese were the heaviest drinkers I'd ever met, as well as the greatest lovers of music. Everybody played an instrument, and every social occasion called for singing. Their pop music was incomprehensibly awful; at the time it was called City Pop, aptly pronounced *Shitty Poppu* in Japanese. But the traditional music really knocked me out. One of the greatest musical experiences of my life happened completely by accident when our group went to Kyoto for a week. Most of the time we were under the thumbs of the Japanese professors who dragged us from one tourist spot to another, but one night we were released to prowl around on our own.

I paired up with a Hawaiian girl who later became a stuntwoman in the movies. We chose a little bar at random to have a beer or five before we hit the town. When you enter a Japanese bar, the employees all bellow *"Irrashaimase!"* ("Welcome!") at the tops of their lungs. It can be very startling. At this bar the two young guys doing the bellowing were the rare smart-alecky Japanese. Ninety-five percent of Japanese are bowing, smiling machines, while 5 percent are sarcastic iconoclasts who like giving you a hard time, probably because they know they can do it only with foreigners. The two waiters in their short blue *happi* coats served us our beer and quizzed us in English, repeating our answers in mocking, drawn-out shouts.

"Where you live in America?"

"Los Angeles."

"*Laas Aaaaaaaaanjelessss!* What you doing in Japan?"

"Studying."

"*Staaaaaaadyeeeeeeeeng!*"

We'd had just about enough when the two waiters abruptly went to a tiny stage. One picked up a *shamisen* – a three-stringed banjolike lute – and the other a *tsuzumi,* a hand drum. They began playing *min'yō,* Japanese folk music. Until that moment, I didn't know how the style should be correctly performed. Those two young ball busters were absolute virtuosos of the genre. The complex and ardent melodies of the singing, the syncopation of the drumming, and the plaintive chords and notes of the lute created an alternate universe, transporting us back centuries. We imagined harvest festivals, illicit romances, village life, the daily rituals of farmers and artisans, and the thousands of deities that inhabit the islands.

The Hawaiian girl and I spent the entire night in that bar, listening. I wish I'd recorded it. Nearly thirty years later, I still remember it as though I heard it last night.

What struck me about Japan besides the drinking was the nation's interest in the bass guitar. Everyone knew about the bass. They didn't have guitar heroes; they had bass heroes. The three most popular were Hojin Egawa, Tetsuo Sakurai, and Yoshihiro Naruse, all of whom were famous for the thumb-slapping technique, called "chopper bass" in Japan. Everyone wanted to play chopper bass.

I'd brought my Rickenbacker bass with me to Japan, along with a battery-operated headphone amplifier called a Rockman, designed by guitarist Tom Scholz of the band Boston. By that time I'd developed a much higher level of skill on the bass and didn't want to spend six months not playing. The day I helped my sixteen-year-old host brother buy an electric bass was one of the two times he spoke to me. After he brought the instrument home, he was too shy to let me give him lessons. I wanted to tell him to do what his father did: Get plastered and lose all your inhibitions, my host dad's nightly ritual. We'd sit in the kitchen drinking beer while he monologued in heavily accented English. A chain-smoking heart surgeon, he gave me the impression that nobody in his life listened to him. His wife certainly didn't.

The person who should've haunted me the most from this period ended up not doing so. She was another Hawaiian I'll call Sophie, a singer with a beautiful heart-shaped face and the demented sense of humor that I go for. She was an incredible mimic and had a Wildean wit, seeing the absurd in everything. Before our group had gone to Japan, we'd had a retreat on the Oregon coast, where we prepared for our sojourn by drinking. The guy who led the trip – the adult in charge – got smashed and ran through the bonfire, scattering embers and gobbets of flame everywhere. He took off down the beach, trailing sparks like a meteor. Later, we retired to communal sleeping quarters, drunk and exhausted. After someone turned off the lights, I said, "Pardon me while I unzip my pants." I then slowly unzipped my sleeping bag, which took about thirty seconds.

Out of the darkness, Sophie called, "Grandmother, what a big crotch you have."

I was too bashful to say, "All the better to – "

During our stay in Japan, we immediately became involved. I'd go to her host family's house in the daytime when everyone but Sophie was out, and we'd spend hours in bed, laughing as much as anything else. She had me in stitches when she told me about how a Japanese student at the university hit on her and she walked away.

"So he starts yelling, 'Hey! *Hey!* Where you going? Come back here!' Then he starts following me, and he steps on my *heels* and gives me two *flat tires*, man! Now I can't run 'cause my shoes gonna fall off, I'm *shuffling* away, and this little *worm* with glasses and an armful of books is right behind me, still yelling, like I'm suddenly gonna say, 'You know what? You're *right!* Let's go on a date! How can I turn down a man who has to hobble me like a donkey so I can't escape?'"

Soon it went bad because we were young and addicted to drama. We started fighting like insane people and then making up in bed. She was my first fully consummated love. Though I mourned the passing of our relationship, she left no bad memories. I think of her only with affection. What we fought about was stupid, histrionic, and absurd. It was fighting for its own sake. All of that is out the window, leaving me with the way she made me laugh when she did her various voices, spoke in Hawaiian pidgin ("No can moi moi. I come stay go, you no stay come. Got choke grindz, brah.") and taught me the funniest word ever: "katonk," what Hawaiian-Japanese like Sophie called mainland Japanese-Americans. It described the sound a mainlander's head made when hitting the floor.

Later I learned that the term originated in World War II, in the 442nd Regimental Combat Team, made up entirely of Japanese-Americans. It's the most decorated unit in the history of the U.S. armed forces, earning twenty-one Medals of Honor among its mind-blowing total of awards. Two-thirds of the men were Hawaiian-Japanese, called

"Buddhaheads" by the mainlanders. Both groups fought each other, and the Buddhaheads began calling the mainlanders katonks because they knocked them down so often.

In bed one afternoon, Sophie told me that everyone on the trip made fun of me behind my back for bringing my bass to Japan. They thought it was pretentious. That hurt. I just didn't want to lose my hard-fought skills, which every year brought me closer to my goal of someday duplicating note for note Ray Shulman's live version of "Free Hand."

The most disturbing aspect of Japan was that the place was overrun with massive, primitive-looking crows. They were about three times the size of American crows and had bulging, tumorous foreheads, like they were diseased caveman-versions of the bird. Their voices were so deep they sounded human, and instead of cawing, they said as clearly as my father, "Tom!" I discovered this phenomenon walking home one evening. As I trudged through the snow for several blocks, I heard a chorus of malevolent men calling my name over and over: "Tom! Tom! Tom! Tom!"

It was crows in the trees, watching me. As freaky as that was, it wasn't as strange as what I had to do when I worked on the shore-support base in Norway. Part of my job was to write the Norwegian word "empty" on acetylene and oxygen cylinders in chalk after they were shipped back from the drilling platforms. In Norwegian, "empty" is... *tom*.

I still get a little twinge whenever I sign my name, particularly on books. It seems like an admission of failure.

The Ghost who Exorcised Himself

During my final year in college, I became close friends with a guy I'll call Mike, who'd been one of my fellow exchange students in Japan. Our friendship was as unlikely as the one I'd forged with Joe. It was based on a mutual love of music and our bizarre senses of humor. He was hilarious. When I got an earring, he copied me, but he somehow managed to pull it out just a few minutes after the piercing. I had to put it through the raw, bleeding hole again. We sat in my car, laughing with horror because although I got the peg in, it wouldn't go all the way through to the other side and just sort of gouged around inside his flesh, getting hung up.

"Hurry! Hurry!" he shouted. When I finally got it back in place, he said, "Christ, I'm absolutely *bathed* in sweat. Why would some little pinprick in your earlobe make you sweat so much?"

We went out one night, and without warning he said, "Do you ever think about just crashing your car so you get killed, and then everyone will sit around talking about how sorry they are that you're dead and how they wish they'd been nicer to you?" And we laughed hysterically at what ridiculous, self-pitying buffoons we were.

He was a drummer who never had any money. In a fit of generosity, I bought him an entire drum kit. We were going to start a band, but after our exchange program the Japanese girl he met in Sapporo, whom I'll call Yuki, came to Portland and they got married. I wasn't able to attend the wedding due to a family emergency that kept me by the phone the whole day. After they got hitched, Mike, Yuki, and I lived together in an apartment. It was absolutely cataclysmic. They fought all the time. On my twenty-second birthday, Yuki baked a cake and then she and Mike got into a vicious argument. I asked them if they could please not do that on my birthday.

"Shut the fuck up and eat your goddamn cake," Mike said. That made me so angry I wanted to punch him out. Before he and I got into a confrontation that would've ended in my death, since he was a weightlifter who studied martial arts, Yuki attacked him and began tearing off his clothes. Mike just stood there.

"That's right. Tear off my clothes, bitch."

And she did, yanking and shredding until he was naked. She cackled and yowled in Japanese the whole time. The problem they had was that she was a virgin when they met, and after they were married he told her about the dozens of women he'd slept with before he met her. She thought it was unfair and wanted the freedom to even up the score. He didn't approve of her proposal; they couldn't arrive at a compromise, and the result was daily high-volume conflicts followed by frenzied rutting. After a fight and a bout in the sack, Mike would grin and say, "There's nothing like make-up sex, Tom. Am I right?"

The night of my birthday, they patched things up and we went out drinking. I was so depressed by what a flop I was at everything, especially picking friends, that I got loaded on Long Island Iced Teas and we had to stop on the way home so I could kneel like a congregant by the side of the road and throw up for half an hour. Back at the apartment the quadriplegic neighbor downstairs called and asked if I could help him.

I staggered down and as soon as I opened the door, I knew by the smell what had happened. Drunk and reeling with nausea, I cleaned him as well as I could with washcloths, lifted him out of his bed even though he was six-foot four, put him in the tub, washed him down, changed his bedding, carried him back to his bed, dressed him in clean pajamas, and then washed his soiled clothes and sheets. As I worked I told him about my day, and he kept saying, "Happy birthday, Tom! How do you like my gift to you?" So we were able to laugh about it, especially after he was clean and tucked in and we smoked one of his huge medical-marijuana joints.

Mike and Yuki's fighting cost me my job at the college library. It was impossible to get any sleep with all the screaming followed by passionate moaning, which resulted in me being a few minutes late every morning. My boss, the library archivist, was a pipe-smoking graybeard who sang nautical tunes all day. He was the meanest bastard I've ever met. Two weeks into my employment, he let me know we had a problem by interrupting one of his shanties and hissing, "Is there a pattern?"

Today, at age fifty, I'd say, "Yes. Polka dot." But at twenty-two I didn't have the weapons I've developed over the past three decades. I stuttered, "I don't – I – I'm not sure what you mean."

"Is there a pattern to the time at which you choose to show up for your job?"

I knew enough to not make excuses. Instead, I simply apologized and promised to do better. Getting only two or three hours of sleep a night, I began making more and more mistakes. My overall ineptness didn't change the fact that my boss was completely off his rocker. He once told me to photocopy an entire yearbook; I therefore did so. When I handed him the massive stack of paper, he roared at me, "I didn't tell you to copy the whole *book!* Why would I do *that?* All I need is the *index!* What's wrong with you? Can't you *think?* I'm not paying for this! *You* are!"

Screaming and orgasmic moaning by night, roaring and sea shanties by day. After a month, my boss said, "This isn't working out, I'm sorry to say." I wasn't sorry. He had one of those terrifying paper cutters, a metal platform with a scimitar attached, absolutely perfect for decapitating rotten old pipe-smoking sailor sons of bitches. By the time I was fired, I had a fantasy on an endless loop in my brain, that I'd somehow trick him into bending over the paper cutter.

> *Oh, the hog-eye sailors roll and go*
> *When they come down to San Francisco*
>
> *With a hog-eye, ho*
> *Railroad navvy with a hog-eye*
> *You roll ashore with a hog-eye, oh*
> *She wants a hog-eye man*
>
> *Hey, open hand and primed is he*
> *He'll spend his money fast and free*

With a hog-eye, ho
Railroad navvy with a hog-eye
You roll ashore with a hog-eye, oh
She wants a –

Cha-lunk. And then exquisite, blessed relief.

A few days after my termination, Mike and I went to a bar to talk about whether or not his marriage could be saved. I was paralyzed by fear of the future and had an unbroken string of catastrophic or inane relationships behind me. The conversation was a complete waste of time. However, he was my friend, and I felt obliged to give him my worthless advice. On the fourth or fifth round of drinks, Yuki suddenly appeared behind us, clad in a bathrobe. Since she couldn't drive and barely spoke English, and since there were thousands of bars in Portland, I have no idea how she materialized there. My gut tells me she hitchhiked. Wearing a bathrobe and unable to communicate with the guy who picked her up, he deposited her at exactly the bar where her husband sat drowning his sorrows. That has to be how it happened. Mike turned around, and before he could say anything, Yuki pulled out a pair of scissors and raised it over her head, preparing to stab him in the face.

As unearthly as Yuki's abrupt manifestation was, it was instantly eclipsed by the gigantic bouncer's similar feat. He just as magically burst into existence behind her, grabbed her scissors hand, and shouted, "I *knew* it! I *knew* it! The second I saw her, I knew she was trouble!" Yuki began her usual shrieking, but the bouncer did something Mike never tried: He covered her mouth. "You guys get outta here," he said. "The cops are on their way."

Portland was unique in my experience, in that when you dialed 911, the police always showed up in under a minute. It was uncanny. Mike and I walked out, and sure enough, squad cars were already screeching to a halt in front of the bar. The bouncer turned Yuki over to the cops, and as soon as he took his hand off her mouth, she screamed, *"Mike! Doan go! I rub you! Mike! Mike! I rub you! Doan reeb me! Mike! Mike!"* It was exactly like the final scene of the movie *A Face in the Crowd.* I've never been more shocked and disgusted in my life, but I also had to fight to keep from laughing because it was so stupid, especially when Mike started crying.

"I can't leave her," he blubbered. "I love her!"

"You're done with her," I snarled and tried to frog march him – a grown man – to my car. "She's demented. Fuck her."

He shoved me away and went over to beg the cops to release her, which they did. After we all drove home in silence, Mike and Yuki had their usual session of chattering, caterwauling make-up sex while I lay in bed with pillows jammed against my ears. Soon, however, he saw it my way and divorced her. He and I then decided that the best thing for us to do would be to move in together for the summer and then go back to Japan to seek our fortunes. Mike got a job as a bartender at a restaurant, while I tried working as a bartender in a club. I was fired my first night, when a customer ordered eight different drinks and then claimed I'd gotten them all wrong after I poured them. I argued with him; he started yelling; and I was canned on the spot.

When Mike wasn't working and I wasn't trying to find work, we went to strip clubs. I found them depressing beyond belief because the strippers obviously loathed the customers, who were fat, howling blue-collar guys and their slutty dates; half-dead pensioners spending their Social Security checks; yuppies carrying on like baboons; and priapic smirkers like Mike. At his insistence I bought a lap dance once. It was unspeakably mortifying to have a nude woman sit on me, grope me, and engage in frottage with me in front of a roomful of leering anthropoids. When it was finally over, she kissed my cheek and said, "Thank you, mister. I'll always remember you as the first man who gave me a break."

The next day I escaped to Los Angeles, where I stayed with Tim. About to embark on another madcap adventure, I decided to make a memory box. I built it out of pine, which

I stained dark walnut. It had niches for objects that represented my background, interests, accomplishments, and goals. Included were my high-school and college graduation mortarboard tassels, hanging in two long niches; a shot glass to commemorate my four-hour career as a bartender; a tiny pencil to signify my urge to be a writer; a photo of a lip-synching contest my dorm floor had won by adopting my idea of wearing white lab coats and dark glasses and carrying white canes while miming Thomas Dolby's "She Blinded Me with Science"; a little oil derrick I constructed from styrene rod, mounted in a niche in front of a photo of Lake Maracaibo; a photo of our house in Tyler, with a Lone Star State lapel pin on it; and a plastic model World War I biplane I'd built as a teenager.

I also put in a photo I'd cut out of a magazine and glued to poster board so I could give it a three-dimensional effect as it stood proud from the background inside the niche. Since my first left-handed bass was a Carvin, I cut the figure of a bassist from a Carvin ad in *Guitar Player*. The bass player was unknown to me; I just wanted the Carvin instrument. I was quite satisfied with my memory box. It looked very professional.

After saying goodbye to my family, I drove back to Portland, where for the rest of the summer I took care of my quadriplegic former neighbor from the previous apartment. All I had to do was drive him around and prepare his meals. He didn't have any more accidents, and a trained nurse bathed him. It was a nice, relaxing job. He was remarkably positive, despite having been in his wheelchair for over twenty years. We got along because he taught me how to cook and he was a writer. He wrote everything in longhand, the pen in his mouth and the pad of paper in his permanently clenched fists.

One night I went to Mike's restaurant to pick him up, since his car was in the garage. Business was slow, and we got into a conversation with one of the sexy waitresses, a short, busty brunette I'll call Angela.

"You guys ever had a threesome?" she asked.

Neither of us had.

"You wanna have one? Tonight?"

I didn't, but Mike's face lit up. When the bar closed, Mike and I got in my car and had Angela follow us back to our house. As we drove along, Mike tittered and said, "Um, how are we gonna do this? Is it gonna be me on one end and you on the other?"

"No!" I barked. "Let's do it one a time. You go first."

"Yeah. That's what I was thinking. Both of us together in the same bed would be..." He trailed off.

Yes, it would. At our house, we all smoked pot and then Mike and Angela went into the bedroom. I realized I'd have to take off my clothes. Even with the THC coursing through my system, all I felt was dread. I turned off the lights, stripped, then sat on the sofa and waited. After about twenty minutes, Mike came out of the bedroom naked. He dropped into an armchair and said, "Your turn." I went to the bedroom and slipped under the covers. Angela lay there, staring at the ceiling. I put my hand on her bare belly; she didn't react.

"You don't want to do this, do you?" I asked.

"No."

"That's okay. I don't either."

She gave me a rueful smile and said, "I'm sorry. It sounded like a good idea in the restaurant, but now that it's happening... I just had an abortion a few days ago. I shouldn't have suggested this."

I wrapped myself in the sheet and went out to the dark living room, where Mike sat with a cushion over his groin. Angela came out of the bedroom a few minutes later, fully clothed. "See you, guys," she said and left. Mike sighed.

"Well, *that* was the grossest thing we've ever done, wasn't it? You're lucky you didn't fuck her. Something's wrong with her pussy. It felt like oatmeal."

In July he met an eighteen-year-old and spent the rest of the summer with her. We bought our airline tickets to Japan and guidebooks to finding employment. The plan was to go there and land lucrative jobs teaching conversational English while we learned the ropes and perfected our Japanese. Then something exceptional would no doubt come up.

Two days before we were scheduled to depart for Tokyo, Mike told me he wasn't going to go. He'd fallen in love with his eighteen-year-old and had to stay in Portland. To say I was stunned doesn't begin to express the outrage and volcanic fury that gripped me. Mike's new girlfriend was a dolt. All she had going for her was a nice body. I honestly couldn't understand why he'd chosen her over our adventure, but I said nothing except "Okay, then." He spent that night with his girlfriend, and the next day he came back to our house, shook my hand, and wished me luck. I then flew to Japan by myself. We wrote each other twice. In his second letter he asked me what to do with the Rickenbacker bass I'd left in his family's care. I told him to sell it. We had no more contact; he never offered to repay me for the drum kit.

In 2010 I got an e-mail from Mike. He said he'd been looking for me for ages, and we had tons of catching up to do. In that message he asked me what I'd been doing since the last time we saw each other. I told him, and he wrote, "Jesus, you've had an interesting life. I run a scrap-metal business. I don't have any stories to tell you about anything." He had no recollection whatsoever of our mishaps, including my loathsome twenty-second birthday. He didn't remember our trips to the coast, our burger barbecues, the time he pierced his ear, or any of our mutual friends. He truly had nothing to say to me. E-mailing me seemed to depress him, as his messages became shorter and shorter. After only five exchanges, I let our relationship die again.

But I still have the memories of our friendship, and they give me pleasure. His humor was exceptional. He could always make me laugh, and for that I'm grateful.

If Mike reads this memoir, I'd like to tell him that Joe Cady and I are still friends because whenever we talk, we simply pick up where we left off the last time. He's the most consistent person I've ever met. Joe and I would probably disagree on everything if we talked about politics and social issues. All I care about when I talk to Joe is my friendship with him. All he cares about when he talks to me is his friendship with me. We don't tell each other stories; we *talk*. We discuss everything on our minds, and the conversation flows, sometimes for two hours without us knowing it. Since 1981 I've never had an awkward moment with him. In July of 2012, I asked Joe if he had a photo of me with my Fender Musicmaster. He didn't, but he drew a cartoon instead. Even after thirty years, he was able to summon completely from memory a shockingly accurate representation of not only me but also my essence.

Joe is an order of magnitude more successful than I am, and he lives in *Paris,* for God's sake. He has a stable marriage, tons of friends, and he's on the cusp of something great in the tech world. I hope he becomes a billionaire and lives to be 175. I'm just happy for him, that's all.

Good for you, Joe.

Interlude with Scott Thunes
Zappa

I went directly from parking cars to working with Frank. Going down to L.A. and working with Frank in 1981, I was a puppy: I kept my mouth closed and my ears open. Being a puppy means you don't put yourself out because if you do, you get crushed. The older people who'd been in the band for a while will piss on you. Frank's a fair guy, but if you are stupid and say stupid things, he'll nail you immediately. So you either don't say anything at all, or you are very tentative in what you say. You don't want to say anything that's too drastic, too opinionated. According to lore, it was obvious that I was tweaked in some way, that I was a goofball. Even though I didn't put anything out in a huge way that could be construed to be really psycho, Frank could tell I had some energy there that he wanted to be a part of his band.

I saw his band that previous year, and there was no energy there at all. It was Dullsville. I hated it. It drove me bananas, and I didn't want to have anything to do with them at all. I wasn't ever going to listen to Frank's music again. I had nothing to listen to. I listened to *Joe's Garage* and it was sterile. So when I went and actually started playing with them, I kept my mouth shut. I was hanging out with Tommy Mars and Ed Mann, who were very, very funny, and very intercommunicative, and very boisterous, very intelligent. Their humor was really severely weird and odd, and so I got to hang out with two or three older people who were really cool. I definitely, once again, was hanging out with the older guys, which I've always done. Ended up getting out of my peer group and moving forward. It wasn't really hanging out with them but more experiencing them and understanding how much you could get away with.

I wasn't in any way at that point caring about whether or not my communication needs were being met. I was very happy to just be in this experience and keep my mouth shut, listening to music on my headphones, driving around and seeing things, and going about my business. There wasn't really much going on that I could change. I wasn't affecting anybody or anything yet. So it was very good for me to just sit, learn, and listen, and I did that in '81. At the end of that tour, there were about three months where we didn't do anything, and Frank said he was gonna go out, but he didn't know when, so I came back up to the Bay Area. Finally, he calls me up and three days later, I'm down in Los Angeles getting ready for a tour. We had only a month to rehearse and then we went out. So by the time the '82 tour was over, I'd been in the band for about a year, and there's a videotape of me being obnoxious and annoying.

When I was in high school, I invented a personality that got me attention. At the alternative school where I went, the hippies would go outside and smoke pot and their cigarettes, and if I spotted anybody with a cigarette, I would grab it out of their mouth and smash it. "Uh-oh! Here comes Scott Thunes!" I got beat up once and didn't do it ever again. But for three or four months, I was a scourge. None of the high-school girls would look at me twice. They were all older than me, and the ones I liked that were my age were going out with the older guys. The only way that I could get any attention was to be over the top, and once I realized that I could apply that personality perfectly in rock and roll, I just fell into it. I expanded to fill up that space because I was with Frank Zappa, for God's sakes. I couldn't disgust him in any way, but I could pretty much disgust everybody else. One of the first things that Chad Wackerman said to me was, "Don't say fuck off to me." I'm like, "Oh-*kay*." I'm in rock and roll, but there are normal humans here, too.

The '82 tour ended, and then there was a year and a half where we didn't do anything, what I consider the finest time of my life. For a year and a half I was a rock star at home, back in my environs in the Bay Area, surrounded by tons of really cool people and surrounded by tons of beautiful girls. And they didn't care that I was a rock star at all. Most of them didn't know who Frank Zappa was. But I had a boisterous personality that had been honed to a sinister touch. I could utilize it to get what I wanted. I didn't even realize it at the time, didn't know what the hell was going on. But still it was fun. I could communicate; I was hanging out with people who were smarter than me; and I was holding my own. I had definitely found my niche.

Even so I was depressed most of the time. I would find myself pretty much depressed one day a week, just completely down. Very much *Sturm und Drang, Weltschmerz,* adolescent bullshit. I was finally doing some of my adolescent stuff that I hadn't done before because I didn't have time. I was learning and soaking in, and I realized I'm not getting what I wanted. Nothing's going forward; I can't get a job. I've been in rock and roll, and spent all my money on sushi, and now I can't even fucking get a job. So I got a couple of cheesy jobs. I was a busboy; I worked at a liquor store; I taught guitar for a while. I was completely and utterly poverty-stricken for a year and a half. Didn't do anything at all, and I was living in the City but coming into Marin every day. Bus fare was $36 and I was making $30 a week. It was very weird, that whole year-and-a-half period.

I was deliriously happy with my environment, though. I was surrounded by very cool people; I was boning beautiful girls; and I was in three or four bands, playing really cool music with my friends. It was the ultimate experience that a musician could have, really just prime. I didn't care what happened for the rest of my life. I didn't think Frank was ever going to play again. I was just playing in bands and working cheesy jobs. And finally when the cheesy jobs got to be too much and nothing else was going on, Frank called back, and I went down to L.A. again.

Nineteen eighty-four was the pinnacle and last bastion of my obnoxiosity. I was really full on. I'd just had a year and half of enthwartenment of my outward-going-ness, and in 1984 I was Frank Zappa's bass player again. I was twenty-four, at the height of my powers, emotionally and musically and humorously, and Frank let me do anything that I wanted. Couple of weird things happened, but for the most part, I was king of the world. I could do whatever I wanted. I could say whatever I wanted. I was a golden boy. Frank never voiced any complaints about anything I did, and it was maniacal. Smack dab in the middle of that tour, I fell in love with this girl who was gorgeous. Frederika Kesten, a New York babe, seventeen. I fell in love, ended up moving to New York to be with her for a year. We were in love for three and a half years. She moved out to Los Angeles, which is why I moved there.

I was golden. I had the most beautiful girlfriend in the world, and I was twenty-four, and I had tons of money, and I was traveling the world. It was the ultimate expression of what rock was all about. I didn't know what I was doing. I was just a fucking kid going along with the flow.

In '88, I was so rich and frivolous that instead of staying in Orlando for three days, for example, I decided to fly back to New York on my own dime. I booked my own flights, flew back to New York, hung out with my girlfriend for three days, and then flew back. Had an absolutely wonderful time. Couple weeks after that, we were about to leave for Europe. We had two days off before we left. Everybody else had to stay up in Woodstock. I flew to New York again on my own money. I stayed in New York with my girlfriend for two days, and then met everybody at the airport, and that was really cool.

That was one of the better experiences of my life because she was pretty snobby. Not necessarily rich, but her father was a movie producer. Not a megabucks one, but just enough to make things happen. She was a club goer and had pretty good values. I had to fly back with the guys for some reason, and she decided to meet me at the airport, at La Guardia, in a limousine because I had three hours to kill. There was no reason to go back into town, but since she had a limousine we could make out in the back. She rented a limousine, bought me a six-pack of Heineken, and met me at the airport. Frank's limo didn't show up, so he had to ride in the van with the guys.

It was a complete and utter turnaround. Absolutely amazing. I got to hang out in the back of this limousine, drinking beer and making out with my incredibly beautiful, big-titted girlfriend. Everybody else was tense out of their minds because we're about to go to Europe, and I'm like virtually getting laid. I was massively in love with this girl. It was really, really sweet. That's one of the cool things that can happen every once in a while: Your girlfriend can be cooler than anybody else.

We went to Europe, had two and a half months there. Came back and had a week off, so I flew her out here and we hung out in Marin for a week, and then we had rehearsals. Our first gig was in Worcester, Massachusetts, so I flew her out there. She got to hang out with me for two weeks straight in the middle of this five-month tour. After every rehearsal, we had the rest of the day off. Unfortunately, Worcester is a boring little town. That's kind of one of the things Frank does. He starts in these small towns so that if the gig is bad, it's not that much of a disaster. There wasn't that much to do in town, so you can't go crazy every night. So, for two weeks, I got to hang out with my incredibly beautiful girlfriend, right smack dab in the middle of the tour, five days of which are in this hellhole out in middle of nowhere. I would've gone completely insane, but here I am living with this incredibly beautiful girl in the hotel.

The night of the concert, she gets dressed up in this beautiful black dress. The show is in this old theater, and along the side wall on stage, up here back in the corner, is some kind of old ice box or some kind of office, and it's got a window. So she's sitting up there, with her head out the window, being a beautiful girl, watching, and after a while, Frank's bodyguard motioned her to get her head back inside because she was attracting too much attention away from Frank. It was really funny. That was part of the beauty of having a really beautiful girlfriend.

We went to Europe and were in London for five days. She flew out and hung out with me for five days. It was kind of a disaster. These things happen. Sometimes timing's bad, communication is off, desperation ploys come into play. You have no idea where the tension is coming from. It didn't work out so good, but there was still some fun there. It was fine. Ended up being together for three-and-a-half years. But girlfriend stuff? All the time.

Mike Keneally brought his wife Vivian along in the 1988 tour because he'd never been to Europe. He knew he'd probably never end up in Europe again, but he knew that it wasn't cool to put girls on the bus even if they were spouses, so he got her a Eurail pass, and she followed us around. It was great. Vivian's great, and it was absolutely fun to have her around. People do that all the time. As a matter of fact, I heard that one of the major misplays that Terry Bozzio did was he brought Dale along for a European tour that they had done in the middle seventies, but he bought himself a Eurail pass so he could be with her. They would always show up late and he would always be burnt out from an overnight stay in a train. There's a million girl stories – a million, billion of 'em, all different.

Most people I have ever hung out with never had the experience of their spouses or girlfriends getting jaded about the guy being in a rock band. Definitely never had that experience. My friend Alex Kirst, who is in the band the Nymphs, was married to Tracy, who I used to go out with a long time ago. She was a very diligent rock wife. Made sure that she was at every single show. Completely and utterly juiced out by every rock thing that happened. Any good thing. I mean, he was signed to Geffen. They were supposed to be the golden band. She was definitely basking in the rock adoration. Unfortunately, their lead singer was insane and hated her, so there was always tension. And Tracy's kind of a tension-filled person anyway, so it was always interesting to see that affect.

But no, I would say that generally more of the people that I have hung out with, or been with, that their spouses and significant others always stayed interested. I would say a large percentage of them definitely took part in it. I mean, that's the only glory that 98 percent of them are ever going to get. Patti Hansen: Does she ever get bored going to a Rolling Stones concert? I'm sure she'd much rather stay in the Bahamas or wherever the hell she lives. You know? But it's different when you're a kid and you don't know how long this gravy train is going to last. Gotta go out there and get as much glory as you possibly can.

Women are very interesting on the road, because most of them are twits. Most of them aren't nice people. Most of them just want to be with their particular mate, and every once in a while, you find some really, really cool people. Others turn out to be weird fucking spaced-out shrew-persons. There is a lot of not-nice stuff that happens on the road. When we were finished in Worcester, Massachusetts, we were going to hop on the bus and drive down to Connecticut, and then drive down to New York. I figure, why not have Freddie come with us? Frank knows her. Frank's been hanging out with her the past couple of weeks. He knows exactly how cool and how smart she is and how beautiful she is, but he says, "No, you can't bring her on the bus because of this insurance thing. If anything happens, we're dead." So I put her on a bus to New York. "Goodbye. I'll see you in two days. You can't stay on the bus with us."

That night someone else brings a girl on the bus. And there was a lot of tension about that because I said, "I can't believe this." And they said, "Well, to be honest, we know how smart Freddie is. We know that if we make her sign the release, that it doesn't mean anything. The release doesn't mean anything. She could still sue us, and she'd probably be able to do it. But this other twit doesn't know that." So the other guy and his pick-up ho get to ride on the bus to New York for two days, and Freddie – who I'm in love with, and who is one of the finer, smarter people in the world – has to take a different bus and leave me alone for two days. The first night, we come in to whatever city it was, and as I'm walking past the guy and his ho, I say something really nasty, akin to, "Well, it's a good thing your girlfriend is never going to find out about this," or something like that. He had just supposedly fallen in love on the road with this really great girl that I really liked. And I pretty much just stuck it to him as much as I could. He called me about four times. I talked to him on the phone a couple of times. He came down and banged on my door and told me he was going to beat the shit out of me. But I didn't open the door, and the next day, I made sure to get on the bus only when everybody else was already there. It was pretty good.

From that point on, there was a massive feud and we never spoke again. When he came to the '88 tour rehearsal, as soon as I saw his outline, I left. I got the hell out of there. Not from any sense of danger to myself; I just disliked him so intensely. "Hi. Goodbye."

Frank said one thing to me, a long time ago. He said when he's at rock concerts, when he's playing, he looks at everybody in the audience and everybody on stage. They all have a thought bubble above their head that says, "Blowjob," or something like that. It was "Head," or "Blowjob," or "Cum," or something like that, and unfortunately that stuck with me. I don't know if I agree with it, but when I think about these rock people, well, I think definitely, "Money." I think, "Hit." I think, "Blowjob." All this rock-band stuff – it doesn't matter. I've seen rock bands where the people don't actually look like they want to make any money, but even some of these punk bands – they look like they want a hit! They want to be a punk band with a hit. That's their goal in life. Hardly anybody is in a rock band just because they love the music. The whole subtext is, you're going to get rich and famous. And Frank never put that out. This is the pinnacle. Even if you got rich and famous, you may want to quit that band so you could play with Frank. It was more important to play with Frank than to be rich and famous.

Frank himself was rich and famous, sure, but he never gave his musicians any of that glory. It never rubbed off on them. The only thing that they could do – the pinnacle of rock experience – was either to make a million dollars, or play with Frank. If you play with Frank, you're not going to make a million dollars. He paid less than anybody, ever. For that kind of arena gig, he paid less than anybody.

My sister Stacy was working at the Rainbow Bar and Grill on Sunset, and the night I first got hired in '81 I went there and had a burger. I celebrated by going to the Rainbow, hanging out with my sister, and having a beer. I was poverty-stricken; I was out of my mind; I didn't know what the hell was going on. But I went; I had a burger and a beer, talked with her and the two guys that ran the place – I guess two Italian guys, something like that; they'd been around for a long fucking time – and Stacy said, "Yeah, my brother just got hired with Frank Zappa," and one guy goes, "Oh, congratulations," and the other one says, "Yeah, he doesn't really pay very much, does he?" Ohhh-*kaay*. A thousand dollars a week I thought was pretty damned good, but it's not the $5000 a week that a rock band gets. That's a rock band. Frank is not a rock band.

I don't know that I "carried the show" in '88. I could easily agree that in 1984 I was the only person who was doing anything up on stage. I was probably the only person who was doing anything at all on stage from 1981 to 1984 and for ten years previous to that. In 1973 and 1974, he had a couple of really great bands. He had Napoleon Murphy Brock, who was doing some crazy-ass shit. There was interesting communication on stage. There were some stories; there were puppets; there was poodle madness – anything that could go on. I was easily the only person who had done anything since 1978. As soon as Terry Bozzio was out of the band, I was definitely the only person. I took his place in that regard. There was now something to watch on stage besides Frank standing around doing funny voices.

In '88 I don't remember carrying that band. You can tell me that, but I am as about as removed from that physical experience as a person can be from anything that they've done. I don't want to know. I wasn't there. I very much gladly tuned it out. I have absolutely no interest in reliving any of that – which doesn't mean to say I'm not going to answer your question, but the point is, I don't remember carrying anything. I don't remember standing up on stage and being the most powerfully intense person. Unless you mean you look up there and go, "The show is being ruined because this bass player seems like he doesn't enjoy himself."

You stick around in a band when you're not enjoying yourself because Frank needs you. I have absolutely no problem with Frank. The only thing I can think of, in terms of carrying the band – if at all I was – is the idea that I'm solid. I am golden. I haven't done anything wrong. I am exactly myself. I am the exact same person that Frank hired. I haven't gotten a huge ego. I haven't changed my communication with the band on purpose. I knew that I was doing stuff that was not run of the mill. Absolutely.

Anthology Two
First Light
1985-1991

Mystic shadow, bending near me,
Who art thou?
Whence come ye?
And – tell me – is it fair
Or is the truth bitter as eaten fire?
Tell me!
Fear not that I should quaver.
For I dare – I dare.
Then, tell me!

The Cat-faced Ghost in the Rising Sun

Upon landing in Tokyo in the early fall of 1985, the first thing I did was find a place to stay. At that time there were guesthouses that catered to tourists and foreign carpetbaggers like me. I chose a place at random from one of my guidebooks and took a taxi there. When I went in through what I thought was the entrance, I found myself in the communal kitchen, in the nook reserved for the garbage can. Several young western women at the dining room table stared at me in silence.

"Is this where I check in?" I asked.

"No, that's where you stand in garbage," a blonde answered. I looked down and saw that I was indeed standing in garbage. Since she pronounced it *gaahbeej,* I knew she was Australian. "Go up one door. That's where Mr. Yoshioka will sign you in."

I followed her instructions and was given my own room, about the size of our cedar closet in Tyler. A bare bulb hung from the ceiling, and the walls were so thin I could hear people coughing, laughing, belching, breaking wind, and having sex all around me, the sounds of a Manila whorehouse. It occurred to me that I'd made the biggest mistake of my life.

For a few days, I just explored Tokyo. The crowds were unbelievable. Riding the subway one night, I estimated that ten people were crammed against me at once. If that doesn't seem possible, imagine me as a wagon-wheel hub and all those Japanese as spokes: hot, soft, impassive, xenophobic spokes. Soon I fell in with a fellow resident of the guesthouse, a Canadian man in his thirties who traveled the world taking photos for a famous series of books. We went to the imperial palace, the Yasukuni Shrine, the Tsukiji fish market – everywhere a photographer would want to capture images. We talked about our lives and confided in each other about our hopes and fears. After about ten days, I came down one morning to find him in the kitchen putting on his giant backpack.

"Well," he said, "Gotta go. It's been great knowing you." And he strolled out the door. It sent me into a deep funk because I thought we'd become if not friends at least close acquaintances. He didn't shake my hand or offer to keep in touch; I don't even remember his name. He was a nomad, the way oil-industry children were. I didn't want to revisit that lifestyle, but most foreigners in Tokyo were like that. Here today, gone tomorrow.

One of the residents of the guesthouse was a twenty-three-year-old Japanese-American woman with a striking catlike face and long, frizzy hair. She was a fellow Californian, from an upscale beach community. Like many Sanseis, or third-generation Americans, she had a western first name and Japanese middle and family names. She wryly told me she hated both her first and middle names, so I promised I'd address her by her family name, which I'll say is Nakamura.

She laughed. "Excellent! And I'll call you Wictor! How come I never thought of that before? I could've saved myself years of angst!"

We began spending all our time together. She was extremely funny and bright, short but long-legged, bosomy, and possessed of a big, muscular, round bottom, a feature hardly ever seen on women of Japanese ancestry. Her easy conversation and humor made her great company, as did her beautiful ass. I thought we were just pals, but then one day when we bought soft-serve ice-cream cones, she performed fellatio on hers, gazing steadily at me. It's still one of the most erotic performances I've had the honor of observing. I was thrilled and confused, especially after discovering that her tongue was abnormally long and supple. She could touch her chin with it or make it ripple in waves.

The next day I tried to kiss her, but she laughingly pushed me away. "Wictor, I'm not here to find a boyfriend," she said. "Chill, buddy." It was all right with me. Though I liked her a lot, I thought we'd make a terrible couple. She was a natural-born heartbreaker, I could tell. Still, I bought a set of watercolors and painted a sailboat at sea under a setting sun for her. I had it framed and gave it to her for Christmas. She slipped a note under my door.

> Dear Wictor:
> Thank you so much for the lovely picture – I am so impressed!!! I feel like I have been given a gift fit for a queen. I don't know how to express myself, I am so embarrassed. It is so beautiful – I can't stop staring at it. I had a wonderful Christmas. Thank you! I want to run into your room and give you a big hug, but it's too difficult right now. Do you understand? I'm so glad I've found a friend like you, Wictor, among the 11 billion people living in Tokyo.
> I wish I had a purple pen to write with. After all, purple is cosmic. You've made me a very happy person.
> You're very special, Tom. Merry Christmas.

I moved out of the guest house to live with two British hostesses. That lasted only two weeks because they worked all night, came home at two in the morning, and woke me up as they raucously unwound from their evening of pouring drinks for and flattering swinish Japanese businessmen. I returned to the guest house and got a job teaching conversational English. Nakamura became an administrative assistant at a Japanese manufacturing firm, since she was bilingual. She asked me if I wanted to share an expensive two-room apartment with her, on a strictly platonic basis. In Tokyo you're expected to pay six months' rent up front when you sign the contract: first and last months' rent, two months' rent for deposit, and two months' rent as a tribute to the landlord for granting you the privilege of tenancy. I'd never lived one-on-one with a woman and figured the experience would come in handy for the future, so I accepted Nakamura's offer.

Sliding wood-and-paper shoji doors separated the two bedrooms, and there was a kitchen and a bathroom with a bathtub shower. As soon as we moved in together, I bought a cheap Japanese J-bass copy and a small practice amp. Nakamura liked it when I played softly in the evenings. I'd gotten much better in the past year, and she hadn't known any bassists. At night we lay in our futons and talked for hours through the closed shojis before nodding off. As she moved closer to sleep, her voice became sweeter and more childlike, unlike her normal near-baritone.

One day she gave me an envelope and told me to open it at lunch during work. It was the most flattering letter I'd ever read.

> Dear Wictor:
> I'm really not very good at expressing myself sometimes, & this character flaw, if that's what you want to call it, gets me into lots of messes – w/people I get close to. I've been trying hard for the past few years to develop a way to be open but it's still pretty difficult to me. Maybe it's that I'm not open enough in the way it s'posedly counts to others – I dunno. And well, w/you I feel like I've come a long way in a pretty short time – that scares me... but I know that everything we've shared has been good for me and I can't remember the last time I felt so well tuned in w/another person. I guess I feel threatened because of my feelings for you. As you know, my mental and emotional health has been in sad shape recently, but as trite, dumb, & retarded as it sounds, I get a lot of my strength from being w/you.
> I don't know how what I'm saying will affect us, but it's just a chance I have to take. Our living situation has been a real dilemma and that is mainly due to my weaknesses. Before, when we first met and talked casually about getting a place together, it was OK. I wanted a clear-cut idea of space needs recognized and it would've been fine – a platonic, palsy setup. But as the months passed and I got much closer to you I couldn't trust myself to live with you. It would be too dangerous and I saw it as a threat to our friendship because I could just see us @ the inevitable – "together," "in the sack," or however you want to put it. You left and went to live with those two British chicks and then came back to the guest house and I realized you meant more to me than just a friend to cruise around Tokyo with. And so I thought "Well, what the hey...!" This is really hard for me to say but I decided to get an apartment with you because I thought I would lose you otherwise. I hate to ever say or admit to myself that I need anyone but realistically – if you were to vanish from my life right now I'd be a pretty sad Nakamura.
> Oh, Mr. Wictor, I didn't think I'd feel this way about anyone I was to meet here in Japan, but I was wrong. As corny as it may sound, I think about you constantly. I'd like to feel you holding me in your arms – I can imagine how good and right it'd feel from just thinking about it.
> I'm not even sure I want to give you this letter – even tho' I know it would probably be for the better if I did since it'd clear up a lot of misunderstandings, I think. But having written this I feel so incredibly vulnerable and am more sad than before I wrote it. There is so much more I want to say, but I'm starting to feel overwhelmed by the waves in my brain and my *kokoro* [heart].
> Nakamura

When I came home, I thanked her for her letter and told her everything would be okay. I was impressed by the courage it took her to write it. Also, it was beautiful, written in several different colors of ink in her careful, rounded printing; she never used cursive. I told her that we should just take things one day at a time and not pressure each other. She agreed and seemed to relax.

About three weeks later, we woke up one Saturday morning in our bedrooms as usual. I yawned, and Nakamura called, "Wictor, come in here." From the undertone of laughter in her voice, I knew exactly what she wanted, and it was what I wanted, too. When I slid open the shoji, I found her lying naked on her futon, propped up on one elbow, smiling. I lay down next to her and in about two minutes began the most blatantly carnal relationship of my life.

She was a sexual athlete. I've never been with someone who wanted more sex. The instant intensity of that first time set the tone for all our subsequent couplings. Although the best kisser I've ever encountered, she was impatient with the preliminaries and preferred going right to the main event, smiling broadly the whole time, as though watching a particularly funny stand-up comedian and anticipating the next great joke. She liked to put on solo shows for me before and after, and when she was finally satisfied I'd see by the clock that two hours had gone by. She wanted to try everything.

"How's *that?*"

Shrug. "Eh."

"What about *that?*"

Frown. "Yuck."

"That?"

Wide-eyed smile. "Oo, yeah! Right *there!* Keep right on doing that, mister!"

I called her "Nakamura-face" and she called me "Wictor-head." She'd scuttle up to me on all fours, wagging her round bottom like a dog's tail, and chortle, "Wanna fuck?" Her favorite pastime was giving me haircuts naked, swinging her ample breasts into my face and giggling. Once on a train, we managed to find seats. She sat and crossed her legs, her umbrella between them, and proceeded to masturbate right there in public, smiling at me and making occasional cooing sounds. Though Japanese cities have the highest population densities on earth, the countryside is empty, which is why on our weekend hikes she'd strip naked and trot along in her boots, smiling and making her breasts and buttocks bounce for me. Then we'd find a secluded grove and go at it.

I found that it was too much. All we ever did was have sex or talk about sex. Having a girlfriend with an insatiable sex drive had been my fantasy, but the reality of it was exhausting and tedious. Most of her stories from college were about how she and her girlfriends did things like put little rubber penis-covers over the light switches and shout out the dorm window, "*I want cock!*" Her nickname in school was "Tits." We'd get letters from college friends addressed to "Tits Nakamura." Her best friend at school was a guy who liked to come up behind her or other girls as they sat in chairs, unzip his pants, put his penis beside their neck, and croon the opening line from Paul Anka's "Put Your Head on My Shoulder." Everybody thought it was side splitting. I wondered how many times you could do that. Wouldn't it be utterly played out after just once? And was it actually funny in the first place?

She also began constantly mugging for me and making weird sounds. "*Doyng!*" or "*Meep!*" or "*Feeeyuuuuuu!*" She'd twist her mouth into a sideways slash or talk like Scooby Doo for minutes at a time. Her most disturbing characteristic was that in the dark, as she fell asleep, she went into sighing, whispering recitations of her hypnagogic hallucinations.

"I see a clown, and he's in midair, and he's got cables attached to his feet, knees, wrists, and elbows, and they're slowly pulling his limbs so it looks like he's running, and he's bathed in a golden light that shines down from the upper right, and he's wearing a pointed dunce cap with a 'π' symbol on it, and he's got red circles painted on his cheeks, and he's made of wood with jointed limbs..."

Another one I remember.

"I see you as an 1890s baseball player, and you're totally fit and muscular, with your mustache waxed into two curly points, and you're wearing a light-gray pinstriped uniform with red knee socks and a flat-topped cap with horizontal red bands, and you're tapping the soles of your shoes with the bat to knock the dirt from your cleats, and the crowd is roaring, *hhhhhhhhhhhhhhhhhh,* and you take your first swing, and it's a strike, and you shake your head and take the second swing, and crack! you round first base, second base, third base, home..."

She had two distinct personalities. One was quietly humorous and elegant, the young woman in a business suit who visited me at the school where I worked and whom everybody there called Nakamura, since that was how I'd introduced her. This was the romantic, sensitive woman who wrote long, funny, cultured, sweet letters for me to read in my lunch breaks. The other persona was the mugging, *meep*ing, Scooby Doo-voiced sex maniac in jeans and no underwear. Her dualism scared and frustrated me so much that the relationship began to sour after only a few months.

Looking back from my current vantage point, I realize now how I felt about her: She embarrassed me. The letters from her friends addressed to Tits Nakamura, the funny faces and cartoon noises, and the need to be naked as often as possible made her seem like a coarse nitwit, which she wasn't. I thought she was better than the way she behaved, and I tried to hold her to higher standards. What attracted me to her in the first place was her ironic sense of humor, which matched her sly cat's face, and now she did things that made me think of her as a trailer-park pig. She'd become a burping, farting, whooping party-girl and frightening nighttime blatherer with an audience of one: me. It was simply a bad fit, something I refused to accept.

She knew it though; she once slipped a note into my pack of cigarettes. I found it when I lit up after getting off the subway before work. It said in part, "The reason I don't think you know me is because – now don't hit me – is I think you see me in a higher light than I'm due."

We began fighting, always about her doing something that upset me. I learned she had a terrible temper. One letter she wrote in cosmic-purple ink expressed perfectly how our relationship deteriorated.

> You've made me realize and admit something to myself – something I am so ashamed of and feel so terrible about. There is a viciousness in me. It is a kind of cruelty to others that comes from my weakness and fear of being even in the least bit under the control of another. Because I always have to be the "maker of my own destiny," when I come into contact w/an agent that might possibly have so much influence over me that I could end up doing something, being someone, going somewhere not for me and not even for them either, necessarily, but just because I feel I should – not because I want to for them or for myself, I freak. Understand? Pretty garbled, wasn't that? Well, Wictor, it's that I constantly feel like I'm out of control over you and you can accept my reasons or whatever, asshole, but the reason I'm so terrified of getting closer & closer to you is because you count.
>
> I'm finding this too fucking frustrating to write. Y'know, even when I want to not see you or not talk to you, I miss you, and it hurts.
>
> I'll meet you at the train station tonight.
>
> Love,
> Nakamura

The fights eventually got physical on her part. One time I tried to push past her in the stairwell, and she kicked me in rear. It's still the hardest blow anybody has ever landed on me. Things escalated until the night I woke to find her kneeling over me.

"I've been here for an hour," she said with a grin. "I could've cut your throat while you slept. With this." And she held up a giant, serrated kitchen knife that gleamed in the moonlight.

I moved out a week later and found my own tiny apartment. After a month or so, someone rang my doorbell at two in the morning. It was Nakamura, drunk and sheepish. She asked if we could talk. Since I still liked her even though I was afraid of her, I invited her in, and she collapsed onto her knees next to my futon, her hands lying palm up in her lap.

"I just had my first threesome," she said. "I don't know what I'm gonna do. I really, really like these people, but it was just too weird. I don't wanna be a bisexual. Am I bisexual? Did you ever get that vibe from me?"

Actually, I love butch women. Not truck-driving, *yeehaw*ing man-women, but attractive females who assert themselves, wrestle with me, and swagger. I never liked precious girly-girls with heavy makeup. I didn't tell Nakamura that what drew me to her was the combination of her beauty, wit, elegance, low voice, and macho way of walking. To me it wasn't a bisexual vibe she gave off, but I'm not the right person to consult on any matters in this realm. I knew the woman Nakamura had just slept with; she was a fat, obnoxious cornball, with one of those ghastly asymmetrical hairstyles, long and ladylike on one side and a buzz cut on the other. I had no idea how either gender could find her attractive on any level.

Nakamura and I reconciled, and she got me a job at her new place of employment, one of the world's first online newspapers. We edited copy for an arrogant, unpleasant, bearded American man in his forties. Nakamura told me that she hated people whose eyes showed the white *under* the iris. It made them look like dead bodies. He'd hit on her repeatedly in a clumsy, unsocialized way, and now that her boyfriend worked with her, she hoped he'd leave her alone. He did, but I became his sworn enemy for butting in.

The second time around with Nakamura wasn't as volatile because we each had our own apartment, though we still suffered from the same issue of me expecting better of her. I told myself I simply wanted her to achieve what I saw as her full potential, but the truth is – sadly for me – I wanted a more fitting partner. I liked her deeply and was obsessed with her, but I wasn't in love with her. I was more concerned with my own desires than hers.

Soon after we got back together, she went on vacation in Thailand and sent a postcard that made me laugh and wince. It had a photo of a crowd of bald monks in orange robes; on the back she'd written a typical Nakamura-face message.

> Hey Wictor-head!
> Dig the skinheads! This convention was sponsored by the Blind Barbers' Association of Thailand.
> Things have been pretty hip. Spent 3 days on a beautiful, tiny, primitive island just SE of the capital – where I burnt my tits off! The life here (on the beaches) is so GREAT! If things don't work out in Tokyo, come enlist in the orange clan! Will see you soon w/the rest of the tale.
> With much love... tho' now w/o tits,
> Nakamura.

It took us almost two years to fully disengage. I should've let her go when I left the first time, rather than pursue her and keep trying to make her into something she wasn't. It wasn't fair or considerate to her. When we parted for the second and final time, she gave me a copy of Shel Silverstein's *The Missing Piece*. On the title page, she inscribed in her beautiful penmanship, "For Wictor. Someday, maybe we'll both find our 'missing pieces.' Love still, Nakamura."

I did, Nakamura. But it turns out that sometimes being so lucky can almost kill you. I hope in your case you found and kept your missing piece and lived happily ever after.

A Nice Former Butthole

During the slow unraveling of my relationship with Nakamura, I worked at a conversational-English school. It was a horrendous job. The students were color coded according to their skills, purple being the equivalent of Epsilon-Minus Semi-Moron. The best students were red, virtually bilingual. Each class lasted an hour. The system was set up so that the files of the next hour's students were simply put in a box that the teachers chose on a first-come, first-serve basis, which resulted in an unseemly stampede from the room as everybody fought for the few reds and tried like hell to avoid the many purples. After the struggle for the files, everyone lit up cigarettes and filled the small teachers' room with a dense tobacco fog. A smoker myself, even I found it vile.

One of the teachers was a gracious Texan named Terence Smart. He struck me as ex-military because of his crew cut, erect posture, politeness, and spiffy suits. Extremely funny and articulate, he said he was a bassist like me. In fact, he'd once been in a band called the Butthole Surfers. Had I heard of them?

I almost fell out of my chair. They were legendary for their consumption of LSD; their ferocious, absurdist humor; their uncategorizable, Dadaist, avant garde, punk-psychedelic music; and the many names of their band: Ashtray Babyheads, Fred Astaire's Asshole, the Vodka Family Winstons, the Inalienable Right to Eat Fred Astaire's Asshole, etc. Terence was the first musician I met in person whose records I owned. He'd played bass on the EP *Cream Corn from the Socket of Davis,* on the tracks "To Parter" and "Tornadoes."

When I asked him why he taught English in Tokyo, he said, "I'm a daddy now. I cain't be a Butthole anymore."

He quit soon after I joined the school. As a parting gift, he gave me a tape he'd labeled *Smart Mix-up One* that contained his work with the Buttholes, including "100 Million People Dead." His own original compositions – "The Dog Needles," "Sounds of a Pregnant Woman," "Why Don't We Try" – were brilliantly twisted. He played all the instruments and manipulated his voice electronically into demonic rumbles and high-pitched squeaks. Terence's songs were even more gleefully demented and creative than anything the Butthole Surfers had done; the Residents would've been disturbed by his music. I laughed for hours listening to that tape.

On the cassette case, Terence put a little paper label that said, "Thanks for listening!!! Watch out for killer earthquakes!"

Thank you, Terence. Although I scrupulously watched out for killer earthquakes, they got me anyway.

The First Ghost Who Released Me

After Terrance left, two new teachers were hired. One was a Brit who was a guitarist. During a smoke break he asked me who my favorite bassist was; I answered Sting, because he had a completely original sound.

"Not if you ask any Jamaican," a voice said. I turned and saw the second new teacher smiling at me. His name was Steiv Dixon, a tall, lanky, exceptionally handsome man who looked like the young Gary Cooper. He had the same vulnerable Barbra Streisand smile as my drug-addicted lost love Jennifer. Despite his looks and fashionable clothes, he was quite friendly to me. I wasn't used to that. He was from Sarnia, Canada; the name of his hometown made me think of Orcs and Hobbits. We began going out every night after work, to drink and talk. I don't know how it is for women, but for average-looking men like me, it can be very flattering when very handsome guys befriend you.

He was extremely funny and seemed genuinely interested in me. We'd hang out at his apartment and talk about utterly esoteric topics such as underwater volcanoes, old episodes of *The Outer Limits,* how adhesives worked, Japanese superstitions, and the world's most bizarre houses. Once he tried to persuade a crane fly to get out, telling me that he'd been trying to catch it for days, but it would hide and then come out and go whining around his ears as he tried to sleep. When he cupped his hand to trap it against the wall, it evaded him and zipped behind the fridge.

He waited and then said, "Fine. Just stay there now. Out of sight, out of mind. Keep away from my ears and I won't flatten you, okay? You've got the entire world to fly around in, so you don't have to keep trying to go inside my ears."

"Why do they always go for our ears?" I asked.

"Well, considering what insects eat, an ear hole is probably their version of a five-star hotel."

Steiv was a guitarist, singer, and songwriter. His favorite singer was Peter Gabriel, and he loved bassist Tony Levin. Soon I did, too. Eventually, Steiv convinced me to play in a band with him. We'd put together a group and clean up in the millions of Tokyo live houses, the "Engrish" phrase for clubs that played live music. Steiv could play; his demo sounded like faster, bouncier Roxy Music. My favorite was a song he wrote called "Far Tortuga," the title of a Peter Matthiessen novel about turtle catchers in the Caribbean. From the other teachers we rounded up a lead guitarist, a keyboard player, and a drummer, all Americans who'd lived in Japan for years. We rented out a practice studio – which like the live-music clubs are found on every street corner – and tried a jam session. It seemed to work.

We cobbled together about thirty original tunes and started getting gigs, but we didn't play three shows with the same band members. The original keyboardist and lead guitarist left immediately, replaced by Kazuo and Miki, the two who stayed with us the longest. Though Kazuo was a great guitarist, he was so paralyzed by stage fright that he'd stand in exactly the same spot the entire night, staring at his feet. Often he missed his solos because he was frozen in terror. In photos taken of us, he looks like a cardboard cutout, a band prop. Miki was a fair keyboard player, but she always turned her volume down *after* the sound check, rendering her inaudible during the concert. Both Kazuo and Miki were extremely nice people who made me want to wring their necks. I dealt with my own chronic stage fright by drinking and taking off my glasses; Kazuo had perfect eyesight and was the only Japanese man I ever met who was a teetotaler.

Steiv said we'd be known as A Window, a name I hated. I wanted to call us Geyser Head, after a movie review that described a scene in which a guy was shot in the cranium and sprayed the room with blood. Steiv refused, even though he laughed at my suggestion and drew me a fake leaflet advertising a concert for Geyser Head. In Steiv's rendering the bassist looked like me, with a red column jetting from the ruptured top of his skull.

Tom Hojnacki, our original drummer, played only a handful of gigs with us before leaving. We then worked our way through a conga line of drummers from almost every nation on earth, most lasting no more than two engagements. One of them, a Senegalese, never bothered to show up one night, forcing us to perform an unscheduled acoustic gig in a dance club. While we took our intermission, I was at the bar ordering a triple scotch when I heard someone behind me ask, "How's the band?" His friend blew a huge raspberry that went on and on, echoing in my head for weeks.

We finally recruited our best drummer, a Dutchman named René. Though he taught me how to slap my bass like Louis Johnson, he was dangerously unstable and had the strength of ten longshoremen. The walls of his apartment were riddled with fist holes, evidence of the violent scuffles he had with himself. If a wolf or bear could speak English, it would sound like René. "You're so bad," he'd grunt. "Why are your lines so boring? I'll show you something better!" And with that he'd tear my bass right off my body, knocking my arms up into my face and sending my glasses flying across the room. Once I stupidly resisted his lesson. Our tiny keyboardist intervened before René compressed me like an accordion.

An incident that made me want to jam his drumsticks up his nose was the time he pinched my upper arm for no reason and said, "We're the same size, you and me, but I don't have as much *grease* on me." I slapped away his fingers, which left two angry, red marks in the grease of my arm.

On August 7, 1989, I wrote my parents a letter. Here's an excerpt.

> I practice the bass two hours a day now. The drummer I'm working with is phenomenal and I'm not, but I want to keep trying. Playing music is the most satisfying experience I've had – when it goes over well – and I honestly can't see myself finding enjoyment doing anything else except maybe writing. Of course it goes without saying that to be good in the music business you have to be VERY good, but I know I'm already above average, a B-minus kind of bass player. If I can get to A-minus, I'll be able to make it as a pro. Not a rock star, mind you, but a

professional musician. I don't want fame. The best bass player in the world today is a guy named Tony Levin, and he can walk down any street in the world and not be recognized by anyone except other musicians. That's the kind of life I'd like: money, security, and privacy. For now, that's what I'm shooting for. It might change, but I'd like to give it a try.

The most infuriating aspect of our band was that Steiv, the front man, refused to learn the formats of his own songs. Every performance included a moment where he'd launch into a chorus while the rest of us played a verse or a bridge. After the twentieth such fiasco, he told us, "You gotta back me up out there! If I mess up, follow me!" So the next time it happened, we switched over to the chorus, just in time for him to go back to the verse. After the show, he said, "What the hell's wrong with you guys, anyway? Don't follow me if I mess up. Play what you're supposed to!"

Steiv and I had a love-hate relationship. He was incredibly kind sometimes, but he could be horrendously insensitive, too. Often when we went out together, he'd see a sexy Japanese girl, say, "Catch you later, Tom," and dump me. It made me feel worthless. He was very narcissistic, but he was also hilariously funny. He could make me laugh until I was crying. Once we had trouble ordering at a McDonald's. The Japanese word for cheeseburger is *chiizubaagaa*. The poor young clerk had no idea what we wanted. I blew my top, of course, but Steiv was always more laid back. When we finally got our burgers and sat in a booth, I raved about how could it be hard to differentiate cheeseburger from *chiizubaagaa*.

"Maybe it's an intonation problem," Steiv said. "Maybe to her, we were saying 'cha-*heez*-boo-*gah*.'" He used his singer's voice to make it sound like one of those 1930s custom musical car horns with several notes.

He also called me "guy." For some reason, I liked that. He had no friends except for me. I could never figure out why. Maybe despite his looks, he was shy. He told me a lot about his background, and it wasn't pretty. His terrible asthma didn't prevent us from smoking tons of hash together. Sometimes he had attacks that left him speechless. He'd simply sit there, wheezing, trying to play it cool, though I could see the terror in his eyes.

Steiv earned my total respect when I played the live version of "Free Hand" over the PA system at one of the practice studios. Everybody stopped in their tracks, and the jaws of all the bassists dropped. Steiv said, "Man, that tone is just *nasty*. Nobody played bass like Ray Shulman, huh?" I was so proud of him.

The one thing he did that still rankles me was to introduce me to one of the students at our school, a young woman who spoke perfect, unaccented American English, even though she'd never been out of Japan. She looked, sounded, and acted exactly like Judy Davis in the film *Naked Lunch*. I guess Steiv thought I'd hit it off with her. He knew I'd broken up with Nakamura and was pretty lonely. When I went to the woman's house for dinner, she got a phone call. Her end of the conversation – in English – went like this:

"I don't know when I can see you again. Yes, I know you love me. It's just not working out. Your wife is getting suspicious, and this has gotten way out of hand. No, I never said that. What I said was I didn't want anything serious, and now it's gotten to the point that you're calling me day and night; you're crying, the way you are now; and you're getting drunk and making a fool of yourself. Listen to yourself, Bill."

My boss at the school where Steiv and I worked was named Bill. There were strict rules about dating students. Bill had fired several teachers for just having coffee with students.

"Bill, I'm going to hang up now. No, I have a guest. No, he isn't one of your teachers."

Perfect.

She hung up, sat on her bed, put her hands in her lap, and began silently weeping. Tears poured from her closed eyes and down her cheeks as though from tiny faucets, her lovely mouth forming an impeccable, downward-turning crescent. I asked her if there was anything I could do; she didn't answer. After about twenty minutes, I told her I had to go. She didn't respond. I gathered up my coat and gloves and left.

When I told Steiv about it, he said, "Yeah, she did the same thing to me. She's nuts."

"So why the hell did you think we'd get along?" I demanded.

He snorted. "You *like* 'em nuts, Tom. C'mon! We both know that."

In the three years that A Window existed, we shed personnel like autumn leaves. Among the sixteen or so non-drummers who graced our stage was a great guitarist from New Zealand. His spectacular looks drew the massive college-age female audience, and he owned forged press passes that allowed us backstage for every major act that toured Japan. We hated to lose him. We also hired Steve, a British sax player who'd melt quietly into the background when the rest of us fought, something we did on a daily basis.

Once Steiv brought in a Japanese fashion designer to watch one of our practice sessions in the studio. The idea was that he might help dress us, since except for Steiv none of us had any taste at all in clothes. He was a nice young guy who seemed interested. After switching on the tape recorder, we launched into one of our songs, and about a minute into it the designer pitched forward and hit the floor face first. He writhed around, kicking and flailing. We stopped playing; when nobody said or did anything, I yelled, "He's having a seizure! Somebody tell the staff to call an ambulance!" The designer came out of it before two surly, gum-chewing paramedics arrived and walked him downstairs. We were all deeply shaken.

As we sat smoking in the lounge, Steve the saxophonist said, "You know, at first I thought he was just getting into the music and sort of going a bit over the top."

I have a tape of the whole episode. It really is terrible to hear, especially since in Japan there's a social stigma against epilepsy. The designer had hidden his affliction from all his friends and colleagues. He came back to the studio a week later to show us ideas for costumes. His right eye was full of blood, where he'd hit a knob on a guitar effects pedal. He was still mortified, so we accepted his drawings and he fled. He envisioned me wearing a ruffled white shirt, a purple foulard, and pleated gray pants that would've made my hips look three feet wide.

The band was on its last legs, no matter what we wore. Every promise of a record deal fell through, and we couldn't keep a consistent lineup. For our final few performances we took on a Chinese-American percussionist-keyboardist. Sticks flying, she danced and strutted, whipping her hair. Drunken Australians gathered next to the stage and bayed at her like basset hounds.

Eventually, it was clear that we all hated the sight of each other and were going nowhere, so A Window fell apart in early 1989. A few months after the formal breakup, we attended a Battle of the Bands that included several local groups. Near the end of the three-hour thrash-fest, the emcee asked us to do a number. Overcome with beer and nostalgia, we stumbled onstage and did "The Dinosaur Song," a silly, two-chord slapping riff I came up with that Steiv turned into a song about an ex-girlfriend making him feel like a dinosaur:

> *Sometimes*
> *I feel like a dinosaur.*
> *Great big body*
> *And a real small brain.*
> *Sometimes*
> *I feel like a polar bear.*
> *All that ice*
> *But no ice cream*
>
> *What I tell you*
> *Is all I wanna tell you.*

What I tell you,
Is what I wanna say.

No sight
No sound
No taste
No touch
Can keep me from you baby[1]

Like former lovers having an unexpected fling, we connected like never before, all our fears, hopes, and inhibitions gone. We blew the roof off. Steiv was in perfect pitch, and we followed his every improvisation without hesitation. Kazuo gyrated across the stage like a madman as his howling solo put Adrian Belew to shame. René was sublime, trading off with our slinky percussionist in a frenetic question-response that left them both panting. Miki deafened us with a rousing honky-tonk piano, and gentlemanly Steve blasted out the raunchiest, filthiest saxophone break ever. For my part, I slapped my bass to pieces, doing the only bass solo of my entire playing career. We stretched a three-minute pop ditty into a quarter-hour of crowd pleasing, totally self-indulgent exhibitionism, and when we were done, the audience literally screamed for more.

That was our only live performance we didn't get on tape.

The Things People Say in Foreign Countries

At a meet-and-greet in Tokyo, at which I was the only non-Japanese, an American bass legend started talking to me because the organizers forgot to provide an interpreter and he got tired of just sitting there with forty Japanese staring at him in silence. Soon he began to confess all his sins without knowing it. He told me with no sense of self-irony or ruefulness that he stopped his practice of inviting bass players in the audience onstage to jam with him after a young kid turned out to be a better player. And this artist is one of the biggest of the big, someone whose massive talent is so apparent you'd think he'd never be threatened by anyone. He showed me how he made the cut-across-the-throat gesture to his roadies and said, "Get him off. *Get him off!*"

I always wondered if it was like those scenes in movies where the Secret Service mobs the actor playing the president and whisks him away from the podium in a fast-moving scrum.

Imagine being that kid, invited up onstage to play with your idol at a concert – "I'm on the top of the world, man!" – and suddenly all these ogres with flattened noses bum-rush you off stage, down the stairs, and out the back door, where they yank the bass off you, knock you down, kick you a couple times for good measure, and then slam the door, and you're lying there bleeding, going, "What just happened?"

I guess it's like what I read Tony Curtis said on hearing the news that William Holden had died: "Screw him. One less guy I have to compete with."

Since I was born without the competition gene, it isn't a sentiment I understand. On the other hand, I'm about .000000002 percent as successful as Tony Curtis was. Or this bass legend is; he's still famous and still raking in the dough.

Soon after I attended that meet-and-greet, the online newspaper where I worked went bankrupt, being decades ahead of its time. Steiv quit the teaching business and turned to voiceover work, acting, and – since he was a talented artist – animation.

Then I met the ghost who's had the most impact on my life.

So *There* You Are

In November of 1987, I landed a position at another English-conversation school. My immediate supervisor was a Scottish man I'll call Conan. When I was hired, I had to sign a contract that made me promise to never reveal the proprietary teaching methods of the institution, techniques invented by Conan. Therefore, I won't say anything about them. But they were ingenious and incredibly effective.

Conan was pretty much a maniac. He spoke at three times normal speed and said things that left you gaping. The day I met him, he asked if I had any kids. I told him no.

"Well, I have a daughter," he said in his Glaswegian burr. "She's four. The other day I got together with my Italian friend who I hadn't seen in years, and he said, 'Ah, daughters. Aren't they great? Doesn't it make you feel good as a father to know that someday she's gonna meet a guy who'll shove his big *cock* up inside her?'" And he bellowed curry-scented laughter in my face.

He was a curry fiend. In restaurants, he'd ask the cooks to make his curry thirty times hotter than normal because he loved the sensation of sweating through his shirts. An aikido master with abnormally wide, square shoulders, he enjoyed demonstrating his deadly skills by grabbing your hand and twisting it in such a way that you'd be instantly brought to your knees by some kind of diabolical principle of leverage, as though he'd quintupled the force of gravity.

Before I actually began working, the man who convinced me to apply to the school invited me to a party where I met several of my now-colleagues. They were a friendly bunch – Americans, Brits, Canadians, Australians, and Kiwis. I hoped things would work out. A strange moment occurred when I met an attractive American woman who shook my hand and didn't let it go. She was black but had light grayish-green eyes, exactly like the famous Afghan girl on the cover of the June 1985 issue of *National Geographic*.

"Oh," she said, gripping my hand with both of hers and leaning in close to examine my face intently. She looked puzzled and then smiled. "You're going to be so happy."

I didn't know what to say except, "I hope so!" She didn't seem drunk; there was something motherly and reassuring about her, even if what she said to me was bizarre. She let go of my hand, gave me a complicated look of affection and what seemed to be sympathy, and walked away.

"I see you've met our witch," a guy said to me. "She's psychic. It's creepy how right she is."

"Well, she told me I'm going to be happy, so that's all right with me."

On my first day at work, Conan introduced me to Carmen, a fellow teacher. She was small and stunningly beautiful, with a magnificent mane of black hair; dark eyes; and a pale, freckled face. We shook hands.

This is what I wrote in my journal a few weeks later.

> The second I saw her, I fell instantly in love. *Kaboom*. I saw her, and I said to myself, "Oh. *There* you are. I've been looking all over for you. Where the hell have you *been?*" It was as though we'd known each other many, many times before and had been waiting to reconnect again in this life. There was an instant recognition; I even recognized her scent, which was all her own because I knew she never wore perfume. As soon as I saw her, I remembered what her body felt like. She had the most amazing flared-out hips, and as I looked her over in her faded jeans, I knew exactly what it was like to sit on the edge of a chair as she stood in front of me, leaning into me, her arms around my shoulders, my arms around her pelvis and my cheek resting against the warmth of her stomach. This was a memory, not a fantasy. As I was being introduced to her, the nerves in my face and forearms began tingling as they recalled what it felt like to touch her. It was as if I were waking up.

What was even more striking than that sense of recognition was the fact that I actually relaxed when I met her. I breathed a sigh of relief because I knew that everything was going to be all right. A transformation came over me; I was a different person than I'd been only seconds before. I knew I was now complete. The missing piece had been found. To me there was nothing monumental about this discovery or the changes it would make. I felt that everything in my life had led up to that moment. It was simply a logical culmination.

Carmen and I had a nice, casual conversation about music. I told her that I was a bassist, and she said she was a singer-songwriter and multi-instrumentalist with her own recording studio set up in her apartment. "You should come over and see it," she said, merely a friendly invitation to a fellow musician. I knew I'd go because that was what was supposed to happen. She was twenty-six, a year older than I was.

We talked during every break for about a week, and that sense of being absolutely familiar and comfortable never left me. She was one of the most attractive, charismatic, intelligent, good-natured people I'd met, and I should've been a stuttering wreck, but I was calm and happy instead. We'd been through this so many times I had no reason to be nervous. Everything about her awoke another memory in me: her expressions, her cheeriness, her body language, the timbre of her low voice, her smile, her smell. I knew her the way I knew my own face. Worrying about what she thought of me was as nonsensical as being anxious over the impression I made on myself. She already knew everything there was to know about me. I was so glad to be back with her again that I don't even remember much of what we talked about. Mostly, we discussed music. Each night I'd go home happier, knowing that our restoration approached. Every minute brought us closer to where we'd been so often before and where we'd left off.

My first visit to her apartment was exciting, but it was the anticipation of getting to re-experience an old pleasure, such as sitting down to watch *Bad Day at Black Rock* again, a movie I've seen dozens of times. When Carmen let me in, she said wryly, "I'm sure it really *stinks* in here." Actually, it smelled great, like her. She was gracious and self-deprecatingly humorous about her recording setup, which included keyboards on a rack, a tape deck, a mixer, a microphone, and a drum pad. She had an acoustic guitar for recording basic melodies, which she'd then flesh out with her other instruments.

"It's more a hobby than anything else," she said. "I mostly do it because it's fun and it lets me get things out of my system. I don't have any big dreams or anything. Would you like to hear one of my songs?"

"Of course," I said.

She played the tape for me, the first song of hers that I experienced in this life. I still remember it note for note; I can sing it anytime I want. It was very good, a bouncy pop tune with an unusual melody and sophisticated vocal harmonies that she did herself. She had a terrific voice, fully formed and mature, as though she'd been performing professionally for years.

After an hour or so, her live-in boyfriend came home. I'll call him Hazim. He was a Tunisian, friendly and polite. I wasn't upset at meeting him, because he didn't matter. He literally had no role in this. Since I knew Carmen wasn't ready for me yet, I left without a twinge at the two of them being together. There was no hurry.

I invited her to join my band A Window. We began meeting at her apartment once or twice a week to listen to music and play together. The second time Hazim came home and found me there, he was noticeably unhappy to see me. Again, I bade them both goodnight and left. A block down the street, I heard a male voice calling, "Tom! Tom!" At first I thought it was the giant, demonic Japanese crows, but it was Hazim, running after me. I stopped and waited. A tall, handsome, powerful-looking man, he stood very close to me, almost nose to nose. Though I was afraid he was about to punch or stab me, all I could think about was how none of it mattered. It was utterly trivial. Even if he put me in the hospital, it wouldn't change anything. I found it hard to concentrate on his words.

He said, "Tom, you shouldn't be doing what you're doing, you know? Carmen and I have a relationship. It isn't right what you're doing. Why don't you think of me? There's more than just you and Carmen involved in this situation."

"Hazim, Carmen and I are just friends," I said. "I'm not doing anything except listening to her music. I'm a musician, too, and we're just enjoying music together. You have nothing to worry about. Nothing's happening." Which was true. Everything had *already* happened. The thing was done.

He seemed mollified. "All right, then. I just wanted to say that to you."

We shook hands and I walked away feeling no guilt because Hazim may as well have been telling the moon to not rise. The rising of the moon is neither right nor wrong; it simply occurs, regardless of how anybody feels about it. I knew what was coming. Hazim had no role one way or another. Besides, it was true that all Carmen and I had done was play and listen to music together. We'd spoken almost exclusively about music and our mutual love of Art of Noise, Peter Gabriel, the B-52s, the Thompson Twins, Fishbone, Boys Don't Cry, Thomas Dolby, Level 42, Frankie Goes to Hollywood, Murray Head, Talking Heads, Duran Duran – on and on and on. She was extremely knowledgeable about the bass and explained to me why different bass lines were more creative than others. We'd listened to several of her own compositions and one day talked about her new kitten, which she thought was sick because she'd thrown up and spent the day sleeping in a drawer.

"Cats do almost nothing except vomit and sleep," I'd told her. "And eat, scream their heads off at night, and claw your walls, the way she's done here. I'm sure she's fine."

Carmen was relieved. She didn't know much about cats. I told her I preferred them to dogs because cats don't suck up to you. I liked that. Carmen said she did, too.

When Hazim had confronted me, the reason I didn't admit that I was utterly, irrevocably in love with Carmen was that she and I hadn't acted on it or spoken about it. She hadn't betrayed him in any way. Hazim didn't have to know that every time I saw Carmen I left her apartment more at peace with the world, as though I were being restored bit by bit. I'd taken so many wrong turns in my life, but now I'd arrived at the place meant for me. It'd been set aside for me, like a seat at a vast banquet; it was mine, but not through any action of my own. I was born with hazel eyes, and I was supposed be with Carmen. These were simply facts.

About five weeks after I met Carmen, she told me at work that she'd broken up with Hazim.

"I'm sorry," I lied.

She nodded. "The romantic side of it ended a long time ago. We were sort of living together out of convenience."

We didn't speak about it again. She'd leave nice notes in my mailbox at school and sometimes call me at home to chat. The next time I went over to her apartment, we had our usual discussion about music. I sat in a chair in front of her recording equipment and she sat on the floor. Her kitten pounced on my ankle and raced off to hide. When a fat gray tomcat appeared outside the sliding glass door on the side of the apartment, Carmen said she'd recently befriended him. He liked to drop in for visits now.

"Would you like a beer?" she asked.

"Sure. Thanks."

She went into the kitchen and came out with a glass and a bottle, put them on the coffee table, and then straddled me in my chair, face to face. She linked her wrists behind my head and pulled me forward until our lips met. It was as inevitable as moonrise. I was ecstatic but not surprised. A natural law had simply come into effect.

After we went to bed a few days later, she told me that as soon as she saw me, she'd been walloped with the same realization that had struck me: We were meant to be together.

Love is *Not* all You Need

Although reuniting with Carmen – as I thought of it – was without question the most profound and fulfilling experience of my life, we had our problems. We both drank heavily, as did nearly everybody in Japan. The nation was awash in booze. There were beer and whiskey vending machines on every street corner of every neighborhood. The Japanese relied on the honor system to keep the underaged from using the machines. Carmen and I drank every day, usually beer or wine with dinner, but sometimes whiskey.

One night at a restaurant, we both got drunk and she dumped an entire freshly baked pizza into her lap, topping-side down. When I tried to help her, she yelled, "You *hate* me now, don't you?" Two Japanese girls sitting behind Carmen stopped talking to watch. I glanced at them, and Carmen snarled, "What are you looking at *them* for? You wanna *fuck* 'em?" That prompted me to pay the bill, take her outside, and aim her toward her apartment. I went in the opposite direction.

She called the next day and apologized. "I can't say I'm sorry enough. I don't know what happened. This is all so new and I think I was just so intimidated that I lost control. It won't happen again." And it didn't for a while.

The night I introduced her to Steiv and a mutual friend I'll call Hideki, it was a catastrophe. Carmen fell down on the dance floor. Her feet went out from under her and she did a pratfall, with a rollicking bellow of laughter. Hideki took me aside and said in Japanese, "Tom, she's unbelievably drunk!" He was mortified for me. Steiv simply watched and smiled knowingly. His words echoed in my head like in a scene from an old movie, in which the hero hits rock bottom: *You* like *'em nuts, Tom. C'mon! We both know that. You* like *'em nuts, Tom. C'mon! We both know that. You* like *'em nuts, Tom. C'mon! We both know that.* I'd cover my ears and shout, "*Stop it!*" and then there'd be a fade-in to me waking up in a jail cell or mental ward.

I was too angry to talk to Carmen when we left the club. We rode the first leg of our subway trip in silence, changed trains, and arrived at the station two stops from hers. On the way down the stairs to the platform, she stopped dead and slurred, "Aw, doan do thish! Doan be like thish! Lesh talk."

"Not here," I said. People silently walked around us, ignoring our little drama.

She shook her head so vigorously she almost fell over. "No! I wanna *talk!* Right *here!* I'm not goin' anywhere until we *talk* about thish!" Her half-closed eyes, slack mouth, and the way she swayed back and forth made her look like an alcoholic, skid-row prostitute. I'd had a similar scene with Jennifer in Norway, after she became a full-time drunk and druggie.

I said, "If you don't come with me, I'm going to leave you here." She was two stops from home, and I was fairly sure that she wasn't as drunk as she seemed. There was an element of playacting in her conduct. I couldn't quite put my finger on why I felt this, but I thought she was testing me.

"*No!* I'm not goin' 'til you *talk* to me!"

So I left her there and went home. She phoned the next morning and apologized.

"I'm really sorry, Tom. I know I said it wouldn't happen again, and I screwed up. I was just nervous about meeting your friends, and when I get nervous I don't show good judgment. I drank too much and made a fool out of myself. I'm sorry. Please forgive me."

Of course I forgave her. We were going to be together the rest of our lives, I knew, so I had to accept the ups and downs, the bad with the good. It was hard at times because I'm not naturally forgiving, nor am I patient. I reintroduced her to Steiv and Hideki, and they came to love her as much as I did. It was inevitable; she was unlike anyone we'd ever met. She spoke Mandarin Chinese, Japanese, and some Arabic. Although a petite, stunning beauty with delicate features, she was very butch, exactly the way I liked. She walked like a man, preferred jeans, had no women friends, and liked to wrestle. Her laugh was deafening, an actual bray: *Aaaaa-aaaaa-aaaaaaaaaaa!* That took some getting used to. It scared me at first, then it annoyed me, and finally I came to need it.

She'd given her kitten a truly bizarre, utterly original name for a cat. "Well, it sounds like the name of an all-powerful, inter-dimensional, galactic being," she explained. It was a perfect moniker. When the cat grew up, she was so smart she figured out the principles of leverage: The shrimp we bought kept disappearing out of the refrigerator, so one day Carmen and I made a big production of going out, but we left the front door open a crack and hid in the hallway, peering into the apartment. After a minute or so, the cat sauntered over to the fridge, squatted, and pulled open the door by using both paws on the bottom edge under the handle, not the edge under the hinges. She then stuck in her head and helped herself to the shrimp, blocking the door with her body until she'd had her fill. Carmen and I had to run out of the building to laugh without the cat hearing us.

During our first Christmas after we got together, Carmen flew to the U.S. to be with her family. When she returned, she told me that on the voyage back, the Korean Air flight attendant asked her if she wanted beef or pesher for dinner.

"What's pesher?" Carmen asked.

"Pesher. *Pesher!* Ep-ai-ess-aitch. Pesher. Live in ocean!"

Carmen shouted, "She meant 'fish'! I was *dying!* Pesher!" She hugged me, shoved her face into my chest, and brayed her deafening donkey laugh into my heart. Ramming me with her head was one signature move; the other was to suddenly rush into my arms without warning.

She was the most curious person I've ever met, which I adored. She wanted to know everything. Nothing was too esoteric for her, and nothing I said ever made her give me that what-are-you-weird-or-something look. She was a fellow weirdo. Our conversations meandered everywhere. We were both musicians; we both loved history; we both loved knowledge, languages, movies, food, walking, talking, daydreaming, clowning, and laughing. She was a great cook who introduced me to Indian food. If for nothing else, she'll always rank among the most influential people in my life, since she's the one who guided me to the miracle of tandoori chicken.

We played word games. One was based on the old poster "Be alert: Your country needs more lerts." We determined that our country needed more gressives, goraphobics, stutes, pallings, fflicteds, ffiliateds, bnormals, propos's, postolics... She was like a human thesaurus. We discussed Alexis de Tocqueville's concept of dualism in America, which explains how people can manifest two diametrically opposed characteristics simultaneously. This led to our trying to come up with the most crippling dualisms: prudishness *and* lechery; pretension *and* ignorance; ambition *and* insecurity; unhappiness *and* smugness; hypochondria *and* denial.

When she did household chores, she hummed incredibly complex, discordant pieces by Sergei Prokofiev, her favorite composer. Sometimes I'd stand behind her, pretending to dust but actually just listening. I was nine inches taller than she, which scared her, she said, because she'd read that couples with seven or more inches of height difference never lasted. When we went out together, she always commented on couples with a large discrepancy in height.

One of her many skills was racking up unimaginably high scores at video games. We'd go to arcades and I'd sit and watch her play *Tetris* or *Splatterhouse* for hours. She'd need only one coin to keep going indefinitely. As she played, we talked; it had no impact on her game. It was as though she had two separate brains. Watching her I remembered reading that in World War II, one training exercise for German *Luftwaffe* fighter pilots was to lie on a spinning turntable and solve math problems in their heads while also counting the revolutions.

She was also as overly sensitive as I am, our mutual Achilles' heel. We had the same spiritual beliefs, the same sense of humor, the same views about friendships and humankind in general. Our core values were identical. I've never been more in sync with someone, which was as it should've been, since we were supposed to be together. She was simply the other half of me.

In keeping with our gender-role reversals, our problems stemmed from my complaint that she wouldn't open up emotionally to me. Our disagreements and fights were the result of our inability to communicate. I constantly pushed for more closeness, and the more I pushed, the more she withdrew. There were also occasional public episodes of drunkenness that frightened and angered me. Even so, I was confident we'd overcome these issues. No matter what we went through, I knew we'd always survive it. We were two halves of a whole, and that would solve everything in the end. We'd find a solution somehow. Now that we'd found each other, we'd never let each other go again.

She loved movies as much as I did, and her eye for detail was astonishing. When we watched *No Way to Treat a Lady,* she noticed the entire film crew and director reflected in the mirror for a fraction of a second in the scene where Rod Steiger, disguised as a waiter, tries to murder Lee Remick. I missed it, so she paused and rewound the tape, froze the frame, and sure enough, there they all were, as clear as day. I'm sure nobody else, including the editor, caught that gaffe, but Carmen did the first time she saw it. She had incredible powers of observation.

I introduced her to one of my favorite films, *A Patch of Blue,* and she cried all the way through. She loved the way Elizabeth Hartman delivered her lines, conveying overwhelming emotion in so few words. I handed Carmen the remote, and she replayed certain lines again and again, savoring them and then diving into my arms to hug me tight enough to hurt. Though unable to talk about her feelings, she expressed them physically without reservation; it was unnerving for someone as stunted and thwarted as I was. I liked it, though. It was different and exciting.

Unfortunately for me it also led to our demise because as I grew into an ability to communicate, she adamantly refused. The dichotomy of a woman who wore her emotions on her sleeve but could not discuss them was simply too confusing and frustrating for me. I had the evangelical zeal and righteousness of the new convert; I expected too much, and it wasn't realistic or fair. If given the chance to do it all over again, I'd be content with what she could offer instead of forever demanding more. The unavoidable outcome of my militancy was years in the future, however. At this time I was still the happiest I'd ever been.

We once went to an exhibit by an American artist. He himself turned out to be a disappointment, an Aspergerish savant who couldn't engage in conversation. Among the many things he'd created were life-sized silhouettes of men in wood. They had moveable lower jaws powered by electric motors that slowly moved them up and down, and on the side of the profile hidden from the viewer was a small speaker. Each of these wooden men stood motionless, their lower jaws moving up and down, and they said, "*Pecha pecha pecha pecha. Pecha pecha pecha pecha. Pecha pecha pecha pecha.*" They were called the Chattering Men. Carmen loved them, and for months afterward she'd say, "*Pecha pecha pecha pecha*" out of the blue and we'd laugh.

She once gave me an article about instructions written in English on the side of a police box in Aoki Prefecture.

When a passenger of the foot hove in view, tootle the horn; trumpet at him melodiously at first, but if he still obstacles your passage tootle him with vigor and express by word of mouth warning, "Hi. Hi."

Give great space to the festive dog that shall sport in the roadway.

Despite the turbulence and episodes of outright deceit that characterized our early relationship, how could I not love someone who gave me that?

Voiceover and Editing Work for the Japanese

Along with teaching conversational English, I recorded for audio books, documentaries, and taped lessons that needed a native speaker of American English. Japanese wrote all the scripts.

I never threw tantrums over what I was asked to read, the way Orson Welles did during his legendary frozen-peas and fish-fingers commercials. Instead of arguing, I simply read the copy and pocketed the money. There were lots of voiceover "actors," as we were called, who emulated Orson Welles. Recording often had to be delayed while some preposterous American prima donna demanded changes. It was beyond inane and monumentally ungrateful to boot.

Here's part of a script I once read. I was "Japanese Boy," which makes sense, since I'm American. This script was some kind of wish-fulfillment fantasy on the part of the man who wrote it, I think, because very few foreign women in Tokyo dated Japanese men, but all Japanese men wanted to date foreign women.

Anyway, the script.

Japanese Boy: How would you feel about beefsteak for dinner?

American Girl: Sounds like a good idea. But might it be expensive?

Japanese Boy: You might be right. How about hamburgers?

American Girl: That's allright.

Japanese Boy: And sherry?

American Girl: That's great! I'd love to sip some sherry!

Japanese Boy: Waiter! Some hamburgers and two sherries, please.

Mmmmmm, burgers and sherry.

I also was also a freelance editor of technical manuals and instructions. They'd send me the hard copy and I'd correct it with a red pen and send it back, after which money was deposited in my bank account. Incredibly easy and funny work. Some examples of sentences I had to correct:

Warning: The blade of this hobby knife is extremely sharp. Keep out of children.

Determine the number of workers needed and, if necessary, alter their members.

Mount a dog-legged dog on the mounting platform and screw it.

Let's see you do *that* with your altered members.

First Brush with a Psycho

In June of 1989, I broke up with Carmen for the second time because of an incident that finally made me lose trust in her. It hurt me greatly to let her go, since I still believed in my soul that we were supposed to be together. However, I wasn't emotionally equipped at that time to handle situations I could easily manage today. She was ashamed, and that made her angry and say cruel things that she immediately regretted and tried to take back, but it was too late. Our parting was sad, not acrimonious. I even helped her move to a new apartment just ten minutes on foot from mine. Although she insisted that I'd misunderstood what I'd seen and what she'd said, blaming what happened on alcohol and not her real motivations, she was as tired of the rough patches as I was.

It was the lowest period of my time in Japan. I drank whiskey and smoked hash every night, watching stacks of rented videos. When I managed to sleep, I had the worst nightmares of my life. I witnessed the butchering of children; I wandered alone in dark, underground rooms the size of sports arenas, knee deep in excrement; I looked in the mirror and saw that my head was shaped like a volcano and my eyes were on different levels; I lay in the street at night, paralyzed, as passersby emptied my pockets and dogs ate my face; I approached people and tried to speak to them but could only produce the thick, labored moaning of a stroke victim, and they ran from me in terror.

Some nights I went out with Steiv, who tried to comfort me in his brusque way, which only made me feel worse. He truly liked Carmen and was sorry that we hadn't been able to work it out, but he was neither sentimental nor romantic. His advice was for me to plow through an endless succession of willing young Japanese beauties, which would've been extremely easy. The problem was I just wasn't attracted to them. They were like dolls, and as Steiv informed me, they were terrible kissers and utterly passive in bed. After Carmen, being with a Japanese would've been like trading in a Lamborghini for an oxcart. I may be the only heterosexual, unmarried, male, long-term, foreign resident of Tokyo who never slept with a Japanese woman.

A month after I left Carmen, we were both invited to a party by a mutual friend. When I told him that Carmen and I were no longer involved, he asked if I could call her anyway, since he was her friend as well as mine. I did so; it was awkward and painful. She said she really wanted to go and asked if I'd mind. For her sake I said I wouldn't.

The only people at the party were happy couples. Carmen and I were so miserable and out of place we soon left. Outside, we spoke alone for the first time in a month. Neither of us eager to go home, we went to a live house near my apartment, but the band was just awful. We gave up after ten minutes and while saying good night suddenly found ourselves in each other's arms.

"Let's go to your place," she whispered in my ear.

There was no way I could resist her. I prayed that this would be a new beginning.

At about 5:00 A.M., my phone rang. When I answered it, I heard only whimpering, the sound of a small child in pain. I hung up. The phone rang for the next hour, always with the whimpering.

Finally, Carmen answered it while I was in the shower. I emerged, and she told me it was Hazim. I already knew she'd gone back to him at least temporarily; why wouldn't she? They had a history together, and she was lonely. It didn't upset me, because I'd left her. What she'd done since I'd broken up with her was her business, not mine. I had no claim on her anymore. But I was angry at his harassment of me. Telephone stalking was endemic in Japan. Some of my friends had endured years of it. The next time the phone rang, I picked up the receiver and said, "Go fuck yourself, Hazim."

He screamed, "*Go fuck myself? Okay, now I kill you! Just wait, you bastard! Now I kill you!*"

I hung up and took the phone off the hook. Carmen swore she didn't know how he got my number, an avowal I didn't believe. I asked if she wanted me to walk her home, but she said that wasn't necessary. She seemed to regret that she'd spent the night with me. I let her out and went to sleep.

At 10:30 A.M., Carmen called and told me that Hazim had broken into her apartment while she'd been with me, which meant he'd been watching her. He'd ransacked the place, stolen almost all the photos she had of him, and left her address book open to the page where my number was written. She thought he'd called me from her apartment. I asked if she was all right. She said yes, and that we shouldn't be afraid. He wouldn't hurt us; his threats were just empty words.

Too depressed to do anything, I stayed home and played my bass. At 5:30 in the afternoon, the phone rang. I picked up the receiver and an inhuman howling blasted into my ear. It sounded like a dog having its paws crushed, the worst noise I've heard a living creature make. I realized it was Carmen. She was utterly incoherent, producing a series of gabbling, gasping, choking screams.

"What's happening?" I shouted. "Carmen! What's happening?"

"*Don't go out! Don't leave your apartment! He's coming after you! He's going to kill you!*"

She was at a police kiosk near her home, crying so hard it took her several minutes to tell me what'd happened. Hazim had come over, and she'd let him in when he said he wanted to apologize. Once inside he immediately commenced beating the stuffing out of her with his fists and the butt of a large knife. Telling her the knife was for me, he demanded my address. When she refused to give it to him, this strapping six-footer knocked her down and kicked her all over the kitchen floor. She was five feet, three inches tall and weighed 100 pounds fully clothed and soaking wet. He then yanked her up by the neck and choked her until she gave him a fake address. One hand around her throat, he dragged her out of the apartment, shouting, "Come on! Let's go! You're going to watch me kill him!" Outside, she tore away from him, ran to the police kiosk, and called me.

The cops told me to lock my door and wait. They escorted Carmen back to her place and stayed with her until Hazim was arrested at his apartment at 10:30 that night. Under interrogation, he denied saying he'd threatened to kill me, but he admitted beating Carmen "to scare her." When the cops asked her if she wanted to press charges, she declined, saying she was too afraid and didn't know what would happen if she did. In Japan, arrestees were generally released on their own recognizance. Domestic violence was not considered a crime serious enough to hold someone on a bond. Hazim signed a statement of apology and a pledge that he'd never attempt to contact Carmen or me again. He was allowed to walk out of the station forty-five minutes after he was brought in.

I went to Carmen's place at about midnight. Her injuries included a black eye; split and swollen lips; lumps on her head; a cauliflower ear; purple finger marks around her neck and throat; and red, yellow, green, blue, and maroon bruises all over her face, arms, legs, back, and stomach. She was the most severely beaten human being I've ever seen in person. It was astounding that despite what he'd done to her and the terror she felt as he did it, she hadn't given him my real address. I was in awe of the core of strength she had to have, somewhere deep inside.

There wasn't much we could say to each other. I told her how sorry I was about everything, and she told me she was sorry, too. I've never been angrier with anyone than I was with Hazim. Part of me hoped he'd come after me, because he didn't know that I'd studied *shotokan* karate for years and was confident that I could bring him down with one blow, using the heel of my palm against his chin. I practiced that movement frequently and could snap out my left arm with the speed of a mantis shrimp clubbing its prey. Opponents generally don't anticipate a blow with the left hand. Once Hazim was on the ground, I'd jump into the air as high as I could and land on his face with my 200-plus pounds. Since force equals mass times acceleration, that would mean more than 800 pounds coming down on Hazim's brave, manly mug.

Carmen and I didn't see much of each other for a while because she soon quit the school and became a DJ at an English-language music station. I'd listen to her smooth, deep voice at night, missing her. One of her favorite songs was Chris Squire's "Lucky Seven," off his solo album *Fish Out of Water*. It was a bass tour de force I'd introduced to her.

On several levels I was glad that she'd quit the school. Mainly, I was tortured by the memory of the day our boss Conan lost his mind and demonstrated an Aikido technique on her. He'd taken her to the floor and used her as a mop, swishing her around at his feet as she desperately held her skirt in place with one hand. Not only did I do nothing to stop him, I didn't even *say* anything. I couldn't forget the flash of helpless mortification and genuine terror on her face before she masked it with her donkey laugh. Not defending her was one of the many ways I let her down.

For foreigners, Tokyo is a village instead of a giant metropolis. Inevitably, Carmen and I ran into each other at a bar one night and had a wistful conversation. It hurt so much to be with her that after a few minutes I told her I had to go. When I hugged her, she clung to me fiercely, and without knowing I was going to do it I kissed her. She responded enthusiastically, crying and laughing. We took a taxi back to her place, and I stayed with her. For the next four years.

Farewell and an Order that Was Obeyed

The happiest extended period of my life began in July of 1989. The reason for my joy was not only that Carmen and I were back together, but also that we'd finally stopped fighting. It seemed that we'd discovered the ability to love each other unconditionally. We even said it to each other, words that never came easily to me. Before July of 1989, saying those three words to anyone made me feel cheesy and sheepish, like a self-deluding ham actor reciting lines that nobody could possibly believe. My flat head, narrow shoulders, wide hips, and fatness also made me feel ludicrous. Who'd want a pear-shaped flathead declaring his love for her? I stopped asking that question after July of 1989.

It's not a coincidence that after Carmen and I reunited and achieved a healthy, mutually supportive, and respectful relationship, my ability to play the bass improved exponentially. She had her own bass, and we practiced the thumb-slapping technique. She became far more adept at it than I, but I was no slouch at it myself. We tried every way we could to play the bass line in "Close to the Edit" by Art of Noise but agreed it was not humanly possible. Since the band used a sequencer, they'd cheated. Even so, it was still our favorite song. We listened to it almost daily.

During my lunch breaks at the school where I taught English, I'd go up to the empty auditorium at the top of the building and play my bass through an amplifier I brought with me. I learned the two-handed tapping technique and improvised soaring melodies. For years I wondered if I did it to show off to the teachers and staff who often took the elevator up to find the origin of the music, but now I know I played simply because I was so happy that I had to express it. I no longer feel conflicted about those shows I put on.

My happiness reached a crescendo when Carmen lent me the money to buy a right-handed MusicMan Sting Ray bass. I then had Japanese luthiers build me a left-handed body, to which they mounted the right-handed neck and all the pickups and electronics from the original instrument. I finally had my Sting Ray, after ten years of pining for one. It was the best bass I ever had, and I owe it all to Carmen.

My drinking and drug use tapered off dramatically. One day Carmen and I went to a giant outdoor reggae concert with some American friends. They introduced us to their Japanese buddies, a dozen or so men who were part of the iconoclastic 5 percent of the culture. One of them was a guy who did 500 pushups and 500 sit-ups every day. That was all the exercise he ever got, he said. He was shirtless and looked like Michelangelo's *David*. We all started drinking beer and smoking hash at ten in the morning, but I didn't eat anything. Carmen won everybody's hearts by doing perfect gymnastic forward and backward walkovers, and I was struck all over again by what a privilege it was that she was with me. I missed most of the show because I got so drunk and high I had to leave early. I told Carmen to stay to listen to the music and be with our new friends. She happily agreed. I rode the many trains home by myself, stopping at every platform to get out and throw up in trash barrels until it looked as though I were relieving myself of bright green Gatorade. That was the last time I got vomiting drunk and the last time I got high.

Carmen came home hours later and told me what I'd missed. The main reason I'd gone was to see drummer Sly Dunbar and bassist Robbie Shakespeare. Carmen said they were brilliant. She'd barely had anything to drink, so she was in great shape. First she surpassed me in the thumb-slapping technique on the bass, and then she surpassed me in abating terrible, self-destructive behavior. She made me want to go up in a mushroom cloud of pride.

Despite our drastically reduced drinking, we frequented a Belgian bar run by a hilarious Walloon, meaning a Belgian who speaks French. His name was Alain, and he's the only person in the world who's made lamb chops I could eat. A music fanatic, he had the same wacky sense of humor Carmen and I shared. We went to his bar to laugh, listen to great European tunes, eat lamb chops, and have a Chimay.

One night a Belgian pop band touring Japan came in. They were all Walloons except for one backup singer. She was a Fleming, a Belgian who speaks Flemish. A tall, stunning blonde, she had a slightly nasal voice that made her sound like Al Stewart singing "The Year of the Cat."

Men always flocked to Carmen. When she'd go to a guitar store and thumb-slap a bass, every guy in the vicinity would gather and watch. She liked the attention. People involved with truly beautiful women know that this is just something that is. We can pretend it's not so, but beautiful women like being beautiful. If you choose to be with a great beauty, you have to be prepared for that. You can't have a jealous cell in your body. Many of the problems Carmen and I had before July of 1989 didn't stem from my jealousy, but rather Carmen's *assumption* that I'd be jealous. She'd concealed things from me, and when I'd found out and gotten angry, she thought it was jealousy at play. In reality, it was anger at the deceit and lack of trust.

Carmen had never understood why I didn't ask her how many men she'd been with before me or during the periods she and I were apart. I simply felt that it was none of my business and also irrelevant. How could I resent someone for what she'd done before she met me? How could I resent her for what she'd done after I left her? It didn't matter to me. The gender role reversals came into play again in this dynamic, in that physical acts didn't mean much to me in comparison to emotions. It would've upset me more to learn that she were in love with someone than to find out she'd slept with him.

But by July of 1989, we'd put all of that behind us. In the Belgian bar, handsome Belgian men – members of the band, its road crew, management, and entourage – immediately boxed in Carmen while I sat there and watched. Sometimes she'd look over and smile goofily at me. I can honestly say I was never jealous. I was grateful that she was with me, and I knew that at the end of the evening she'd go home with me. I was the one she chose. That realization regularly humbled me.

The stunning blonde backup singer joined me at the bar, and we talked for hours. She was incredibly nice and friendly, especially for such a beautiful woman. Well into the conversation, she asked, "Are you Belgian, by the way?"

I said, "No, I'm just fat like a Belgian guy." I have no idea what that means.

She laughed a throaty laugh, stroked my forearm, and purred, "Well, you're not fat. But I like fat guys anyway."

Soon before we parted, she gave me her name, address, and phone number in Belgium, written on the back of a Chimay beer coaster. I still have it. That Belgian singer probably won't mind me revealing her first name, Virginie. I kept the coaster as a memento of that fantastic night, in which the woman who chose me above all others was mobbed by far more desirable and successful men but still stayed with me, and a beautiful, talented, smart, glamorous singer told me she thought I was attractive. I also kept it to remind me why I made the right decision to leave Japan. Not only was it easy to stay there forever, surrounded by adoring Japanese, but other foreigners – overwhelmed by the weirdness – reached out to you in ways they wouldn't in different countries. It was too seductive.

In April of 1990, I finally moved in with Carmen, getting rid of my own apartment, and soon after that Hazim began stalking us. We'd find the sentence "Someone is watching you" written on our utility bills in our mailbox. One morning we found it in heavy felt-tip ink on our front door. It hadn't been there the night before. Detailed itineraries of our days and nights were left in our mailbox, along with the times we'd been to these places. He followed us everywhere, and we never saw him. He was like a special-forces operator doing reconnaissance. It terrified Carmen and caused her traumatic flashbacks to the beating he gave her. Whenever she saw one of Hakim's messages, she'd burst into tears and wail, "Oh, no! Oh, no!"

I'd begun doing voiceover work almost every day. Most of these jobs took place early in the morning, before I put in my hours at the school. As I left the apartment at around sunrise on a Wednesday, Hakim pedaled past me on a tiny pink girl's bicycle with a white basket and tassels on the handlebars, his knees pointed out to the sides in a grotesque, insectoid way. He wore a full tuxedo and a leer. It was like a scene out of a surreal Italian film from the early 1970s. After much deliberation, I told Carmen; she cried and trembled.

I began fearing for Carmen's cat, convinced that one day we'd come home and find that sweet, eccentric, trusting, oddly humorous little animal hanging from our balcony or cut open and nailed to the front door. Japan had soured on me for many reasons, the two main ones being I was the only antiunion holdout at my school and was under constant attack for it, and I was tired of the culture's endless debauchery. I knew Carmen loved her job at the radio station; I'd stood beside her in the wee hours as she interviewed bassist Brian Bromberg from a telephone booth, taking notes for her on a pad and pencil. She also interviewed Suzanne Vega and Marcus Miller, two more of my musical heroes. Miller had complimented her on her thumb-slapping technique, an incredible honor and confirmation of her skill. But it was time for me to leave. Japan had lost its luster.

When I raised the possibility of us moving to San Francisco, one of the American capitals of voiceover work, Carmen agreed. I felt I pressured her, but she insisted that she wanted to leave as much as I did. I wasn't sure. I'd never seen her happier than when she worked as a radio DJ. We made our plans and began the long process of wrapping up our time in Japan. I'd lived there for five years, Carmen for six. While she'd been home several times, I hadn't seen my family since 1985. I was nervous about reconnecting with them face to face, and I was worried that they wouldn't approve of Carmen. It wouldn't have made any difference to me if they did or didn't; I just wanted to spare her as much as possible for the rest of our lives. I couldn't shake the image of her beaten to a pulp. And now that Hakim had reappeared, I was afraid of what I might do to him.

The hardest person to leave was Steiv. We hadn't seen each other very often after the demise of A Window, but I still liked him a lot. As I discussed him with Carmen, she flabbergasted me by saying that Steiv had once told her that he loved me. I found that almost impossible to comprehend. He simply didn't love people. The fact that he said he loved me almost made me cry. We had a last beer together in August, a day before I left. Although we were comfortable, I think we both knew we'd never see each other again. He wasn't a letter writer. We talked about my plans to pursue a career in voiceover work and maybe writing someday, and he wished me luck.

"It's been really great knowing you, guy," he said as we clinked bottles.

"Likewise," I said, trying not to weep.

Carmen left Tokyo in October, taking her cat with her in a carrier that they let her bring into the cabin. We'd bought special kitty tranquilizer pills that ended up only making the cat meow in a much slower, lower voice – a kind of low-energy howling – for eleven straight hours. The passengers on the entire airliner were crazed with hatred by the end. There was nothing Carmen could do because she wasn't allowed to take the cat out of the carrier.

Steiv did send me one letter after Carmen and I found an apartment in San Francisco, but I never heard from him again. In 2011, I Googled his name for fun and was horrified to learn that he'd died of an asthma attack in Tokyo in 1997. I remember those episodes and the barely concealed terror they induced in him. It broke my heart to imagine him dying in panic, suffocating and alone because he didn't let people get close to him. I was the only one. And I'd abandoned him.

In August, after weeks of feeling just horrible about Steiv's death, I had the most vivid dream of my life. Steiv and I were walking down a street wearing long, heavy coats. It was fall; the trees were bare, and a gentle, cold breeze blew, ruffling our hair. He gave me his vulnerable Barbra Streisand smile as I told him I was so happy to see him, and I'd missed him for the past twenty-one years. He looked off into the distance, listening without looking at me, the way he did. It was one of his many idiosyncrasies. When you spoke to him, he became a ship's captain scanning the horizon.

We halted beside a low concrete wall. On the other side there was a large field covered with orange and yellow leaves. Steiv faced me and said, "Look, you have to stop being upset. I'm fine! I'm much happier where I am. Don't worry about me anymore. Seriously, now, Tom. *Stop it,* okay?"

He gazed at me with a warmth and open affection he'd never shown in life, and I realized that he did love me after all. That was the only time I've ever dreamed about him. Steiv was so vain when I knew him that he dyed his prematurely gray hair jet black; in my dream, his locks were as white as Einstein's.

I think he really is fine, and I've stopped being upset, as he demanded.

Endnotes
   [1] Although Steiv Dixon was the lyricist for A Window, he never wrote anything down and he never sang the same song the same way twice. He liked to improvise. These are, to the best of my recollection, the lyrics he used most often for "The Dinosaur Song."

Interlude with Scott Thunes
Music

At the College of Marin, I studied jazz and classical. The problem was that I was at school every day, but I don't know exactly how much I actually learned because I cut so many classes. I did learn about four-part harmony. The way they teach you classical music is: soprano, alto, tenor, bass. They teach you a very rigid way to learn the connection of chords.

Rock music is a homophonic type of music. Homophonic is one of the three types of music. Monophonic: Gregorian chant. One line. One sound. Homophonic – which is what most music is, especially songs – is melody with accompaniment. Polyphonic is many sounds or many lines. Bach is the king of the polyphonic universe, and his sons started really deeply getting into the homophonic. From that point on, it's been relatively massively homophonic. Any kind of other lines that are gonna go in there, are gonna be countermelodies to whatever else is going on in your melody and in the accompaniment universe. Rock is virtually, strictly, a homophonic art.

What they teach you at the College of Marin is how to connect voices, so that every line in the middle is its own melody. That's classical music's job, when you go and actually learn it. That's what you're supposed to learn. I never learned it because I dropped the ball in actually digging in and trying to get that knowledge into my brain. I can write melodies, but the whole idea is that you write a melody, then you write another melody, then you write another melody, and they all work together. They create good chords, as you're looking vertically, but they're also beautiful in a horizontal sense. Most people can't do that. It's very difficult to make it work. In the modern world, it's a lot easier because you can accept a lot more dissonance. A funny thing about a lot of modern music is that these rules are very rigid, and you know exactly what that melody is doing and why it's doing it, but if you play it for somebody who doesn't know modern music – someone who only knows classical music or only hears the major and minor chords of rock – they're going to think, "It's madness! These people don't know what they're doing. I can't hear where the sense is."

I skipped over all the stuff that I needed to know. I didn't learn any of the basic rules. I just immediately said, "This dissonance sounds good to me. It reminds me of the weird rock music I used to listen to." But those rock guys got their shit from the polyphonic music that I was listening to, so it's like, first I have to learn the 1600s, but instead I wanted to learn the early 1900s. But I was raised on music that was written in 1970 and performed by the best musicians of our day. So I didn't learn all the shit that gave the people of the modern classical period – from the 1900s on – their information. That's the stuff that the people I listened to got. I'm kind of like this mix-up of 1900 on, without knowing most of the rules that went on before.

Even today, I still don't know most of the rules. I know a lot of them, and I know how these people applied them, but they're the logical extension of all the stuff that came before. But I kinda jumped in at the next level. The whole problem is going back and learning all the rules. That's why I went back to this teacher, David Scheinfeld, in around 1980. I wanted to go back and learn most of these rules. My brother Derek had been going to him for three years and David was diligently, rigorously giving him all of this really early information, really hardcore. Spending weeks and weeks and weeks on, like, two pages of the book, instead of like at the College of Marin, where you'd go through a chapter a week kind of a thing. That's what David's speed was. He was really trying to diligently make Derek a great composer. But when I said I just wanted to conduct, David said, "Okay, well, we'll just go through the basic rules," and I went through what Derek did in about three weeks, and then I ended up not being able to take lessons anymore because I got the Zappa gig and I had to quit.

I'm still at this ancient impasse, where I still need to go back to school and learn all those rules that I never really learned. I know a bunch of it. I can try and analyze harmony in certain classical pieces of music, but most of them don't relate to any of the modern stuff. They're based on different rules and different needs. I know a lot of the modern rules, but I don't have the ability to come from underneath, to build those structures. Even writing classical music for films would be tough for me because I don't have the knowledge of orchestration that most of those people need to make that shit happen. Most of that stuff's very polyphonic. A lot of it – the Danny Elfman stuff – you can tell how it came from the keyboard: *koon-chang, koon-chang, koon-chang, koon-chang.* You know, put a melody on top of something silly. But anything from *Batman* on has been pretty juicy, and pretty complicated, and it's between Elfman, his synthesizer, and his orchestrator that determines how thick that shit's going to get.

I'm pretty much at an impasse where I am very happy to just sit and play the piano. I'm very, very afraid to touch the keyboard if there isn't some music in front of me. It would take me months of just actually sitting down, and really honestly not caring what I played or what I was trying to do. The last time I tried to write a piece of music, I choked after about five bars. It was something I was going to do for Georgia's birthday and I just totally dropped the ball. That was over a year ago. I can't do it. I'm not interested in it. Right now I guess you'd say I'm acting in really bad faith. I'm not writing classical music, and I'm not performing any kind of music at all, and the kind of music I am performing – the Brahms, and the Schuberts, and all that kind of stuff – I'm performing very badly because

I have no piano technique. I really could possibly spend the rest of my life being a really bad classical piano player.

I didn't get into the conservatory, but I studied jazz and classical on my own. If I'd really applied myself and had all that knowledge at my fingertips, I would've gone ahead with the classical, definitely. I rue the day I started working with Frank. I would've infinitely preferred to spend the rest of my days dealing with David Scheinfeld, especially since now that I've done all that rock shit, I'm still working in an office. I could still go spend an hour a week at fucking David Scheinfeld's house in San Francisco learning the in-depth rules of classical music. Now that I'm thirty-seven years old, I've got all this mental energy just burbling under with nowhere to go because I've got no rules. Beethoven, Satie – all these people went back and took lessons after they were famous. Excellent composers. Went back and took theory lessons, a lot of them. So I'm just prime for that right now.

The rules I learned are not even really rules. They're just what music consists of. When I was a kid, when I put a third in the bass, it sounded bad. I did not like the sound of it. That's a very powerful sound, and can be very useful, but not in rock. In rock, it sounds not very good. In classical music, one of the best chords in the orchestral suite *The Planets,* by Gustav Holst, is in the movement titled "Jupiter." It's just a regular major chord, with a third in the bass. It's heavy. Stravinsky thought that the first-inversion major chord – which is the third in the bass – is so different from a normal major chord that it should be classified as a different chord. He firmly believed that. One of the world's finest instrumentalists and creative minds thought that the third in the bass, the simplest operation you can possibly do, should be classified as a different chord.

A major chord, first inversion, the third in the bass, sounds weird in rock. It was so weird that in one of my classes – a small composition class at College of Marin – it was being taught by one of the major jazz guys. He said, "The third in the bass is a very distinctive chord, very powerful, and should be very rarely used. Scott? What do you think? Should the third be used in the bass?"

"Fuck, no," I said. I actually said the wrong thing. This sixteen-year-old kid telling everyone else in class, "Fuck, no. Never use the damned thing. Sounds weird." All the chord and notes that I use that make songs sound weird are not the third. They're the fourth and the flat six. Those are my two big ones because they really do change what's happening on top. The third is just the third in the bass. Especially out of the third in the melody. One of the creepiest sounds in the world. The double third – a melody in the bass – is one of the biggest no-noes in classical music. Whenever I hear it in rock, I freak. I shudder. Really gives me the heebie-jeebies. But I use it all the time. As a passing note, I was using it in "Black Napkins." I use the third in the bass all the time.

I know it's true that notes or chords create an emotional reaction, but I never think about it. Not while I'm doing it. I just think, "Here's something different that I can do. I have the choice of twelve notes, but eleven of those might be really severely wrong. I can pretty much use four or five with utter freedom – the root, the third, the fifth and the flat seventh. I can use those pretty much at any time, with ultimate freedom, at any point in time because people have heard seventh chords for three hundred years. That chord can be really messed around with. The third in the bass sounds different. It changes the whole quality of everything because you're getting the harmonics, especially with a loud rock bass. You're getting all the harmonics off of that, which is going to change the quality of the harmonics that are going on above it. It sounds completely different.

What if you put the fifth in the bass? I don't know why that is different and more emotional. All I know is, it has its place. It's very, very powerful, and has to be used sparingly. Most people don't use it at all, which is why you don't hear it. The first reason I can think of is that it's so rare is that it's changing the face of the song for you. Another reason is that it is so pungent that it sounds different, just by itself. The amount of times it's used and the actual sound of it.

That's all that is, is a first-inversion chord. Sometimes it's useful, and sometimes it's not. Sometimes you're not supposed to even touch that damned thing at all. But when I'm playing it, I'm very rarely thinking of the emotional impact of it. I'm not thinking, "I'm trying to make you cry." I'm thinking, "What are my choices? How interesting can I get, while still keeping the basic meat of the song alive? How can I keep the song recognizable, and play more stuff?" Most of the time, if it's just accompaniment of a melody, I can do whatever I want. If it's rock, there's going to be a riff-based song, and I'm going to have to pretty much stick to that. The riff is what it is. Sometimes the riff itself can have that third in the bass, and you don't know why you love that riff so much.

I didn't throw *anything* away. Anyone can play like I do. Anyone can do it. *You* can do it. I just learned a couple of simple rules and applied them. Give me five minutes with you, baby. I'll teach you how. Yeah, go ahead and smash me in the head with that bottle. *Anyone* can do what I do.

Yes, I will admit to having good taste. You haven't been asking the right question. I had no idea where you were going with this. But that's absolutely true. I have impeccable taste. Musicians can have good taste, and it is innate, my friend. I've been shoving taste down my friends' throats for years, and they have not changed an iota. I have very many, very excellent friends who have absolutely rotten taste. But I love them dearly because they have other elements where they're strong. The problem is that when you're not being tasteful, it stands out. Oh, Jesus hell! That's the joy for me of listening to my music: the shuddering of when the un-tastefulness is going to pop out. Most of it is very useful, but if I play one pattern that sounds trite, or I do one note in a scale that sounds banal, I freak out.

The only reason anybody gets good in anything is to seduce people with their talent. What else do you have? If you're a talented talker, you talk. If you're a talented lover, you try and get people to love you as soon as possible. The problem with musicians is that most people are talent and no person. Ninety-eight percent of all musicians have no personality. They're all just their musical stuff. People don't fall in love with somebody because they're great musicians. They fall in love with somebody because they have a certain type of power. In music, it's a surface power because music can't be used anywhere else. If you're a great composer, your pieces of music are great, but you don't bone a piece of music. You have to get past the music to get to the person.

The three women that I was with during the Frank years were very much based on that whole period of trying to be this rock person that I was never meant to be. The same thing happened with all three of them. Their communication was horrible from the get-go. I was with them only because of the fact that I was in music. There wasn't any true love of who I actually was. They didn't ever get anywhere near there. Anything that they saw in me scared them out of their minds. They never really loved me. Everything I said as Scott Thunes the person scared the hell out of them. Very weird.

Frank wrote a piece of classical music for a rock band called "Envelopes." The first two thirty-two bars had no bass in it. I had to memorize it. It was a classical piece of music with lots of atonal stuff going on. But the first two thirty-two bars, about the first minute-and-a-half, I didn't have to play. During the course of the night, that was the only time I wasn't playing. It was two hours of constantly playing. Anybody else, as far as I could tell, would probably just sit around and shove as much beer down their gullet as they possibly could, but I couldn't just stand there like a fool. So every night I would choose something else to do. Everything from putting my leather jacket on backwards and wandering around like a fuckin' robot, to pretending to eat spaghetti with Frank's guitar and mic chords, juggling two oranges.

The famous thing is the mayonnaise experience. That was my first claim to fame. The last two weeks of the '81 tour, we played Salt Lake City. It was a pretty small, comfy little club and for my thirty-two bars, I decided to bring a metal steamer tray full of mayonnaise out beforehand. During my thirty-two bars, I took my shirt off, and scooped out a bunch of mayonnaise with a spatula and placed it all over the top half of my body – my face, my hands, my arms – and then I had to jump onto the bass and play the rest of the song. Frank was staring back in amazement. I was very famous for years because of the mayonnaise incident.

Frank actually had Tommy Mars improvise a little afterwards, so that people could come out and wipe all the mayonnaise off of my body and give me my other bass so that they could wipe the mayonnaise off the first bass. I definitely couldn't have played the rest of the set like that. I kind of ruined the set. But before the next set, Frank said, "That was one of the funniest things I've ever seen in my entire life, so go for it!" It wasn't until almost four years later that Frank mentioned off the cuff that I had ruined the show because he had to stop it and get Tommy Mars to do some improvisation.

Taking chances like that was not a change in my personality. It was purely finding my ability.

Anthology Three
Beginnings and Annihilation
1992-1995

Thou art my love,
And thou art a priestess,
And in thy hand is a bloody dagger,
And my doom comes to me surely –
Woe is me.

Your Voice is Stupid, so Go Write Porn

In August of 1990, I arrived in Los Angeles, setting foot in the U.S. for the first time in five years. My mother, father, and brother Tim met me at the airport. I was amazed at how Californian my brother sounded, like a surfer. Driving home was frightening and disorienting because the streets were so wide and there were so few people. I felt as though I'd fly off the face of the earth. Tokyo is so overbuilt that you can't really even see the sky. Los Angeles seemed to be nothing *but* sky.

My sister Carrie sold me her '80 Toyota Corolla, and on October 21 I drove to San Francisco to reunite with Carmen, who'd found us an apartment in the Sunset District. We'd been apart for two months, and when we got back together I tried to hug her tightly enough to fuse her into my flesh. The apartment was beautiful, with a back deck that overlooked a vacant lot. It was surrounded by Chinese markets, which meant we could continue our habit of buying the ingredients for the night's meals on the way home from work. I attached a ladder to the outside of the apartment next to the bathroom window, so the cat could climb down to the deck into the vacant lot or go up on the roof and gambol on an acre or so of tar and gravel, since all the buildings were connected.

The best time was the night, lying in the large double bed with Carmen in my arms, listening to the foghorns in the bay. I didn't think it was possible, but I was even happier in San Francisco than I'd been in Tokyo. Carmen and I seemed to have bonded permanently, the way albatrosses mate for life. We laughed all the time. Once, as we drove across the Golden Gate on our way back from a hike in the abandoned antiaircraft sites of the Marin Headlands, the topic of scream therapy came up. Since neither of us had tried it, we screamed as loud as we could and gave ourselves instant headaches. The way she held her head, moaning and bellowing her deafening laugh and then moaning some more because now her own laugh made her head hurt – she was caught in vortex of self-inflicted, agonizing mirth – almost made me crash the car.

I shuttled back and forth between Los Angeles and San Francisco a few times, bringing up pieces of furniture. Once fully settled in, I sent my résumés and sample tapes to voiceover agencies and was shocked to receive no response at all. The same thing happened when I sent out résumés for editing jobs. I discovered the truth of the sneer "big in Japan." My strangled not-quite-baritone wasn't desirable in the U.S. They preferred men with giant *basso profundo* voices achieved from decades of booze and filterless cigarettes. For editing jobs, they wanted the proper academic credentials, not hands-on experience.

Carmen and I separated for Christmas. We didn't seem to have a choice. It'd be the first Christmas I'd spend with my family in five years.

At the beginning of 1991, I gave up on voiceover work and editing. Although I had my savings from Japan, they were rapidly depleted by the astronomical cost of living. I began answering all sorts of want ads. Some were unbelievable. One asked for somebody "interested in art and people." That was me! I drove out to Marin County and sat down with a fat man who gave me a Vaudeville routine about himself: "Fifty years old and I just got my ear pierced. My wife says, 'Whattaya gonna do next, learn the lambada?' I'm joking, of course." He refused to tell me what the job was about, saying it was easier if I just showed up the next day and met my "trainer." I'd spend the day with him, and if I liked what we did, I'd be hired.

The trainer was a kid with blond hair and an Errol Flynn mustache. His name was Ace. He, too, refused to tell me what the job was. He'd show me instead. We got into a van and drove... somewhere. Ace monologued about two topics: His wealth and his diverticulitis.

"I'm the only twenty-two-year-old guy I know with a boat. Got it doing this. You know what else I got? Silver coins. Tons of 'em. They're a great investment. My wife Tracy is always shocked at the jewelry I bring home for her. 'Here's some more jewelry, babe,' I tell her, 'cause she *is* my babe. I'm the only twenty-two-year-old guy I know who can afford to bring his wife jewelry every night if he wants. Oops, sorry for farting. This fuckin' diverticulitis bloats you up, and then the gas has to go somewhere. Roll down the window. You know what else I got? A whole collection of silver certificates. You know what they are? Old bills with different-colored seals and serial numbers. Worth a fortune. I keep finding them in the change I get. I'm just a lucky guy. Good things keep happening to me. Oops, sorry."

He still wouldn't tell me what the job entailed, though, no matter how many times I asked. I'd decided it was something nefarious and was about to demand that he turn the van around when we pulled into a commercial zone full of offices. We got out, and as we walked to the first establishment, Ace said, "Just watch and listen." We went inside, and he asked for the manager. To this suspicious-looking man in his forties, Ace said, "Hi, we've just finished decorating a couple doors down. You know Mr. Anderson? Short guy, bald, with glasses? Well, it turns out he ordered too many framed prints for his office, so he suggested that we come and offer them to you, which we can, at a 75 percent discount."

The manager had begun shaking his head at Ace's third sentence, and now he said, "No, thanks. We don't need any framed prints today."

Ace dropped his hands and said, "Aw, shit. Fine." And we left. We hit every office in that lot, and Ace used the exact spiel, word for word, always referring to the short, bald, bespectacled, mythical Mr. Anderson. We didn't make a single sale.

I spent the entire day with him. "The secret is in the pitch," he told me; it was secret even to him, apparently, because we didn't sell anything in eight hours of trying. When he brought me back to the fat, ear-pierced, Vaudevillian's headquarters at 5:30 P.M., Ace said, "I don't think you're cut out for this line of work."

"I don't think I am, either," I said. I wanted to kill him for holding me hostage and making me waste the entire day listening to him brag, break wind, and tell me that a 98 percent failure rate in sales was normal.

Things went a little better when I applied for the job of copy editor for an "entertainment publication." The woman who called me said she was impressed with my résumé. "Now what we are is a porn magazine?" she said briskly. "You'll be writing caption for the photos? You know – sexy, dirty, pornographic things?"

Regretfully, I declined. I was terrified of becoming an insensate block of cement when in bed with Carmen.

We both applied for jobs at the Central Intelligence Agency and made it past the first interview. It was fun and scary going to the hotel and seeing a fake convention sign in front of the room where we met with the recruiter: very cloak and dagger. The man who gave the presentation looked and sounded exactly like the actor Tim Reid from the TV sitcom *WKRP in Cincinnati*. Everyone in the interview except for Carmen and me were freaks. Some appeared to be homeless. What made the experience quite sobering was that the Tim Reid lookalike had a big poster on an easel listing the four Directorates of the CIA: Intelligence, Support, Science and Technology, and Operations. Three had descriptions of their functions and duties, but Operations was completely blank.

"We don't say anything about Operations until you actually join the Company," the recruiter said. Carmen and I voluntarily screened ourselves out when they told us some of the potential disqualifying factors.

In desperation I signed up with a temp agency. They gave us a test:

1. 25 + 18 = _____.

2. What do you call a large body of salt water?
a. Ocean
b. Windshield
c. Pie

3. A man married to a woman is called her _____.

About twenty such queries. People came in, looked at the single sheet of paper, said, "Nobody told me there'd be a test," and walked out. I got hired to help clean out an office building; I mean, toss all the furniture, filing cabinets, carpets – everything – out the windows and into dumpsters. One of the guys working with me was young and articulate. It turned out he was a jazz guitarist. I told him I played the bass, and we had lunch together.

It was a one-day job, but he and I kept in touch. He eventually invited Carmen and me to see his band. They were great. I really hoped they'd make it. His female singer got signed a few years later and became internationally famous. He's now teaching at a prestigious music college, and he's a studio guitarist who's played with everyone. I'd love to identify him because his is a story of perseverance and triumph, but he might not want people to know that at one time he was doing work that was beneath the dignity of a Nepalese cow-dung patty collector. Even so, I salute him for never giving up.

On August 1 I took Carmen down to Los Angeles to meet my family. They loved her, of course. She and Tim got along especially well. We slept in separate bedrooms, but that was all right. We agreed beforehand that we'd do it out of respect for my brother and sister, in whose house we stayed. Mom and Carmen liked each other immediately. Sometimes they'd sit on Mom's porch and talk, just the two of them. I was glad that everybody reacted so positively toward her, since she was destined to be their daughter- and sister-in-law. Even my father liked her, telling her about the fun times he had at the Mark Hopkins Hotel when he was in the Coast Guard. The lounge was called the Top of the Mark. He asked her if the hotel still existed, but she didn't know.

Here's the letter Carmen sent my parents in her gorgeous, precise, round handwriting.

> 9 Aug 1991
> Dear Mr. and Mrs. Wictor,
> These are to express my appreciation for the wonderful time I spent in [withheld].
> The Mark Hopkins, Ed, is still **THE** place to be seen on Nob Hill. I hope the enclosed matches are a suitable memento.
> The Bella Coola Sun Card is for you, Cee-Cee. I thought it might help inspire you for future mask-making projects!
> I hope to be seeing both of you again soon.
> Sincerely,
> Carmen

In September I was hired as a driver delivering payrolls and Carmen was hired at San Francisco International Airport. Both jobs required that we go to bed at about eight at night like toddlers. We spent our second Christmas in the U.S. separately. I asked Carmen if I'd ever meet her parents, and she said of course, but not just yet. Though they called a lot they wouldn't speak to me. If I answered the phone, they'd just say, "Is Carmen there?" without even a "Hello." On her birthday they'd leave singing messages on the machine. It hurt that after I'd introduced her to my parents, she hadn't reciprocated. I asked Carmen to marry me, and she said she'd think about it. That was fine with me. We were still trying to find our way.

Birth of a Music Journalist

In January of 1992, I sent a proposal to Jim Roberts, editor of *Bass Player,* offering to write about the Japanese obsession with the bass guitar. Jim accepted, and "The Bass Gods of Japan" was published in the March 1992 issue of the magazine. It was my first article in any publication. I began to wonder if maybe I had a future in that line of work.

One morning in February, Carmen left for work and then came running back into our courtyard. It was still dark. "Tom! Tom!" she yelled. "Someone's breaking into your car!"

I ran downstairs and saw a short, stocky man in a hoodie waddling down the street with his arms full. Carmen took off after him.

"*Carmen, goddammit!*" I screamed. "*Come back here! What're you* doing?"

The guy had stolen my fire extinguisher, Thomas Guide, and various other goodies, all of which he dropped and Carmen recovered. I was terrified but proud. She was fearless, and she still made me laugh. Her infatuation with Susan Rook of CNN culminated one night when she blurted, "God, she's so cool! I wanna marry her!" Then she drove her head into my middle and hugged me, guffawing and hiding her face.

In April I quit my job as a delivery driver. They offered to double my salary to keep me, telling me I was their best employee. That made me furious. I was about to turn thirty, and I was as terrified of the future as I'd been when I graduated from college. The only thing that kept me from falling to pieces was Carmen. Lying in bed with her at night, listening to the foghorns in the bay, was magical. We hiked, had picnics, watched the fog roll in under the Golden Gate, and took walks in the exclusive neighborhoods of Pacific Heights. She was the sole source of my happiness.

I began to build model World War I biplanes again, something I hadn't done since high school. Carmen joined me and naturally turned out to be better at it than I was. She loved the German aces' personal insignia and painted entirely by hand the detailed werewolf face used by *Leutnant* Franz Buchner, commander of *Jagdstaffel 13,* on the sides of his Fokker D.VII. That means she painted it *twice*. With all the paints and brushes lying around, Carmen began rendering self-portraits and abstract designs, something she said she'd never done before. They were breathtaking. She had a fully formed style right from the beginning.

My second *Bass Player* article, "Is Left Right for You?" was published in the May/June 1992 issue. It was about whether or not bassists should play left-handed instruments, the way I did. I interviewed Doug Pinnick of King's X, studio legend Mark Egan, and Jimmy Haslip of the Yellowjackets, musicians I'd admired for years. It seemed entirely possible that I might actually become a music journalist.

On June 3 I was hired as a Field Representative in a document-retrieval service. I'd copy legal and medical documents for use in lawsuits. My duties were to drive around all day, visiting hospitals and government offices with my portable microfilming machine. I'd give the work order to the custodian of records; I'd be handed the document; and I'd feed it through the machine. My writing background and photography skills got me the job, the interviewer said.

The best way to encapsulate the job of Field Representative is the following: As I walked down a hallway in a hospital, I saw two workmen fixing an overhead fluorescent light. The one on the ladder was fat and middle aged, while the one standing below him was young and slim. Their voices echoed off the shiny surfaces, one a deep, hoarse rasp honed by decades of whiskey and cigarettes, and the other a light, pleasant tenor. When I got close, I saw that the fat, middle-aged worker spoke in the light, pleasant tenor, while the clean-looking young man had the wrecked barfly's growl

I once drove past a man sitting on a bench at a bus stop with his legs stretched out in front of him. He idly scratched his nose and looked at his feet, which were on fire. They gave off twin columns of black smoke. He didn't seem bothered, and nobody else stopped, so I kept driving. Another time I saw an elegant woman walking down the street in a suit jacket and dark glasses, wearing high heels and carrying a chic handbag. She was nude from the waist down. This time I stopped and found a cop getting a cup of coffee in a doughnut shop. Really.

"Asian woman?" he asked. "Really good looking? About thirty-five? Dark glasses?"

"Yeah, that's her."

He shook his head. "We can't get her to keep her pants on. There's not a thing we can do with her. Don't worry about it."

My favorite place was the hospital built into the side of a cliff. It was eight stories tall, with the entrance on the top floor in the back. When I parked in front, I saw nothing but a towering wall with darkened windows. There were no doors anywhere. I finally figured out that I had to go up a curved, eight-story-high stairway on the side, which was especially fun when lugging a fifty-pound copier. Inside, the entire hospital was deserted. No patients, no staff, nobody. There were also no directories. It took me an hour of systematic floor-by-floor searching to find the custodian of records. As I should've expected, he was in the basement. His thick glasses magnified his eyes to three times their actual size, making him look like a Humboldt squid. I asked why he was the only person in the building.

He blinked his squid-eyes and muttered, "How should I know?" He wasn't belligerent, but I knew that if his skin started flashing from white to red I'd be in trouble.

After I copied my one document, I had to take the elevator back up to the eighth floor, go out the front door in the back, and walk down the stairway to the parking lot in front, which was the rear. I'm positive that either this building didn't actually exist, or it was an experiment by some shadowy government agency.

Forbidden Knowledge

In August I had a conversation with Carmen that destroyed our relationship. If I could do everything all over again, I would've kept my mouth shut. In my defense, what I told her was about me, not her, but I understand now that there are many things better left unsaid. Compelled by my obsessions for emotional closeness and righting injustice, I asked her to drive us to one of her favorite spots in Pacific Heights, where we parked and spoke. I thought she'd appreciate that I loved and trusted her enough to finally share a formative experience that is central to my character, personality, and mindset. It defines me, despite my best efforts to make it not so, and it provides context. My disclosure made her cry harder than I'd ever seen, except for when Hazim beat her to a pulp. My intention was to explain; I did incalculable damage instead. I've since learned that it's possible to have intimate relationships without discussing everything on your mind. One of my closest friends is a Russian army colonel whom I've never met in person. We disagree on all the things you'd expect, but we solve the problem by skirting virtually every issue that might cause friction between us. So what do I talk about with a Russian army colonel, then? You'd be surprised.

It's almost certain that even if Carmen and I had avoided that conversation, we wouldn't have escaped our ultimate destiny. Still, my choice today would be to not have had the talk because it would've given me more time with her. That would've been worth any price.

Everything changed after my disclosure. She became distant at first, and then savagely antagonistic. It took me almost twenty years to understand her reaction, but now I do. It's a natural instinct to recoil from and resent the person who unnerves. When someone introduces intense unpleasantness into what you thought was your safe harbor, you can easily come to hate them for demolishing what you worked so hard to create. I believe that's what happened. Though my intention was to help her understand me, the end result was that I lost her forever.

Soon afterward she got a job in the broadcasting industry, and we entered the worst period of our time together.

Always Have a Plan B

In March of 1993, I sold my first article to a modeling magazine. Several others followed. I began to think that if the career in music journalism didn't pan out, I might have a future as a professional model builder, working for museums and private clients. It's quite lucrative. In March Jim Roberts also approved my proposal to write an article about ten bassists I thought were criminally overlooked as stylists. I titled the piece "Unsung Bass Stylists." After I turned it in, Jim called me and said they'd decided to break the article up into single sidebars and put them in ten issues, like a monthly column. I was aghast.

"Who's going to read those little articlettes?" I asked.

Jim loved the coinage, and forever after called them articlettes. He also sent me a mockup to show me how they'd look, each with an album cover and my paragraph. I was still upset, but his magazine, his rules. The first "Unsung Bass Stylists" column was published in the May/June issue of *Bass Player,* followed in the next issue by a correction, since I hadn't done my homework. For any young people reading this, you can't comprehend how hard it was in those pre-Internet days. Everything had to be done by snail mail, fax, and phone calls.

The responses to my column were gratifying. Here's one.

> Dear Mr. Wictor:
> I've been an avid reader of your "Unsung Bass Stylists" column since its debut in *Bass Player.* I agree wholeheartedly with its purpose, and my only complaint is that it could be a little longer (is half a page asking too much?). I'm writing this, though, to let you know about a bassist that I think should have a spot in the column, Peter Hook.

I never featured Hook in my column, but he's one of the artists covered in my book *In Cold Sweat: Interviews with Really Scary Musicians.* The introduction to that interview contains some of the best writing of my career.

While things were looking up in the employment field, my relationship with Carmen was clearly swirling the drain. We fought like we did in the beginning of our time together, our new arguments separated by days of not speaking to each other. She began seeing a therapist, and one day she said that when she told her therapist about me, they both laughed. I can't describe the sense of outrage, helplessness, and injustice I experienced hearing that. The feeling of being the world's most ridiculous patsy came crashing down into me again, where it stayed until 2012. I knew at that moment that I'd lost her, and she genuinely hated me. She told me that I was a dictator who tried to control every aspect of her life. There was no sense in arguing, because it was so off base that it almost drove me out of my mind.

I'd willingly stake my life itself that since July of 1989 I'd done nothing but appreciate her for exactly who and what she was. We'd fought years earlier about our inability to trust and her deliberate deceit, but I'd never tried to control her. I wanted to tell her that I could barely control myself, so why would I want to take on the added burden of controlling someone else, too? But I knew it was over, and I was paralyzed with anguish.

Before everything fell apart, the beach had been our favorite place. We'd have picnics – roast beef sandwiches on crusty baguettes with grainy mustard, baby spinach, and tomatoes – or we'd run for miles on the hard sand at the water's edge. There was a strange, miniature inlet no more than fifteen feet wide, where sea glass and polished stones abounded. We could find them only in this stretch of beach, the result of a freak current that brought us these treasures from beneath the waves. At our apartment, we filled a wine bottle with alternating layers of blue, green, brown, and clear sea glass. Carmen displayed her collection of stones on green glass plates, some on the mantelpiece and one on top of an antique wooden ashtray stand.

"Let's go to the beach," she'd say. After a few hours of breathing in the scent of the ocean, running on the sand, listening to the roar of the surf, and collecting sea glass and polished stones, we'd return home relaxed and happy. Like me, she preferred the beach when it was gray, cloudy, and cold. It was another way we were uncannily in synch.

The last great moment of beauty I shared with Carmen was at the beach. We walked morosely along a cliff, heading toward a wooden platform from which hang gliders took off. A hang glider flew past and Carmen waved at him. He circled back and zoomed right over our heads, checking her out, and then he did aerobatics for her for several minutes, culminating in an audacious James Bond landing on the cliff right in front of her. What could I say? I applauded him, and she was flattered silly because she was thirty-three and he was about twenty, a great, handsome, muscular, wild-haired, daredevil of a boy, and it was just what she needed. It was great performance art. I returned to that cliff six years later, but other than that I haven't gone to the beach except for the times I went with Carmen in San Francisco.

God bless you, daredevil, wherever you are. You made a troubled woman happy and you gave me an indelible memory of how unexpectedly funny and gratifying life can be.

Lowlights

I asked Carmen if she understood what I was trying to say, and she said she did. A few days later, when we had a fight about the same thing all over again, I reminded her that she'd told me she'd understood. "Of course I didn't understand," she replied. "I just said that to shut you up."

She'd completely ignore me for days, walking through the apartment singing to herself or humming as if she couldn't have been happier. The phone would ring, and she'd have long, laughing conversations and then not speak to me for another three days.

In the midst of a fight she looked away and chuckled. I wanted to know what was so funny. "I can't tell you," she said. "You just wouldn't get it."

I asked her why she was being so unpleasant. No response. I asked her again, and she picked up her journal and began writing in it. When I demanded that she pay attention to me, she looked up, smiled, and said, "Oh, sorry. I wasn't listening."

As I struggled to find the unfamiliar words to explain how much it hurt when she ignored me, how it made me feel that I was nothing to her, and as I tried to swallow down the horror and humiliation of even having this conversation with her of all people, she suddenly leaned over and sniffed loudly at me, saying, "Does something stink? Smells like sweat."

After a week of silence from her, in the middle of me telling her that this was absolutely killing me, she began mimicking me in the most fiendishly lisping, sniveling, whining voice she'd ever used, her chin jutting and her eyebrows squinched into a hurt little chevron, her mouth pulled down at the corners in a lampoon of grief: "*Ith it too much to aaaaaathk for you to jutht thay hello to me, Caaarrmehhhhhhnn?*"

I said, "All this shows is that you're really angry at me, and I don't even know why."

She got up and walked away, muttering, "All this shows is that you really need help. It's *so* sad!"

The Ghost who Clarified

One afternoon in June of 1993, as I drove across Market Street going north on 4th Street, the tan Nissan pickup in front of me stopped and the driver put on her signal, preparing to make an illegal left-hand turn in front of the sign prohibiting the maneuver. She blocked me, and she wouldn't be able to make the turn for a long time because there was so much traffic. I honked my horn at her, a polite tap, and she sped ahead, stabbing her middle finger back at me out her window. Simply put, I snapped. I drove around and got in front of her, and since we'd come to a red light, I slammed on the brakes, got out, went back, and told her that she should be very careful about who she flipped off. S*he* was the one doing the illegal maneuver, holding me up, and she had no right to give me the finger. Even so, I tried to keep my voice under control.

Slumped in her seat, she was small and dark-haired, about my age. She stared at me blankly for a second and then screamed, "*Fuck off, asshole! Get back in yer fuckin' car!*" right in my face.

And with that, I was transformed. A switch clicked in my head; a white-hot rush hit me; and I went out of my skull. I was in an awful mood, having already dealt with three extremely dense and hostile civil servants, dodged four pedestrians who casually drifted out in front of me, and experienced two very near misses with cars that sped through their red lights.

She screamed, "*What makes you think I don't have a gun, asshole?*" spraying my face with droplets of saliva, since I stood about eighteen inches from her open window. Her twisted, blanched features made her look repulsive and non-human, something that had to be crushed.

I developed tunnel vision, as all my consciousness centered on her nose. Everything around it darkened. As she shouted, "*Just because I'm a girl doesn't mean I can't beat the shit out of you,*" all I could think about was how satisfying it would be to crash the heel of my right hand against the bridge of her nose as hard as I could, the blow I'd wanted so badly to land on Hazim when he assaulted Carmen. I'd piston my arm straight out like a battering ram, putting all my 230 pounds into it. I'd bawl, "Didn't expect that, did you?" Then I'd yank her by the hair right out the window, because she wasn't wearing her seat belt, and stamp her into the asphalt next to her vehicle.

Sweat poured out of me, my hands and legs trembled, and I was so happy I started laughing. In a surprise aural hallucination, I heard my father's voice as clearly as over a loudspeaker: "She's *defying* you." She *was* defying me, so she deserved everything she got. Her shrieking was an invitation; she just *begged* for it, and she had to be punished. We were about to connect in one of the most fundamentally intimate ways, and I'd love it. I looked quickly to either side to make sure no one was watching and cocked back my right arm. My face was rigid and cold as a brass mask and the top of my head tingled and seemed detached. The world became very quiet, and I felt light as a feather, immortal. I felt fantastic.

At that moment, the man in the car behind her, whom I hadn't even noticed, let out a long warning blast on his horn, shattering our universe of two. I realized, in the second before committing to the blow, that I was a large, heavy, thirty-two-year-old man with a beard, about to assault a woman half his size in the middle of the street. In front of fifteen or twenty people and in broad daylight, I'd initiated a deadly altercation. The police would arrive and I'd be hauled off to jail like Hazim, except I'd do hard time.

I dropped my arm and went back to my car, my euphoria evaporating. As I drove away, I pondered several questions: What if I'd had only one more lousy encounter before I met my terrified victim? Because that's all she was, a pint-sized dipshit talking trash and scared out of her wits. In her jabbering fear, could she have said just the right thing to push me over? Would I really have killed her over a finger gesture? Would I have reacted the same if she'd been a man instead of a woman? Am I really capable of murder? The answer to the last question was, yes, I am. I was Hazim. I knew I'd reached critical mass. Changes had to be made.

Let's Take a Little Time Off, Forever

By July I'd been sleeping on the living room sofa for months. Carmen and I hadn't had sex since soon after the conversation of August 1992. We'd barely even spoken. One morning I found that someone had smashed the rear window of my Corolla and punched out the ignition slot. They hadn't stolen the radio because my sister had epoxied it into place when she owned the car. I was too depressed to have the ignition slot fixed, so I just started the car with a screwdriver for a couple of weeks. It was time to go. I gave notice at my job and left San Francisco in August. The plan was for me to go down to Los Angeles while Carmen stayed in our apartment. We'd take some time off from each other because we'd been inseparable for five years. We didn't even hug when we parted. I felt doomed and panicky. None of it was conceivable.

Three weeks later Carmen called and told me she'd met someone and was seriously involved with him.

In September of 1993, Tim and I drove back to San Francisco in his '75 GMC Jimmy to get my things. Though I felt as though I were dying, with an intense pain in my chest and neck, Carmen was casual and cheerful, the happiest I'd seen her in ages. It was surreal. I have no idea how I held it together because I knew with every fiber of my being that we'd never get back together, in exactly the way I knew when I first met her that I was supposed to be with her. What our five-year relationship had proven to me was that fate can be altered by decisions. Nothing's set in stone. I still believe that things are destined to happen, but now I know that ultimate outcomes are never guaranteed.

She was utterly indifferent to me. Our time together was so trivial to her that she wasn't upset. Actually, *I* was so trivial to her that she wasn't upset. She couldn't even be bothered to mourn, since apparently this wasn't an occasion for sadness. It was just another day. She wore a short, tight, black miniskirt ensemble, high heels, and heavy makeup; she glowed, like a billionaire's high-spirited girlfriend.

As Tim and I packed, I caught Carmen trying to hide some of my CDs. "Those are mine," I said.

"Oops!" she said and laughed.

I credit Tim with helping me through what was essentially an amputation of half my body and half my soul. He was pleasant and friendly to Carmen, and we loaded up the vestiges of my life with her in about forty-five minutes. I said goodbye to her for what I thought would be the last time. As usual, I was wrong.

Tim didn't say much on the way home. Since 1993 he's never badmouthed Carmen, either. Like everyone who meets her, he likes her immensely.

An Englishman in Los Angeles

Living with Tim and our sister Carrie in our late grandmother's house was difficult for all of us. Carrie moved out almost immediately, leaving Tim and me. We didn't know each other very well at the time, and I was a basket case. My sadness and shock slowly transformed to rage. I didn't want to be angry, but that final scene of happy, miniskirted Carmen hustling me out of her life was nearly impossible to process. It wasn't the fact that she was now with someone else; it was the cosmic unjustness of her so utterly misunderstanding me, coming to hate me, and then becoming indifferent to me.

My "Unsung Bass Stylists" piece on John Taylor of Duran Duran appeared in the April 1994 issue of *Bass Player*.

> Lost amidst the pop megastardom and recent resurgence of this group is the fact that John Taylor is a brilliant bass player, consistently pushing the envelope of his genre. He has a clear, metallic tone and plays somewhat unorthodox patterns, and he adds color with subtle effects and sophisticated, if only occasional, harmonics. Taylor's lines are evocative and carefully crafted, which helps to produce the exotic jet-setting atmosphere for which the band is known. "New Religion" showcases Taylor's work on faster cuts, while "Save a Prayer" displays an amazingly sensitive approach to ballads.[1]

I chose "New Religion" because it was Carmen's favorite song off the album. It was my secret tribute to her. The letters immediately began pouring in.

> You have my undying respect and gratitude for your exceptionally insightful and greatly appreciated mini-profile by Thomas Wictor of one of the greatest 'Unsung Bass Stylists' of our time, John Taylor of Duran Duran. It was solely his remarkable talent that first interested me in the bass guitar, and my happiest moments are spent playing along with his inspired bass lines.

Another one.

> When I leafed through the April issue of *Bass Player,* I actually got goose bumps to see that you had chosen Duran Duran's John Taylor as one of your 'Unsung Bass Stylists.' I've reveled in John's hook-laden grooves for years; in fact I cut my teeth on 'New Religion,' and Rio is still my all-time favorite album.

And another.

> I am writing to tell you how much I enjoy reading Bass Player. April 94's issue was most excellent, because I received a shock on page 12 in the Bass Notes section. I have always liked John Taylor's 'unorthodox' bass playing. His style is one of a kind – and very much underrated! How nice to see him finally recognized in your magazine.

One more.

> I would like to thank you and Thomas Wictor for last month's "Unsung Bass Stylists" on John Taylor. Even before I picked up a bass, Duran Duran's music was an influence on me. The curious listener without "Duranic" hang-ups should also be pointed toward the first album for cuts like "Girls on Film" and "Planet Earth."

The letters were gratifying on many levels. Of course it's nice to know that one's work is appreciated, but I was also pleased that so many others recognized John Taylor's unique voice on the instrument. I don't understand the "John Taylor isn't talented" trope. To this day, I've never heard anyone play the bass lines from "Girls on Film" or the Power Station's "Some Like it Hot" exactly the way Taylor has played them live countless times. It's a completely original style, a signature sound. In Taylor's case it was always the combination of note choices, attack, tone, and his ability to play slightly ahead of the beat that make what he does all his own. He's a natural. The exceptionally talented bassists of the Mexican band Molotov told me that of all the bass lines they copied as youngsters learning to play, John Taylor's were the most difficult to duplicate.

The letters also confirmed the rightness of my tribute to Carmen, her taste, and the good if deeply painful memories I had of her.

Clipped to the letters was a note from Jim Roberts: "Wow... You really struck a nerve with John Taylor. Want to interview him?" That was Jim. He always knew exactly where to go with the magazine, and he was bold and imaginative. I nearly had a heart attack, especially after contacting Jim and having him tell me he wanted a feature-length article, my first as a music journalist. I didn't know a thing about John Taylor the man, so I was horribly intimidated. I thought he'd be like David Bowie: enigmatic and impenetrable. I called his publicist, and she shouted, "*You're* the guy! John's assistant sent me that short thing you did where you said he was a brilliant bassist. He called me and said he couldn't believe that *Bass Player* thought he was brilliant! He's going to flip when I tell him you want to do a feature article on him!"

The publicist arranged for me to go to Taylor's house in an exclusive Southern California neighborhood on April 26, 1994. It was some kind of hallucination. His *house?* I was given his home phone number in case there was a problem. Naturally, there was. I got hopelessly lost because of the winding roads and lack of numbers on the curbs and mailboxes. When I was fifteen minutes late I reluctantly called Taylor, expecting him to be furious.

"Mr. Taylor, it's Tom Wictor from *Bass Player,*" I said. "I'm so sorry, but I'm lost. I can't find your house."

He laughed and said, "So where are you now?"

I told him, and he said, "How the *hell* did you get *there?*" but humorously, as though sharing an observation of something absurd with a friend, like, "Is that crazy or *what?*" He very patiently gave me precise directions, and when I got to his home and he opened the door, I said, "Mr. Taylor."

"John. Please," he said, shaking my hand.

He made me fresh coffee while we talked about Britain, where I'd once lived. Though he was calm, open, and friendly, I sat there feeling like a cheap hoaxer about to be exposed. "Please don't let me screw this up," I silently begged whatever patron saint of interviewers there might be. "Please don't let me screw this up." We then sat down and did a perfectly civilized, fun, funny, and – for me – poignant interview. He was touchingly humble, and I could tell it wasn't an act. My favorite line of his was that Duran Duran's first album was the sum total of their musical knowledge. They couldn't have played "Johnny B. Goode" even if they'd wanted to. He explained in painful detail how his fame had overwhelmed him, mentioning mind-boggling sums of money, drugs, and unscrupulous characters who took advantage.

Taylor was the only mega-famous musician I interviewed who appreciated honest praise and rejected fawning. I read him a quote from a reviewer who said that "Working for the Skin Trade" was "the finest three minutes in pop-music history." He scoffed with what seemed to be genuine annoyance and rattled off a list of great pop songs, asking if "Skin Trade" was better than those. Although I wasn't afraid of him by then, he appeared – in a campy way – ready to get into a fist fight over it, the way men in movies throw down on each other: "Okay, *that's* it, pal! Let's go!" He said the most noteworthy aspect of the difficult bass strumming at the beginning of "Some Like it Hot" is how out of time it is.

What really struck me was his lack of melodrama and self-pity. He had the knack of relating truly devastating failures and disappointments in a matter-of-fact way. I'd say of all the musicians I interviewed, he was the most objective about himself. If a young musician on the verge of mega-stardom asked me to name the best person to talk to about handling fame, I'd say John Taylor.

I called his signature bass the Ibanez; I knew it was the Aria but brain-fartedly said Ibanez anyway. The second time I did it, he very politely raised his chin, opened his mouth, and took a breath, the way well-bred people do when they want to interrupt you. I paused, and he said, "Aria." He waited until I made the mistake twice before correcting me. I asked if he was angry about his change in fortunes.

"Sometimes," he said. "Not consistently. The anger that started to surface was probably more as a result of being shunned by the public that put us on these pedestals. That's really weird to deal with. I reached the age of thirty, and I was back in London making the *Liberty* album and I started to look around me and started to look at what other people had, and I started to get really angry. Not at their success, because so much of it is based on how you measure success. I now think that success is measured by the amount of time you get to spend with the people you want to be with. That goes way, *way* beyond Oscars or Grammys or things like that. If you're really successful, then you're in control of your life, and that means you get to be where you want to be and with whom you want to be."

He let me stay in his home as long as I wanted, which was about two hours, and he shook my hand firmly and thanked me as he saw me out. When I sent his publicist the article for him to preview, she asked if he'd be allowed to ask for changes. "Of course," I said. "The article is about him, not me." Taylor called me personally a day or so later and told me the article was perfect and to not change a word. He said it was the best interview with him he'd ever read, and he thanked me profusely. It was by far the proudest moment I experienced as a music journalist. The article, "John Taylor: Learning to Survive," was published in the November 1994 issue of *Bass Player.*

I interviewed Taylor a second time on September 19, 1995, for his solo album, *Feelings are Good and Other Lies,* which wasn't released until 1997. Since his publicist represented several other artists, we worked together a few times. If she asked, "How're you doing?" she was one of the few people who really wanted to know. When I spoke to her in January of 1996, in regard to a different artist on her roster, she asked how I'd been, and I told her that just six nights earlier someone had tried to murder me at my bookstore. She wanted all the details, which I gave her. We then concluded our business.

When *Feelings are Good and Other Lies* was released in February of 1997, I got a copy of the CD in the mail from John Taylor. He'd written on the cover, "Dear Tom, Glad you're alive. Love to ya, John, 1997." He'd sent it more than a year after I'd had the conversation with his publicist about a different artist, which meant that she'd told him about me and it'd stayed in his mind for all that time.

I was floored but not surprised. That seemed the sort of person John Taylor is. I was privileged to have spoken with him, not only because he's a great artist and he warned me that I was on the wrong track, but also because he's at the center of so many good memories I have of music, the bass, music journalism, and my time with Carmen. He also set several terrific examples for me, which I'm finally able to follow. Although I wasn't ready to hear it at the time, he showed me by his words, demeanor, and actions how to handle setbacks.

Thank you, John.

Apocalypse

In May of 1994, Carmen called and said her boyfriend had dumped her because she was too much work. She told me she wanted me sexually, needing to feel me on top of her and inside her. "Just get up here," she whispered." I drove to San Francisco the next day. When I arrived at our former apartment, she let me in and said, "I've changed my mind. I don't want you after all."

It didn't upset me, because I hadn't driven 350 miles to just have sex with her. I wanted to see her, talk with her, be with her. We'd been apart for a long time, so I didn't blame her for not wanting me. I told her it was all right and suggested we drive around for a while. We cruised through some of our old haunts in my rented car, but she wouldn't talk to me. I chattered like a mockingbird while she stared out the window. After an hour or so, she asked me to take her home.

At the apartment, I lay on the sofa and held out my arms to her. "Come on," I said. "What'll it hurt? You're not involved with anyone. It'll just be two old buddies having a fling. Get your ass over here."

She stood by the window, not making eye contact. "No."

"Come on! It'll be fun!" I was actually – God help me – in a good mood. I thought at any second she'd smile and join me. We'd be together again, and we could junk all the pain, cruelty, and misunderstanding. I knew I could forgive her anything. She was still my world.

"I'll fuck you if you buy me a mountain bike," she said.

I laughed. "Sure. What color?"

She snapped her head around and glared at me with a level of hate I've never seen directed at me by anyone. "You always sucked in bed," she hissed. "Jason was much better at it than you ever were. He fucked me the way I needed to be fucked. With him I was wet twenty-four hours a day."

I didn't need her to tell me that I was lousy in bed. It wasn't news to me. Criticism of my sexual incompetence never bothered me. I also still didn't care that she'd been with someone else. Of course she had, because we'd broken up. What cut me like an axe blade was the uninhibited, unrestrained viciousness of her attack. She still loathed me, and at the time I didn't understand why.

"The whole time you were just waiting for something better to come along, weren't you?" I asked.

"Your problem is you never made enough money. It was a total bummer having to put up with all those years of struggling. For what? Nothing."

"You always told me money didn't matter to you. You told me that for years."

She shrugged and gazed out the window again. "I lied. I just said all the things you wanted to hear because of your need to dominate me and control me. Our entire relationship was a lie. I literally danced with glee the day you left."

Though she actually said much, much more, this will suffice.

I nearly lost my grip on reality. Everything we experienced together had never existed, and I'd imagined the whole thing? I'd been such an inept, oblivious ninny that I loved a mirage? The brutality of the attack sent me into shock. My limbs tingled and my head felt as though it floated a few inches above my body. I couldn't understand her desire to obliterate me. All I'd ever done was love her.

It's impossible to describe the totality of the despair I felt at that moment. It robbed me of my very humanity. If I were so defective that I could be deeply, utterly in love with a figment of my own imagination, then I wasn't even a person. There was no hope for me at all. What would you call what I was? A humanoid, I suppose. Something that resembled a human but wasn't.

I utterly lost control and said, "You know what you are? You're a cunt, a self-centered, gold-digging whore who's only good for fucking."

She wore her habitual tights with no underwear; spreading her legs, she jammed her finger up inside herself and said, "That's right. Oo, *baby!* Here it is. Come fuck it." Then she made squishing noises with her mouth and laughed at me. She'd never done anything even remotely like that the entire time I'd known her. The Carmen I'd loved was gone or never existed. This was a demoness.

I got off the sofa, walked past her, and drove back to Los Angeles, having spent exactly seven hours in San Francisco. Two days later a letter arrived.

> Dear Tom:
> I feel the wound I opened this time will never heal. I am surprised you're even reading this letter. Tom, I knew your trip to SF would end in disaster, because you came to see me & not the city. I am agonizing about the way I treated you but I know I am not capable of treating you any other way at this point. You are still attacking me with partial truths and I can't buckle under your provocations ever again. The problem is I did love you and probably still love you, but I don't ever want to see or talk to you again. There is too much pain involved.
> Carmen.

There was an arrow drawn next to her signature, pointing to the right, instructing me to turn over the paper.

> P.S. As schizo as this may sound, I have a strong desire to visit you in L.A.

Her letter may as well have been in Sanskrit for all the sense I could make of it. Did she mean she wasn't done yet and wanted to come down here to flense me some more? I wrote back that we should have no further contact. Two weeks later another letter arrived asking me to send her a partially finished World War I model airplane of hers that I'd accidentally packed and brought home with me when I left in 1993. She wanted to finish it. I sent it and a British model-building magazine that featured one of my articles; in a spasm of regret I also enclosed Suzanne Vega's CD *Nine Objects of Desire*. I told Carmen that after a lot of reflection I wasn't angry anymore and asked her to listen to the track "World Before Columbus." Since our time together was over, we no longer had to be enemies. Maybe we could even be friends.

Carmen responded with a four-page letter that actually made me nauseated. She related that my offer to be friends had completely thrown her; that her better judgment told her I was just trying to manipulate her again; and that she felt she should quietly walk away from any involvement with me. Describing our time together she used scare quotes around the word "relationship," and then she calmly spelled out why we'd failed.

> I didn't want to leave you because I really thought we had a chance together. When you told me that's a lie and that I was just waiting for something better to come along, I think that's your way of feeling sorry for yourself. You want so badly to believe you're worthless & that the world hates you... I admit that I didn't open up to you from the start and maybe I hated you for finding out about my real self. I felt all along that you would be disappointed in who I really was. You're a very critical person & I felt too vulnerable to your criticism to open up to you. It was a no-win situation. Part of my problem is that I aim to please and with you I felt I could NEVER please you. I understand that you didn't want me to please you. You wanted me to be myself. Well, the reality is that the pleasing side is a part of me! You couldn't accept this.

It was true: I couldn't accept her the way she was and I insisted on trying to change her the way I had with Nakamura, the Cat-faced Ghost in the Rising Sun, almost ten years earlier.

What I didn't know this time was if it was for selfish reasons or because I honestly wanted her to achieve her full potential. My head began to spin.

Did I act out of a need to manipulate and control, or a desire to help her blossom? I'd read that the desire to change people is inherently selfish; could an impulse be both selfish *and* altruistic? Didn't our five years together show Carmen that I hadn't been driven off by disappointment in her real self? If you aim to please, isn't *that* letting others manipulate you? And what happens when they're no longer pleased with you? Is it controlling to want someone to be in total control of her own life? What's the difference between someone trying to change you in order to please themselves and you trying to change yourself because you know they're not pleased with how you are? Isn't it being critical to call someone a very critical person?

My mind simply cratered. It seized up. The only thing I understood was that I'd done everything wrong. And she was right that I felt worthless, which made me nonviable for her or any other woman except maybe a mail-order bride from Tajikistan.

She ended the letter with a roundhouse to the jaw.

> Thanks for the CD. It's too bad that you had to have a song express how you used to feel rather than tell me yourself how you were feeling when you were feeling those things.

Now stars circled my seized-up head. I thought *I'd* expressed *my* feelings to her constantly, and that *she* was the one who didn't open up to *me,* as she said in this very letter. Instead of writing a furious response, for once I restrained myself. It was time to leave her alone. I sent something that amounted to "message received" and began eating nonstop, putting on fifty-five pounds in four months. Astonishingly, I didn't fall off the wagon, though I couldn't think of a reason in the world why I shouldn't. In a repeat of what'd happened in June of 1989, when I broke up with Carmen, I began having terrible nightmares about her every night. In all of them, I'd gone back to Japan to find her. Either I couldn't and ended up wandering empty streets at night, or when I did find her, I was never able to see her face. She'd be standing in shadow or just out of my line of sight, and some invisible force would keep me from turning so that I could look at her.

The way my relationship with Carmen ended was the second-worst experience of my life, surpassed only by someone trying to murder me eighteen months later. In July Carmen sent me a friendly, chatty letter telling me she'd met someone at her place of work. I tore it up, threw it away, and didn't reply.

Moving Closer to the Collateral Ghost

On February 13, 1995, Jim Roberts sent me a letter.

> I've got another assignment for you. The bassist for Z (Ahmet and Dweezil Zappa's band) is a very talented young guy named Bryan Beller. Great kid and an excellent player. I think he'd make a great 'up-and-coming' Bass Note."

I called Bryan himself and interviewed him on March 28. He's an amazing bassist, a man with the wacky sense of humor I love, and an all-around sweetheart of a cranky-pants who'd come in and out of my life for the next seventeen years. We had a great time in that first interview. The article, "Bryan Beller: On the Fast Track to Joe's Garage," was published in the September/October 1995 issue of *Bass Player*. My brother Tim took the photo of Bryan jumping like Marilyn Monroe in one of the many Philippe Halsman portraits.

During the interview, Bryan described his favorite bassists.

My main influences can be traced directly like this: John Paul Jones first and foremost, Flea, John Patitucci, and then Jaco Pastorius, Scott Thunes. *Invitation* by Jaco is the most amazing record. His groove and his sound are just so unreal. Scott Thunes is my biggest influence now. That's it![2]

I was so clueless that in the original transcript, I wrote "Scott *Tunis*." I'd heard of him, but he was connected to Frank Zappa, whose music and public persona I didn't like. Of course I corrected the spelling for the article, but I didn't bother looking into Thunes until later.

Bryan is the only bassist I ever asked to sign a copy of the article. Here's what he wrote.

Tom –
My parents were very impressed w/your writing style. Considering their standards, you must be proud. Can't thank you enough – great work if I say so myself.
Love and kisses,
Bryan

Nosferatus and Buddhas

Going to recording studios and musicians' apartments in some of the worst parts of Los Angeles, I came across massive numbers of gangbangers. I never had any problems with them, but it was deeply uncomfortable to come in close contact with such an alien culture.

There were two kinds of gangsters: Nosferatus and Buddhas. The Nosferatus scared me more, with their tiny heads, pointed ears, spindly limbs, and sharp teeth. They wore the same enormous shorts, white knees socks, numbered football jerseys, and tattoos as the bosomy, more placid Buddhas, but they seemed a lot more unstable. Skinny and quick is always more frightening to me than big and trundling. It has to be a primeval fear, related to a horror of arachnids. The clicking, scrabbling Nosferatus were human tarantulas, capable of anything.

The gangsters and their girls developed what biologists call "sex-limited traits" so that males and females can be instantly distinguished. Instead of growing bright plumage and red wattles, male gangsters enlarged and lowered everything: their pants, their shirts, their cars, and their bicycles. They also adopted squatting, hunching, and crouching postures – the Crip Walk, pimp roll, and gangster lean. The girls, on the other hand, went for scantiness and height. They clopped around in seven-inch platforms with stacked heels; they tied their hair into swaying palm trees that added another five inches; they yanked their tiny halter tops up to show cleavage under their breasts; and they wore microscopic shorts that disappeared up their bottoms, squeezing out luscious banana rolls from the leg holes. And while males shaved their entire heads except for their eyebrows, females shaved *only* their eyebrows, reapplying them so lightly in pencil that they were invisible from six feet away.

I never made eye contact with any of them. Once, as Tim and I drove down a street on our way to an interview at a studio where Tim would be the photographer, we saw a Nosferatu ambling toward a giant Lincoln lowrider. As we passed, he glanced at us, flexed his mouth in a snarl or smile, kicked up his right leg, and – in one movement almost too fast for the eye to follow – leapt sideways through the driver's window into the front seat of the Lincoln, snapping his head, arms, and left leg after him. He was like a hermit crab retreating into its shell. *Click*, and he was gone.

"*Eeeeeeeeeew!*" Tim shouted. "Did you *see* that?"

How to Ask Somebody if they Wouldn't Mind Moving

At a club I attended at the behest of a struggling band, I sat at the bar because my back hurts when I stand too long. It's the result of my job as a Field Representative for the document-retrieval company, lugging around the fifty-pound portable microfilming machine. One day my back just gave out because I very stupidly carried the thing by its handle instead of putting it on a wheeled cart like the smart Field Reps did. Things were never the same, back-wise.

Rather than stand at this club, I sat on a stool at the bar. There was one empty stool next to me. Two biker-looking guys came in and one sat on the empty stool. His friend stood next to him, gazing around the room for a while and sipping from a bottle of beer. After about five minutes, the standing biker clapped his hand down on my shoulder and spun me around.

"I was wonderin'," he yelled over the music. "You been here for a while now. Don't you wanna go in and check out the band? You might be missing somethin'."

When I didn't respond, he jerked his chin toward the door. "Hey, look! There's your girlfriend! I think she wants to talk to you." He smacked my shoulder several times, the way people pat horses, then he grabbed it and shook it. He'd begun to look more businesslike, the corners of his mouth turning down in impatient little tucks. I slid off the stool.

"You know what?" I said. "I think I'll go check out the band."

The biker pounded my back and roared, "Ya! Ya! Why don't you do that? That's a *good* idea!" He hopped up onto the stool next to his buddy as I left. I gave in to him because the situation reminded me of the time I'd done something incredibly stupid in college. I was at a bar with my friend Andy Hatfield, of the Hatfield-McCoy Hatfields. He was a large, intelligent, loud rock climber who tried to teach me to rappel off a water tower while I was drunk. I wasn't afraid until I actually started going over the edge; at that point I panicked and made the classic error of trying to climb back up the rope, which proceeded to slip effortlessly through the carabiner. "*No! No! No!*" Andy shouted. He knew what was about to happen. Some sympathetic providence saved my idiotic backside by giving me the presence of mind to grab both ropes at once, preventing me from dropping 150 feet.

But that was a *different* incredibly stupid thing I did with Andy in college. The *really* stupid thing was sitting at a bar next to some snickering loon who engaged us in conversation for a few minutes before pulling an automatic pistol out of his jacket and showing it to us.

"Put that away!" Andy snapped, and the guy obeyed. Then we sat there right next to him, drinking, for the next hour.

By the time I was thirty, I'd figured out that some things, such as drunk rappelling off water towers and potentially deadly confrontations with strangers in bars, were not necessary.

A Warning Ignored, from the Ghost who Never Was

After the success of my feature-length interview with John Taylor, I pitched Jim Roberts a feature with Andy West, formerly of the Dixie Dregs. Jim readily agreed. I interviewed Andy at his home in Arizona, on July 17, 1995. "Andy West: How Not to Sell Out in One Easy Step" was published in the January 1996 issue of *Bass Player.* My photo of Andy was also published, a first.

An exceptionally talented bassist and easily the most skilled pick-wielding player I've ever seen, West had recently recorded *The Mistakes,* with guitarist Mike Keneally, guitarist Henry Kaiser, and drummer Prairie Prince. I struggled for days to try and define the CD's sound in as few words as possible, and finally came up with something.

A pure collaboration, the record contains melodies, fragments, poems, haikus, and not-quite-commercial cuts that defy categorization. One way to describe the CD might be to say it sounds something like Gentle Giant and King Crimson jamming with Alice in Chains and Tim Buckley, with solos by bluesmen and musicians from South Africa and the Middle East.[3]

West replied that my description was very apt. He was a pleasant, completely down-to-earth man who made me feel right at home. I instantly forgot that he was a high-ranking deity in my bass pantheon, someone whose music I'd bought and whose career I'd followed since my college days. He was one of the bass players who'd hooked me for life the first time I'd heard him, yet drinking lemonade with him in his house, he was just a nice, interesting, humorous guy who effortlessly put me at ease.

Like John Taylor, he'd experienced dramatic reversal of fortune, but West's Plan B had been computer programming, something that had always intrigued him anyway. Although he considered himself a software engineer now instead of a full-time musician, he was happy and spoke with no trace of bitterness. He used his Plan B to provide the freedom for occasional excursions back into music on his own terms, without worrying about commercial viability.

When I asked him the main difference between the music industry and software engineering, he spoke frankly but without anger.

"One of the frustrating things I've found being a technically competent musician is that the more you know, the less likely you are to get paid for it, to a certain degree. In the entertainment business in general, we've gotten to the point where there isn't much respect for what people have done. In the computer business, what I've found is that the more things I have on my résumé, the more things I know how to do, the more respect I get, and the more I'm paid. That's not true for the entertainment industry. We can just give the whole thing a big wash. Respect is an important quality to try and have, and people just don't. They just treat people like shit. There's no reason for it."

That disturbed me. Scared me, to be more accurate. It sent a chill down my spine. I clearly remember thinking at the time, How horrifying to be in a situation in which it's arbitrarily decided that you're not going to get any respect for your impressive body of work. What would you do in that situation? How would you cope?

West did haunt me because I felt it was unjust that his jaw-dropping, unique talent was not on display everywhere. This was offset, however, by the fact that he was one of the most content people I've ever met. Though he freely admitted that he would've preferred being a full-time musician instead of a software engineer, he didn't look back. Everything he said indicated that he thought only of what might be, not what had been. A student of Buddhism, he emphasized the constant changes of life. He said he always asked himself, "What am I trying to do here?" Through this question he was generally able to avoid finding himself trapped in situations not of his liking. "I don't believe in solidification," he said, a statement I simply couldn't grasp at the time.

I wish I'd taken everything he said to heart, although in hindsight I know it wouldn't have been possible for me to have done so at the time because I hadn't lost enough yet. But I still should've realized that he knew what he was talking about. After all, he said Gentle Giant was one of his biggest influences, and he'd listened to them forever.

Vainglory

I interviewed the bassist in a well-known but non-mainstream band that played niche music. They were great and I loved them. I sent their CDs all over the country and even to Britain, but nobody bit. They finally got signed to a major label. I was ecstatic. Almost immediately, the lead singer quit and struck out on his own. The rest of the band tried to carry on, but without the lead singer's charisma and abilities as a lyricist, they didn't have a chance.

The lead singer completely changed his appearance, leaving behind his deliberately goofy persona and becoming on the outside a suave, handsome devil. But he was still a nerd, as I read in his interviews. He was the type of person with a one liner for every occasion. If you said, "Nice to meet you," he'd say, "Nice to be met!"

As a solo artist, he contacted me and asked if I'd pitch an article about him to a music magazine. They agreed, and we conducted the interview. I'd seen that all his interviews as a solo artist were identical, so I tried to do something different, but he would not be deterred. Nothing I asked got him off message. Same jokes, same observations about his writing process. Word for word, he repeated everything he'd said in all the other interviews. So I gave up and let him deliver his canned answers. To me, it was already clear he was doomed. I wrote the article; it was published; and I wished him well.

Of course his career soon crashed and burned, since the strength of the band was their ensemble performance, like the show *Seinfeld*. In ancient Rome, it was the custom for a general or emperor celebrated in processions to have a slave standing beside him in his chariot during the ceremony, whispering in his ear, warning him about vanity, reminding him that he was only a man, this was all transitory, and someday he'd die. Too many people in L.A. never had that voice whispering in their ear, and it cost them everything.

Another August; Another Piece of Great News

In August Carmen told me in a letter that she was getting married. I tore it up and threw it away. In fact, I'm ashamed to admit that I threw away nearly all of my photos of her. I didn't melodramatically rip them to pieces or cut them up with scissors; I simply tossed them in the trash, the way I felt she'd done to me. The only ones that survived were a handful that I'd tucked somewhere and blocked out. Some of them appear in this book. Whenever I thought of that final scene with her, I felt myself losing control again. I kept a dream diary at this time, recording the endless nightmares I had about her.

> I'd gotten word that Carmen was ready to take me back. I found her in a dark, gloomy apartment that seemed to be made of one enormous vacuformed sheet of plastic. Everything was dark green, aqua, or black, and there were clothes piled everywhere. Carmen looked stunning, and when I first saw her I was so happy I thought I'd drop dead from sheer emotion. She greeted me at the door naked, holding a towel in front of her against her breasts. It hung down and covered her waist and hips and thighs. She was expressionless, and through my immense joy, I felt remorse; she'd still not opened herself up to me. Even after all we'd been through, together and apart, she still wouldn't open up to me.
>
> The thought of her just barely tolerating me, never to smile or joke around or be genuinely happy to see me, made me shudder in horror. I knew getting back together with her would be a huge mistake, but I couldn't help myself. I caressed her; she seemed rounder, her flesh more dense, than I remembered. As I reached out to take off her towel off so I could fondle her breasts, I suddenly understood that she had several videotapes containing moments in which I'd suffered total blackouts. During these blackouts, I'd beaten her. I had no memory of doing this, but I knew she had the tapes to prove it.
>
> A chorus of women's voices began accusing me of being a batterer. There was nobody else in the room with us, but I knew we were being observed. "Yes, you did do it," the voices said. Though they sounded sympathetic, even friendly, I knew that I deserved no sympathy if it were true. "Turn her around," the voices suggested. I gently grasped Carmen's warm shoulders, the touch of her making me

ache with desire, and turned her around. Since she was naked under the towel, I could see that her buttocks were scarred and covered with bruises. I knew I wasn't responsible for the fresh marks because we'd been apart for so long, but I was still horrified. I realized that after we'd split up, she'd found someone even worse than me, so it was my fault after all. I'd made her accustomed to being abused.

I turned her around to face me again. She stared into the distance with total indifference. The utterly blank look on her face convinced me once and for all that we'd never get back together emotionally, even if we did physically, so I walked out of the apartment. I wandered the dark streets, wishing I had the courage to kill myself. Eventually, I went to my brother Tim's house. I was exhausted and had no idea what I'd do now. I felt worse than I had before I'd gotten back with Carmen because now I knew I was an abuser. At Tim's place, I saw a photo album lying on a coffee table. Tim approached looking wary and uncomfortable. He sat me down and said, very gently, "Listen: Carmen's gone. She went away for good."

I was unable to respond. "She left this photo album," Tim went on. "She said she wanted you to see how happy she is. It has pictures of her family." He handed me the album, which had a bright aqua vinyl cover. I opened it to a page full of snapshots of a baby. It was a boy, and he was obviously dead, because he had an autopsy incision on his chest, sewn up with heavy black thread. His blue eyes had withered in their sockets, giving him the dry stare of a pig's head in a butcher shop. The baby's whole body looked shriveled and leathery, as if it had been preserved in formaldehyde. Whoever had taken the photos had propped the corpse against walls, next to a wadded up towel, in a crib, and so on. The baby's arms and legs were drawn up against its body, and its mouth was twisted into a smile. Its orangish hair stood up in an ugly tuft.

Looking at the photos, I felt such horror, guilt, and sorrow for what I'd done to Carmen that I knew I was going insane. It was too much to bear. On the next page, the photos were even worse. "This is her husband," Tim murmured. These pictures showed the mummified remains of a man sitting upright in a chair. His eyes had swollen into black plums and the skin of his face had been sliced away, exposing the musculature and cartilage underneath. He, too, had a ghastly smile on his lipless mouth, his teeth exposed like those of a rodent. He looked as if he'd been heavily varnished with polyurethane. Since I knew that I was responsible for this abomination too, I got up and hurried outside. I began running down twisting brick paths, sobbing uncontrollably, but the faster I went, the stronger and more physically fit I felt. I knew I'd never see or touch Carmen again, that I'd ruined her life, but now my body felt better than it had when I was a teenager.

Coming to a stairway set in the path, I saw a middle-aged woman loom up in front of me. She had long gray hair and was dressed for gardening in shorts, a wide-brimmed purple sun hat, and dark glasses. I slammed into her, knocking her over backwards. Her head-over-heels tumble down the stairs made me feel guilty, but I also knew she deserved it. I launched myself into space, gazing down at the stairs that dipped away from me now, several hundred feet below. I'd taken off and flew like a bird. Flying was easy; I'd always known I'd someday be able to do it, once I'd achieved the proper mental state. I felt incredible, free and clean and blameless.

As I arrived at the first peace of mind I'd felt in years, a man abruptly shot like a rocket up from the ground, aiming directly for me. He whooshed right into my face, making me cringe back. His hair was dark and tightly curled; his nose was enormous; and his eyes were squinty little slits. He whispered, "Remember, now: Don't tell anyone." I realized that I'd been about to reveal the secret of flight to the other people floating aimlessly around me in the sky. I'd been about to tell them how to achieve control, but I understood that I no longer merited the knowledge. I lost my buoyancy, sinking slowly down to the ground and feeling dirtier than I had even after I'd seen Carmen's terrible photos.

My Guides in Hell

In September of 1995, I met a married couple I'll call Roger and Dolores. They worked in the entertainment industry. For the next nine years, they shepherded me through Hollywood, involving me in astonishing, revolting, soul-killing spectacles. Sometimes they were true friends who supported me and seemed happy for my few, early successes. Other times they abused me mercilessly and caused me such pain that I felt they wanted me dead. In other words, they were entirely typical Hollywoodians.

During my first dinner together with Roger and Dolores, she suddenly said to me, "Roger really likes you. He really, really does. And he hates *everybody!*" She had a strange, beautiful, hiccupping laugh, which she now directed at me as I squirmed.

Dolores was just my type: small, dark-haired, funny, brilliant, quirky, and a trained dancer. She once deftly explained her entire life to me by showing me a gorgeous, sepia-toned photo of herself. "Nice, huh?" she asked. It was. She was a classic Jewish beauty, with sky-blue eyes and a strong nose. I told her it was a terrific photo. She smiled and said, "That's my mother, when she was twenty-five." They could've been twins. Nothing more needed to be said, and I instantly understood everything she wanted me to know about her.

Roger always called me wearing a headset. I'd answer the phone, and I'd hear, "Just a sec," followed by the sound of typing on a computer keyboard. I'd just sit there, listening. Finally, he'd say, "Okay. Wanna go out to dinner?" Once I listened to him type for three whole minutes. I told him to call back when he was done. "Oh, sorry. I'll call you right back." I didn't hear from him for a week, and when he did contact me again, he'd forgotten why he'd called in the first place.

He once phoned me on my birthday. "Happy birthday, Tomás. Before you know it, you'll – Whoa! Aaaaaaaah, dammit. Just a second. I've got a little problem here." Endless silence.

"Everything all right?" I finally asked.

"No, my damn machine just booted. Or something. Whatever. Uh... Oh, Dolores wants to say hi. Hold on."

I heard her in the background talking the whole time he was on the phone with me. She had thousands of pet names for him, "Bumble Bee," "Pooter-wooter," "Boo Bear," "Schweety," and "Poindexter" among them. Her voice increased in volume as she approached his workstation.

" – and do you know what she wanted me to do? Thanks, Boo Bear. I'm almost done, and then we can eat. She wanted me to pretend like she'd never said anything about it. Can you believe it? After an hour of spilling her guts about it to me – hi, Tom, happy birthday – she wants me to forget she ever told me about it. See you soon, Tom."

At home, she habitually spoke to three people simultaneously: Roger, the person on the phone with Roger, and the person on the phone with her.

Back to the Scene of my Death

Since leaving San Francisco, I'd had to return to the Bay Area several times on business. One such trip was a visit to Subway Guitars in Berkeley, California, to do an article on their amazing, dirt-cheap basses. I interviewed the owner, Fat Dog, who was gruff but extremely cooperative. After the interview, I told him that the magazine would send a photographer in a couple of days.

Suddenly, I was grabbed by the arm and yanked around to face a middle-aged guy with a gigantic mustache. He looked like the latter-period Friedrich Nietzsche, except with a soiled baseball cap. "I'm a photographer!" he yelled in my face. Fat Dog – who's extremely tall and powerful – pried the guy's hand off my arm and said, "Take it easy. What's wrong with you?" The guy grabbed me again and pulled me toward him, as though he were trying to fold me into an embrace. Fat Dog gripped my other arm and pulled me in his direction. "Let the fuck go!" he shouted. The grabby mustache guy screamed, "Hey, man, I'm just tryin' to get some work, man!"

Fat Dog yanked me out of the guy's hands, stashed me behind his bulk, and said, "Yeah, well, that's not the way to do it. You can't assault people in my store!" He then belly-bapped the mustache man, knocking him about fifteen feet across the room. "What the *fuck*, man!" the would-be photographer shouted. He stomped out in a fury. Fat Dog shook my hand and said, "Sorry about that. Some people are hurting in this economy, so they do nutty things."

Outside, I looked at my upper arms. They were both red and blotchy, as though I'd been given Indian rope burns.

What it Feels Like to be Murdered

In October of 1995, Tim and I went to work at a used bookstore where we'd been customers for years. It was run by an old man I'll call Larry. He could barely walk, and his store was a shambles. We offered to get everything shipshape for him because he specialized in a field that Tim and I both love, and he often had incredible treasures. His store was a magnet for hooting, growling, cawing, rumbling mental patients, which made working there unpleasant. It sounded like the African Savannah at night, when territory is staked out, mates are sought, and the predators and prey keep the wheel of life in motion with their gruesome struggles.

Larry soon began opposing our attempts to help him; it took me years to figure out that he didn't want the responsibility of having a functional business. At the time, I believed his daily mantra: "If I only had a chance!" When we went to work for him he was eight months in arrears to the landlord, but he began to resent Tim and me for holding him accountable for his choices. We were too unschooled in the ways of the professional con man to understand that Larry played us like a master violinist.

On December 28, Tim and I spent the day unloading boxes of books from a storage facility. Larry claimed for months that this was his stash, and if he could only get it into his store, all would be well. Tim and I finally forced him to take us to the storage unit. The books were in boxes that had been attacked by termites, rats, and some unknown creature that had puked a gray, cementlike secretion all over them. Inside the boxes, the books had rotted into mulch. They were worth about thirty-six cents. We decided to take them to Larry's store anyway, in case there were a few undamaged volumes hidden in the compost.

Tim and I unloaded the U-Haul truck in the store parking lot after night had fallen. We were too exhausted and short-tempered to be alert to our surroundings. Besides, Larry was there, blaring about all the terrible things that'd happened in his life and how today he had a bad case of the "drizzlin' shits," interrupting himself only to give us contradictory orders. When he was around, we always tuned everything out.

The work was a mind-numbing cycle of carrying books from the U-Haul, piling them on two wheeled carts, transporting them into the loading dock of the store, and shelving them or stacking them in the aisles. As I came out of the truck for the thirtieth or fortieth time, I noticed a car parked in the alley behind the building, next to the open roll-up door of the loading dock. It just sat there, idling softly, the brake lights on. I felt a chill. Since there was only one spotlight on the rear of the store, I hadn't seen the car even though it was only five yards away. I grabbed Tim's arm and said, "Look! There's a car right there!" He shook off my hand and said, "Well, don't worry about it."

I got so angry at him that I decided to do what he said and not worry about it. Fine, I thought, and as I took a step toward the carts, a man popped out of the alley in front of us. He was dressed in black – ski mask, heavy jacket, pants, boots, gloves, and body armor, the bulky flak vest that SWAT cops use. I could see his eyes very clearly; they were dark and twinkling and slanting downward in a nest of laugh lines, as if he were about to tell us a really good joke. He lifted his right hand, and up came an enormous gun. It was an Intratec TEC-9, an assault pistol with a perforated jacket over the barrel and a long clip that holds thirty-two nine-millimeter bullets. It looks like a one-handed machine gun.

The gunman began weaving and feinting like a boxer. It was so unnatural that all the blood in my body froze. I could feel my veins everywhere, like ice-cold wire coat hangers. Tim said, "Oh," a small sound of total comprehension; he knew exactly what was happening, and suddenly I did, too. It set off a delirious babble in my head: *There he is. I knew you'd come. Here we go. He's here. This is it.*

The man pointed the gun at my face. He looked two-dimensional in the orange light, like a cardboard cutout outlined in black Magic Marker. There was an aura of squiggly lines radiating outward from his body like heat waves, some kind of visual distortion caused by the thirty gallons of adrenaline dumped into my system. The darkness intensified until all I could see was the gun aimed at my right eye, the muzzle less than two feet away, a ring of bright metal around a black hole.

I went completely deaf, but I could also hear a strange cacophony, almost like a Tibetan religious ceremony, with gongs and horns. Everything around me seemed to have been sucked away, leaving me in a vacuum. At the same time, there was a tremendous sense of imminence, as if the air itself were about to burst wide open. *The circus*, my mind gibbered. *Ferris wheel. Boston Pops. Happy New Year. God save me. Orson Welles. Nazi bastards. Christmas lights. Pinwheels.*

"Don't *fuck* with me, man," the gunman squealed. "Hah? Hah? Don't *fuck* with me!"

That broke the spell. I heard "You are going to die" as clearly as if someone had spoken it aloud, and then my body took over. Without conscious thought, I turned and ran, dropping my books. Deep inside my head, in an isolated bubble of calm, a countdown started.

Five.

I glanced back over my shoulder. The man in black ran after me, still pointing the gun.

Four.

I ran so fast that the wind whooshed past my ears. I seemed to cover twenty feet with each stride. The world tilted as I leaned to the left, sprinting around the back of my boss's van. *I'm a motorcycle,* I thought. *Zoooooom.* I wasn't moving fast enough, though. I wasn't moving at all. The sound of my shoes hitting the asphalt was a dainty *chip, chip, chip, chip* in the whooshing but somehow dead air. Directly behind me, I felt a gathering, an expanding force catching up to me. The Tibetan music turned into an orchestral swelling like in the Beatles' "A Day in the Life." I knew that it was the sound of my life ending. I had only seconds to live.

Three.

High above me in the cloudy sky, from somewhere off to the right, I heard someone wailing, "I'm not fucking with you! I'm not fucking with you!" It was a shrill, hopeless, pleading screech that echoed across the empty parking lot. That's me, I realized. I'm screaming because I'm being murdered. Another part of my brain spoke up, inventorying my surroundings as they flew by like stark Polaroid images: *Burnt-out street lamp. Store front. Stars. Clouds. Tree. Goodbye, street lamp. Goodbye, clouds. Goodbye, tree.*

When the countdown reached One, the gunman would shoot me in the back of the head. I knew it with complete certainty. I'd see teeth, bone fragments, and pieces of my brain spray out in front of me. I'd feel it, too. It would feel like water up my nose and an electric shock, but it would also be cold and crunchy. It would be pulpy and probing and intimate. That was the amazing thing about being murdered: It was so intimate, much more intimate than sex. And sad. I was incredibly sad that my death was going to be so ugly.

Two.

On the back of my head, directly above the nape of my neck, a dot of supersensitive nerve endings awoke in preparation for the bullet. All the sensation in my body concentrated into that tiny disk of skin. The slug would pass through my head so quickly that I'd still be alive as I flopped across the asphalt, my skull mostly empty, the cool night air burning into the rawness. I'd feel the pebbles gouging my palms, my knees, and my cheek, and then I'd be gone. It was just about to happen. *Lab rat! Marshmallow pie! I love you, Carmen! Sapphire! Golden rod! Welder's fees! Samsonite! Here I go! Here I go! Here I go!*

Overhead, an airliner swooped in toward Los Angeles International Airport. The passengers were safe, unaware of what was happening to me. I was being murdered right under their feet, right under their big, fat, safe asses, and they didn't even know. They'd all get to live. I hated their guts and wanted the plane to explode into a ball of flame.

One.

I closed my eyes. Nothing. *You didn't why there's no teeth alive what*

The gunman hadn't shot me. Some kind of emergency time-expansion had come into play, because I had all those thoughts during the two seconds it took to circle my boss's van. When I came around the front of it, I caught a glimpse of my brother in midair, leaping like Mikhail Baryshnikov over a pile of books. He plowed into me, the top of his head breaking my nose and sending my glasses flying. We untangled ourselves, scrambled into the store, and slammed the metal front door. I'm ashamed to admit that we forgot about our boss. We left him in the parking lot with the gunman.

While I turned off all the lights, Tim dialed 911. I remembered that the loading dock was open and ran to the back to close it. That was much worse than the initial attack because now I knew what was out there. It's not possible to convey the fear I felt standing in the loading dock, totally exposed as I rolled down the door, waiting for the bullets to rip into me. It was more than fear, actually. It was a level of negativity and hatred of my fellow humans that I can't afford to ever feel again. And since I didn't have my glasses, I couldn't see a thing. I didn't know if the gunman had slipped into the 8000-square-foot store and was hiding in the aisles with his assault pistol, ready to hunt me down. I didn't know if my boss had been shot or was about to be shot. I couldn't think. I didn't know if I was still alive.

The police took fifteen minutes to come. During that time, my boss ambled in through the front door, unhurt, shouting that he was too angry to be scared. The gunman and his driver had apparently left when Tim and I dove inside the store, but they returned twice and cruised by the enormous front window, close enough for me to make out the blurs of their faces. We called 911 three times. A police captain later told me that the tapes of the calls were unnerving because of all the screaming. When the cops arrived, the gunman and his associate were gone. Tim and I gave a report to a couple of uninterested officers who said, "If I were you, I wouldn't stick around here any longer than I had to, okay?" and then took off. After unloading the U-Haul, Tim and I quit. We turned in our keys, apologized, and left our boss to fend for himself.

When Tim and I got home, I didn't go to sleep until three in the morning because I was afraid of the nightmares I knew I'd have. I eventually nodded off and dreamed that I was interviewing G. Gordon Liddy in a busy hallway. He was patient and considerate as I fumbled through my questions. The more he spoke, the more I liked him. After he gave me a particularly sensitive answer, I said, "Why, you're not at all the bugaboo you're made out to be in the press!" He lowered his gaze, blushing like a teenager, and I felt a blast of love for him.

This incident – the near murder, not the Liddy dream – taught me that traumatic flashbacks are real. I've had several. When young men have looked at me with a certain twinkling, challenging expression or walked with a bouncy cockiness, I've run blindly into the street. Once, two teenagers on bicycles approached me on the path where I was walking, and without any control over my actions I dove headfirst into the bushes. They almost started crying.

"Don't do that, mister!" one of them called to me. "We don't mess with people!"

Tim and I found out later that it was almost certainly an insurance scam. Larry planned to have us murdered and then the guys he hired would drive off with worthless books Larry could claim as golden. A young soldier-bassist I know who served at Guantanamo Bay tells me that the TEC-9 is a notoriously fickle weapon that requires careful cleaning or it'll jam; in fact, it's called the "Jam-o-matic." Criminals like big, scary, macho, Hollywood automatic weapons, but if you take a TEC-9 out to a range, shoot it once, and then don't clean out the gunk, it won't work the next time you pull the trigger.

I believe that's what happened. Tim and I were saved by Hollywood. A smart murderer would've used a small, reliable revolver.

Thank you, Hollywood. I owe you my life.

Tinseltown is Really Nice

Roger and Dolores took me to lots of parties in Hollywood. They seemed to know everybody. I usually had no idea who these people were. The only time I recognized someone was the afternoon I found a famous TV and later movie star sitting in the kitchen with Dolores, talking about her day.

"So then this nigger bitch says, 'Yo, what the fuck,' I think to myself, Why is it that everywhere I go now, niggers are overrunning the place, ruining everything for everybody? I can't even go to gym now without some nigger giving me shit for something I didn't even do."

At one of the first big parties I attended with Roger and Dolores, I eavesdropped on a troika of Industry big dogs. The man was handsome and tan, with a white goatee; one woman was short and conservative looking, wearing wire-rimmed glasses and a suit, and the other was outfitted in jackboots, brown leather pants, and a green button-up sweater.

"He dates only black women now," the man said.

"Why only black women?" the jackbooted woman asked.

"They froth." He sipped his wine.

"They *froth?* What's that mean?"

"Their pussies," the suited woman said. "Their pussies froth." She may as well have said, "It's ten o'clock" for all the emotion she put into it and the reaction she got from the other two. They were all as impassive as mannequins. At another party, Roger and Dolores dumped me on an actress who they'd warned me was "very sensitive about her age." I had no idea why; she was young and beautiful. She told me a litany of failure stories, how she'd screwed up this and that, ruined this and that relationship, gotten fired here and fired there, and just couldn't seem to find her footing.

I said, "Aaah, we're both mentally ill," thinking she'd laugh.

She sighed. "Oh, Tom. Don't ever call me that. I've worked so hard on myself. I've tried for years now to work beyond my history, and I think I've done a pretty good job, despite my problems, *so don't ever call me mentally ill!*" Her voice went from a murmur to a banshee scream that scared everyone, especially me. It was identical to the scene in John Carpenter's *The Thing,* where Donald Moffat explains that he doesn't want to spend the winter tied to the fucking couch.

I said, "I'm – "

She put her head down and held up her hand like a cop stopping traffic. We stood there in silence for almost a minute until Roger and Dolores rescued me.

After every party, I'd write down snippets of conversations I'd heard.

"How'd you like our little fag director? Didn't he seem a lot faggier this time, what with all the faggots he's surrounded himself with?"

"So I said, 'I wanted strawberry shortcake, not this fuckin' shit! Get me the manager! I want the manager!' And let me tell you, did I have *that* cocksucker standing at attention!"

"She's got Jewish credibility up the old wazoo, and boy, does she use it."

"They all suffer from what I call the Elephant Syndrome. Know what that is? They work for peanuts. That's the Elephant Syndrome. That's what I call it."

"Bulldog clips, but it didn't hurt."

One of the most satisfying moments of my expeditions into Hollywood came when a guy and his writer wife – a woman who'd told me I'd never be a successful novelist because I didn't have a master's degree in English like she did – asked me if I wanted to see their prize possession, an original clown portrait by John Wayne Gacy.

"Of course not," I said, and they were agog. They were flummoxed. I'm sure I was the first person who'd ever refused.

"Why would I want to see a painting done by the hands of a man who inflicted such pain on others?" I asked.

They had no answer. And I've learned that the would-be novelist wife with the master's degree in English has never published a single book. This memoir is my fifth.

I don't look it, but I'm part Mexican. My surname is Luxembourger; my father is a lily-white Midwesterner whose hardy genes wiped out my mother's Latina contribution in terms of my skin tone. Those Luxembourg-German chromosomes couldn't hide my Jewish ancestry; I've got a big, hooked nose and hazel eyes. At these parties, everyone was white, and after they got drunk enough, they told three types of jokes: antisemitic jokes, antiblack jokes, and antigay jokes. All I heard about was kikes, Hebes, niggers, coons, fags, and faggots. Everyone was obsessed with Jews and gays. The Jews and their slaves ran everything. After 9/11, someone told me that we'd gone to war against the wrong people.

"How come not a single Jew died on 9/11? Besides, no airplanes crashed into the Twin Towers or the Pentagon. In the video footage from New York you can see parts of the airliners disappearing and reappearing before they hit the towers. Those were holograms projected by orbs that also broadcast the sound of jet airliners. They 'hit' places in the buildings where they'd prepositioned explosives. A missile was used on the Pentagon, and Flight 93 was shot down by the U.S. Air Force."

I was unaware of the holograms and orbs, but several Hollywoodians – including a brilliant bassist I interviewed – asserted that not a single Jew died on 9/11. Only once did I respond that the roll of the dead included Ackermann, Bergstein, Bernstein, Birnbaum, Eisenberg, Feidelberg, Glick, Goldberg, Goldstein, Greenberg, Greenstein, Horowitz, Kappelmann, Kirschbaum – about 300 surnames that are obviously Jewish.

"So what?" I was asked. "They could've just been married to Jews. You don't know they were Jewish."

"Okay, now you're saying no Jews died, but they let their gentile spouses die? And most of those names I mentioned were men. Are you saying they were gentile men married to Jewish men?"

"Where'd you get those names, anyway? Fox News?"

One night Roger and Dolores invited me to a restaurant in West Hollywood, where we met Julia, a reporter from the *National Enquirer,* and her two friends, a gay couple named Jim and Bill. Julia's new boyfriend Terrance was late.

We were seated at a big table, and everyone except for me immediately started drinking. Julia asked the waiters if we could hold off ordering until her boyfriend arrived. More drinks were consumed. After about twenty minutes, a blond man walked in. He looked like an utter psycho, with a big smile and feverish eyes. There was something smeary and deformed about his face. Seeing him gave me a jolt of fear. He marched over to our table and sat next to Julia. This was Terrance, an ex-pat Brit. He shouted, "Gimmie a fuckin' drink, somebody!" over his shoulder at the waiters of that very upscale, quiet and homey restaurant.

Dolores suddenly said in a loud voice to Jim and Bill, the gay couple, "I hate fags. You'd never know it from looking at me, but I'm really conservative."

Jim said, "I'm a Republican and I don't hate fags."

"Why do you hate us?" asked Bill. He was amused.

"Because you always say things to women like, 'Eeeeeew, get that stinking pussy away from me! How can you have one of those disgusting things?'" She put up her hands in a warding-off gesture, mincing and squirming in her chair and using a screechy falsetto. She looked angry enough to kill.

"Is someone gonna give me a drink or what?" Terrance roared.

Our waiter came over and took Terrance's order. Everyone else asked for another round. When he got his vodka tonic, Terrance drank it all in one gulp and handed the empty glass back to the waiter. "Another," he demanded. The waiter left and returned in about ten seconds with it. His fresh drink in hand, Terrance turned to Jim and Bill. "So, you're fags? What, like a couple, like a man and woman?"

Bill – who was bearded and powerfully built – said, "No, honey, we're both men."

"Fuckin' sick if you ask me," Terrance said.

"That's why I didn't ask you," Bill answered.

More drinks were brought, but no menus. I started wondering if I'd died and gone to hell, where I'd have to spend eternity with drunks raving about fags. Dolores finally turned to Roger and snapped, "Why aren't they serving us? We've been here an hour already. If you had any balls you'd go tell them to serve us!" Roger laughed into his glass and said nothing. Bill and Jim left after about an hour. I finally got up and went to the waiters' station. This was West Hollywood, so I knew that every single man working there was gay. I found the young waiter who served us our drinks and said, "Look, you've seen that I'm not drinking or taking part in any of the conversations, right?"

He hesitated and then nodded. "Yeah."

"So, could you just tell me: Are you boycotting our table?"

"Absolutely."

"Okay. Thanks."

I walked out the door without saying goodnight to anybody. The next time I saw Roger and Dolores, they didn't mention it.

You may wonder why I didn't protest all the fag baiting. It's because the waiters did just fine. They served our group drinks but didn't even bring us menus. Roger, Dolores, Julia, and Terrance stayed two hours and ran up a massive booze tab but never got to eat. They left drunk, starving, and humiliated. It was a perfect punishment that made them look like dumb animals not worthy of attention. Plus, I don't know if you've ever been to West Hollywood, but almost every single guy there is built like Arnold Schwarzenegger in his prime. They're pretty tough and don't need others to protect them.

Shocking Act of Fakery Witnessed in Los Angeles

A musician who toiled for years in the L.A. music scene before giving up told me the following story.

"We played a showcase thing on TV a year ago. It was for unsigned bands. We put on a great show, one of our best. People were going crazy. The last band to play was a ska band with a female singer. Really, really lame. It was a long night, and after each band played, it went to the front dressing room to wait for the winner to be announced. Someone told me, 'It's all fixed, you know. The band that's on the major label is going to win.' Well, I didn't believe it. I said, 'It's unsigned bands. No one's on a major label because it's an unsigned-bands contest.' And he looks at me really pityingly and goes, 'Okay, you're right. See ya!' and runs off.

"So in the dressing room, after everyone is finished playing, this girl singer for this lame ska band is yelling for a makeup person to fix her up. She's yelling, 'I *have* to go down and accept the *award!*' And I said, 'Um, they haven't announced the award yet.' She rolled her eyes and went, 'Yeah, right.' See, everyone except for us knew it was fixed. I just couldn't believe it.

"They announced the winner, and of course it was this lame ska band, and a week later their record was playing on the radio. They'd recorded a whole album in a week, right? Wrong! They'd already done the record a year before the contest, but the network and the label wanted everyone to think they were a great unsigned band that got discovered in this TV showcase like Lana Turner at the Top Hat Cafe. And I was saying to everyone, 'It *can't* be fixed! They wouldn't *do* that!'

"But they did."

Endnotes
 [1] Thomas Wictor, "Unsung Bass Stylists: John Taylor with Duran Duran," *Bass Player,* April 1994, 12.
 [2] Bryan Beller, interview with author, March 28, 1995.
 [3] Wictor, "Andy West: How Not to Sell Out in One Easy Step," *Bass Player*, January 1996, 48.

Interlude with Scott Thunes
Rock

Frank Zappa wasn't rock. It wasn't a rock environment. It was very much jazzbos playing in a rock environment. Frank is definitely one of the classic split personalities: raised in R & B, played guitar, but was writing classical music when he was fourteen. He knew from the very get-go that he was split down the middle. He wanted to rock – and he could. He played the bars, smoked cigarettes, but he was a classical musician, and before classical music he played rock. That was what you did, if you were intent on being a musician. This is the kind of music you went out there and did, and you could be a debauched individual and play classical music. It's not that way anymore.

To be in Frank Zappa's band is very much akin to being a classical musician or a jazz musician, but you're playing arenas. You gotta be the Modern Jazz Quartet or something like that to play arenas, and even then, what are you going to do with that? What kind of power is that? What kind of power is playing jazz? You can get laid out of it, obviously, but by whom, or by what? And I mean, I wasn't in jazz in the forties, or the thirties, or the fifties, or even the sixties or the seventies, so I don't know what that experience was like, but every musician wants to get laid. Everybody does everything in order to get laid, and musicians more so than most people because that's their whole purpose.

Rock is bigger than anything else. Arenas are bigger than anything else. To play for 70,000 people is a high, but most people would utilize that power to get laid. How many times a night? Once? Twice? Very rarely did that happen. A lot of times in the eighties I got laid on the road, but not as much as I would've liked, and not as much as I'd heard other people had. And the whole idea of going out there and playing this kind of music in front of that type of audience, it's – I don't want to say it's an anachronism, but it's something very weird because it isn't related to the rock that we knew. It's something wholly "other," and it gives you a sense that you're a better person than anybody else in rock, because you're able to play really great music and still play arenas. But it's not the same thing as having a power hit on the charts. There's no way that you can relate to those things.

We had "Valley Girl" on the charts, but we were in Europe. We didn't get any glory from "Valley Girl." I never got any massive amounts of millions of dollars or got laid off of that song once. So it's not like rock and roll, where everybody goes out and has to play a specific part because they were trained. That's what they were trained for. I was trained to play bass. I trained to be a musician, and I went out, and that's what I did. I got paid to play, and anything else was secondary. It didn't really matter if I got laid. It didn't really matter if I got glory. That's not the whole point of the exercise. Nobody learns how to play an instrument to become the best musician that they can possibly be. They all want to play good enough to get in a rock band, make a million dollars, and do whatever the hell they want with that.

Every single time I see a video, an article in a rock magazine – *Rolling Stone,* anything – I look at this filth and I say, "They're all totally insane." Every single last one of these people is not even human. They're absolute machines for glory. They're glory robots. There's nothing there that has anything to do with human interaction. It drives me crazy to see a rock band, and the only reason they're doing that is to get a hit. Somebody has said, "I want you on this label because you are going to give us a hit." And everybody's wrong, and nobody knows anything, and it's the best thing in the world to not have to worry about that shit anymore, because it is a mono-directional, mono-thematic, one-single-idea'd concept that all these people have. Every single-ass one of those people, I swear, has said, "I wanna do this someday."

The problem with Dweezil's band, Z, was that it's also an orchestra. Dweezil started his career with me being his bass player, and you get a feeling that possibly you're pals, and that you're in this together. But a million things go on during the course of that – I don't want to say that *relationship* because that's not the most important aspect. That *business* relationship, I'll say, that shows you that you are just as easily replaceable as anybody else has ever been in the Zappa universe. They hire you and use you for your usefulness, and as soon as you're not useful anymore, they get rid of you.

The entire time, working with a person like that, you think, "I could be replaced." You don't think it constantly because you know he really doesn't want to go search out another bass player. I'm helping him a lot. I'm his arranger. He's got a bunch of guitar parts, and if he doesn't have me to say, "That part really sucks," or "We really have to put something else around it, surround it," he just has a little guitar riff. We turn it *into* something. He really needed me. I was really good for him. But he wasn't going out and playing out in the world, so it was very much self-contained. We would hang out; we would do demos together; and then we would do the albums.

At any point in time, he could've easily said, "I want you to be my coproducer. I want you to do all this stuff," but he always got these rock producers that wouldn't allow any kind of leeway like that. So I was very much an appendage. I was like a butler? A valet? Something like that. A Man Friday. I was hired; I was considered part of the family; but I was separate. Like a Man Friday, a person who is there every single day, and you confide in him, and you talk to him, and sometimes even cry on his shoulder, but he's still an employee.

A factotum. Yes. Thank you. A go-fer. Very rarely was I asked to actually go out and get things for them, but I did have to pick the kids up at school. When I was still working with Frank and Dweezil was thirteen, I went and picked up the kids every once in a while. I didn't have a problem with that. I had a car. I wasn't doing anything that afternoon – it was fine. But working with Dweezil was also not like being in a rock band because it was very much being a valet, being a Man Friday. If he had something he needed to get done in a musical realm, I was always there to help him do it.

During the course of those four years, I stopped being necessary when we hired Mike Keneally, because Mike had arrangement quality, and he took over all the voices that I normally played in the music. He would play them differently, but he would also jump in and take them. So after about a month of rehearsing with Mike, I wasn't needed anymore.

And that's where the tension really came into play. We did a bunch of rehearsals – rehearsed for a year – but I knew I wasn't necessary anymore. So from that point on, I knew my days were numbered. I knew there was going to be a replacement eventually because I wasn't Scott Thunes anymore. I was just a bass player in a rock band.

It wasn't like it was a rock band where we all wrote the songs together and we all paid the price and shared the profits. You were very much an appendage. So trying to figure out whether you were a rock band or not – you weren't. I knew I was not in a rock band, but I wanted desperately to be in a rock band my entire life. I wanted to be in a rock band, and this was my last stab. I was in a band, and we were playing rock, and some of these people were my friends – Josh and Mike were my friends. So it was the last stab at it. Worst thing that happened was Josh quitting and me having to play with this other drummer. I only had one person to hang out with in the band.

I knew I wasn't in a rock band. I knew I still hadn't made that – not intuitive leap, but that functional change. I still was not in a rock band with some friends doing and supporting music that we all wrote. I helped arrange some tunes, but I was the arranger. It wasn't the same thing. Still a total and utter lack of regard, going out there, and realizing that everyone was looking at Zappa's son.

When we went on tour, it was the first time I ever shared rooms. I never shared rooms with Frank. They try to make it a little easier on you by doing the A, B, C thing, switching you around and letting one person have his own room. That would've worked if they hadn't forgot about me for the first two weeks of the tour. I always had to room with somebody. For two weeks, I had to room with either Mike, who's a nice guy, or with this drummer. Absolutely impossible to hang out with for more than thirty seconds without wanting to punch his fucking lights out. And I had to spend five nights in a row with him in a London hotel room. Fucking drove me nuts.

Once or twice a week, we'd have to do in-stores, and the in-stores were bad because my acoustic instrument was the only one that you couldn't plug into an amp. The pickup was bad. They tried working on it for ages. So everybody could plug in their electric instruments and get sound out of the PA. I had to have a mic, and that caused a lot of problems. So I felt down, and then afterwards – it seems stupid but it hurts me to this day – I'd walk around the store, waiting for the ride to leave. You know, you hang out in Tower Records for an hour, and I'd come back to join the rest of the band, and they'd all have CDs in their hands. It'd be time to leave. You know, they got a chance to get them, but I didn't. Immediately after the concert, I'd wait around for five or ten minutes – *doot dee doot dee do,* nothing's going on – and then I'd leave to go browse. I'd come back, and they'd say, "Oh, we told you that we were going to get CDs. Why didn't you stay?" That happened three or four times.

We did some concerts in California. Went to a radio station. Did an in-store there, and afterwards, the guy opened up his cabinet, showed all the CDs. "Hey, take whatever you want." Mike and me are about to get on our knees, and Dweezil says, "Don't take too many. It makes me look bad." Like, fuck you, asshole! You're fucking telling me now, in front of this guy, shit like that? You never knew when he was going to do something completely and utterly robotically anal. That whole tour was at that level. You knew he had trained us to not want to do anything outwardly that would make our lives more beautiful. Nothing. He never allowed us any chance to do that, except once when he rented a van and we all went to Edinburgh, when we were in Glasgow. We went up to the castle and hung out up there for a day. It was very cool that he rented the van. If he'd asked us, we all would've put in twenty bucks to do it, but he did it on his own. Excellent.

Everything else was taken care of by everybody else. I definitely got the feeling, with the tour manager that we had, everything that ever had anything to do with the Zappas, their shit was taken care of and you were a lowly person. The worst thing was that they would always stay in really great hotels, and our hotels were Holiday Inns and stuff like that. Some of them in London and Europe were absolutely fine, but the idea was that we were all supposed to be in this together, and they couldn't afford to pay us anything, but then they would fly first class and stay in better hotels. There was always some kind of excuse for why they needed to that. They needed to come in quicker, or something like that. So always there was this tension that, you know you are shit.

You're playing, and most of the time you're driving around in buses, while they're flying first class. I never flew first class under any Zappa or Steve Vai. Never once was that even a possibility. The only time I flew first class ever in my entire life was coming back from England after doing the Waterboys TV-show thing, and even that was a fluke. We should not have done that but it was luck.

You're humanly undervalued on purpose because the Zappas had no sense of what other people are like. "Everybody" was *them,* and they looked at you as if you were a freak. And you were. You would always prove yourself to be a freak by saying something that they didn't like, or didn't understand, or some joke that they wouldn't get. It's like, "Well, Scott's cool. He's okay to deal with, but he's a freak, and I'm getting rid of him as soon as I possibly can." You know? And as soon as I became uncomfortable, as soon as I became a nuisance, as soon as I put out any emotion whatsoever, such as saying to the drummer, "You fuckin' stay the fuck away from me. I'm going to fucking kill you! I'm going to fucking knock your lights out," as soon as I put some emotion out that was more than "Ha! Ha! Ha! Great gig, guys!" I was out of there. I apologized. I did the best I could, but it wasn't good enough. Everything was training to make you feel that you were not at all necessary. Everybody explained that you could be replaced with absolutely no problem.

I did two tours with Dweezil. One was for two weeks, and we did three gigs. We went to Europe and did three gigs. So we had four, five days off apiece. It was really great. I was hanging out with Josh. We were having a wonderful time. Josh and I were roommates – loved it. We did a couple of things in the United States – went up and down California – Fresno, Sacramento, couple of other places like that. It was very cool. We drove around in a van. It was fine. I was roommates with Josh, everything was great. Sharing rooms with Josh was a piece of cake. I loved it. We were great friends. East Coast, we did some dates there, rooming with Josh, driving up and doing a gig. It was cheap and fine and guerrilla and we loved it. We felt we were really trying to do something good, but I didn't mind the lowliness of it. It was fine. Got to stay in really nice hotels. I shared rooms with Josh. It was like having a great friend.

I quite often took my girlfriend with me. Almost everybody else did, too. Everybody talks about their experiences, who's fucking who, but I kept my mouth shut. I don't say anything about that regard, as far as any personal experiences, only because I stayed so far the fuck away. Others have done everything. I've listened to tapes made the night before, with certain women on the road – orgasm tapes, lots of them. Tons of them. Once I actually got to listen to one while the woman who made the tape the night before was sitting right there. Sometimes the tapes were played in concerts. The women seemed to enjoy it. They'd giggle.

Don't tell me you're not being judgmental. Sure you are! I'd play along to a certain degree. When someone tells me that the girl that he was with last night blew him for two hours and he wasn't even hard, I think, "God, I'd like to be him, just for a couple of minutes." I know how often he gets boned during the course of the tour. I would like to do that. That's why I'm in rock. I would like to get laid once a night. I would like to be Wilt Chamberlain. I would like to have four women outside my door come in, one after the other. But I know that my stamina isn't that good because I drink too much beer. And I'm a young kid, and I'm out of shape, and stuff like that.

Someone else, all he does is bone. That's great. That's exactly what he should be doing. I'm glad he's pleasing so many women. But I don't know what the women are thinking. Why would a woman want to blow someone for two hours? She was beautiful and blonde, very secretarial, very normal, worked in an office, wanted to bone a rock star. This is the perfect rock star to bone, you know? But why would you blow him for two hours? What are you getting out of that? I have no idea. Almost everybody I know in rock has gotten massive amounts of blowjobs. I've never actually gotten a blowjob from a girl. Never. Not once.

As a matter of fact, I missed out on a pretty good one in one band because one time in Memphis I heard that there was this girl who had a crush on me from just listening to my records. She was a bass player. Wanted to meet me. So she showed up at the rehearsal during the sound check. She was very cute. I was hanging out; I was going, "Yeah, she's pretty cool." This was really great, but we're gonna go eat. You gonna go eat with us? Naw, naw, I'm gonna stick here. Drummer says, "Yeah, I'm gonna stick here, too." So we go and eat; we come back. We find out that she's blown him twice in the time that we've been gone. So she'd come to see me and I let the ball drop because I don't look at women in a sexual fashion. She's gorgeous! I'd love to bone her. I wish she'd give *me* a goddamn blowjob, but I leave and she blows the drummer, maybe because she's got to blow somebody? And of course, he won't bone her because he's got a girlfriend and can't bone anybody.

He can't bone anybody because he's like a politician. Everybody who knows anything about politicians knows that they get blowjobs all the time because they don't consider them cheating on their wives. And yet this girl in Memphis was still kind of being nice to me. I've got videotape of her. Very cute. She called me a couple of times in Los Angeles. One night I called her up, and I was just so frustrated and pissed I said, "Well, I gotta go bone my girlfriend now. I'll talk to you next week." She says, "Oh." Never called back. No idea what a person like that wants, or thinks, or does.

Nothing's changed in rock in the past thirty, forty years. Gotten worse. It's all I see nowadays. It's a big cartoon – that's exactly how it is. Every article, every picture, every song I hear, no matter how quirky the song is, I think, "This is the weirdest thing. That's all these people are thinking about." I never even thought about it. Well, okay, if I thought about it I'd probably like it myself, but I never went out and functionally tried to achieve it. I didn't know that I was supposed to do it. I thought I was supposed to be a good musician. Go out and get my glory just from the mere fact of being good. I never once got laid because of how good a bass player I was. I've been using that quote for years. Never once got laid because of that. I had that chance in Memphis, but I dropped the ball.

While everybody else was out doing their stuff I was going off by myself, sitting at bars, bringing a score or a book, headphones, checking out the world. Definitely looking at beautiful girls going around, getting my blood pressure raised, walking around with massive erections in beautiful cities where there are nothing but beautiful young girls going around and I was going totally, absolutely, absolutely crazy, knowing that I couldn't get any of it because they all spoke a completely different language than me. I know it'd be impossible for me to apply any of those normal rules of rock stardom, which I saw applied constantly.

One of my best friends was so desperate to get laid he'd use the line, "Hi! I play in the [withheld] band! You wanna come see us play tonight?" I mean, I don't blame him. He's cute; he's got a high sexual content; and he didn't get any glory, ever, for being a keyboard guy, so anything that he could actually use to get laid, he would. And, you know, absolutely! Go for it. I did not fault him for it. I made fun of him, but I knew that if you gotta get laid, that's the only way to do it. But I had already been on the road for eight years, I can't do that. I couldn't actually say, "I'm in the [withheld] band." I'd hate being in the [withheld] band. I wouldn't want anybody to know that I'm in that band. I want to get laid because I'm cool. I'm *me*.

So he would do that constantly, and he very rarely got laid. Even the real struggling types very rarely got laid. It was always at the whim of the woman. But of course from the nineties on, the whole AIDS thing got really bad. There wasn't really much you could do. You know, nobody is actually frivolously going out and boning, unless they're morons. And if they aren't morons and they're using condoms, where are they? I heard that they're around. There are women out there who like to have sex. I would like to be with one of those women. I always hear about these women who like to have sex, and they bone pretty much whoever they want. They don't come up to me. I don't know how to talk to them, and I don't know which ones they are, and I haven't asked for sex from a woman on the road since 1984. Actually saying, "Would you please sleep with me?" maybe you get, "Oh, okay." That's one kind of element.

But for the most part, it's way different. Way different. It's virtually impossible to get laid. A woman looks at you and says she wants you, and then you get laid. But unless you're actually trying to seduce someone, you're going to be stuck with morons. I don't fuckin' know. I would definitely appreciate somebody falling in love with me for my art. But I know that in a second – especially since my personality's so abrasive – that as soon as they met me, they wouldn't like me anymore.

Romance doesn't exist in rock. Rock is life. Rock is normal stuff, and rock has to coexist with all the other crap. There's no romanticism at all, as far as I can tell. Never was, even when I was out on the road. I was just like, "I'm out on the road! I'm making some money!"

Anthology Four
Summit
1996-1997

A man said to the universe:
"Sir, I exist!"
"However," replied the universe,
"The fact has not created in me
A sense of obligation."

Gene Simmons

Since *Bass Player* had never written anything about Gene Simmons, I pitched him to Jim Roberts. Jim agreed, telling me it would be another feature article, my third. I contacted Simmons's publicist, who asked if Gene would get the cover.[1] That decision was out of my hands. Jim said he never made deals and had to see the interview first. The publicist and I called back and forth a few times until I threatened to move on to another project.

Simmons himself called me without warning a few days later and wanted to do a phoner, which I refused. The point for me was to meet him and hone my chops. He abruptly hung up, called the next day, and asked if I could meet him in half an hour. When that didn't work, I cleared my schedule and waited until he called a third time and we worked out a deal to talk at the studio where Kiss put the final touches on their new album. I interviewed Simmons on January 26, 1996.

The interview began with him actually taking my tape recorder out of my hands and cradling it in his lap as he sat on the sofa with his legs stretched out on the coffee table. He went into his standard interview, which I let him do for a while, and then I started in with questions I'd never heard anyone ask him before. I don't know how I figured this out, but with someone as famous as he is, it's a complicated dynamic: You can't be too deferential, or they get bored because everyone kisses their rumps all the time, but you also can't be too familiar, because then you're disrespecting their hard-earned position in society. The key is to simply be perceptive. I took my cues from my interview subjects; they always let me know exactly how to interact with them.

When speaking to Simmons, I remembered a story I'd read about the actress Ethel Barrymore, who was a legend in her day. At a party, a stranger kept addressing her as "Ethel." Finally, she shouted, "Ethel, hell! Just call me 'Cuddles'!" So you have to show that you're not a sycophant, but you're also not in any way taking liberties. I can tell you the exact moment I won him over: I referred to myself as an insignificant insect, and he whistled the way you do when you witness a terrible disaster or something you simply can't believe. At that point he knew I was camping it up for him, and he knew that *I* knew *he* was camping it up for *me,* and everything was going to be okay. It was something neither of us acknowledged, of course; if I'd punched him on the arm and said, "Aw, ya nut!" he would've rightfully cut me off at the knees.

Initially, the Gene Simmons interview was the most difficult balancing act I performed in my career. When I asked him my most combative questions, I actually got out of my chair and sat cross legged on the floor at his feet, like an acolyte. From this position, I could then really challenge him. An extremely intelligent man, he knew exactly what I was doing and appreciated my strategy. All was well, as long as I didn't overstep my bounds by acknowledging the art we created together. That would've been boorish and disrespectful, and would've shown unearned familiarity. It also would've put *me* at the center of the story. My goal was to telegraph to Simmons that he was entirely the focus; he'd set the agenda; and I'd make him shine by playing the straight man. He got it – understanding that in no way was it manipulation – and ran with it. I always shudder at interviews I read, thinking, No, no! Why'd you ask him *that?*

Though the interview was originally supposed to last no more than an hour, he gave me two. We had a huge, shouting fight over tone when I told him I could tell different brands of bass by the sound, and he said I was full of it. The fight wasn't real, but we had to pretend it was. It's very hard to be deferential while yelling at someone, but it can be done. I told him that *he* was full of it because the tone of the bass in his songs changed and so did his instruments. If it didn't matter, he wouldn't have changed tone or basses. He eventually admitted that tone is important, but he refused to tell me a thing about his equipment, settings, or anything technical. At least twice in the interview he said he needed to be on the cover; what I did to allay his concern was to present him ever more opportunities to say outrageous, entertaining things. It was up to him.

My policy as an interviewer came perfectly naturally to me, but I soon discovered it was almost unheard of in the field of journalism: I always offered the musician the opportunity to read the article before I submitted it. If they had any problems, we could talk about them. The article was about *that* person, after all. For the vast majority of the artists I interviewed, this rarely resulted in anything noteworthy. Their people would contact me and say that everything was fine, or they'd ask for a tweak here and there, and I'd turn in the article.

At the end of this interview, I asked Simmons if he'd like to see the article before I submitted it. He closed his eyes, turned down the corners of his mouth in an expression of colossal indifference, slowly shook his head, and went, "Naaaaaaaaah." I thought, "Why you – " But years later, I realized that he knew it was going to be great, so he didn't have to worry. Gene Simmons was the only artist I ever interviewed who didn't ask to see the article before I submitted it. I now recognize the huge compliment he gave me.

When the interview was over, I called Jim Roberts on the studio pay phone and told him Gene Simmons had just concluded the most exceptional interview I'd ever heard him give. It would blow everybody's socks off, but he wanted to know if he'd get the cover. To show you the measure of the man who is Jim Roberts and to demonstrate a supreme example of his skill, savvy, courage, and perception, as well as his trust in me – the insignificant insect – he said, "If the interview is as good as you say it is, then yes, he'll get the cover." I put him on the spot, and he came through for me, just like that. I asked a studio staffer for a notepad and wrote, "Dear Gene: I just spoke to my boss on the phone. You got the cover. Congratulations and thank you. Tom Wictor."

The Kiss reunion tour with the original lineup was announced in April of 1996. Simmons hadn't said anything about it, and I wondered how that would bode for the new album, parts of which Simmons had played for me during the interview. I actually loved the song "Hate," which in my opinion is Kiss's best work. The lyrics, vocals, and bass are outstanding. My article, "Gene Simmons: Call Him Doctor Love," was published in the July 1996 issue of *Bass Player,* creating a firestorm. The most gratifying letter in response to it was from music journalist Matt Resnicoff, a writer I admired greatly.

> Congratulations to Thomas Wictor for an interview that does justice to a personality as colorful and routinely ignored by the "credible" press as Gene Simmons. It was likely the best Simmons piece ever. And the fact that Kiss's underrated recordings were analyzed by Karl Coryat with such literate care makes

a strong case for *Bass Player* as one of the most insightful and important music magazines.[2]

I seemed to have pulled off the impossible. Winging it every inch of the way, I'd transformed myself into a serious music journalist to whom Gene Simmons would speak for two hours and whose work was worthy of praise from the likes of Matt Resnicoff.

In 1997 I ran into former Kiss guitarist Bruce Kulick at the NAMM (National Association of Music Merchants) show in Anaheim. I identified myself and asked if the CD I'd heard during the Simmons interview was finally in the can. He said, "It's in the can, all right. The garbage can." I discovered to my sadness it was canceled. Fans, however, began passing around bootlegs of the album, so it was officially released in October 1997 as *Carnival of Souls*. I reviewed it for *Bass Player*. Here's an excerpt.

> Many believed *Carnival* would sit in the vaults indefinitely, but it was eventually released, augmented by a skimpy insert and adorned with photos of the band looking remarkably glum. The CD seems to be an embarrassment to everyone involved, which is a shame because it features Kiss's strongest, darkest material to date. And Gene Simmons has never played better. His melodic sense and rhythmic sophistication show yet again that he is a terrific bass player with a unique style.
>
> *Souls* opens with its best cut, the churning, angry "Hate." Gene dominates the song with his clanking-yet-snarling tone, busy fills, and perfectly timed slides. He also handles lead vocals, roaring the bleak lyrics with fury and passion. As a performer, Gene's greatest strength lies in using the abilities he has to maximum effect. Many "better" musicians could do worse than follow his example.[3]

• • •

A few days after the Simmons interview, I phoned him to ask follow-up questions that he refused to answer. At the end of the call he asked me again if he'd actually gotten the cover. I promised him he had.

In response, he said, "I'd like to say I think you're a great guy and a lot of fun to be with, and I had a lot of fun talking to you. I really enjoyed myself. I hope you go on to write lots of best-selling novels and make lots and lots of money. More than *enough* money. Make tons of the stuff and find happiness and success. Go out and write; get everything you want; do everything you want to do; have a great writing career. Goodbye."

Thank you, Gene. It took a long time, but I've finally managed to achieve some of what you so graciously wished for me.

Promotion

On April 16, 1996, Jim Roberts made me a Contributing Editor at *Bass Player*. He told me I was only the third person given the title. In the letter, Jim said, "You've written a lot of quality stuff for BP and helped to shape the magazine's identity. From now on, your name will be on the masthead to acknowledge this[.]" My future in music journalism seemed assured.

Thank you, Jim. I still remember reading that letter and being suffused with pride and gratitude.

Your Soul for Muffin Tops

A monstrously talented band that'd been knocking around Los Angeles for at least five years invited me to a show. They were extremely nice guys whose publicist always got one of the following three aspects of her clients' shows wrong: date, place, or time. A sweet woman, she surely contributed to the band's inability to make it. This gig would supposedly be at nine on Saturday night at a club on Santa Monica Boulevard.

I drove the forty minutes there and found the band's name on the marquee and my name on the list. Things were looking good. Inside, a quartet of thirtyish white men in jeans and J.C. Penny button-front shirts played "Johnny B. Goode." The audience of twelve pumped their fists and let loose with an occasional "Ow!" After a fifteen-minute version of the song, complete with bass and drum solos, the band launched into "House of the Rising Sun." The guitarist kept hitting the wrong fret and quickly correcting himself, producing a Charles Ives effect that made my teeth hurt.

In the front lounge, the bartender – a twentysomething woman in a tank top and ripped loose-fit jeans – stood behind the bar, smoking. She'd adopted a ridiculously contrived stance, her right leg and buttock on the counter, her left foot planted on the floor, like a composite photo of one woman sitting in a lotus position and the other standing at attention. She had an enormous Carly Simon mouth and long streaky-blonde hair, and her low-cut top displayed her deep cleavage to a babbling middle-aged drunk on a stool in front of her. He poured out a flood of incomprehensible sounds, just *mah-meh-bleh-mah-meh-mi-bluh* as he kept his eyes locked on the bartender's magnificent chest. She ignored him, a woman patiently waiting for a bus.

I went out and checked the schedule tacked to the front door, which I should've done earlier, and saw that my band wouldn't go on at nine; it would go on at midnight. That meant that after the hour-long show, the schmoozing, and the drive, I'd get home at three. Ever since I stopped drinking seven years earlier, my stamina had steadily decreased. Who knew that active alcoholism kept you in shape? I'd have to tank up on Diet Coke to make it through the night. I ordered my first from the wide-mouthed bartender and tipped her a dollar. "*Think* you," she said with a smile, her eyes lowered demurely as her hand snatched the money with the speed of a chameleon's tongue.

Two more bands played before the one I was there to see. The first was a Rush cover band whose lead singer kept saying things like, "So this is L.A.!" and "We've heard so much about L.A. audiences, so give it up!" That meant they were *touring*. I was gobsmacked. They were popular, too, because as soon as they started playing, the room filled with cheering people. This despite the fact that the vocalist-guitarist didn't hit a single note dead center the entire show. He'd adjusted his microphone to tower over him; to reach it, he had to throw his head back, making him look like a plucked turkey on a butcher's hook. I could hear his vocal cords shredding, every vein and tendon standing out on his neck and forehead.

Another bar faced the stage. I sat at one of the tables in front of it and eavesdropped on the conversations taking place around me. Everybody bellowed and roared to be heard over the music, spitting in each other's faces.

Most of the activity centered around a tall woman in a black cocktail dress that half-concealed the large tattoo on her right shoulder. She had a nest of porn-blonde hair and was somewhere between thirty and fifty. A roll of back-fat slopped over the top of her dress and her gigantic breasts were balanced by a gigantic rear. Her fishnet stockings showed off her dimpled thighs. Two men interacted with her. One was a fat biker with sleeves of tattoos peeking out from under his black T-shirt, and the other looked exactly like Peter Hook, with the same leather pants, surfer's hair, and sleepy expression. These two joked with and hugged everyone around them, but they gave off waves of imminent violence, a kind of radar that scanned the room for targets.

I've taken lessons from Tim on how to deflect this sort of attention. It's very easy: Sit or stand as tall and as straight as you can; hold your head up; don't look anyone in the eye; and don't swing your arms when you walk. Humans slouch, make eye contact, and swing their arms when they walk; creatures that are other, don't. Since the brains of most human males will register only rivals or possible mates, you – a member of a different species – won't even be noticed. I sat up on my stool and stared into the middle distance, and these men no more than two feet away didn't see me.

The tall blonde shepherded a flock of girls who looked to be no more than sixteen. Most had nose-rings and baby tees, which distinguished them from the Original Rockers, older ladies with big hair, skintight jeans, and black T-shirts. Skinny sideburns and gas-station attendant shirts differentiated the young males. The boys and girls looked touchingly childlike next to their craggy older brothers and sisters, but both age groups pounded beer, sucked on cigarettes, and went "Ow!" together. It's called "modeling," something I thought about a lot because my three-year-old nephew had recently begun calling me on the phone and asking me to come over and play. When I did, I had to be careful because he'd copy everything I did. If I cleared my throat (one of my many nervous tics), he'd do it too. If I crossed my legs, he'd cross his legs. It was a terrible responsibility.

In front of me, Peter Hook took his hands off the shoulders of the two teenagers he'd tucked under his arms and brushed his fingers down the front of the tall blonde's dress. She arched her back, her breasts popping out like ICBMs. She'd been playing with a cigarette for five minutes, mouthing it and caressing it but not lighting it.

"Hey," Peter yelled. "Don't be wearin' dresses like that."

"Why not?" she screamed. Her voice was not possible, a piercing croak.

"Well, you don't wanna go showin' yer... yer... *titties* like that."

"Why not?" she asked again. "You already seen the whole package."

She lit the cigarette, inhaled massively, and released only a tiny wisp of smoke. The nose-ring girls swiveled their heads back and forth. Peter stared at the blonde for a few seconds, his lips moving. Finally, he came up with an answer.

"'Cause I might wanna see the whole package *again!*" He spun away and did a head-bobbing hula victory dance, his face scrunched up, snickering with his tongue jammed into his lower teeth like Robert De Niro: *A-hyih-hyih-hyih-hyih!*

The blonde rolled her eyes and told two of the nose-ring girls to ask me if they could sit at my table. My humanity was obviously showing, so I stood and bore down on the girls, my arms hanging at my sides like dead things. The girls scattered and I went up to the VIP lounge to see if anything was happening. I'd been given an "All Access" sticker, which was funny because there was no backstage or dressing rooms, just the tiny bar upstairs. A gargantuan bouncer grabbed me on my way up, and I thrust out my own chest so he could see the sticker. He leaned in and peered at it, his brow knitted; I wondered what would happen if I shook my shoulders and squealed "Boop-boop-be-doop!" Upstairs the crowd consisted of bloated, sweating, florid, older men and their heavily made-up robot trophy companions.

I went back downstairs just as the Rush cover band finished, the singer's cracked *"Eeeeeeee-yay-yuh!"* causing my face to tingle and my spine to chill in vicarious humiliation.

The next act was a Led Zeppelin cover band. They all appeared to have had cosmetic surgery to look more like their idols, and their milling crowd of a road crew wore T-shirts that proclaimed them "The Best Zepp Cover Band Touring Today." Introducing each song, they used cheesy *Spinal Tap* British accents, saying things like, "This is oaf ah fird owbum," or "We 'ad a loat a fun recoadin' this tewn." For someone with as tenuous a grip on reality as I have, it was terrifyingly disorienting, especially since they were tremendous musicians. They brought in an even bigger crowd, most of whom were in their forties. There were a few very young fans, the girls all showing muffin tops under the hems of their baby tees.

My band went on at midnight, and the room instantly cleared. They killed; nobody was there to see it except me. My heart ached for them. After the show, I spoke to them, telling the bassist that it was the best show they'd ever put on. He thanked me the way a mourner accepts condolences. I was out of the club by 1:30. On the drive home, I pondered the fact that I'd had absolutely no idea – even after five years as a music journalist – that there were cover bands that toured the country. And after the show they'd go up into the VIP lounge, meet with some boozy Industry hangers-on, and then go back to their Motel 6 with some muffin-topped groupies before hitting the road again the next day. It was as though they'd sold their souls to an incompetent, delusional Beelzebub, a big-talking loser-devil whose two-bit powers could grant them only a cruddy, piddling version of stardom. But they went for it anyway.

Model, Actress, Whatever

They were known as MAWs. I was told many stories. One guy I knew was hired as second assistant to a famous photographer for a one-day shoot of an up-and-coming MAW. The MAW said her thighs looked elephantine in her dress; the assistant laughed and said, "No, they don't!"

Instantly the photographer marched over and roughly grabbed the assistant by the upper arm, slipping his hand into his armpit the way my father used to do to me. He shoved his face in close and snarled, "Don't talk to my talent, understand? That's *my* talent, and you're not to talk to them. Do you hear me? I said, *do you hear me?*" And he shook the assistant's arm, expecting an answer.

"Yes, I hear you," the assistant replied, his shoulder rammed up into the side of his neck.

Here's what the problem was, I learned: Clients are supposed to remember only the photographer, not his assistants. A terrible sin had been committed.

At every photo shoot, every MAW would flash the photographer. "I'm not wearing any underwear!" she'd squeal. "Wanna see?" And she'd briefly lift her skirt with a "Whoopsie!" or a "Woo-hoo!" or an "Ow!"

Since MAWs all starved themselves, they were always on the verge of passing out. As emergency rations, they all carried tiny cans of tuna fish in their purses, the smallest portions, like tins of cat food with pop tops, which they'd gobble with pink Baskin-Robbins spoons. It was 100-percent consistent: no underwear, flashing, tuna fish, and Baskin-Robbins spoons.

The Woman Who Lived in Disneyland

Roger and Dolores once accompanied me to Disneyland for a project. We were introduced to a woman of thirty-four I'll call Lindsey, who showed us around the Magic Kingdom. She was not an employee; she had a lifetime pass to the place and spent all day, every day, at Disneyland. Tall, blonde, and muscular, she'd been doing so for almost two decades. She'd learned the complete history of the park, the heights of all the structures, the speeds of the rides, and the inconceivable variety of merchandise available in the millions of shops. We, in turn, learned every bit of this information.

Lindsey spoke with breathless awe of "Mister Walt Disney," always referring to him by his title. Mister Walt Disney banned facials on his employees, a rule that was enforced to this very day. When Dolores gave me an incredulous grin and asked if workers were getting public facials in the park, Lindsey explained that mustaches and beards were considered a sign of hooliganism.

"Disneyland does not allow facials on either male *or* female employees."

That made Dolores cover her mouth with both hands and stomp her foot. She went behind me and rested her forehead against my back as she tried to suppress her guffaws. Roger was enthralled.

"This is just great, Tom," he said. "Thank you so much."

Lindsey never went into the character dressing rooms, even though she had access, because she didn't like to see Mickey and Minnie with their heads off. It upset her to be reminded that they weren't real beings after all. She had the voice of a Southern bell. Not a *belle*, a *bell* – ringing, tolling, and clanging endlessly. She showed me where I could buy a soft drink. It was a place called "ay concession stand," she informed me. She pointed out what they sold.

"Now, this is ay 'Diet Coke,' and this is ay 'Coke,' and this is ay 'bottled water,' and this is anne 'orange drink.'"

When I tried to pay the concessioner on my left, Lindsey literally screamed, "*No! No! Tomiss! Pay over here, Tomiss! Over here!*" as she flapped her arm at the other clerk. It was terribly frightening, like the scene in *Rain Man* where Dustin Hoffman refuses to get on the airliner.

She showed us the secret Mickey Mouse faces hidden all over the grounds, helping us see how this or that smudge or bush or shadow or pile of rocks represented the ubiquitous rodent. Also, she knew the words of every spiel of every ride, display, voiceover, robot, song, and announcement. She'd recite or sing in time with whatever we visited or walked past, the lyrics or patter seamlessly incorporated into what she'd been saying at the time: "And did you know, Tomiss, that Mister Walt Disney only decided *All abooooooard!* to expand his original concept of *Hurry-hurry-hurry-step right up!* an eight-acre park to 160 acres after his brother Mister Roy Disney *Are ye feelin' brave, mateys? Arrr!* convinced him that the extra acreage *It's a small world after all* was absolutely necessary?"

I'd had it after about an hour, but Roger and Dolores were fascinated by Lindsey and wanted to spend the whole day with her. To keep from losing my mind, I began claiming motion sickness every time Lindsey dragged us over to another ride. I'd sit on a bench and chain-smoke my throat into jerky as I counted the seconds until we could leave.

After six hours, Dolores conceded that the charm of the situation had waned. She took to sneaking out and sitting with me while Roger and Lindsey continued their tour. Dolores clearly knew the effect she had on most men. She liked to play with me, complaining about how her husband was too busy, too silent, and thought she was fat. I listened and took in the flawless skin white as cream, the sky-blue eyes zapping out bolts of sad electricity, the full smiling lips, the dimples, and the strong, competent hands delicately holding a cigarette or touching my shoulder in a way that promised all sorts of adventures, if only...

We finally left after eight hours. Lindsey walked us to the gate and stood there almost in tears, calling, "Bye-bye! Bye-bye!" I got home an hour later. The second I walked in the door the phone rang. I picked it up and my ears were assaulted by a clanging Southern accent, ding-donging out, "Tomiss? Hi! It's Lindsey! I just wanted to tell you I had such a nice time and I wanted to know when's the next time we can all get together?"

With no idea how she'd gotten my number, I swivel-hipped my way out of a commitment. In revenge for the eight hours of my life stolen from me, I then called Roger, since I knew that on a Friday night he and his unappreciated wife would be out carousing. I left a message that Lindsey had phoned and wanted their number, so I'd given it to her and they should expect to hear from her soon. Of course I hadn't, but it was worth Roger's panicky, enraged call the next afternoon.

Phone Call to the Cardinal Ghost

In June of 1996, I had occasion to call Carmen to tie up a loose end. I was seriously involved with a woman at the time; I'll call her Noreen. She was a small, dark-haired, intelligent, and wickedly funny musician. I took her to San Francisco with me for a week, the plan being to exorcise myself and the City of Carmen's ghost. It seemed to work. I introduced Noreen to my friends in the Bay Area, and they liked her a lot. Noreen was quite a catch. She could paint like you couldn't believe, play any instrument, and was a wildcat in bed. I hadn't been with anyone since I left Carmen, but Noreen and I made up for lost time. She also cracked me up with her bizarre sense of humor. Once when awoken before she was ready, she grumbled, "Why are you waking me up, you *sow?*" She made up new names for popular songs: MC Hammer's "2 Legit 2 Quit" became "Do the Hitler Jig"; the chorus of Duran Duran's "Is There Something I Should Know?" morphed into "Please please smell me now"; and Pat Benatar's "Hit Me with Your Best Shot" was rendered "Hit Me in the Wet Slot."

The day I called Carmen, I was deeply in love with Noreen. I expected to handle the conversation with dignity and aplomb, ending this whole terrible chapter of my life for good. Carmen had given me her work number a year earlier, in a letter I'd kept because all it said was, "My new work number. Carmen." I dialed, eager to tell her tell her that I'd finally found what I wanted, too. To be perfectly frank, there was also vengeance in my heart. Carmen had always been deeply jealous; my call would upset her, I knew, no matter how strong her marriage was. I intended to let her know that Noreen was hotness incarnate and made me as happy as I'd ever been. It would be Carmen's punishment for the way she treated me the last time we spoke.

As soon as I heard her deep, creamy voice again, I got a whole-body chill. All my plans were blown into dust and I numbly stuttered, "Hi, Carmen. It's Tom Wictor." There was silence, and then she gasped, "*Tom?*" with an emotion I never, ever expected. It was elation. "Oh, my God, I can't *believe it*. It's so *good* to hear your voice. How've you been?"

She was so happy to hear from chronically underemployed, fat, marginalized me, the loser she'd eviscerated daily for months, that she was briefly in tears, laughing at the same time, the way she did when we reunited in July of 1989 after Hazim had assaulted her. And the way she did when I gave her the MusicMan Sting Ray bass for her birthday. "Sorry," she sniffled. "You just really caught me by surprise. I didn't think I'd ever hear from you again."

In a rush, she told me that the last concerts she'd been to were with me; she never played her instruments anymore; and she never wrote songs or sang anymore. She said she'd gone to a guitar store with her future husband once, and when she pulled a bass down from the wall, plugged it in, and began thumb-slapping it, all the young dudes in the building came running tumescently up, the way they always had when she and I went to guitar stores. Her future husband got embarrassed and told her to stop. "People are *watching* us!" he said.

"I haven't played my beloved Sting Ray since I don't know how long," she said.

There was nothing I could say except that I was sorry. We quickly recovered and dropped into a breezy, utterly impersonal conversation, concluded our business, and hung up. But the damage was done. I knew that my relationship with Noreen was a sham. I was still on the rebound, three years after the breakup with Carmen. After that phone call, the sense that I should be with her was as strong as it'd been the day I met her. My chest began to ache, the way it had for almost a year when I realized that I'd lost her. For some reason I didn't start drinking again, but I began remembering things that I'd blocked out, such as our first home-cooked meal together in her Tokyo apartment.

It was chicken, garlic, mushroom, carrot, and broccoli in a yogurt sauce on white rice. She ate gigantic portions. In answer to one of my questions, she started to speak with her mouth full, stopped, chewed and swallowed, and said, "God, I'm sorry. I have to be on my best behavior all day, so I tend to be a pig at home, at least where food is concerned. I love to eat, as you've probably noticed." I was actually amazed that such a small person could eat so much. "I just hope you don't think I'm a pig *all* the time," she said, waving her fork. "It's just that this apartment is the only place in the entire known universe where I can be myself. This is the only place I don't have to pretend I'm something I'm not."

"I don't think you're a pig," I said. It was the most peculiar thing I'd ever said to a woman in my life. It made us both laugh. We fell over and rolled around on the floor. "Stop! Stop!" she begged. "My stomach's killing me. I'm going to throw up."

I said, "Please don't. I'll throw up, too. I mean it."

"Calm down. I'm not *really* going to throw up. I'm fine. Get a hold of yourself. And get me some more wine."

I remembered her PTSD, too. One night in San Francisco she came home in tears and told me that a wild-eyed man had followed her for blocks, telling her to button her blouse or he'd kick her ass. She'd brazened it out until she got to her car and then locked herself in and had hysterics. It was hard for her to drive home, she was crying so hard.

She bought pepper spray when we moved to San Francisco from Tokyo. On the way back up from the one time we visited my parents in Los Angeles, we took the Pacific Coast Highway, which winds and twists like a road in the Swiss Alps. Carmen got carsick and begged me to stop to get her some Dramamine. We pulled into the parking lot of a drugstore and I ran in, leaving her squatting next to the car, ready to vomit, clutching her pepper spray. I've never felt more protective.

On a foggy day in San Francisco, as we crossed the street, a car ran a red light and plowed right into Carmen. She went up on the hood, her legs over her head, and when the car slammed on the brakes she slid off, flew twenty feet, and slammed into the asphalt. Before I could reach her, she bounded to her feet, braying her donkey laugh. About fifty people must've called 911 simultaneously because an ambulance and the police were there in seconds. Carmen swore she was fine, but the paramedics told her that tomorrow she'd be so sore she couldn't move. They were right. The next morning she could barely get out of bed. I fed her, helped her dress, and half-carried her to the bathroom, terrified at how close I'd come to losing her. I knew I couldn't live without her.

She was caught in the Oakland firestorm of October 20, 1991. As she cruised along Highway 24, a gigantic wave of flame washed over all eight lanes from left to right, no more than fifty yards ahead of her. She slammed on the brakes, made a U-turn, and drove back against traffic, weaving, flashing her lights and honking her horn, warning others. Saving lives.

"It looked like the biggest flamethrower in the world," she told me as she lay on top of me on the sofa and I held her. "I can't believe I'm not dead. If I'd gotten there a few seconds later, I would've been barbecued."

In 1992, a block from our apartment, I looked up and saw Hazim standing on the sidewalk. He smiled at me and stepped back off the curb, turned, and crossed the street. I have no doubt it was the courageous, pious woman beater himself. When I told Carmen, her face crumpled and she began wailing, "Oh, no! Oh, no! Oh, no!" We called the cops and when an officer arrived, we gave him a photo of Hazim.

"There's not much I can do, you know," the cop said. "Speaking off the record? Buy a gun." We didn't. Guns scared me to death at the time.

I never saw Hazim again, but I know he was there. The way he followed us for a year in Tokyo without us ever noticing him showed his preternatural skill in stalking. My fantasy is that the cop – a Russian émigré – told some very dangerous friends about this terrified young woman he couldn't help. Maybe somebody strapped Hazim to a chair and used a power drill on him before weighing him down with an anvil and dropping him into the bay. Or maybe one of the Chinese triads in our neighborhood got wind of him and gave him the Death of a Thousand Cuts. Whatever happened, I hope it was slow and painful and he had time to wish he'd done things differently.

Right before Carmen became my enemy, another car almost killed her. We went to a book store in the Castro District and then decided to find a place to eat. As we walked down the sidewalk, we heard car horns honking frantically nearby.

"Wonder what that's all about," I said.

Carmen said, "Someone got married."

The honking got closer, and then half a block ahead of us a Chevy Impala drove up on the sidewalk doing about seventy miles per hour. Two men holding hands in front of us leapt in opposite directions. The younger man grabbed a metal crowd barrier – the kind that looks like an antique headboard made of bars – and flung it at the car. The barrier hit the vehicle, shattering the headlights and cartwheeling into the air. Everybody's seen nearly identical scenes in hundreds of movies. All that was missing were boxes of fruit for the car to smash into.

The Impala raced toward us; I realized the honking came from two other cars in the street chasing it. Carmen stood there, frozen, her mouth open in the puzzled smile that she always produced when witnessing absurdity. Without thinking, I grabbed her with both hands by the front of her jacket, swung her into the doorway of a video store, and hurled myself after her. A second later the Impala roared past, missing me by about five feet. The driver was fat and unshaven, with a black mustache and a long ponytail. He wore a white T-shirt and a jeans jackets with the sleeves cut off, the standard biker ensemble. There were others in the car, but I couldn't make them out. The Impala flew off the curb and swerved into the street again, trailed by the two other cars and a motorcycle. All four vehicles disappeared.

"What the hell is going on?" a man in the video store asked me.

"Someone just tried to run us over," I said. Actually, I think I screamed it.

"What, again?" the man said. "Did you get his license-plate number?"

"Part of it."

"Well, come upstairs to my apartment. Let's call the cops."

He took us up to his apartment, and while I reported the incident to the police, he and Carmen had a conversation about music, since he had a piano and several electric guitars on stands. He looked and sounded exactly like Richard Simmons; even his tank top and hot pants were the same. After my call I asked him, "Why did you say, 'What, again?' when I told you someone tried to run us over?"

"Because they come up here and try to murder us all the time," he said.

"Who does?"

"People who hate fags."

"They try to run you over?"

"They don't *try;* they *do* it."

I didn't know what to say. He didn't seem particularly angry, while all I could think of was putting a shotgun into that fat driver's mouth and letting him sweat for a few seconds before I pulled the trigger. Years earlier I was tormented almost out of my mind by the sight of my boss Conan using Carmen as a mop. The new unbearable image was her standing there, open mouthed and helpless, seconds from being reduced to offal, all her humor, intelligence, talent, quirkiness, and beauty taken from her by an obese, ugly, hate-filled fuck.

On the way back to our car, she said, "Things keep happening to us, don't they?"

I said, "The important thing is we keep surviving them."

We'd endured some truly horrible experiences, most of which I've omitted from this memoir. All they did was reinforce our bond and my conviction that we were meant to be together. Like a samurai sword, we'd begun as two different alloys, but the Master Smith had pounded us into an integrated whole.

As it turns out, the call to Carmen was a blessing because the relationship with Noreen was in fact the worst of my life.

How a Ghost in Los Angeles Said Goodbye

Noreen broke it off by phone. She didn't like the fact that I preferred to come home instead of spending the night with her. I didn't want to in effect live with anybody again; she'd initially said she understood and preferred such an arrangement herself, but now she'd changed her mind. "It's too much like you fucking and running," she said. "I need you here with me at night. I've been in enough relationships to know exactly what I want and exactly what I need, and I'm not getting it from you. I don't feel fulfilled."

"You said you agreed with me at the beginning."

"Yeah, I did. I know. I'm telling you I can't deal with it anymore. It's too much like being in high school. In a real relationship people spend the night. They don't get up and leave after a couple of hours. This is just not working out. I'm just telling you my feelings."

She always pronounced it *relayship*. Everyone in Los Angeles does.

"Well, I don't know what to tell you. I'm doing a lot of writing right now. I do my best writing at night."

She snorted, "Tom, you're not making any money writing. You're always broke."

"True. But I've always wanted to be a writer, and writers always struggle. You said you admired me for pursuing my dream instead of settling for some safe, easy job."

"I *do* think it's great that you're pursuing your dream, but there are guys out there ten years younger than you making ten times as much money."

"I know. But you told me that as long as I was happy, it didn't matter."

"For *you*. But since you never have any money, we can't do the things I like to do. I like going out. I like being treated in a certain way. I don't like having to suddenly stop doing those things because there isn't any money. I've worked very hard to get where I am, and I don't need any more stress or problems in my life. That's not what I want."

I said, "You told me you were tired of going out all the time, tired of the parties and night life. You said you liked staying in and having a quiet meal with me. It was more satisfying, you said."

Long pause. "I think I was wrong. I'm thirty-three years old. I know what I want and I know what I need in my life. And my needs aren't being met. I like eating in expensive restaurants. I like going away for the weekends. I like going to the best clubs. You and I haven't been able to do any of those things. I need to be with someone who has enough money to do everything I like to do. You could spend the next ten or twenty years fucking around at the same level you're at now. I don't have time to wait, Tom. I've already paid my dues. I need something better."

"Well, look," I said. "You knew at the beginning that I'm committed to trying to be a writer now. It's too late for me to change careers, even if I wanted to. I'm in it for good."

"But *I'm* not."

"You have tons of money. If going out and traveling and eating at ritzy places means so much to you, why don't you pay for it?"

"*No!* No man is ever going to use me for my money. I can't pick up the tab for someone who's not capable of paying his own way. Everyone's got to pay their own way. I can't support you. I won't be used that way."

"I'm not asking you to support me. I'm just saying that if it means so much to you, and if you can afford it – which you can – why not pay for it yourself? Lots of people have situations in which one person helps the other out, as long as that person is making an honest effort to – "

"*No!*" she shouted. "*No!* I don't know *anyone* who does that. None of my friends do that. I will *not* be used by someone. Everyone I know works for what they have, just like I do. We're out there in the real world, working every day. If you want something, you're just going to have to work for it like the rest of us."

"I *am* working. I'm not a total failure yet."

"I didn't *say* you're a failure! Don't put words in my mouth, and don't get defensive. It's great that you're working toward what you want, but it might take you years to get there. I can't wait that long."

"Well, then maybe you should find someone who's already made it."

"I think I have to, Tom."

"Maybe you'd be better off with someone making enough money to take you wherever you want to go in the style you need."

"I think I'd better do that. I mean, this is my *life* we're talking about, Tom."

"You're right. It's your life we're talking about."

"Well, okay, then."

After a long silence, I said, "Okay. Take care of yourself."

"You, too."

"Goodbye."

"Bye."

About three weeks later, she called at seven one night and said, "We can't leave it that way."

"We can't?" I asked.

"No, we can't. I miss you, Tom. I miss being with you."

"You do?"

"*Yes,*" she hissed. "I've just been thinking and thinking about you, lying here alone at night, and I had to call you. It's just been terrible. I feel so bad about everything."

"I do, too," I said.

"It's just been so... so *lonely.* I'd really like to see you."

"I think that could probably be arranged."

"I know this is really short notice – no notice, really – but can you come over right now?"

"Right now? You mean tonight?"

She laughed throatily. "Yes, tonight. I really want you *bad.*" She sucked air past her clenched teeth. "And you don't have to stay the night. I get that now." Then she switched to a broad Valley accent, "The praaaablam *ihhhhhz,* I'm *not* getting *laid.*"

"I'll be right over," I said. I drove the forty-five minutes to her condo and spent almost three hours in bed with her. When I told her at 10:30 that I had to leave, she demanded one last go-round, which she said would only take a minute. It took about four. The next night I called her. "Hi, it's me."

"Oh." Very long pause. "Hi."

"I just wanted to tell you how nice it was to be with you last night."

"Mmmmm." She took a sip from a bottle.

"I was wondering if I could come over again tonight."

"Tom, I hope you don't think last night meant that everything's all right between us now, because it isn't. Nothing's changed."

For the only time in my life, I actually took a phone receiver away from my head and stared at it. Since that was a completely pointless thing to do, I put it back to my ear and said, "I thought you wanted to give it another try."

"I didn't say that. I said I wasn't getting laid."

"Ah. Well, that's right," I agreed. "You did say that."

Silence.

"So you were just using me," I said.

"Mm-hmm."

"That's really great. What a fantastic thing to do. Thank you."

"Tom, I'm only human. I'm not perfect. I'm weak."

Since I had absolutely no response to that, I sat and listened to her breathe and take sips from her bottle. Eventually, she said, "This is really boring. I have to go. Goodbye." She hung up. I sat there for a few seconds and then punched in her number.

"Hi!" she said cheerily after the first ring.

"I don't understand what's going on," I said.

"Nothing's going on. I felt like getting fucked last night, so I called you. It was just sex. It didn't mean anything."

"Why are you doing this?"

"Doing *what?*" she snapped.

"Why are you treating me this way?"

"Treating you what way, Tom?"

"I don't know. You're being so... so... mean."

"*Mean?*" she screamed. "What are you, a five-year-old? *Mean?* What kind of a word is that for an adult to use?"

"You know, you talk a lot about being an adult, but I would never treat you the way you're treating me."

"Oh, just save it, Tom. I'm *light years* ahead of you. There's not a thing in the world you could tell me about anything. You have no idea how adults act or treat each other. I swear, you're such a little boy it's hilarious. You're really not to be believed."

I digested that. "Could I ask you something?"

She laughed. "Sure! Why not?"

"What happened to that jeans jacket I gave you?" She'd told me that she really liked my faded old Levi's jeans jacket, so I'd given it to her.

"Well, I think jeans jackets are tacky. I'd never wear one. I asked you for it just to see if I could make you give it to me, since you loved it so much. I threw it away. I'm a little *devil,* aren't I?" She snickered.

After a while, I said, "It was all just lies, wasn't it? Everything you said to me about how I was the kind of person you wanted. None of it was true."

"Look, I never lied to you once, Tom. Whatever I might've said I meant it at the time. But that was before I really got to know you. You're not the person you pretend to be. You think you can fool people with your sensitive act, and yes, I suppose you fooled me for a while. I'm a very trusting person. I mean, all that shit about how you had to tell me about all your bad points up front because you wanted me to have no misconceptions about the kind of person I was getting involved with? What a crock. What a load. It was just a way for you to get into my pants."

"That's funny," I said. "I remember you saying you were grateful I'd told you. In fact, you said it was the best compliment you'd ever gotten."

She laughed, a piercing bark. "You know what it was like, Tom? It was like someone coming into my apartment and taking a big dump on the rug. That's what it was like. You spoiled it from the start. Who wants to hear all that negativity from the beginning? You're so negative it's really depressing. You have no idea how to deal with women, do you?"

"Probably not."

"Well, I'm sick of this whole stupid thing. Don't call me anymore, okay? Goodbye."

I didn't. And I've never owned another jeans jacket.

How I Said Goodbye to a Ghost in Los Angeles

Dear Noreen:
And so it comes time to say goodbye for good. When you called the second time and told me you wanted to try again I hoped it wouldn't come to this, but

this is what you chose, so now you have to live with the consequences of your actions. There's a lot of good in you, Noreenie. You're funny, intelligent, and so damn attractive. Deep inside, there's a person who's kind, sweet, gentle, and empathetic. That person was the one I wanted to be with and get to know.

The reason I told you I wanted no more contact with you is because you will not control yourself. Notice my choice of words. I'm not saying you *can't;* I'm saying you *won't.* The last time I spoke to you, you said I was a Menendez brother, I was the King of Chaos, and that I was crazy. Not only that, you told me Tim thought I was crazy, too. You weren't satisfied with trying to hurt me, so you tried to poison my relationship with my brother as well. The really sad thing for me was to hear how miserable and unhappy you sounded saying it, like you were dying. You knew what you were doing was wrong, but you went ahead and did it anyway. You're not miles ahead of me in terms of development, Noreen, because I would never try to hurt you and spoil your relationship with someone close to you that way.

It's bad enough that a 33-year-old would do that, but when she's a trained therapist, it becomes obscene. You've used your ability to find peoples' weaknesses for destructive purposes, not for healing. You've perverted what you've learned, and you should be ashamed of yourself. I know you are, and you deserve that feeling because nothing I did or said justifies the sort of rabid attacks you've subjected me to. I wonder what it was you learned in all the therapy you studied that taught you it was acceptable to do that? Good therapists don't act as out of control and viciously as you do. I hope you realize that all this fallout was totally unnecessary and entirely your doing. I didn't ruin your life or your relationship with Tim; somebody else did. And you know who that was.

I'm sorry for all of this. I never wanted to hurt you. I refrained from attacking you with everything I know about you because I'm trying to make myself a better person. If I had wanted to, I could have really made you suffer. You have no idea what I'm capable of. I spared you that because I didn't want to add to your problems. I like you, and I hope – I sincerely do – that someday you find happiness. I hope you find what you're looking for. I hope you knock 'em dead with how together you are. Someday, it all might happen for you, and when it does, I'll be as happy for you as you'll be yourself. As for right now, I'm sorry you're hurting. I'm sorry you feel so much pain. I feel pain, too, but I'm not going to try to destroy you because of it. I learned a lot about myself from you, and you helped me get over some lingering hang-ups I had. I'm not entirely regretful I was with you for a little while.

Not to be cruel, I'll leave you with this thought, in the hopes that you'll come away from this having learned something: This situation, as it stands now, is entirely your doing. All I wanted was some time to readjust, because I really, truly loved you. I never said I had to stay away from you forever. You told me to not call you again, remember? Now, even though I'll think of you with affection, I can't see or talk to you because I can't have contact with someone who acts with such total self-centeredness, viciousness, and complete loss of control. My life has had and continues to have such ugliness in it that I have to limit my exposure to people like you. Even though you can't really hurt me anymore, because your opinion of me no longer matters, you've proven to me all by yourself that you're capable of astonishingly toxic behavior. I'm trying to move beyond that, and I hope someday you will, too.

When I think of you, I'll remember your great sense of humor, your sweetness, your alertness and energy. I'll remember making love to you on your leather couch as you said to me, "I like it that you're so into me." I *was* so into you, Noreen. Really and truly, warts and all. I knew you had problems. It wasn't a fantasy. I connected, for a couple of weeks, like I hadn't connected in years, and that was real. You can't revise that. I only stopped loving you when you proved to me that you have to destroy everything you can't control. Also, you took the absolute worst thing that has happened to me and used that to try and hurt me. You jeered at and ridiculed me for [withheld]. You hit me right where you knew I was most vulnerable. Think about how low and gutless that is. Think about how ugly that is. Think about what that says about you as a person, to do such a thing. Finally, think about what you can do to change, before it's too late for you.

Good luck to you and take care of yourself.

Tom

A Component of my Distant Early Warning System

In August of 1996, I interviewed Guns 'n Roses bassist Duff McKagan about Neurotic Outsiders, a band that grew out of friends jamming in Johnny Depp's club, the Viper Room. It included McKagan and drummer Matt Sorum of Guns, guitarist Steve Jones of the Sex Pistols, and bassist John Taylor of Duran Duran; McKagan played guitar for Outsiders. Since Guns 'n Roses had spectacularly imploded in 1994, I asked Duff if he considered it a setback to go from playing stadiums to small clubs.

It was really a gift to me, just to start playing in a club again, with this band that just reacquainted me with why I started doing this in the first place. It was needed. For me, it was needed. It just gets... *out there* doing stadiums. It gets really surreal, man. Playing to the horizon. I mean, as far as you can see, it's people. It just becomes like, "That's not really happening." You know, you go back to your hotel room and turn on CNN and you go, "Fuck! I just played in front of a hundred thousand people." It's fuckin' weird. It was hard for me, after being so busy in music for fourteen years of my life, to all of a sudden just stop. But it let me take care of some health issues. It's just been kind of fortunate how everything has worked out so far.[4]

He's another in the long list of artists whose words I heard over ten years but didn't absorb. What others – including me – saw as calamity, he recognized as deliverance from the dangerous path he was on. He was genuinely grateful for having his eyes opened, despite what it took for him to achieve that awareness.

Letter to the Cardinal Ghost

After the horror show with Noreen, my nightmares about Carmen began anew. In desperation I finally wrote a letter.

Dear Carmen:

It was nice to talk to you again. It's been a long time since we last saw each other, and it's probably not my place to say this, but for what it's worth, I just wanted to tell you that I'm sorry for all the awful things I said to you the last time we saw each other. I'm sorry about the fighting and ugliness. I had no right to say the things I did. I was trying to hurt you, and it was wrong. None of what I said was true. I hope you know that. I don't mean to stir anything up by telling you this. I just had to say it because I feel bad about the way I acted.

Take care of yourself,

Tom

I didn't expect a response. Four days later a letter addressed to me in Carmen's distinct, rounded handwriting arrived in the mail. I left it on the kitchen counter off to the side for two days before opening it.

Dear Tom:
Thank you for your letter. I was very surprised to get it, but I was also very grateful. For what it's worth, I said and did a lot of horrible things myself, so I can't let you take all the blame. I'm sorry for what I said and did too. I hope you know that I didn't mean it, either. [Sentence withheld.] That's no excuse, but there it is.

It's very hard for me to talk about this with you, so I hope you understand if I ask that you don't bring it up again. I think these things are better discussed with a therapist. I've been seeing one for a long time now, and your letter has given me a lot of food for thought. Please take care of yourself, and I hope you're doing well.

Carmen

I remember thinking, so this is what they mean by closure. It isn't bad. I was wrong, as usual. That night I had this dream, which I recorded in my diary.

I was in a seedy motel room, waiting for Carmen. I knew that we had to get back together because I was dying without her, but I also knew that when we did reunite, I'd lose something forever. I didn't care. The arrangement was for her to spend the weekend with me, seventy-two hours of nothing but sex and reconciliation. I was terribly afraid, aroused, and ashamed.

Suddenly, she breezed into the room. She was much taller than I remembered, and she was blonde. I looked down at my body and felt loathsome as a toad, but she rushed me the way she used to and kissed me, her tongue snaking around inside my mouth. Even though I was almost comatose with happiness to be with her, I noticed that she was preoccupied, not really paying attention. She was seeing someone else, I knew, but I was still happy that she was with me. I hugged her, and she pulled back and said, "If we're going to do any fucking, we'd better start now!" I was shocked; she'd never spoken like that before.

Then we were both naked in bed. She squatted on top of me and guided me into her with her hand. I thought I might die from the sensation. She bucked violently, panting and moaning, her eyes closed, and she screamed, "You're fucking me! You're fucking me!" I felt utterly panicked. What was wrong with her? She'd never acted this way before. She howled like a siren and then it was over. I didn't climax.

"If I were seeing someone else," I said, "what I'd do now would be to go to him and get some from him, too. That way I could do two guys on the same day."

She nodded at me in a mock-rueful way, fluttering her eyelids. "Yeah, I guess you're right. That's what you'd do, all right."

I said, "You're not going to spend the weekend with me after all, are you?"

She shook her head and gave me a grotesquely fake apologetic smile. "No, I'm not. I'm really, really sorry."

I watched her get dressed and leave, and in a few minutes I put on my own clothes and went outside into what looked like a renaissance fair. There were large pots of food sitting on long tables. I loaded up a plate with stew, cornbread, and vegetables while everyone around me stopped what they were doing and stared at me in silence. They all knew what had just happened in the motel room. I looked up and saw Carmen approaching; she'd donned a dark trench coat and carried a briefcase. Stopping next to me, she filled her own plate with food and then faced the silent crowd.

She held up the plate and said, "This is my boyfriend; my *real* boyfriend." Then she looked at me with a phony wince of alarm, pretending to be horrified at what she'd just said.

"All right. If that's the way you want it," I said. I threw my own plate on the ground and marched away from her, literally, swinging my arms and pumping my legs like a mechanical toy soldier while imitating a military snare drum: *dt-d-dt, dt-d-dt, drrrrrt-d-d-d-d-dt, d-dt.* It was a pathetic, demented performance, but I couldn't stop. People turned away in disgust; I kept on marching and making snare-drum sounds. I began physically shrinking in size. The further I got from Carmen, the smaller I became. At the same time, my buttocks expanded and my hair became a cap of tightly permed white curls. In seconds I'd become a fat, middle-aged German *Hausfrau* in polyester stretch pants and a sleeveless blouse. I couldn't bear to look back at Carmen's reaction to my transformation, so I kept on marching until I was less than an inch tall.

We wrote each other several letters, exclusively about music, and I sent her copies of *Bass Player* and some model-building or military-history magazines with my articles. It was indescribably painful, but she seemed happy for my writing careerlet. I have a letter from her dated October 10, 1996, in which she said she could meet me for lunch when I was in the Bay Area the next week. I canceled my trip instead, because I didn't trust myself to not break down the second I saw her. The last letter she sent is dated November 6, 1997. After that we had no contact for almost two years, until I finally went online and sent her an e-mail. She responded, and we again talked about music occasionally. It petered out in late 2000.

A paragraph from one of the messages she wrote during this period.

> I'm going to force myself to pick up my treasured Sting Ray and PLAY. I'm dying to create music... but I feel bottled up and scared... I'm getting OLD... but I'll always remember Tim telling me that Madonna will always be older than I am.

Meet the New Boss

On October 1, 1996, Jim Roberts stepped down as editor of *Bass Player*. The new editor was Karl Coryat, a man I knew. Though I was sorry to see Jim go, I had full confidence in Karl. He was weird, funny, highly intelligent, and extremely open to unorthodox ideas. Like Jim and me, he cared more about the quality of the material than putting his own stamp on it. With Karl at the helm, I felt I could do anything.

In his letter to me announcing the change, Jim wrote, "I'd like to thank you for the help you've given me during my tenure as Editor. It's been very gratifying watching the magazine grow up, and I will always be indebted to the many people who have helped to make it possible."

The Collateral Ghost

As soon as I moved to Los Angeles in 1993, people began telling me I had to interview Scott Thunes.[5] Not only was he an exceptional player, but also his personality was so extreme and his story so tragic that it would make for un-put-down-able reading. I wasn't all that interested, because I never liked Frank Zappa. The only Zappa music I'd heard was

Joe's Garage Act I, which my floor mates in college played incessantly, singing along to "Catholic Girls," "Crew Slut," "Wet T-Shirt Nite," and "Why Does it Hurt When I Pee?" I'd heard all the arguments that Zappa was a brilliant satirist, but I could never understand that. Satirizing wet T-shirt contests? Shooting fish in a barrel, as far as I was concerned. To me, brilliant satire was *Monty Python's Flying Circus.* The Ministry of Silly Walks. The Four Yorkshiremen. Self-defense Against Fruit. The Black Knight. *That* was satire. Since I also hate the xylophone and utterly despise the *Phi Zappa Krappa* poster of him sitting naked on a toilet, which every single infantile, conventional, self-described iconoclast in my college had taped to his wall or door, Zappa was just never my cup of tea.

And then I heard the intro to "What's New in Baltimore," off Zappa's *Does Humor Belong in Music,* a compilation of live performances recorded in 1984. It contained the best one minute and forty-three seconds of bass I'd ever heard, packed with more creativity, emotion, and beauty than most musicians achieve in a lifetime of playing. It reminded me of the bass passage in the middle of Gentle Giant's "The Moon is Down," from *Acquiring the Taste,* evoking the same emotions in me: a sense of awe and exultant admiration for such originality on my chosen instrument. Scott Thunes's playing had the same impact that Ray Shulman's had when Joe Cady played me the live version of "Free Hand" in 1981.

Karl approved the interview, and after much intrigue and much help from songwriter and guitarist-keyboardist Mike Keneally, I arranged to drive back to the cursed Bay Area and meet with Thunes at his house on the afternoon of October 6, 1996. If we could get along, he'd consent to be interviewed the next day. It was an intimidating plan – an audition, in fact. I was never more terrified of anyone in my entire life. The idea of me interviewing such a consummate musician was surreal. It wasn't his infamous antics; it was the fact that he was a human incarnation of musical knowledge. He understood music in a visceral way, down to a cellular level. I'd watched hours of video tapes of him playing and listened to dozens of his recordings in preparation, and the closer it came to the actual interview day, the more panicked I became. I even thought about deliberately crashing my car on the way to his house.

He was the first person I'd meet in my life – as far as I could tell – who had absolute knowledge of a subject, and I was expected to talk with him, intelligently and productively, *on his level,* about it. I was terrified that after just a few minutes with me, he'd stop and say, "You're nothing but a fraud, aren't you? Why are you wasting my time?"

I can tell you the exact moment I realized it wouldn't happen: When he said to his wife Georgia, "Good. He's comfortable," and she left the room. Whatever happened next, I knew he at least took me seriously enough to let me interview him. The sense of relief was overwhelming. I didn't allow myself to think about what would happen the next day, when the actual interview would take place. All I knew was that this person who had risen to a level of accomplishment that I couldn't even begin to comprehend had decided that I wasn't a phony or dilettante. Emotionally, it was a turning point for me as a professional writer.

Though interviewing Thunes was stressful, it was actually a breeze – if that makes any sense – because he showed me exactly how to engage him. We created a performance together, and as long as we played our parts and I respected his desire to communicate in the abrasive, outlandish way he'd chosen, he'd answer anything I asked. He was actually by far the least difficult of my interviewees.

The article, "Requiem for a Heavyweight?" was published in the March 1997 issue of *Bass Player.* Like the Gene Simmons interview, it generated an avalanche of mail. One letter stuck in my mind.

Bravo! Scott Thunes has my gratitude for giving a great interview. Not since Bill Laswell or Anthony Jackson has an interviewee shown the proper disdain for the effusive and sycophantic ways of writers like Thomas Wictor. I sincerely hope this magazine can bring us more such material – either by interviewing more musically conscious people like Thunes, or by sending writers like Wictor back to *Tiger Beat,* where their slack-jawed efforts are more at home. *Bass Player* could do with fewer interviewers who are primarily seeking validation for their mindless worship of their interviewees. On his way out the door, perhaps Wictor can take his annoying list of '80s-albums-now-mostly-unavailable (known as Unsung Bass Stylists) with him.[6]

Once again my pathological need to address what I saw as an injustice kicked in. The letter infuriated me – not because of the gratuitous savagery, but because my purpose had been so utterly misunderstood. I asked Karl if I could write a response, but he told me I had to learn to let these things roll off my back. The letter ate at me for years. I mentioned it on my long-defunct Web site in 2002, in a mile-long blatherfest I wrote about the nature of happiness. To my utter shock, the writer of the letter contacted me by e-mail and apologized. His apology was one of those "I'm sorry if you were offended" things and by the end of it he seemed to be backtracking, so I just wrote back "Buy my book and all is forgiven."

Today, looking at that letter that hurt me so much in 1997, my immediate reaction is, "Oh, so you're saying, 'Thanks for the great article. Now fire the guy who wrote it.' Brilliant!" Also, the letter writer didn't know that Thunes and I had achieved the same understanding that I'd arrived at with Gene Simmons. Though unspoken, our arrangement was for me to play straight man to a tour de force.

Both Simmons and Thunes perceived that my ego structure would allow them to use me as their foil. I'd not only let them "insult" me, I'd help them provide readers with an entertaining, informative piece that they'd never forget. My only goal was to create what I viewed as great art. Interviewing *is* an art. Simmons and Thunes understood my approach after interacting with me for half an hour or so. When Thunes saw me to my car after our five-hour interview, I reminded him that in our first phone conversation, he'd told me that I'd hate his guts by the end of the interview.

He frowned. "Did I say that?"

"You sure did."

"What a stupid, useless, pathetic thing to say," he mumbled.

Thank you, Gene and Scott, for providing me with the best interviews of my career.

And a note to the letter writer: Bill Laswell showed the proper disdain for my effusive and sycophantic ways in Tokyo, during his tour with Last Exit in 1986. I wasn't even a music journalist back then, just a twenty-four-year-old fan who recognized him on the street and tried to tell him how much I liked his bass playing. Drummer Ronald Shannon Jackson literally had to step in front of Bill to keep him from physically assaulting me. The man *really* doesn't like sycophants.

I've never met Anthony Jackson, but there's still time. I'll be sure to report it on my Web site if he holds me down and defecates on me or something.

Stealth Basher

At my first punk concert, I was given an all-access pass. I decided to watch the show from the right wing of the stage. The thing that fascinated me was the crowd surfing. To surf, a person climbed up on the crowd's shoulders and got passed around by hundreds of hands, tumbling like clothes in a drier. Surfing for a male ended quickly because soon he'd be pushed toward the stage and the security guards, who pulled him down off the hands and dropped him on his head in the dirt between the steel crowd barriers and the band. The male surfer would then be yanked to his feet and marched away.

Female surfers stayed up much longer, as everyone squeezed, fondled, pinched, and stroked them. The female crowd surfers were always passive, riding the molesting hands with blank faces as dozens of boys fought to reach them and tear at their clothing, groping under their shirts and reaching inside their jeans. Instead of passing female crowd surfers forward to the security guards, the crowd swallowed them back up. Female crowd surfers always sank down into the forest of arms and disappeared.

In the middle of the crowd was the mosh pit, which was just a large number of boys – never girls – running in a counterclockwise circle punching each other. Everybody gave them plenty of room, but even when the flailing fists connected with a non-mosher's face hard enough to poof out his or her hair in a graceful penumbra, like a pulsating jellyfish, no offense was taken. Everyone in the crowd was utterly expressionless. I learned that it's possible to yell, punch, and be punched without showing any emotion.

I saw only one person in that mass of humanity whose face wasn't as blank as a plate. She was a girl jammed up against the steel railing of the security pit. Every time a mosher crashed into her, she turned and screamed back over her shoulder. Male crowd surfers passed along to the security guards went right over her head. When they fell in front of her into the security pit, she showed her teeth and pummeled them with both fists while they were still in the air, landing two or three lightning-fast blows on each before he hit the ground. She was a thin-armed kid in a white tank top, and by the time I left the concert she'd pounded on at least fifty boys, expertly going for their kidneys and ribs. As the security guards escorted them out, the surfers grimaced, holding their sides or lower backs. The girl timed her punches with split-second precision so that nobody noticed what she was up to. I was the only one.

Of course I fell deeply in love with her.

On Writing, Values, and Unfathomable Loss

I interviewed bassist Chi Cheng of the Deftones on November 5, 1996. We got along fine, despite his well-known and justified disdain for music journalists. He showed no sign whatsoever of being ill at ease. Although I appreciated his dedication to his art, privately I wondered if he were genuinely indifferent to critics.

Now I know that it's entirely possible to not care in the slightest how strangers view that which you create primarily for yourself. Such unconcern comes when you finally recognize the what's important and what isn't. I wish I'd been able to cultivate that mindset back when it would've helped me in my own writing career.

However, they grow them tough in Sacramento. Cheng is in a different league from me.

I never do interviews myself, so they're pretty much all quotes from the other guys in the band.

You don't like giving interviews?
I'd prefer to do zero interviews because I don't think the questions people ask ever really get towards the intrinsic nature of most people. They're kind of superficial and they don't really try to get to know you as a musician. I prefer two people to just have a conversation. I think that a lot of interviewers have preconceived notions of what artists are or what they should be, as opposed to just looking at the personality of the musician.

That's why I don't even trust the Bible. See, it *could* be the word of God, but it went through a man. It went through his hand, it filtered through his system, and he put in his own learned behaviors and his preconceived notions, so even if it *was* the word of God, it kind of got flipped around. I do the same thing with my writing. I've been writing for twelve years, and when I write, you'd better believe that it's everything I've gone through and everything that I'm doing. It gets focused into my writing.

What kind of writing?
Poetry.

Does any of it ever end up as a song?
Nah. Too strange. Yeah, it's really crazy. I write a really weird style. It's cool. I had the lucky experience of one of my old professors in college liking my writing so much that she had me come in and tutor one of her advanced poetry classes. It was really cool. I don't fool with iambic pentameters, meters, none of that stuff. I did learn a little bit of it, but it's just another constraint, you know? I mean, if you write honestly, if you write passionately, then everything you write is all right. And I don't write for anybody else.

That seems to be pretty important to you, the idea that what you're presenting has to be passionate and honest and very emotional.
It is. That's how my belief on life systems is. If you're going to do something, jump in feet first and have passion and honesty and love when you do it, or don't do it at all.

So what happens if you put something out there and people don't get it or it bombs?
Oh, I couldn't give a shit. I know I put everything that I had into it, and it was honest and came from the source, and everything I had went into it, so I could really care less. It'd be great if I could be financially secure. You know, I have a baby coming. It would be great if I was able to not worry about bills. But you know what? It doesn't really matter. You know what I mean? As long as I know I'm putting everything I have into it, that's what matters. I used to build houses as a carpenter. You know, frames or whatever. I would put everything I had into it, do the best I can, and not have any regrets in life. It's not really about the end product. It's more about the love and the passion and the honesty that you put into the work. *That* is actually the achievement, not really the end product.

There would be a lot of people in this industry who would say that approach is just opening you up to being smashed on the head because this is a really cold-blooded business.
Yeah. But I would rather be smashed on the head than change the way I am.

Because I'd assiduously ignored the music industry since 2003, I didn't know until I wrote this book that on November 4, 2008, Chi Cheng was nearly killed in a car accident. He suffered traumatic brain injury that has left him in a minimally conscious state. I debated whether or not to include this short story in my book, worried that his family and friends might be upset by the cruel irony of his phrasing. Ultimately, since I believed what Chi said about honesty being vital, I decided I owed it to him to relay his words unfiltered.

The conversation was extremely wide ranging. We discussed things that had little to do with music, and I enjoyed our time together. This scary looking, hard-core player and I had much in common. Like me – and every woman I've loved – he abhorred being photographed.

After a while, material things, monetary things, things that we deem valuable – they don't glimmer anymore. Once you have them, you're like, "Eh." You're unfulfilled. The sense of belonging that you're missing is that traditional, old-school Godhead that you want to get back to. Old harmony that we used to have being at one with nature. We tend to have lost it. We taught ourselves to unlearn everything we already know. Everyone has the answers to everything, but we taught ourselves to unlearn it. It could all be bullshit, but it makes sense to me. When I was framing houses, it was such a beautiful lifestyle.

You know, I'm real camera shy. I don't like taking photos either. The aborigines say the camera steals your soul. It's just another thing taken from you. In this line of work, I do get photos of me taken – I have to – but I hardly ever look the camera in the face. I'm not trying to look like a serious guy. I mean, I'm a pretty lighthearted person. I have a good time. But I don't like to be photographed. It makes me pretty uncomfortable. It's another thing taking a piece of you away. I don't even have that many photos from my wedding.

You have to work within the system. It's like life: You take the cards you're dealt and make with them what you can.

He figured things out long before I did. I hope I was able to change his mind a little about music journalists.

Donations to support his continued treatment can be made at www.oneloveforchi.com.

Second Interview with the Collateral Ghost

By early 1997, I couldn't get Scott Thunes out of my mind. It was imperative that I *do* something for him. First I begged him to let me ghostwrite his memoirs. He refused. I then decided to write a novel about the L.A. music scene, and after months of my harassment he finally agreed to talk to me as a technical advisor. I drove back up to the Bay Area and checked into a motel, just in time for my '80 Toyota Corolla to break down. After I had the EGR valve replaced, I met with Thunes. He gave me a massive, brilliant, funny, wildly engrossing interview on May 4, 1997, as we sat beside a brook in the great outdoors and ate sandwiches.

This was many years ago, and both of us were under myriad pressures. *Bass Player* offered Scott a job as a columnist after the success of our interview, but the deal had fallen through. I believe that my first interview caused him to relive a lot of painful experiences, which was never my intention; I only wanted to tell his story. The aftermath of my first interview contributed to my haunting by Scott because it seemed that I'd only created more problems for him. Part of the reason I pursued him was to make up for both what I'd done and the injustice of his situation. Like me, he was a person whose intentions were often misunderstood. He was ignored and viciously denigrated. I felt an obsessive drive to right the wrongs and help him.

Scott is a man of genius and total recall, so he'll understand when I reveal that the rest of our time together didn't go well. Neither of us handles stress well, and we have trouble reining ourselves in. My original plan was to stay in the motel, but Thunes wanted me to see a concert of Béla Bartók music the day after I was to check out. Since there was a regatta or some such absurdity going on in San Francisco, I couldn't extend my stay in the motel. The Thuneses agreed to put me up for a couple of days. During that period things got so out of hand I had to physically react and then warn Scott that unless he stopped what he was doing, I'd punch him in the face as hard as I could.

"Very nice! Very nice! God, you're so *fast!*" he said, not knowing I'd studied martial arts for years. I also lifted weights and did aerobics. Though fat, I've always been very strong and very quick. After the Bartók concert, I announced that the music had so energized me that I would now drive back to L.A. It was 11:00 P.M. "I love night driving!" I said. "It gives me a chance to think!" A load of crap. I hate driving at night.

Thunes begged me to stay, telling me I was acting crazy, but I was adamant. I tanked up on three cups of powerful, fresh-brewed coffee, accepted a sack of warm, grilled-chicken sandwiches on French bread prepared for me by Scott's father-in-law, allowed Scott to hug me, and hit the road. By myself again, I screamed in exultation. During the nightmarish seven-hour sojourn back to Los Angeles, I stopped frequently for more coffee, put my head out the window into the slipstream, slapped myself, and sang to keep awake.

At 5:45 A.M., outside Pasadena – an hour from home – my car broke down again.

Ghost in the Magazine

During the second day I spent in Scott Thunes's house, I idly picked up a magazine and flipped through it. The fifth or sixth page I looked at showed a photo of my first ghost, Brigitte Cardei from the Netherlands, all grown up and living in Los Angeles. She was an entrepreneur whose business served members of the entertainment industry. It was unquestionably my old unrequited flame and shade: same unusual name and beautiful face. She hadn't changed much at all since 1977. When I got home I sent a letter to the magazine, asking if they could forward it to her, but I never got a response. Though I looked her up, I couldn't find her.

Ultimately, I decided that it was probably a good thing. She was successful and well connected, while I still limped along. We'd have nothing to say to each other. Even so, it was nice to see her again, if only in a two-dimensional image.

A Warning from a Writer? Ignored. How *Strange!*

At around this time, I met a very famous music journalist who told me, "There are no successful freelance writers, except for the ones who write for East Coast publications and are given million-dollar retainers."

Since he was a great writer, I asked him why he didn't try to get a job with a magazine like that.

"Because that wouldn't even be a question of selling out; it'd be entering a stratum of emotional and professional compromise that I literally can't imagine. I'd have to change my entire life. It's a self-contained society, with inviolable rules. Besides, they'd never have me. It's invitation only, and it requires a much better wardrobe than I'm capable of putting together. Writing is a pathetic existence anyway, and in music journalism you have to get detached about something you used to love. You have to write about bands you hate, and you can't be in it for the long haul because there *is* no long haul. You wake up one morning and you're forty-five and you're still making a pittance.

"I know a guy in his forties, and he assesses the value of musical events based on the quality of the free food. He lines his coat pockets with aluminum foil and fills them with brownies and egg rolls and pot stickers and kebabs, watches the shitty new band, and then goes home with enough food for three days. I don't want to become that guy, but the way it is now, no magazine is going to hire me and pay the astronomical rates I deserve unless I know somebody there. They can get a twenty-three-year-old who'll do it for less than a third of what I'd charge. Also, they wouldn't have to put up with him spouting off about music being an important sociological force, the way I do."

He's no longer a writer, but he's happy. I e-mailed him excerpts from this book.

His reply.

I'm glad you've made peace with it to whatever extent is possible. Otherwise, interesting stuff (as expected) and certainly bringing on waves of my own disillusioned nostalgia for that business/time; would love to read more but might ask you for reimbursement if doing so causes a need for expensive self-medication.

Seriously, congrats on all of it and thanks for getting in touch.

Two Pitches, One Strike

While I was in *Bass Player* editor Karl Coryat's office asking him if I could interview Ray Shulman, the phone rang. It was a bassist I'd pitched to Karl by phone a week earlier. Extremely famous in the bass world, he's hardly a household name. He's also a notoriously arrogant, opinionated man, technically brilliant but whose work has always left me cold. I wanted to interview him because I figured we could have a nice, big, theatrical fight the way Simmons, Thunes, and I had. The main topic of discussion would be how he defends himself against charges that his playing doesn't emotionally engage the listener.

I got up to leave, but Karl motioned me to sit. Though Karl didn't put the call on the speaker and I couldn't hear the bassist's voice, it was clear he demanded the cover or nothing. Karl said he didn't make deals.

Then Karl said, "The writer who wants to do the article is sitting here in the room. Do you want to talk to him?"

He didn't.

Nothing was resolved. In the end I didn't get to interview him. I've never asked Karl why my idea was assigned to a different writer, but I believe that somebody didn't want me to be the interviewer. The person or people who made the decision wanted to showcase the bassist's playing techniques and sweeping pronouncements, which didn't interest me as much as his story, personality, and the opportunity to challenge him.

When the call ended, Karl – who was usually a hip, snarky guy – slumped and said, "Sometimes I wonder if it's worth it. You put your heart and soul into this, and people hate you for it." I knew what he meant. One letter to the editor they printed said, "I'm still scratching my head over Wictor's statement that John Taylor is a brilliant bassist." Karl asked me if I wanted to respond. I did, sending in two sentences.

> If you're still scratching your head after three years, you need to see a doctor right away because that means your cholinergic brain synapses have stopped releasing the acetylcholinesterase that neutralizes the neurotransmitter acetylcholine, which is responsible for initiating voluntary motion. You could end up scratching your head forever!

Of course it didn't run. Nobody would've known what to make of it.

I left Karl a pile of Gentle Giant CDs to help him make up his mind about Ray Shulman. A few weeks later he gave me the go ahead.

Noise, Forearms, and Buttocks

In my career as a music journalist, I got to see one music video being filmed. It was the most chaotic scene I've ever witnessed. The set was a fire station's five-story drill tower, the artificial building that firefighters use for training. It was wrapped in sheets of blood-red Mylar and surrounded by blinding klieg lights on stands. In front of the tower, a man and a camera sat on a boom-mounted platform attached to a heavy wheeled base that resembled a sports-utility vehicle. The platform was raised forty feet into the air and then swung rapidly to within inches of the lead singer's nose as he lip synched to the band's single. Hundreds of pounds of metal careened right at the man's face, stopping at the last second, but he didn't even flinch. I was told that those platforms were computer controlled and virtually foolproof.

I thought, *virtually* foolproof?

The band's single roared out of stadium-quality speakers set up around the drill tower. They were cranked up so high my earplugs had no effect. The music competed with shouted directions emanating from somewhere overhead, an unintelligible Zeus-like raging that completely fuzzed out the unseen PA system. Nobody seemed to pay any attention to it.

Maybe nobody could *hear* the director. Every few minutes, the segmented metal doors of the brick firehouses rolled up, screeching in agony, and fire engines exploded into action with whooping sirens and blatting horns. I had no idea how many engines a fire battalion had; there were dozens in this one. The fire station had its own PA system, too, which broadcast beeps, earsplitting clicks, and frantic, roaring gibberish.

Since Burbank-Glendale-Pasadena Airport was only three miles away, jet airliners thundered in 200 feet overhead, the earth-shattering blast of their turbofans drowning out everything else I've described. It was like Armageddon.

Camera platform, lights, and studio PA system required miles of heavy electrical cable, thick black and gray coils strewn everywhere like dinosaur intestines. They snaked in and out of the eight enormous trucks parked around the drill tower. A long table was set up off to the side, covered with plates, bowls, and metal trays full of pasta, potato salad, and sandwiches. According to strict union rules, food had to be available all day.

The brawny firefighters who hadn't been called away stood around with their arms folded. Equipped with Ray Ban sunglasses and huge mustaches, they watched the production assistants, a drove of young, blonde women in revealing clothes. The outfit of choice for the assistants was either skintight jeans and baby tees, or skintight wraparound skirts and platform shoes. Skirted or jeansed, the women all had walkie-talkies tucked into their waistbands, multitudes of clacking bracelets on their wrists, and no underwear.

On one side was a phalanx of immense chests girded by powerful forearms, and on the other a parade of proud, jiggling buttocks. Much smoldering eye contact was made between the opposing forces. I remembered reading that according to surveys, firefighters had sex more times per week than men of any other profession. I wondered if the production assistants knew that. They didn't strike me as the reading types.

One question was answered, the reason why the quality of music videos had gotten so abysmal. Everyone was deaf, stuffed to the gills with greasy food, and swamped by hormones.

Simply Irresistible

After dinner with Roger and Dolores, we stopped on the way home so he could buy them their nightly wine. Dolores and I stayed in the car. She sat sideways in the back seat, her legs stretched out and crossed at the ankles. In her faded jeans, long-sleeved shirt, vest, and motorcycle boots, she looked like James Dean in the famous poster for *Giant*.

"You know, I'm sorry things didn't work out for you with that girl," she said.

"Thanks. It's all right. She was completely insane and evil."

"On the other hand, we were afraid you wouldn't be available to us anymore. It'll happen sooner or later. You'll meet someone, and then you won't hang out with us anymore."

"You're not in any danger of me meeting anyone anytime soon," I said.

She sighed. "You *really* don't know how irresistible you are do you?"

"Irresistible in a repulsive sort of way."

"Don't talk like that. Any woman with any taste will be interested in you, and then after you get together with her, we'll never see you again."

"We could all go out together."

"No. That wouldn't be the same. We want you all to ourselves. Roger really likes you, and he hates *everybody,* even me. You're his only friend. How many women have you slept with, Tom?"

I told her.

"That's not bad. It's the minimum number you need."

"For what?

"Oh, I don't know. I'm drunk. I don't know what I'm talking about. I just said that."

Roger returned with the wine. "What'd I miss?" he asked.

Dolores yawned. "We were talking about how many women Tom's slept with."

"Did you tell him how many people we've slept with?"

"No, because we have no idea, Bunny-boo." She put her cool hand on the back of my neck. "One time we decided to count, to see how many people we'd been with before we were married. It got to the point where we were having to write things like 'girl in yellow dress' and 'guy in Irish bar.' It was ridiculous. We gave up. There was just no way to know."

"You wrote a *list?*" I asked.

"Yes."

"Why would you write it down?"

"To have."

After a while, I said, "Was it fun? Being with so many people?"

"You know, I don't even remember."

At their house, I told them I was convinced I was a total failure at everything.

Dolores looked back over her shoulder at Roger and said in wide-eyed, campy earnestness, "But *we're* failures, *too,* aren't we, Snooper?" He nodded gravely.

"How are you failures?" I asked.

"In all ways."

She stretched, arching her back, lifting her legs off the floor, and making little squeaks. Then she got up and went over to Roger and leaned against him. He slipped his hand into her open collar, gripping her shoulder.

"We're *incredible* failures," she said as she caressed his arm. "But it's not so bad. It could be worse. It *will* be worse because someday we'll be *old* failures."

Conversation with a Giant

On July 14, 1997, I was granted the rare experience of having a dream fulfilled when I interviewed my bass idol, Ray Shulman of Gentle Giant. It was a phoner, but he may as well have been sitting across the table from me in my dining room. I can't describe the thrill it was to finally speak with the person who'd influenced me in so many ways and whose work always cheered me up, no matter how badly I felt about everything. When overcome with the knowledge that my life was a farcical shambles, I'd just put on "Free Hand," "Working All Day," "River," "The Runaway," "The Power and the Glory," or "Mobile," and I'd forget for a while.

To my immense relief, Ray was a perfect gentleman who answered all my questions willingly and without hesitation. Though I was sad that he didn't play bass anymore, he made it clear it was a decision he'd made for himself, and he didn't miss it. That was the only time he spoke with a trace of heat, obviously tired of answering this question from fanboys like me. It was *his* life, he said, and he couldn't live it for others.

He'd been deeply disappointed by the gradual diminution of Gentle Giant, due to the demands of record labels, and by the end of the band's existence in 1980 he didn't even enjoy it anymore. Despite his bad experiences, he'd moved on. He spoke to me without a shred of anger, bitterness, or negativity; interviewing him erased much of the melancholy I felt over the group's demise. Ray helped me see that often it really is better for things to end than continue on for the sake of the past and at the cost of the participants' well-being.

And yet I *still* didn't perceive the stark warning given and the example set for me by another musician, in this case the one I admired the most. If I couldn't hear it from Ray Shulman, then the die was cast. Which it was.

You'd Better Be Nice in My Store

With my additional Scott Thunes material safe on two cassette tapes, I decided to begin writing my novel about the L.A. music industry. One of the characters was a collectibles dealer. To do research I went to a store and asked the owner if I could interview him. I brought copies of *Bass Player* to show him I was a "real" writer, and he agreed. A few days later I showed up with my tape recorder; we chatted as he worked. He was an older man, very muscular, with rimless glasses and a salt-and-pepper beard. After we'd been talking for an hour, he said, "Hey, why don't we lock up, pull down the curtains, and get to know each other better?"

I lied and said, "Well, I'm spoken for."

"He's a lucky guy," he said, and we went on with the interview.

At least now I knew why butch women are attracted to me.

The best story he told is this one.

It's important that my customers be nice, because so many of the dealers are insufferable. They're especially nasty to me because I won't give them a discount. I've taken the time and money to stock thousands of items, and I refurbish most of them, too. A lot of the stock has to be reupholstered, rewired, refinished, polished, or thoroughly cleaned, so I'm not going to give some guy 10 percent off just because he's a dealer. And most of them don't even try to refurbish their own stuff. They pick up an item at a garage sale or estate sale for a dollar and try to sell it as is for fifty, and when they can't, they count it as a forty-nine-dollar loss and whine that they're not making any money. They're an incredibly jealous group of people, too. They hate the idea that another dealer might make a bigger profit, so they'll sell something to me for sixty dollars instead of thirty because they know I'm going to refinish it and sell it for more anyway. They basically hate anyone who's successful. That's fine. If they want to pay astronomical rents on their stores and then stock them with garbage, wonderful. But when they come in my store, they have to be nice or I throw them out.

I've only had to get physical with someone once, when this guy came in and I was talking to another customer, a really nice guy who always buys a lot, and so this other guy starts clearing his throat really loudly – *hruh-um, hrruh UM* – and going "Excuse me! Exkeeeee*youuuuuuuuuuuse* me!" and waving. So I went over and he asked me if some pieces in a glass case were rare. He kept interrupting me as I tried to tell what they were. "Yes, but are they *rare? Are they rare?"* I told him I didn't know. I mean, if you see them all over town, they're not rare, are they? He was really aggressive, and when I asked him what he collected, he didn't even respond. He's picking up stuff, asking what it is, and saying, "Is it rare? Well, is it?" Finally, I knew he wasn't a dealer or even a collector. He was just a moron, so I told him I didn't have time for this and I asked him to leave.

He got all sniffy and said, "Aren't you just the sales clerk?" I told him, "Yeah, I am, and I'm also the bouncer. Now get out." He said, "Okay, I'll take these doorknobs," and I said, "No, you won't. You're leaving," and I took the doorknobs out of his hand and put them on the counter. So he walked to the door, mumbling and looking around, and I knew he was going to do something, like maybe smash something or kick something over, so I ran up behind him and grabbed him by the back of the collar and shoved him through the door. And even then, out on the sidewalk, he *still* wasn't through. He was looking for something to throw through the window, so I went outside and said, "Was there something else?" and he finally went away.

"Is it rare?" All I could think of was the "Is it safe?" scene in *Marathon Man*.

The Letter the Radio Talk-show Host Never Forgot

On August 31, 1997, I heard on the radio that Princess Diana had been killed. A female talk-show host who specialized in mind-boggling sadism announced it. While the news of Diana's death saddened me, the talk-show host's actions were infuriating. She celebrated Diana's death. First she giggled, "Uh-oh! Looks like we're gonna need a new princess!" She said the accident was not a tragedy, because Diana had done nothing except marry well and party, and it was no great loss. "What am I supposed to do?" she'd sneer at angry callers. "Hang black crepe all over the studio? I can't help it. I think this is funny." At one point she sang, *"Diana's dead and I wanna go home"* to the tune of the "Banana Boat Song."

She had a calmly avid glee – a genuine cheerfulness – that I recognized right away. It was the same joviality expressed by Noreen, the cruelest person I've ever known. This talk-show host and Noreen were happiest when inflicting pain. The more outraged people became on the phone, the warmer and more contented the talk-show host sounded. I decided to do something for Diana. And for myself.

First I went out and bought a porn mag and found a full-page, close-up photo of a gaping, larger-than-life vagina, the lips artfully held open by beringed, well-manicured fingers. I then typed up every personal thing the talk-show host had discussed on the air, including her terrible childhood, her ludicrous marriage, and her cosmetic surgery. Here's what I wrote.

> Hi, I'm [withheld]! I like to puke up all my self-loathing on the air! In fact, I hate my vacuous husband even more than I hate myself! I only married him because I knew nobody else would have me. The reason I'm such a sadist is because I'm fat; I'm already thirty-eight; my facelift made me look worse; and all I have going career-wise is this ridiculous show. My life is headed nowhere but downhill from here, so the only thing left for me to do, as I age horribly and become even more mentally ill, is have kids! Yeah, that's it! I'll make them pay for what my own parents did to me, and that way I can be sure that there's someone in this world who's even more miserable than I am. But before I mindlessly breed like the bitter, saggy, desperate cow I am, maybe another person worth five thousand of me will be killed, and then I can whoop it up some more!

After printing it, I cut it out of the paper in the shape of a word balloon, glued it to the photo of the vagina, mounted the whole thing on cardboard, and sent it to her at the station. A week later the talk-show host brought it up on the air. Although she didn't have the guts to read the text out loud and actually hid it from her staff, she spoke of the photo.

"This doesn't bother me at all! I'm a big girl! I can take it! What kind of buffoon would do this? What kind of no-life idiot would send something like this to me? Do you think stuff like this hurts me? I love it! Send me more!"

She spent an entire hour insisting that it hadn't bothered her, and she made it sound as though it were random hate mail unconnected with Diana's death. Finally, she said I had bad taste in porn, because that vagina was one truly ugly orifice, all raggedy, dark, and asymmetrical. Her only concern was that I'd used some lawyer's return address on the envelope, and she felt sorry for the poor schmuck whose name was dragged into this idiotic prank. I'd indeed put a return address on the envelope, which was this.

Bair Akuda, Esq.
Attorney At Law
12345 N. South Street, Suite X
Beverly Hills, CA 90210

I sent her a follow-up card – a Hallmark.

> To My Special Friend:
> Boy, am I flattered! Thanks for spending a whole hour of 50,000-watt broadcast time on my little project. When you say it didn't bother you, you know what? I believe you. I really do. And by the way, speaking of buffoons, "Bair Akuda, Attorney At Law" is not a real name. See, "Bair Akuda" is a homophone of "barracuda," a popular term used to describe particularly aggressive lawyers. And "N. South Street"? I'm sorry it all went over your head. I completely overestimated your intelligence.
> In closing, do you really think I *randomly* chose a picture of the ugliest vagina in the world?
> Yours,
> Bob Dole

Unlike the vagina, this card went unacknowledged.

But now my special friend knows who sent both items.

Bad Mask

A musician friend told me about a great jazz player who used both electric and acoustic bass. He lent me the bassist's CDs, which were terrific. She was a heck of a slapper on both instruments. My friend gave her my number, and she called, excited about getting in *Bass Player*. She said it was a dream come true and invited me to a show in Pasadena. The only problem was that I didn't know what she looked like because the CDs had no photos of her band, just artistic fifties-style designs. My friend therefore gave me a newspaper clipping that showed a young woman with dark hair and a cute, girl-next-door face. Very sweet looking.

The night of the show, I went to the club and introduced myself to the manager, asking where the bassist was. He pointed toward a woman in a dark suit standing with her back to me. I went over and called her name.

When she turned around, I almost screamed. She'd had a total plastic-surgery makeover that included cheek implants the size of Ping-Pong balls, giant trout lips, a forehead lift to give her those angry-eyebrows, Botox, an eyelid job, and a chin implant. Since there was loud music playing over the PA system, she leaned toward me to speak, and I'm sorry to say I recoiled. That sweet, pretty face was gone. I felt so bad for her I wanted to cry.

The show was excellent. Great acoustic and electric soloist. But I was terrified that her new face would make the readers laugh. I didn't want the magazine to print nasty letters about her. We arranged for me to confirm with my boss, and then I'd get back to her about when to set up an interview. My plan was to ask her to provide pre-surgery images if she could.

"Say, if you already have some photos, that'd be cool, you know?"

Karl okayed the article, and then something typically L.A. happened: She would not commit. I called her and she said she was too busy to do it at that moment, but she'd call me back. Weeks went by; I called again and got the same answer. Finally, I made one last call in the afternoon, and she sounded half-asleep. I'd woken her up, she said. She'd been out all night on a gig.

"Okay, I'll call you later. Go back to sleep."

I never called her again, and she never called me. For those of you who don't live in Los Angeles, the weirdest thing about this place is nobody commits to anything, even when it's in their own best interest. You could tell someone, "Meet me at that sushi bar on Sunset, and I'll give you a suitcase with ten million dollars in cash," and they'd say, "Sure!" and then they'd never show up.

That bassist is still playing, and she's still great. Her face is much better today than it was the last time I saw her. I still think, however, that if she'd just let herself turn into a mature woman, she'd look absolutely fine.

In the Closet

I interviewed the bassist of a band that was big in the seventies and had experienced a significant revival. Things had gone so well I was invited to a show as my reward. The publicist said my tickets and a special pass to the after-party would be left for me at the will-call window.

Although I'd appreciated the bassist's skill, I was never a fan of the band. To me, the music was neither fish nor fowl, too bombastic to be pop but too bubblegum to be rock. I always thought of the group as a novelty act with a cult following, like Meat Loaf. On the cusp of forty, I was the youngest person in the audience and onstage. Almost everyone in the audience had a giant beer gut, even the women, and they all went, "*Woooooooo! Woooooooooo!*" the whole time.

The singer, guitarist, and bassist sang as loudly as they could, screaming and straining with every fiber of their beings to hit the high notes. I'd learned at the interview that all four band members were chain smokers. At this performance they kept having to clear their pipes, hawking and spitting constantly. The stage lights illuminated the flying material; it looked like the band spat nuggets of gold.

After the show, the hall emptied instantly, and the people with the special passes were herded into a room the size of a closet. There were about twelve of us: me; a six-foot, three-inch transvestite in fishnet stockings; a couple of elderly women; a 600-pound man; a 400-pound woman; three or four nervous Japanese girls; a woman with two-inch-thick glasses and an LP of the band; and a couple of genderless Goths. We stood there staring at each other for a while.

"Ekthkeeyooth me," the transvestite said to me. He had a giant silver tongue stud. "Do you know where I can find a tekthy?"

"I don't know what a tekthy is," I replied.

"A tekthy. Tekthy. Tee-ay-ekth-ai."

"Ah. No, I don't know where you can find a taxi. Sorry." After about twenty minutes, I stepped out of the closet to get some air. A security guard immediately appeared and said, "Are you with these people?"

"Of course I am," I said. "Who else would I be with?"

"What?"

"Nothing. Sorry." I went back into the closet.

Half an hour later, the same security guard opened the closet door and told us we all had to go because the concert hall was about to be closed.

"Where's the band?" somebody protested.

"At the hotel. They left an hour ago."

"What about the party?" the whole tiny crowd except for me wailed in one voice.

He laughed. "*Party?*" There's no *party!*" I've never seen such amused contempt on a face in my life. He found us absolutely inexplicable, like people wearing clothes made out of cheese slices. So we filed out of the closet, through the empty hall, onto the street, and went our separate ways. Someday we may have a reunion.

Friendships and Marriages in L.A.

One night Roger, Dolores, and I went to see *Sling Blade*. I hated the movie so much it made my head hurt, so I put myself to sleep to escape it. I woke up hearing in my right ear a breathy murmuring of my name: "Tom. Tom. Tom," spoken with such tenderness, understanding, and acceptance. Whispered with the sort of affection you hear only a few times in your life, it was an incantation that flooded my body with a swirling, scalp-tingling rush. I pretended to remain out a little longer, until Dolores settled her hand on my shoulder. She didn't shake it; she just held me, her touch warm and soft, and then I had to open my eyes. Such a smile, from that lush-lipped, cat-eyed, classically Semitic face, only inches from my own.

We went to a Thai restaurant and ordered, and then something happened that caught me so much by surprise I honestly believed I'd instantly gone insane, as though I'd been dosed with some top-secret, colorless, odorless psycho-gas. Completely out of the blue, Dolores began flaying her husband alive, dissecting him, exposing and examining his every fault, foible, and shortcoming.

"You loser," she hissed. "What, are you going to cry now?" She threw out her hand, appealing to me as her witness. Her eyeballs looked hot and glistening but not with moisture. They looked varnished instead.

"Just look at him. He makes me sick. You make me sick, you know that? Huh? I gave you the best years of my life, I gave you my youth, and you took it away and gave me nothing in return. You lied to me, you sick fucker, you bastard. You selfish son of a bitch, you shit. When are you going to get off your ass and do something with your life so I don't have to work myself to death for you? When are you going to do your share, you fucking loser?"

And he sat there, mumbling, "Oh. Okay. Sure. Hmm? Ah. I guess. Well. Huh." It was like one of those old Beat poetry recitations, one person producing a waterfall of words and the other playing a tom-tom. Dinner came and we silently ate. I was dizzy with shock. Counting Dolores, I'd now heard the exact same attack from three different women. The fact that this time it was directed toward someone else made it no less harrowing.

When I left them at their house an hour later, they were cuddled together in a chair. She sat on his lap, her arms around his neck, giving him kisses on the side of his forehead and calling him her "little Pooter-wooter" in a squeaky, baby-doll voice. He leaned back with a big, sloppy grin, his eyes half-closed, chin thrust forward and the corners of his mouth pointed upward in an expression of idiotic contentment. He looked like a perfect imbecile; all he needed was a dunce cap. But I was the real imbecile because it took me years to disengage from them.

Flashback: L.A. in Tokyo

In March of 1988, the lead singer of my band A Window, Steiv Dixon, invited a friend from Los Angeles to visit him. When she arrived, he said he was too busy to see her, so would I mind showing her the sights? I agreed. I'll call her Samantha, even though her real name was so contrived and L.A.-actressy that I'm tempted to reveal it. You'd howl. It wasn't SanDeE* like in the movie *L.A. Story* but something just as laughable.

By the way, *L.A. Story* has one of the most moving scenes ever filmed, when Steve Martin changes the weather and reverses the earth's polarity with his mind in order to keep the woman he loves from exiting his life. The song is Enya's "Exile." Pure art on every possible level. It's on a par with Nicole Kidman returning to rescue Sam Neill in *Dead Calm*. Absolutely wrenching, but in a good way. Watch both scenes alone, because you'll sob.

Samantha was ferociously beautiful, with a big nest of curly hair and a penchant for miniskirts, the better to show off her racehorse legs and high, round bottom. Initially we got along so well that I really enjoyed her company. Since Carmen and I were on the outs after another of her drunken fiascos, I was unattached. Samantha and I hit tourist spots, rented videos, and went out to dinner. Then, as we swayed back and forth amongst silent Japanese on a train, hanging on to the hand straps, she said that our destinies must've brought us together. Ours was a fated meeting of two like minds, an inevitable fulfillment of a preordained encounter.

"Well, maybe not," I said, chuckling.

"Don't you believe in destiny?" she asked.

"Sure, but we're just getting along here. Destiny is when you meet your soul mate or something along those lines." I thought about telling her what I'd experienced the first time I laid eyes on Carmen. Before I could, she started yelling at me.

"What the hell is the matter with you? Are you so close minded that you won't even *think* about the possibility that we were destined to meet? Are you making fun of me?"

Suddenly, I was in another fight with a woman, this time with a stranger, our conflict coming out of nowhere and being about nothing. It was a kind of satire of the endless problems Carmen and I had. Samantha pouted for a few hours before returning to her formerly cheerful self. Years later, when I heard Cornholio on *Beavis and Butthead* say, "Are you threatening me?" I almost died laughing. That's exactly what Samantha sounded like, a gibbering cartoon.

"Are you making fun of me?"

I should've shouted, "*Yes! Because you're like a circus act! What the hell's wrong with you?*"

Two days after our train-fight, Samantha asked, "How come you never open up to me?"

"Open up to you?"

"Yeah. You never talk about yourself. Your fears, your problems, what you're really thinking. You close me out."

When I realized she was serious, I said, "Well, Samantha, you're only going to be here two weeks. I don't know you. I don't open up to people except really close friends."

"Oh, so that's the way it is, huh? I thought you were my friend, but I guess I was wrong. Okay, fine. From now on we'll be totally superficial. We won't talk about anything important since it's so hard for you."

The next day, she held true to her word. The entire time we were together, she said things like, "Nice weather, isn't it? Sunny. Not too cold. Oh, look at that funny dog. Cute, isn't it? Boy, those are tall buildings, aren't they?" All day long. I didn't protest because it was too moronic to do anything about. I just counted the minutes until I could ditch her for the night.

One evening we bought sushi and beer, rented *Eight Million Ways to Die* and *Birdy,* and watched them at Steiv's apartment. Samantha wore a baggy sweatshirt and leotards. In the middle of *Birdy,* she announced, "I need to take off my bra."

I wondered what would happen if I said, "No! I absolutely forbid it!" Instead, I muttered my assent, curious to see what sort of show she'd put on.

What she did was that special trick some women have of somehow slipping the straps off their arms and then pulling the bra out of a sleeve, like a magician producing a rabbit from a top hat. I can always tell the moment when something clicks and people decide to start playing games with me. Samantha and I had reached that crossroads I'd been at hundreds of times in my life. I knew where things would lead from here on out.

A week later, she said Steiv's shower was too dirty for her, so she asked if she could use mine. I watched a video while she washed her remarkable chassis. After twenty minutes she opened the bathroom door and called me over. I found her standing there stark naked, toweling her hair.

"So whattaya wanna do now?" she asked. Her body was incredible, her pubic hair shaved into a racing stripe and the long nipples of her large breasts proudly erect.

"How about going to bed?" I asked. I didn't really want to because I didn't like her at all anymore, but when opportunity knocks...

She frowned. "Tom, are you *hitting* on me?" Standing there naked, with erect nipples, her perfect ass reflected in the mirror behind her, and her big, pink clitoris peeking out at me from under its hood, she projected betrayal and hurt, as though I were the last person on earth she'd expected to behave so inappropriately.

"No, I'm most certainly not hitting on you," I said. "Let's go have dinner and drink a whole lot."

She came out of the bathroom and into the living room naked, slowly laid out her clothes, stepped into her panties, and strapped on her bra while I sat and observed. Then we went out to dinner and drank a whole lot while we talked about trivia, Steiv's life before he came to Japan, more trivia, her life in L.A., and trivia.

By the time her visit ended, I was ready to kick her into the baggage hold of any airliner at Narita. Steiv told me that she said I was too intense for her. About a week after she left, I received a postcard.

> Dear Tom:
> I feel I really made a friend in you. We had a real meeting of the hearts and minds. Please write to me!
> All my love and all myself,
> Samantha.

Since the card had no return address, I wrote her only in my dreams.

No, actually I didn't even do that.

Steiv said that my personality encouraged people to mess with and dump on me. He called me the "Walking Catharsis Generator" because I never told anyone to shut the hell up and leave me alone. I let them get away with everything. Tim says it's a survival skill: placating the monster. Steiv himself never dumped on me, which shows how much he genuinely respected me.

I respect you back, Steiv. After writing this book, I realized that except for those times you'd see some Japanese hottie and eject from our night out together – and who could blame you, really, given that you must've known your time here was limited – you actually showed me more respect than practically anyone in my life, because you never once played games with me.

So thank you.

Endnotes
[1] See Thomas Wictor, *In Cold Sweat: Interviews with Really Scary Musicians* (New York: Limelight Editons, 2001), pp. 19-84.
[2] Matt Resnicoff, letter, *Bass Player,* September 1996, 6.
[3] Wictor, review of *Carnival of Souls: The Final Sessions,* by Kiss, *Bass Player,* May 1998, 72.
[4] Duff McKagan, interview with the author, August 29, 1996.
[5] See *In Cold Sweat,* pp. 163-297.
[6] Michael Wyzard, letter, *Bass Player,* May 1997, 6.

Interlude with Scott Thunes
Bass

If you're in a rock band and there's only four of you, like Bush, the only person that anybody cares about is the good-looking guy in front. If you're the bass player in Bush, you're going to get as little recognition as I did, but you're making so much money you don't give a flying fuck. You know, all that money that's coming in is going directly into your pocket. Most of the money that came in didn't really go into Frank's pocket, but it did help the tour, so I knew that they were paying for Frank, but it didn't matter who he had playing bass with him. People didn't come to see me. If somebody's going to go see Bush, how many people really love that Bush bass player? Do they go to see him?

The only thing that kept me from really worrying that I wasn't getting enough glory as a bass player was the fact that I knew that Arthur Barrow and Patrick O'Hearn were better than I was. They were far better. Patrick was a better technician and a more emotional player. Very good fretless player as well, which you have to look up to, no matter what. Arthur was a better technician. He was a powerhouse of genetically purified bass-playing technique. The fact that he could play these things on an instrument, whether it sounded good, whether it was too plastic-y or guitar-y or what, he was still far better and will always be better than I am. Frank has said the same thing. Arthur's better at the technical stuff, but I took more chances. I did a lot more things.

For some reason, "Black Napkins" is in my mind. The song alone has enough emotional impact for people that it doesn't matter what I do. You have to look at the song itself and find out why those notes are making you feel a certain emotion. Because all I'm doing is creating more of those notes, or creating more notes within an already beautiful structure, depending on what you think of as beautiful, if you think Frank's music is beautiful, or what have you. You would have to show me what part of what bit I'm doing that is beautiful, and I'll tell you why you're probably hearing just the rest of the music. If I was playing what I was supposed to be playing, without any extras at all, it still might sound beautiful to you, and you wouldn't know who did it.

I told you that thing about XTC's Colin Moulding the other day, where all those demos that I heard of Andy Partridge's were all the bass lines that I'd been hearing for years. There was no difference between those demos with Andy playing on them and Colin playing, except that Colin's a great bass player and he made them sound really good. But Colin plays some cool shit on his own songs, material that I know Andy didn't do, so I know he's good. He can create and perform really great bass lines. But at any point in time, you have no idea which is the composer, which is the performer, which is divine inspiration, and which is trying to impress some bird out in the fuckin' audience.

Why would a person ever play? Why am I playing that specific group of notes? What is it about the song that makes me want to play that specific group of notes? Am I playing more on purpose than that song deserves or requires because I'm bored? Am I trying to play a melody that I've heard a thousand times, and I'm just performing for the first time in this song? You know, at what point in time is that thing actually occurring? You don't know, and neither do I. Which is why I can't answer you why something is beautiful. You have to get into specifics with me. The beauty of being in tech support is I can say to a person, "I can't help you with what's going on, why you have this specific problem on the other side of this phone. You're going to have to send me the files. I have to see this."

This one guy was saying, "I've got this thing: I separate this line, and this whole thing shoots out." He sent me the file, and I spent fifteen minutes going *blam, blam, blam,* splitting corners, absolutely nothing went wrong. I looked at the second file, and there was this schmutz that was instantly created by him splitting this one line. Whole bunch of stuff was booted out into space like a dam busting, and I could've worked on that one file for thirty minutes, an hour, without getting that exact same result. But as soon as I saw that one thing, I knew where to punch the button. It happened for me. The people who did the program didn't know that that was possible. But unless I had actually seen the thing and held it in my hand, I couldn't know what the hell the guy was talking about.

You don't know, from instance to instance, why I have done something, and why it gives you an emotional reaction. In that Zappa fan magazine that was produced for quite some time, *Society Pages,* a guy named Den Simms would do all of these massive investigatory pieces on specific albums, and he was trying to give me some glory. All of these magazines came out after '88, and he was a friend of mine. He hung out with me in 1988. I've known him for twenty years, from College of Marin. He was trying to give me some glory. Nine years ago, he mentioned something that happened in one of the *Make a Jazz Noise Here* songs. And he – thank God for CDs – he was able to pinpoint exactly to the second, when I play this one amazing note. And it's just one of those "put the fourth in the bass" moments that makes everything change. He had a deeply emotional response to it.

But I can tell you that all that note does is create a very pretty chord. That pretty chord that I know for a fact is a major seven nine chord, is a very beautiful chord, but you do not expect to hear it there, especially if you're a Zappa fan. You don't expect to hear it there, because I don't know of any other bass players that decided to do that. I was the right kind of bored; I had enough information to make me dangerous; and I had enough leeway to shove in whatever I wanted and have it please the boss. There was never any question that what I was doing was weird. I never thought what I was doing was weird. I thought, "This is exactly what *everybody* should be doing." If I've got a space where I can put something in and make a difference, I'd better fuckin' do it, otherwise I'm not making my money. I'm not earning my cash.

It's *not* prosaic! Music is rules. Some of the most amazing music you have ever heard was based on very specific preconceived ideas by the composer, having nothing to do with whether or not he thought anybody else thought it was beautiful. *He* thought it was beautiful.

[A tiny, pale-blue butterfly lands on the back of Thunes's left hand. He doesn't seem to notice it. I watch in trepidation.]

I very much like a major seven nine chord. Major seven nine chords are excellent. They're fine.

You really expect me to crush that butterfly, don't you? I'm not the kind of guy who crushes butterflies. It's nice. It's beautiful. We're watching it. But I didn't invent it, and I didn't invent my bass lines. I can see these big boulders down there, and if I had the strength I would pick up one of these boulders and throw it into the water. All I had was strength to do something that nobody else was doing. To play a note that was already there. No, I did *not* invent my bass lines! What does that mean? You tell me what that means. We'll listen to the CD later at my house.

I really don't know what you're talking about. You'll have to send me the file, sir. No, you're not talking out of your anus. Nor am I out of mine. The problem is that most of the time art gets created by artists in ways that they themselves don't understand. When they do understand it, all they tell you is how they applied the rules that they know. And all I can tell you is that when I play a specific note against a specific chord, it is in general because I know what it's going to sound like, or I *don't* know what it's going to sound like.

Now, obviously I did enough I-don't-know-what-it's-going-to-sound-likes, and I-don't-know-how-Frank-is-going-to-appreciates that after a while, I could do them on purpose because I liked the sound of them. But that honestly depends on what he's going to do on top. I mean, if he played some ugly note on top, my beautiful note isn't going to mean anything. So it is a communication, and being made more beautiful because he's listening to me, and playing something akin to the change. I know that's not what you're thinking. You're hearing something specific in your mind that I cannot hear right now.

I can talk about my three-chord thing that I do in the "Drowning Witch" solo. It's probably all over *Guitar.* Frank's got like seventeen of them. We did one a night, so he's got two hundred to choose from. That is a B-minor chord. I play a B-minor seventh chord. A minor seventh chord is very beautiful. I like the sound of it. It's very pretty. "Black Napkins" is full of minor seventh chords. The minor seventh chord is a very easy way to make something beautiful: B, D, F-sharp, A.

The top part of a B-minor seventh chord is D, F-sharp, A, so if somebody's playing B down in the bottom, all's I have to do is play a D-major triad up on top, and I'll have a B-minor seventh chord. That is very beautiful. Now, what I did in "Drowning Witch" was B, D, A. That structure's really easy on the bass, and it's open because it has this fifth. It's not a closed-form chord. It's not a closed-form triad, which doesn't sound very good on the bass unless you've got a lot of treble. It's actually almost a stacked fifth, in a way. I'll get into that later: E, B, F-sharp.

Now, if I play E, D, F, and then D, F-sharp, C-sharp, that is the first part of the D-major chord: D, F-sharp, A. The next note up is C-sharp, which is a nine in B-minor. So if I play a D-major seventh chord over B-minor, I get a B-minor seven nine, but it's also a D-major seven chord, which is very pretty. So you're getting two separate beautiful chords for the price of one. D-major seven is very pretty. It sounds really good on the bass. It's got that open fifth. It totally rocks, yet there's a B down in the bottom, and you hear it as an extension to B-minor seven. Then I play a C-sharp minor chord: C-sharp minor seventh: C-sharp, E, G-sharp. Now that, over the B, makes a lot of weird notes. Every single one of them is not in the B-minor chord, so it's weird. But you know that it's a passing tone. That is jazz harmony. That's what jazz harmony is all about: filling in the notes on a melody.

If you've got a scale-wise melody, what are the notes that you're going to put underneath it? If you've got the one in the melody, you've got the one chord underneath. If you've got the two in the melody, are you going to keep that stationary, or are you going to move it up so you can have a closed-block harmony? That what trumpets and trombones and all that harmony shit is all about, making sure that you've got the right voice leading amongst all the notes that are going on below it. Have you heard any of that Charlie Parker tribute band Supersax? All that shit is stacked harmonies – diatonic stacked harmonies – and making sure you've got the weird notes in there. There's all these rules for that shit, that I only even slightly investigated back at College of Marin.

But I know that if you play diatonic seventh chords, you're going to get some pretty extended harmonies. It's very simple to do that, but it sounds really cool, and it's really easy. The first time I did it, it sounded really cool and I continued doing it. I made as many extensions as I could. Playing tenths is the same kind of thing. You can make your bass line into two instruments at the same time when you just do tenths. Make sure they're diatonic. Most people don't know how to do a diatonic scale. They wouldn't know how to do a D-minor scale. "I'm in the key of C-major; I'm gonna play a D-minor scale." That makes no sense! Why should you do that? You learn a little bit of jazz. You learn your modes. All the modes are is a way of teaching you how to make sure that your scale patterns are correct, no matter where you start. No matter what key you're in. And if you make a point of keeping your diatonic scale patterns precisely aligned as you play, starting wherever you're going to go, then it's going to sound good to you.

You can play a C-major scale, and then if you play a D-minor scale right afterwards, you're still going to sound like you're in C-major because all the notes in D-minor are in the key of C-major. All you're doing is starting on the two. E is virtually the same way. You're playing in the key of C-major, but you're starting on the E. That's why you have to learn your modes. That's all that means. That's all I did. Learned my modes.

I'm in B and I play a B-minor. What if I start on D? I've got to play a D-major seventh chord. If I do not, I will be outside of the key of D, and it'll sound horrible. Any bass player doing a lot of notes, maybe you don't know why that works. I do. The first note is minor. The two, in minor, is diminished, but most people don't play that. The note is supposed to be flatted. Most people don't play it. It's not that big of a change – it doesn't hurt your ear. You're not expecting whatever that note is to be there. But what most bass players have a problem with is when playing in the major key, they play the D as a major as well. The D has to be minor, to make it sound like it's still in the C-major universe. And most bass players don't know enough to change the mode. They didn't learn their modes. They don't know what a mode is. It doesn't matter. You don't need to know what a mode is to do this change correctly. All's you need to know is your diatonic scale patterns.

If you start on a D, you can't play a D-major scale. You can't. It will sound dumb, and odd, unless the guitarist is playing a D-major and he's supposed to, and you're about to go to the five, and all that kind of shit. But most people don't know enough of the rules to change the diatonic scale patterns enough to make it sound like they know what else is going on in the song. Most people don't know, and they don't care.

You listen to some band like Humble Pie, and that bass player's playing all the time, and the second they change a chord, you know that he's not thinking what that chord is that he's playing over, based on the diatonic realm of what they're playing in. He doesn't know. He doesn't care. He never asked his fucking guitar player. The guitar player couldn't fucking tell him, even if he wanted to. The only reason it sounds okay is because I know what the difference is between a D-major and D-minor chord, in the key of C-major. If I'm going to be playing a D-major scale, there's a very specific reason that I will be doing that, because I want to hear a specific group of notes. But if somebody else is playing in that continuing C-major mode, the notes I'm going to play are wrong. And most bass players do not care. They don't know what the fuckin' difference is.

Nobody's ever said to me that my bass playing was amazing or moved them. If someone did, I don't know if this person knows anything about music. But I would say, "Thank you very much." How did I do what I did? I practiced all the time. I listened to good music. I loved what I did. I'm glad you loved it, too. If somebody said all that to me, I'd try to change the direction of the conversation, but I'd definitely want to bask in my glory for at least thirty seconds.

I'd say something like, "I love what I do. I really enjoy playing the bass. I love playing live. I love performing in front of people. I really get off on performing. I really want to purvey my art to the world, and I think I'm pretty good, and I'm glad that you think so, too. I wish more people thought I was good, but you're the only person who's come up and said anything like this."

Nobody said, "Oh, my God! You're so good!" Happens to guitar players and singers all the time. "You are so good! I loved what you did." That's fine. I can understand that. That's the problem with being a bass player. How are you going to get that feeling from a bass player, especially from somebody who isn't trying to be flashy, whose job isn't to be Bootsy Collins or Jeff Berlin? Please love me because I'm a great bass player? No. I told you I only wanted to be loved because I loved music so much. I wanted to be loved and appreciated and paid lots of money because of how much I loved and could appreciate music. Total Salieri effect. Remember? You saw the movie *Amadeus*? He said, "You know, I thought that if I learned music and praised God enough with it, that He would shower me with more talent."

And He didn't. He screwed him completely, and He gave all of Salieri's talent – all this musical talent – to a worthless buffoon. That was what he said about Mozart. That's just Peter Shaffer's writing, but it's good. It's totally applicable. I never had anyone say, "You're an amazing bass player. I need to be with your life-force." And I wasn't horribly ugly back then, like I am now.

Anthology Five
Wasteland
1998-2003

I walked in a desert.
And I cried,
"Ah, God, take me from this place!"
A voice said, "It is no desert."
"I cried, "Well, but –
The sand, the heat, the vacant horizon."
A voice said, "It is no desert."

The Beginning of the End

In October of 1997, Karl Coryat was replaced as editor of *Bass Player*. The new editor came with impeccable credentials. I had no reason to be concerned. The magazine had become an incredible publication in my mind, with the broadest possible appeal. I had several pieces in the can when Karl stepped down. These included a feature titled "Why Don't More Women Play the Bass?" that consisted of interviews with two legends and two younger, up-and-coming artists, all women; my article on Ray Shulman; and stories on Oleg Bernov of the Red Elvises – a bass balalaika player – and Geezer Butler of Black Sabbath, who'd released an excellent solo album called *Black Science*. I also had several pitches in. Somebody from Miller Freeman assured me that all my work would be published.

As soon as the new editor was firmly ensconced, he killed most of my articles, including my Ray Shulman piece. It's no exaggeration to say that this caused me a traumatic flashback, and I re-experienced all the horror, rage, and sense of monumental injustice I'd felt when Carmen and Noreen went out of their way to inflict as much pain on me as possible. It was almost beyond my comprehension. My interview with Shulman represented so much of what I loved: the bass, music journalism, fantastic artistry, beauty, and grace. By interviewing him, I felt I'd put much to rest, including my sadness at the fate of Gentle Giant and my years of meandering in low-grade terror over the future. The mistake I made was in imbuing that article with so much significance when I had no power to determine its destiny. It was entirely in the hands of another person, and he killed it without the slightest twinge.

I called the editor to try and convince him that the article should be published, but he was completely unmoved. He was a very calm, low-key person who never raised his voice. He told me that Ray Shulman was "yesterday's news" and had no place in the vision that the editor had for *Bass Player*.

My voice cracked as I said, "They told me that all the articles in the can would be published."

He chuckled. "Tom, that's what they always say, and the new editor always kills the leftovers from his predecessor. That's just how it's done."

"Like a lion killing all the cubs fathered by his predecessor when he takes over a pride?" I wanted to ask. "So you're operating on the level of an animal?" I kept my mouth shut instead.

The feature-length article "Why Don't More Women Play the Bass?" was also killed. In fact, I never again had another feature published, even though my career at *Bass Player* sputtered along until 2003. There were several reasons I stayed at the publication, refusing to accept reality. My anger, my need to right a terrible wrong, and my fear of the future played large parts, as always, but the main impetus was that I honestly thought I could write myself back into the magazine's good graces. I'd given them the Simmons and Thunes pieces, after all. That had to mean something to them.

I never had the courage to contact Ray Shulman and tell him that his article had been killed; I was too ashamed. Instead, I gave the transcript of the interview to Daniel Barrett, who posted it on *The Gentle Giant Home Page*.[1]

As a tribute to Ray, an idol who became a ghost through no fault of his own, I now present the unpublished article. This is also my way of bearing witness to the moment when the massive, seemingly unending series of losses began, ultimately bringing me to the place I am today. It's one of the most eloquent warnings I received, which I ignored along with the example Ray set for me.

Ray Shulman: Letting Go

If you love something, let it go. This is one of the hardest things to do in life, especially for fans of groups like Gentle Giant. From 1970 to 1980, this adventurous, fiercely idiosyncratic British band released fifteen albums of experimental music usually called "progressive" for convenience. It's tough to describe Giant's sound, an amalgam of intricate, arpeggiated melodies, dissonant instrumentation, complex vocal arrangements, and diabolically difficult rhythms. Though not as well known as Genesis or Yes, Gentle Giant was usually one step ahead artistically. Its best work is warmer, more organic, and much funkier, abounding with wicked bass-heavy grooves. Quality alone is never enough, however, and the band eventually called it quits because they were sick of fighting record companies over their noncommercial approach.

Since 1980, Ray Shulman has written music for TV commercials, including Nike Air Jordan shoes, and he's produced successful records for the Sugarcubes, the Sundays, and Ian McCulloch, among others. Currently, he heads his own London production company, Orinoco Sound Source, where he composes soundtracks for CD ROMs. The one thing Ray hasn't done lately is play the bass. Since his is one of the most original voices ever expressed through the instrument, his style characterized by eccentric patterns, unique phrasing and prodigious technical skill, this is disappointing. "I know, I know, I know," Shulman laughs ruefully. "People give me shit for it. But it wasn't a conscious decision. Things happen by accident. You're playing keyboards or programming, learning a whole different bunch of skills, and suddenly you realize the bass has been in the closet for years. After the band finished, my interests went back to composition, which was more attractive to me than that single instrument. Bass was meant to be played in an ensemble, and it's been years since I've been in one."

The sons of a professional trumpet player, Ray and his brothers Phil and Derek had their first success with Simon Dupree and the Big Sound, a '60s R&B/psychedelic band that later mutated into Gentle Giant. Having studied trumpet, guitar, and violin since childhood, Ray had intended to become a classical musician, but "... once rock and roll came into my life, that idea went out the window." Yes, despite the medieval and avant-garde influences brought in by keyboardist Kerry Minnear, Shulman does consider GG's music rock. He rejects the title of bass virtuoso, and the slight rawness of his work keeps it from being overly cerebral. "There was never a conscious desire to write perverse bass lines," he insists. "The violin had developed dexterity and technique, and the bass parts themselves were often just Kerry's or my own left hand on the keyboard. The bass was never an anchor, it was just another piece of the whole."

This is a rather low-key description of a style that's impossible to categorize. A superficial overview would be that Ray relies heavily on complicated, highly melodic ostinatos and classical-sounding arpeggios, as well as near-funk riffs, huge and dirty heavy-rock licks, and mutated takes on the blues scale. A pick-wielder, he likes to experiment with his sound, producing an amazing range of tones from his Fender Precision and applying a wah-wah pedal and distortion on occasion. Finally, there's the speed and clarity with which he tackles his many double stops and upper-register fills, a skill necessary for doubling the fast, often odd-time keyboard, guitar, or vocal lines. A purely subjective opinion is that his finest work is found on records up to and including 1977's *Playing the Fool* [Capitol], the best of these being *Acquiring the Taste* [Polydor], *Three Friends, Octopus, In a Glass House* [all on Columbia], *The Power and the Glory* [Capitol], *Free Hand* [One Way], and *Interview* [Capitol]. Most are now available on CD.

So how does Shulman feel about the undying dedication of Gentle Giant's more hard-core followers? "It's flattering in only one way: People remember the band. The rest of the time, it sort of inhibits what I do. Once, a fan even called me and asked, 'What's it feel like to have your best work behind you?' Well, I like change, and I can't write music now like I did then, because it's all about environment. I'm living a different life now. I wouldn't even want to make music like that again. For me it would be a lie. It's easy to be rosy and say, 'We made this lovely music together and it was great,' but sometimes it wasn't. Things were very tense and there was a lot of friction toward the end. The fans can't see how things really were. We were told to be less experimental, to write songs instead of pieces, but the more the music was compromised, the more it suffered. Everything became very serious and life-threatening, a matter of survival."

Ray has indeed survived – even flourished – but on his own terms and with a perspective upsetting for some of us to hear. "One of the things about having a fan base is that they put pressure on you to make the kind of music they want, yet they forget that we always ignored such pressure. We never listened to people who said, 'Why don't you make another record like the one *I* liked?' We had to trust ourselves. I'm very flattered by the continuing interest, but it doesn't determine what I do. It wasn't sad when we ended; it was right. We did one last tour, and that was it. We didn't just fizzle out. I really loved all of it, touring and playing live, and I'd never deny it. But I haven't done either since, and I haven't missed it a bit. Music changes, and you can't go backward."

Portent

The first letter I got from the new editor at *Bass Player*.

> Thomas:
> Congratulations! You get the squeaky-wheel prize this month; I've scheduled Red Elvises for the next issue (March).
> Best,
> [withheld]

No Mutants Allowed

A bassist invited me to a birthday party thrown for him at his friend's house. The guests were mostly musicians past and present, many of whom I recognized. It was a terribly dull party because the people there were awfully timid and said nothing to me. I was the only one there with facial hair, and this seemed to throw them, as though they were 1950s frat boys seeing their first Beatnik. My K-Mart clothes and girth didn't help, either. Another characteristic about life in L.A. is that people can talk only about themselves or their mutual acquaintances. If you know neither, you're out of luck. All you get is long, nodding silences and lips squeezed together in a totally meaningless expression that everyone in the entertainment business has adopted.

Not drinking is a definite strike, too. I wanted to tell people that it wasn't a value judgment. It's just that when I drink, I'm going to smoke cigarettes again, which will lead to smoking pot again, and then I'm going to start doing coke and meth again, and in L.A. that means getting hooked up with people like the Crips, MS-13, or the Zetas. I'd rather watch a DVD instead.

The bassist who invited me announced that he was going to find me a babe. I almost screamed at him not to. I didn't mind standing there in silence. These were people I'd never know or like, so why pretend? Thank God he was immediately distracted and forgot about it, because that would've been one of the most humiliating anti-quests ever. The babes, as he called them, were exactly that. Girls. I was already thirty-five and long past being interested in girls. And what kind of ambitious babe at a party full of L.A. musicians would latch onto a fat, bearded, pushing-forty, non-drinking music journalist in a K-mart T-shirt?

I did try to join one conversation: a guy telling a woman about being a member of a Russian wolfhound rescue society. I didn't know there were so many such beasts being abandoned in L.A. that they needed a rescue society, but during a pause I related the time I was on a beach in Portland, Oregon, at about seven in the morning, and a young woman came strolling toward me. She was friendly and we stopped and chatted. I finally asked if she felt worried out here alone in the dunes, and she smiled and said no. She whistled, and what looked like a polar bear came tumbling out of the high grass beside us.

I realized it had been paralleling us in silence. It trundled up to me, sniffing at me with its monster head three times the size of my own. Its shoulder went past my waist.

"What is it?" I asked the woman as this terrifying animal went over every inch of me with its snuffling nose.

"He's a Russian bear hound," she said. "Take it easy!" And they went off down the beach, this pretty girl and her guardian.

"I've never heard of a Russian bear hound," I said to the guy in the Russian wolfhound rescue society. "You should've seen it. The legs were as big around as my arms and the chest was like a beer barrel. Have you ever heard of such a dog?"

"No," he said, and turned back to his companion to talk about their friend Mike. He never even looked at me again.

After a couple of hours of pretending to be a part of other conversations so that the bassist wouldn't feel bad about having invited me, I told him I had to go. His wife gave me a nice, long kiss on the mouth, thanking me, and then the bassist gave me a nice, long kiss on the mouth, thanking me. When I next spoke to the all-male staff of *Bass Player* at the NAMM show, I mentioned how the party ended for me. There was the earsplitting silence that I imagine would follow a hostess telling her dinner party that they'd just eaten braised grandmother. All those adult men went a toadstool gray contemplating this image, and someone finally croaked, "You always have such, um, *interesting* stories to tell."

I omitted the final detail, that getting kissed by a man doesn't feel any different from getting kissed by a woman. My colleagues had reached their limit and had begun deliberately shutting me out of their awareness.

Death on the Launching Pad

There was briefly an all-female band that I loved. They weren't American. In my ten years as a music journalist, the only person I ever had to yell at was the drummer-leader of this group. I sent her the article on the bassist before I turned it in; she called me and said she didn't like the opening sentence; I explained why I wrote it; and suddenly there was a

General Electric turbofan engine screaming in my ear about sexism in L.A. and what an idiot I was. I kept trying to break in, and finally I roared at her as loudly as possible, using as much profanity as I could cram into one sentence. That made her settle down.

Once we were calm again, she started crying and told me that the label had withdrawn all support. At their first American show – which I'd attended after the interview but before I wrote the piece – the entire band was bombed and singing so out of tune most of the guests left. I've never been so mortified. There were A&R honchos there, publicists, everyone. It was the most spectacular act of career suicide I've ever observed.

In the end the band did the only sensible thing and went on a month-long bender in the U.S. and then broke up, right before the article was published. For the next few years I'd get a call in the middle of the night, and it would be the bassist, phoning from her home country. She just wanted to chat. The first time she called, she used only her given name: "Hi, Tom. It's [withheld]." I could tell from her accent where she was from, but I couldn't remember knowing anybody from there. She burbled on while I thought, Who the hell *is* this? After about five minutes it clicked.

I felt bad because their debut CD was great, so I let her tell me what she was up to. She called me once or twice a year for a long time, promising she'd send me the latest thing she was working on, but she never did.

The Perfect Gift for the Man Who Has Everything

One night at a party I went to with Roger and Dolores, I had a conversation with a film director who has the driest sense of humor in Los Angeles. It was so dry that sometimes I had no idea what he'd just said. The topic of our conversation was the massive fees commanded by a certain mediocre, obnoxious, superstar actor. He was notorious for his life of conspicuous consumption, being a collector of mansions, motorcycles, and cars.

"I just don't get it," I said. "Who needs all that stuff? What more could he possibly buy that he doesn't already have?"

"A chador," the director said.

I chuckled politely and moved on. About two hours later, driving home alone in my car, I suddenly burst out laughing as I got it.

Shutterbugs

I worked with several photographers. They told me great stories.

One of the biggest celebrity photographers didn't know anything about photography. He bought magazines, cut out photos from them, and put them in a book. Before one of his big A-list shoots, he'd bring his book to a meeting with his assistants and tell them, "See this picture? I want the background to look like that. See the front light in this picture over here? That's what I want, too." All his shots were paste-up jobs, each element coming from a different photo and each achieved by an assistant because he was incapable of doing any of it himself.

Instead, his skill lay in buttering up the celebrity, so that's what he did while the assistants worked everything out. Before a shoot, if a new assistant asked him what f-stop he was going to use, his stock response was, "What're you asking *me* for? *You're* the assistant; *you* figure it out." So that's what the assistants did. They used pasted-together collages as a guide, and then the photographer would come in and press the shutter release on the camera. That was all.

Another photographer had her own way of changing lenses during a shoot. Instead of asking her assistant to come over and get the one she'd taken off, she'd simply hold it out behind her and drop it without checking to see if anyone was there to catch it. Her assistants would sometimes have to make flying dives to both keep the $2000 piece of equipment from shattering on the floor and to keep their jobs. They got hematomas and dislocations saving the lenses, but it was worth it working for such a legend.

My favorite story was that in Hollywood, there are photographers who make a very good living shooting only images of bread, which are used in picture books, cookbooks, magazines, calendars, bakeries, department stores, and utensil catalogs. Art directors hire people they know can do one thing really well, and most commercial photographers specialize in only one subject. One bread photographer was up for a job, and the art director asked him for his credentials. After the photographer showed him his book of photos, the art director said, "Your stuff looks good, but it's pretty ethnic. Do you shoot white bread, too? We need someone who can shoot white bread."

The funniest, most entertaining photographer I met was Neil Zlozower. Somebody needs to make a ten-part documentary of him just talking for twenty hours in his incredible voice, which sounds like he drinks gasoline right out of the pump.

Music magazines aren't interested in quality. I mean, they'll publish a photo of a guy if he's striking a really dynamic pose with the guitar, and he could be makin' just the ugliest fuckin' face and have three chins! The magazine doesn't even look at the face and chin. They're thinking, "Wow, look at this guy's dynamic strumming!" They don't care if his tongue is hangin' right outta his mouth. The art directors at most magazines suck pretty bad. All they want are flash photos. When I was coming up, it was unheard of to use a flash when taking live shots, but in the late seventies, early eighties, it got real popular to shoot with Kodachrome 'cause it's so fine grained. You need a lot of light for that, so everyone started using flash units. So here you are, a rock star, trying to be all cool and shit, singing, and you have ten people in the pit all using flash units. You look down for a second, and *ba-ba-ba-bap,* they get you right in the face. So the bands started saying, "Look, we don't want these fuckin' guys flashing in our eyes all night," so they instituted the three-song limit for photographers. It's totally unnecessary. I mean, I never use a flash. I always thought even the lamest photographer would know how to use ambient light, but they don't, so they use a flash, and since you're shooting from below, it can illuminate a lot of ugly shit, like double chins.

Publicists say they want photo approval. Here's someone who knows nothing at all about photography to start with, and now she wants to *approve* the photos! To me, a publicist is nothing but a professional liar. It's pretty funny. The publicist says that her client *needs* all these things. "There are some things we need in order for this shoot to happen." No, they don't *need* anything except to get here and have me take their fuckin' photos. They just *want* stuff. That's cool. I want lots of stuff, too. I just don't make other people get it for me.

The publicist says, "We're gonna need full catering," and I say, "Great! Give me the money. I'm not paying for it outta my own pocket." And they always give it to me. It's the same with makeup artists. "You want makeup? You're ugly? *You* pay for it," is what I tell them. It's ridiculous! "My client *needs* these things." It just shows how fuckin' incompetent most publicists are. We're doing a photo shoot here, not going on a picnic! If the client eats a big ol' ten-dollar turkey-and-Swiss-cheese sandwich from the deli, they'll get all stuffed and then they can't move or pose for me. They'll just want to go to sleep. They're all outta their minds sometimes.

I was at this interview with [withheld]. He's totally fucked-up lookin', all white and pasty, with a shaved head and real grungy clothes like a street person. Every time the interviewer asked him a question, he'd scream, *"Wot a fookin' load o' crap! You fookin' Yank interviewers are all the fookin' same! You all ask the same fookin' stupid fookin' questions!"* But then he'd answer the question all calm. That's how the whole interview went. He was screamin' at the top of his lungs in this thick British accent, droolin' and the veins poppin' out all over his head. Well, I went home and had a nightmare he was in my bedroom doin' that to *me!* It was terrible! I shoved a wastebasket down over his head to shut him up 'cause he was screamin' so loud he was gonna wake up my wife and baby, but then once I got it on him it made his voice even louder, like he was in an echo chamber! He was just sittin' there at the foot of my bed, and all I could see was this ragged suit with an upside-down metal wastebasket on top with these screams comin' out of it. God, it was horrible!

For some reason there's a higher percentage of totally maniacal psychos in photography than in any other business. They burn out fast – photographers, assistants, everyone. I'll be burnin' out myself one of these days.[2]

I could fill several volumes with what Neil Zlozower has to say about the entertainment industry, and I can promise you that you'd read every last word.

The Ghost in the Miniskirt

What follows is the most shameful experience of my career as a music journalist. The new editor at *Bass Player* approved an interview with Anne Kadrovich, who played bass in two bands, Sissy Bar and Tuscaurora. She was also Operations Manager at Larrabee Sound Studios. Anne was a very good bassist with a quirky style all her own. All the big names in the business used the studio; the afternoon I interviewed Anne, Madonna dropped in with her infant daughter, Lourdes. A few days after the interview, a photographer and I came back to shoot Anne at Larrabee. She wore an amazing, purple miniskirt outfit; the photographer made her look ravishing. Anne said this was the happiest moment in her life.

I turned in the article, and the editor called me and told me he'd killed it. I argued with him for half an hour, mentioning all the huge artists who recorded at Larrabee. The point of the article was that Anne – exposed to all these fabulously successful musicians – was a bassist by choice. She was one of us! Though small in stature, she hauled around that heavy axe as an act of love! She knew everything about the recording industry and was a classically trained vocalist, flautist, pianist, and percussionist but chose to be a bassist. Her story was fascinating, and she used a rare medium-scale Fender Precision and a custom Hamer bass she got from Tom Petersson of Cheap Trick, her bass mentor.

The editor was unmoved and indifferent. Since I hadn't had the courage to tell Ray Shulman that his article had been killed, this time I called Anne and let her know the bad news. She started to cry. "But I've told everyone I know that I'm going to be in *Bass Player!*" she sobbed.

I can still hear it.

The Day I Should've Resigned

I wrote a long letter to the editor, complaining about our treatment of Anne Kadrovich, as well as the killing of other articles. I could understand killing articles from one's predecessor – a lie on my part; I had to try and communicate on this man's primitive level – but I simply could not fathom how a publication could survive if it continually did this to people who'd given up valuable time and had consented in good faith to sitting down with me. I mentioned all the other sorts of bassists we'd covered in the past, insisting that this had given the magazine a broader appeal. The editor sent me a letter in response.

Tom:

Thanks for the letter. I can understand your disappointment about the Kadrovich story, but the article I saw did not offer anything I consider valuable for readers. Yes, we've covered street musicians, circus musicians, etc. – players whose positions are either unique or who hold interesting bass jobs that other players might aspire to, (Though I can't say that all of the stories you might be referring to are ones I would have printed.) In the case of Anne Kadrovich, apart from what gear she uses, there was nothing in the story that indicated what kind of player she is, and there was nothing in her experience that I could see that would be instructive for other players. So my decision not to print it stands.

As for [withheld], it remains my prerogative to publish submitted stories in the form I think best serves readers. That's my job as editor. As a freelancer myself I feel I bring passion to my subjects, but once I put a story in the mail it ceases to be mine. Call it zen mercenary if you like, but I can't imagine surviving as a writer any other way. I feel the same way when I play a recording session too (as do any of the actually successful studio players I know). You play your best, but once the signal goes into the board it's out of your hands.

If I sound a bit inflexible on this, so be it. It's my duty to pull the various pieces together to make this magazine a coherent whole, and I'm prepared to take whatever praise or blame comes my way as a result of my decisions. I can promise you that those decisions will be based on what I feel is best for the magazine and the readers.

The fact remains that you are a really, really good writer, and I fear trying to fit what you want to do into *Bass Player's* narrow format may be confining. Nonetheless I'd like for you to keep writing for us if you can accept these constraints. To that end it's important we know where each other stands, so let's keep talking.

Best,

[withheld]

What I want readers of this memoir to understand is that he was absolutely right, and I was wrong. This letter told me in plain English that his control was more important than the actual content of the magazine; he was absolutely unreachable; and he didn't care about the success of the publication, its reputation, or the feelings of the artists we interviewed. He was also indifferent to whether I stayed or left.

I should've resigned on the spot and saved myself the next five years of idiotic rage and the damage it did to me physically and mentally. I was utterly wrong in not taking him at his word when he told me straight out that my services were no longer needed. He explained the terms of my continued employment as clearly as he could, and I refused to accept them.

All that being said, here is a bit of the interview I conducted with Anne Kadrovich, which my editor said "did not offer anything I consider valuable for readers." I present it here to honor her; to show what a contemptible, myopic, incompetent jackass my editor was; and because these warnings are valuable on every possible level. They were especially valuable to me, but as always I ignored them.

I thought the idea was that people want to get a label deal at any price.
That's some peoples' idea. I know what goes into doing a record. I've been very close to it. I've done it myself on a smaller scale. I've been working at Larrabee and seen the way the big record deals go. I know how much time, money, and effort goes into a major label deal, so I want to be sure I'm with the right band if it happens.

Here's what usually happens: You get signed, so you quit your day job. You get a $10,000 advance, but since you didn't ask the right questions before you signed the contract, and since your lawyer represents the record company, too, which you didn't know and he never told you, you find out the money's going to be given to you over ten months. So now you're getting $1000 a month, which you could've gotten working at McDonald's. So you live like a pauper for ten months, and then you find out the label isn't ready to release the record because the legal work isn't finished. Or maybe they've decided to remix it completely. Maybe they want a different producer now, and he's got a whole different vision. So they remix it, master it, press it, do the artwork, go through more lawyers and more lawyers and more lawyers, and then they tell you that they've got three *other* CDs from three *other* bands coming out at the same time, so yours is going to have to wait. They sit on it for six months to a year, and you end up with no record, no money, and no job. When I hear people say, "Woooooo! I got signed I'm on my way!" I just say, "Good luck."

Why was it a condition of your hiring that you not be in a band?
Because no studio wants to hire somebody who's working to get signed and then they're gonna get signed in six months and go away after the studio put all that time into training them. Also, there could be a conflict of interest. I work with Michael Jackson, Madonna, etc. Somebody in that position could take advantage and give their tape to the right A&R person and open up some doors for themselves. The only way I can keep on working there is if I resist doing such a thing. And I have, but there are a lot of people I've already seen, people who come and go, in my business, who haven't been able to do that. They've approached people with their tape or said, "Oh, did you know I'm in a band, too?" They approach the artists, or their A&R people, their producers. There are a lot of important people who come and work there. It's not just a little studio.

Is it frustrating working at Larrabee after all the time you've lived in Los Angeles? Is there envy or other negative feelings involved in working so close to the mega-successful?
Well, there could be, I guess. But for me, what balances out the frustration is the fact that I'm learning. What balances out the envy is I see the reality of what people go through. Everything has a balance, and you just have to find it. Everyone in this town is like, "I just want a record deal," but they don't know that a record deal doesn't do anything. If they're really conscientious about their art, they'd say, "I'd love for a million people to hear my album." That's *way* harder to achieve. Anybody can get a record deal. But after you're signed, the album may never be made. Or you may start making the record but never finish it. Or the band might break up before the record is made. Or the label decides they're not going to release a single. Or the label decides to drop you before the record even comes out. Or the record is released, and then the label does absolutely nothing to promote it.

I have a friend in a band whose first record went platinum, and they put a single from the second record out, and when after thirty days it hadn't reached number one or been picked up by any of the majors, the record company just let that record fall. This was after they were a platinum-selling artist on their first record, and it broke my heart to see them treated so shabbily after they had done so much for the label. They're just sort of scrabbling now.[3]

On May 17, 2012, I did something that took all my nerve: I contacted Anne and asked her for permission to use her name and a photo of her in my book. It was nearly impossible to send that e-mail. She surprised me by instantly consenting and wishing me success with my memoir; I promised her a copy when it was published.

Thank you, Anne, for releasing me.

Even at the Hollywood Bowl

I went to the Hollywood Bowl to interview a bassist after a concert. The original plan was for me to actually see the performance, but somebody screwed up. There was no ticket for me at the will-call window and the show was sold out, so I stood next to the entrance for two hours, listening to the music. As the crowd departed, I saw that at thirty-eight I was the youngest male there. Every man in attendance had a face-lifted female companion at least a quarter-century his junior. Many of the women wore weird one-piece miniskirt dresses and wide-brimmed hats, almost like shallow sombreros. Their faces were so shiny they looked as though they'd had a layer of carnauba wax applied and smoothed out with a power buffer.

The bassist appeared in a small office on the opposite side of the gate. He wore coattails and a studious frown. I waded toward him, through the mass of elderly millionaires, billionaires, and burnished women. Outside the window, I waved to the bassist; he glared and turned away. When I knocked on the glass in the door, he stormed over.

"Tom Wictor, *Bass Player* magazine!" I yelled.

He opened the door and said, "Yes, yes!" with smoldering impatience, as though he obviously knew I was Tom Wictor from *Bass Player* magazine, so why would I insult his intelligence in such an inconsiderate way?

"Here. Sit. Did you catch the show?" he asked.

"From the outside of the Bowl, yeah. There was no ticket at the will-call window." He just stared. After a few seconds of silence, I asked if we could begin.

"Of course!" he barked. He kept getting angry throughout the interview, telling me about the style of music he played and where it may or may not have originated.

"But I don't *know!* Nobody *knows!* Why's it important? It *isn't!*"

Since he'd started the history lesson on the music without me even asking, I didn't know why he was getting so upset at me. He described a traditional way of playing the upright bass by hitting the strings with a bow, "But we won't get into that."

I wondered why not. Would it be considered offensive?

He talked about how boring his parts were, and he became almost apoplectic explaining how people transcribed music. "They write it as a quarter note and an eighth note or as an eighth note, an eighth rest, and an eighth note, but it's *not!* It's an idiomatic *feel!*"

That was how the entire interview went. By the end, I'd had it with him and his artistic temperament. He never apologized for me having to stand for two hours outside the Bowl. I wrote a glowing piece on him that made him so happy he invited me to another show with another band he played in that performed a completely different style of traditional music. I declined. That music was even more idiomatic than the one he usually played; telling me about it may have made him angry enough to strangle me.

Death of a Novel

I began querying literary agents with sample chapters and a synopsis of my completed novel about the L.A. music scene. Since I had no idea what I was doing, I'd produced a gigantic turd that could easily have been broken up into three smaller turds that would each have also failed. Some agents wrote back that the thing was over twice as long as it should be. A few seemed personally affronted and used lots of exclamation marks. One wrote, "As an author, you need to come up with an idea so clever and unique that I haven't thought of it."

Oddly enough, my novel was about a great former musician named Gwen, a bassist. She was small, dark haired, ethnically exotic, beautiful, funny, tragic, and she thumb-slapped a MusicMan Sting Ray bass. The book is an unpublishable fiasco, but I like the title, *The Mermaid Lamp,* which refers to an Art Deco bronze the protagonist Walter bought because the face of the mermaid holding up the frosted glass globe enclosing the bulb looked just like Gwen's. Walter and Gwen had a horrible, acrimonious breakup and she married someone who forbade her to play, but Walter saved her in the end by helping her return to music even though he knew they'd never get back together.

For *The Mermaid Lamp,* I wrote the only lyrics of my life, just the chorus of a song called "Let's Say Goodbye," Gwen's signature tune.

> *Let's say goodbye*
> *You can slip right out the door*
> *Don't leave me! Wait*
> *You're free to go*
> *Let's say goodbye*
> *I can tell you're really bored*
> *Well, I am too*
> *I'm just as sick of you*
> *Let's say goodbye*
> *Come back tomorrow night*
> *Let's say goodbye*
> *Let's go to bed*

Walter and Gwen were together for five years, a period in which she was on the road a lot, touring with her band, Jayne the Baptist. She left long messages on Walter's answering machine almost every night, and he saved them all. Throughout the book, he listened to the messages, each of which triggered a flashback to their time together. He knew he should just throw away the tapes, but he couldn't. To get Gwen playing again, and as a birthday present to himself, Walter pulled a stunt too silly and sentimental to ever reveal.

I blush that I actually thought this blundering lament with its inanely narrow focus had a prayer of being published. When I'd amassed about sixty rejection notices, it was clear that I had another flop on my hands. I told Tim I planned on tossing all evidence of it, including the manuscript; tapes and transcripts of all the interviews I did with musicians, publicists, antique dealers, and commercial photographers; notes I'd taken on interactions; and reconstructions of conversations – fights and arguments, really.

Tim told me with more than a little annoyance that throwing it all away would be stupid, since I'd put so much time and effort into it. Instead of indulging in a melodramatic, self-indulgent action that I'd regret later, I should hold on to everything because it probably wasn't as bad as I thought and someday it might come in handy. What could it hurt? So I sullenly shoved the whole mess into a trunk and left it there for fourteen years. When my publisher approved the proposal for this memoir, I pulled out the manuscript of *The Mermaid Lamp,* the transcripts, and the notes.

Jackpot. Thanks, Tim. Smarter than me, as usual.

Here's the final scene of my first novel. Gwen has left a long message on Walter's answering machine, the first time she'd done so in four years. I won't repeat the whole thing because it's too mortifying. "Dick Cavett" refers to the prerecorded announcements on Walter's machine, which were done by the former talk-show host.

"It was really great seeing you again, Walter," Gwen whispered. "Stay in touch, okay? I'll talk to you later. Take care of yourself, and happy birthday. Bye."

Dick Cavett said, "Wednesday, 9:42 P.M. That was your last message."

So she'd remembered. Walter sighed and stood up. He pressed a button on the answering machine.

"I will... erase messages," Dick Cavett said.

As the machine whirred, Walter switched off the mermaid lamp and went into the living room.

The Best Therapist in the World

His name was Dave. I was extremely uncomfortable about therapy. He asked me why I'd come to him, and I said I was consumed by rage and sadness; I couldn't succeed at anything; my relationships always failed cataclysmically; and my past had apparently robbed me of the ability to make sound decisions.

"I'm unsure about this," I said. "But I'm willing to give it a try if you can promise me a few things. Well, 'promise' isn't the right word, but if you can assure me that certain things won't happen, I'll sign on."

"Well," he said, "first of all, nothing will happen that you don't want to happen. I *can* promise you that."

I said, "The most crucial thing for me is that I can't allow myself to be reduced to a sobbing heap in the corner. I can't do that to myself. I can't come in here and cry and scream and have you just sit there and stare at me, and then I leave and then the next week I come back and do it again. I can't allow that to happen. It's too demeaning."

He smiled. "I don't know what you've been told about therapy. I can't wave a magic wand and reduce you to a sobbing heap on the carpet. That's not how it works. Any sobbing you do, you have to decide to do it yourself."

"I just want you to know that it absolutely must not happen with me. That would be a condition of me continuing here. I'm sorry to be so blunt. I don't know how any of this sounds to you. I don't even know if patients or clients are supposed to have conditions, but I just can't respond to the crying jags and screaming transference. It just really revolts me. It's very important that I not be manipulated or pushed around or examined like I'm some kind of specimen."

"However you wanted to conduct your sessions would be entirely up to you," he said. "Different people respond to different methods. Anyone who says there's only one kind of therapy is, well, crazy. If you were to become my client, I can promise you that I'd never force anything on you. The best way to think of it is this: You say you don't want to be reduced to a sobbing heap on the carpet, and I don't blame you. If expressing or controlling certain emotions like anger or sorrow is hard for you, think of it as learning how to swim. As a swimming instructor, my job wouldn't be to just pick you up and toss you out into the middle of a lake. First we'd walk around the lake and get you used to the sight of it, and then slowly we'd get you used to dipping your toe in it, just for a second, and then later we might try to get you to stand in it up to your ankles, and so on. And we'd talk about each step before we took it. But I don't have a vested interest in your eventually learning how to swim. You have to decide for yourself how far in you want to go. I'm only here to help, not force. I can't do anything *to* you or *make* you do anything, and I don't even want to."

I said, "I was told once that it's a therapist's job to parent me, including hugs and unconditional love and support. That's not what I'm looking for. That sort of approach wouldn't work with me. Any therapist I had would have to be kept at arm's length, at least in the sense that I would never allow myself to be hugged or rocked like a baby or anything like that."

"Well, as I said, different people require different techniques, and what works for one person won't work for others. It's not my place to comment on other therapists' methods, but I'm not a big hugger and rocker. Support I can offer. In fact, support is vital to the process. But love and parenting? No, that's not my job. You already have parents."

"I'm terrified of becoming too dependent," I told him. "You read stories about celebrities who've been going to the same analyst for forty years and have to call them to ask what kind of sheets they should buy. A woman I dated called her therapist in the middle of our fights to get her opinion on what I was saying, even if it was at 11:30 at night."

He laughed. "Well, if you call me at 11:30 at night, you'll get my answering service. As for seeing me for forty years, I'll make a deal with you: I'll see you only as long as I think I can help you, and then we'll agree to end the sessions. How's that?"

So I signed up. It was 1998, and I still had a long fight ahead of me, but I'm absolutely convinced that if I hadn't seen him when I did, I wouldn't be writing this memoir, and I may not even be here today. I saw him for a year, and then he told me it was time for us to stop. The reason he ended our sessions was because he'd come to a conclusion about me that I won't reveal until later. I disagreed with his conclusion, but he was right, of course, because he was the Best Therapist in the World.

To give you an example of his skill, I once told him about a nightmare I had in which I was in a dark room, trying to figure out how to work a VCR. The tape was in the machine and I had the remote, but I didn't know which buttons to push or even how to begin. The room was so dark I could barely see, and I felt a sinister encroachment, a frightening building up of something. I kept telling myself to just smash the stupid thing, but instead of doing that I'd start all over, going through the whole process again and again until I was hysterical. Then I woke up.

"That's a very positive dream," Dave said. "You're in the dark, but you're trying to figure something out. You wanted to smash it and give up, but you didn't. You kept going, even though you felt threatened by what I interpret as your impending, building knowledge about yourself. You had the courage to keep going. The panic and hysteria you felt didn't stop you, did they?"

No, they didn't. So thank you, Dave.

Self-discipline

I interviewed a musician who showed up drunk, three and a half hours late. He jeered at me, picked his nose, belched, and farted for nearly thirty minutes while ten feet away cooks shouted in Spanish and tossed pots and pans that produced earsplitting, echoing, metallic crashes. The noise and my fury caused adrenaline rushes that nearly made me leap to my feet and turn into a fist-windmill to lay everyone out dead on the floor. Not only would the cooks finally be quiet, the farting, belching, nose-picking, drunken, laughing, sneering, smirking man sitting in front of me might experience a moment of fear.

Or maybe, since he had quite a reputation as a brawler, he would've leaped up himself and smashed my head down into my body, and for a moment I'd be looking up out of the red tunnel of my own flesh he'd created, and I'd see him peering down at me as though I were at the bottom of a well, and he'd laugh even louder, the sound turning into a hideous, rheumy, croupy cough that faded as the lights went out forever.

I caught all his farts on tape. Nine. Yes, I counted them.

Another Approval; Another Killing

This one pained me almost as much as the killing of the Ray Shulman piece. I was supposed to write a feature-length article on Curt Smith of Tears for Fears, the first I'd been allowed to do since my editor took over eight months earlier. I simply can't remember if there was even a reason given for not publishing it. By now my boss was in the habit of not using my work whether it was one of my own pitches he'd okayed or someone he'd assigned me because he allegedly wanted that artist in the magazine. Tim says it was gaslighting, pure and simple. My brother remembers the many hours I spent on the phone with the editor, trying to convince him to not murder another article. Tim once told me something that I didn't believe at the time: "People like to hurt you because when they cut you, you bleed."

Curt Smith is a gentleman, and his solo CD *Mayfield* is fantastic. I had no idea he was such a great bassist. His is a story of grace and dignity in the face of adversity. One song on *Mayfield* unequivocally expresses anger, but the target of the tune – a miserable, bitter recluse consumed by rage – clearly deserves it. "Sun King" is a passionate indictment of people who give in to hate. As much as I loved the song, it disturbed me greatly. The lyrics are about what a waste of time it is to engage angry, sad, lonely losers who refuse to take responsibility for their own failures. I listened to it at least thirty times in a row.

In 2000, after ten years apart, Curt Smith and Roland Orzabal were able to put their turbulent breakup behind them and record a new Tears for Fears album together, aptly titled *Everybody Loves a Happy Ending*. This has led to several successful tours and a resurgence of interest in the band. Curt Smith also released a second solo album, *Halfway, Pleased* [KOOK Media], in 2008.

Since there was no rational reason to treat Smith as shabbily as my editor did, I present my unpublished article on him, based on the interview I conducted June 10, 1998.

Curt Smith: No Tears Here

In 1985-86 you couldn't turn on the radio without hearing Tears for Fears' "Shout," "Head Over Heels," or "Everybody Wants to Rule the World." The duo had memorable videos – the millions of paper airplanes in 1983's "Pale Shelter," for example – and an instantly recognizable sound, a mighty synth-pop thunder that produced monster hits, one of the last being 1989's "Sowing the Seeds of Love." Tears for Fears (the name was taken from psychologist Arthur Janov's book on primal scream therapy) consisted of bassist Curt Smith and guitarist Roland Orzabal, school chums from Bath, England. Both were born in 1961 and they first collaborated in 1979, as members of the short-lived quintet Graduate. In 1990, after much success and some disappointments, the pair split up, apparently with considerable acrimony. Smith departed after a final tour and Orzabal carried TFF on by himself.

These days, Curt Smith fronts Mayfield, whose eponymous debut was released earlier this year on his own label Zerodisc. Encyclopedias of pop music always mention Smith's "teen-idol looks" and his supposed status as Orzabal's second banana, but they rarely describe his sophisticated, highly original style on the bass, a laid-back yet motile approach that is amazingly expressive. *Mayfield* brilliantly showcases this ability, "Sorry Town," "Reach Out," "Mother England," and especially "Sun King" each by themselves being worth the price of admission. The record retains some of the flavor of Tears and the songs tend to be mid-tempo rather than blistering, but it's clear that Smith is currently in a different musical place, one that emphasizes guitar, bass, and drums more than sequencer.

Curt Smith says much in his life has been simplified and pared down, including his music, his equipment, and his career. Fittingly, he himself appears much slimmer. Not diminished, but wiry and spare. He looks pretty tough, actually, which he probably is, having once ruled the pop world, disappeared for a while, endured publicly flung brickbats from his ex-partner, and then come back with a new take on it all. Very few musicians could survive such a wild ride, much less grow artistically and retain their sense of humor. Curt Smith has done all three.

• • •

Do you have a preference between stringed and electronic instruments?
No. I think they all have their place. Also, any preference I have will change. During the Tears time, my interest was in technology because everything was new. When I started writing for this record, I wrote on acoustic guitar and was more interested in the singer/songwriter aspect. Because of that, I felt the record would be more suitable for a band, so I formed one and we played everything live before ever recording it. So right now, I'm not necessarily into technology because I'm loving playing live. I think as a result, Mayfield sounds much more organic than Tears for Fears.

Do you do all your writing on acoustic guitar?
At the moment, yes. It's not the way I used to do it. With Tears, music was very much a studio creation, in that we'd always start with a drum machine or a sequencer. Prior to *The Hurting,* we wrote on acoustic because we had no money, but once we got equipment, that was it. Then everything was created in the studio.

How did you decide to start writing on guitar?
It was a natural process. I decided to stop playing and writing for a while because I was so disillusioned with the industry. I wasn't getting joy out of it anymore. I think music should always be something you have a passion for, but it'd become just my job. So I consciously stopped and decided that I'd only ever pick up a guitar again if I felt I just had to. I wasn't going to allow it to just be my job again. After a while, I had an acoustic guitar in my apartment, I had this idea for a song, so I started writing and it's gone on from there.

How does bass fit into your songwriting process?
The songwriting process for me is almost always based on melody. I don't record anything when I'm writing, so my gauge of something being good or not is if I remember it the next day. It has to have a good melody to really stick in my head. I end up singing that melody and using the acoustic guitar for chords, and I think of bass as pinning down the low end while being melodic itself. I don't think a lot of players really consider bass a melodic instrument, but it can be. In a song like "What Are We Fighting For," the bass starts out holding down the low end, but when you get to the 3/4 sections, it starts to swim. There's a whole different melody going.

Does singing one melody and playing another at the same time come naturally to you?
Not really. I write bass parts by listening to the music and fitting another melody around everything else. It's kind of like syncopation, your left hand doing one thing and your right doing another. In my case it's my hands doing one thing and my voice doing another. It took me a while to learn how to do it. I used to write all these nice bass parts, and then it was like, "Oh, shit! They've got nothing to do with the vocals!" The way I get around it is I just play all the parts until they become second nature and I don't have to think about them. In the beginning, when I'm learning to do them, I try to get into that syncopation because the vocals and the bass are always two different rhythms as well as melodies. Once that becomes natural, I don't think about it anymore and to some degree completely separate the two.

Have you had any formal musical training?
No, I dropped out of music. When I was at school, the musical training consisted purely of classical and nothing else. In my adolescence I found that boring as hell. I really think they should include more modern music as well to make it more interesting for kids. Later on, of course, it was like, "Oh God, I wish I were trained!" There are times when I'm

searching for things I wish I knew. But I basically picked things up by ear. Working with other musicians, seeing bands live, you're always like, "Wow, what's that chord?" Then you go home and do it yourself.

You seem to prefer writing mid-tempo things.
Yeah, I do. I never really think about it. It just happens to be the way I write. I've tried writing up-tempo things and always fail abysmally. It just doesn't feel natural. Why? I don't know, and I try not to think too much about it. I'm way past the years where I'd think, "Oh God, we really need an up-tempo track!" I just play the stuff I enjoy.

Are you strictly a pick-using bass player?
I use both a pick and my fingers, depending on how warm I want it to be. Live, because I'm singing and because of the cross-rhythms and everything else, I find it much easier to play with a pick. In the studio, I go between the two, though I play a lot more with my fingers. It's just a rounder, warmer, sound.

Do you make a distinction between live and studio playing?
Yeah. I used to try playing exactly the same way live as I did in the studio, and it always made life more complicated. For me, timing – keeping the tempo spot-on – is much easier if I have a pick. In the studio, I don't have that problem because I'm not singing, I'm just laying down bass tracks and can concentrate on that. Live, I try and make it so that I'm relaxed. If I'm trying to do too much or if I'm thinking too much about everything around me, I can't give a heartfelt performance.

So when you're up there with your bass and your pick, singing and playing two different melodies, where's your mind?
My mind is always on the lyrics. Once I've written and learned the bass part and the melody and I know them and am very happy with them, then it's all about how much passion I can put into the performance. It's about really meaning it at the time.

Can a bass melody evoke emotions, too?
I think so. Everything in a piece of music should back up the emotion you're trying to get across. The music is your backdrop, and if the backdrop is garish and you're trying to say something intimate, it's not going to work.

Would it be fair to say that as a musician, you're more interested in getting emotions across than rocking out?
Without doubt that would be true. Sometimes live, depending on the night, I enjoy playing so much that I tend to lose some of the more intimate moments, purely because it's a band and it's loud. But my preference is the emotional content of a song. My reason for writing music is not to be in a rock-and-roll band, it's wanting to get something out of my system.

There was a period when Tears for Fears was everywhere, and these days you're playing in small clubs. Has that been a hard transition to make?
Not at all. I actually prefer it. I think it has less to do with the size of the place – though I personally love the intimacy of smaller venues – than it does with who you're with and what you're doing. I've not had this much fun playing live since I was eighteen. I did a tour with Tears in 1990, which was in front of fifteen to a hundred thousand people in South America, and my ex-partner and I weren't even talking to each other. It was one of the most painful experiences of my life. It all depends on what you call success. Success to me is if I'm really passionate and enjoy what I'm doing, and the rest is, "Whatever!"

You said you hadn't played for a while because you were disillusioned, but looking at the state of the music industry today –
I'll be more disillusioned? [Laughs.] Well, that's why I formed my own label. I don't have to deal with all that. I'm doing this for me, not for success. I've had the success. I'm doing this because I want to, because I have a passion for it, and because I feel I have to.

So success isn't your goal in playing again.
Right. I'm not that stupid. [Laughs.]

• • •

Equipment
"I was recently asked to draw a diagram of my bass set-up, and I was sent a bunch of examples. They were all very complicated, with tons and tons of speakers and preamps and amps and loads of effects. So I drew mine, and it was my Warwick 4-string Thumb bass through a tuner into a Hartke 1 x 15 combo. That's all! I also have a Warwick fretless 5-string that I use in the studio. I guess my lack of equipment has to do with how organic the band's sound is. I'm really into the simplicity of everything right now."

Unsung *What?*

The January 1999 issue of *Bass Player,* commemorating the magazine's ten-year anniversary, included a feature titled "10 Unsung Bass Albums of the '90s." A few months earlier the editor had cancelled my long-running column "Unsung Bass Stylists," reviews of albums showcasing players I felt hadn't gotten the recognition they deserved.

I was not asked to make a contribution to "10 Unsung Bass Albums of the '90s."

Tantalizing Glimpse of the First Ghost

Though the year began on a sour note, it improved rather quickly when I attended a St. Patrick's Day party in Santa Monica and met an opera singer from another nation. We spoke about the large expatriate community of her fellow citizens here in California. I told her that I'd known one of her compatriots when I was in eighth grade, and a couple of years ago I'd seen her in a magazine. She lived in L.A. but I hadn't been able to find her.

"What's her name?" this woman asked.

"Brigitte Cardei."

"Oh, I know Brigitte. We're pretty good friends, actually. Give me your number and I'll tell her to call you."

So I gave her my number, stunned that once again I'd been given the opportunity to contact the first ghost of my life. What were the odds?

But I didn't hear from Brigitte. I wasn't surprised; our time together had been short and seemed like several centuries ago. If she remembered me at all, it would be as the boy who looked like a middle-aged Latvian spinster and wrote a love note to her that was divulged to the entire school. I wouldn't really top the list of past acquaintances a successful member of the Hollywood elite ached to track down.

Enter a Hippie

In February of 1999, I went back to San Francisco to visit a friend. She was a musician who could never seem to get her act together. The night I arrived at her row house, she was gone. Her housemate – a woman in her late twenties – cautiously opened the door, broke into a huge smile when I introduced myself, and gave me a crushing handshake. She knew all about me, she said. I'll call her Abby. She told me my friend was at a meeting of a vegan free-love society, which believed that all the world's problems can be solved if everybody just screws as many people as possible, relieving themselves of negative energy. Sex can be completely removed from emotion, and monogamy is destructive.

Abby and I sat in the kitchen and talked. She was very nice and looked almost exactly like Audrey Hepburn, except with frizzy hair. Her black choker, teal hoodie, and loose-fit jeans were hippie-ish but clean, not slovenly. It turned out she was eighteen and only projected as someone in her late twenties. We hit it off instantly because of her calm-but-wacky sense of humor. Her fake Canadian I.D. was in the name of "Chlophelia L. Snaaa," and whenever I used the phrase, "That sucks," she'd answer, "Like *you*" with a teasing smile. She swore a lot; I asked her if she kissed her mother with that mouth.

"I never kiss that bitch," she said and laughed.

She was an ardent fan of the painter Egon Schiele, the only one besides me I've ever known. A songwriter, she let me take a picture of her with her acoustic guitar even though she said she hated being photographed. When discussing our favorite foods, she confessed unprompted to having recently overcome bulimia.

My friend came home late, said hello to me, and went to bed. The next morning she left early for her job. As I ate breakfast, Abby joined me at the table.

"What's on your agenda today?" she asked.

"Just going to drive around and visit places I haven't seen in years. Take pictures."

"Would you like some company?"

"Sure would."

She smiled and said, "Far out!" We both laughed.

First we went to Lands End so I could shoot the Golden Gate Bridge. After that we drove to the hang-gliders' jumping-off platform where the daredevil had landed at Carmen's feet six years earlier. We sprawled on the wooden planks and talked for hours. Lying next to me, Abby gently kicked my foot with hers every now and then. Back at the house we made dinner and had a moment of silent, electric eye contract, the way Audrey Hepburn and Cary Grant did during the pass-the-orange scene in *Charade*. Abby had enormous, piercing, sky-blue eyes that were gorgeous. It was a harmless fantasy on my part, comparing our little spark of whatever to one of my favorite films. I was under no illusions whatsoever. I liked Abby immensely, but she was eighteen and I was thirty-seven, struggling with my weight, my mind, my appearance, my career, my future, my past, my present – everything. While Abby and I did the dishes my friend called and said she was on her way to another vegan free-sex meeting. She came home late and immediately crashed. It wasn't that she avoided me; she was just pathologically disorganized. I didn't take her behavior personally.

Abby and I spent three entire days and nights together, attending a frog exhibit at the Exploratorium, going for walks, talking, renting videos, and cooking. On one walk, I jumped up on a stump in a park, and she immediately joined me and tried to push me off in a game of King of the Mountain. We wrestled a moment and then I let her win. She was amazingly strong; grappling with her was very arousing because her butchness contrasted wildly with her ravishing face and youthful, feminine voice. She also smelled great, like marigolds and something muskier. When we watched *Big Night* – which Scott Thunes introduced to me – we sat very close together on the sofa. After the video was over, she arched her back, linked her hands over her head, and stretched, making a contentment-squeak. Then she dropped her arms, her right hand landing on my shoulder. She stood up, unfolding gracefully off the couch. As she did so, she ran her palm lightly from my shoulder across my back in a friendly, sort of absent-minded caress. She smiled down at me and went off to the bathroom.

We painted together one afternoon, using her acrylics and brushes; she said she wanted to study graphic design in college. I produced a column of red humanoid figures ascending in a yellow cloud. She loved it, so I gave it to her. That night she planned to visit a painter friend who lived nearby, while my newly veganized and sexually liberated pal and I would go out. Listening to a jazz band at a club, my friend told me that Abby talked about me all the time and asked tons of questions about me. When we came home, I let my friend off in front of her house and told her to leave the door unlocked while I parked. By the time I got to the house, the door was locked, as I expected. I tapped on the glass until I saw my friend come down the hall to let me in, but it was actually Abby. She was back from the painter's house because he'd gone from a respectful, funny gentleman of twenty-eight to a lecher who suddenly groped her and called her legs "nice sausages."

He'd demanded that she cook him dinner, slapping her butt and saying, "Get in there and rustle me up some grub, woman!" She'd told him to fuck off and came home. At the kitchen table, she poured out her heart to me. Her frumpy appearance was deliberate, she explained, because every man she'd ever met had crudely, disrespectfully hit on her. She dressed to hide her body; she made sure to never walk with her feet splayed outward like the dancer she was; she didn't wear makeup; and she let her hair look like a tumbleweed, all to keep men at bay. Why were men interested in only one thing?

"Because we're men," I said.

"Well, maybe it's time for me to be a lesbian, then."

"Why not? I love women myself, so why shouldn't you?"

And we laughed.

I left early the next morning. On my way out the door, Abby hugged me and said, "I'm really, really glad I met you. Seriously glad." The afternoon I returned from San Francisco, I told Tim all about Abby as he worked in his garden. He waited until I'd finished, and then he looked up at me, pulled his sunglasses down to the end of his nose so I could see his eyes, and said, "Tom. Let this one go." I got angry and decided not to tell him anything more about her.

Back in New England, Abby sent me a scrapbook she'd made to commemorate our meeting. It was full of weirdly apt images of surprise and beauty, as well as the lyrics of her new song. One photo showed a bullet piercing an apple. "This is how I felt getting to know you," she wrote. We exchanged letters and e-mails for the next eighteen months, two or three times a week. An excerpt from one of her letters.

> I'm thinking about joining the circus. So many bizarre characters to get to know & work with, so many possibilities for repressed, eccentric people like me to reveal their unique talents and be appreciated for them. Lots of exotic animals, colorful lighting, exciting & death-defying stunts to partake in, and NO <u>Mickey!</u> What'chaa think, Tommy?
>
> I've just finished a painting I'd started before I went to San Francisco, and it's by far the best realistic depiction of my face I've ever done. This amazes me, because I haven't tried to do much art (and no realism at all). There were a few things here and there, like the stuff we worked on in SF. I have your painting here in my room, hanging above my desk. I love it, Tom! It'll be with me wherever I go.
>
> Lots of love,
> Abby

On the bottom right-hand side of the letter, she drew a cartoon of herself inside a cannon with a lit fuse; on the side of the gun was printed "WARNING: AIM AWAY FROM FACE." A top-hatted ringmaster stood next to her with a word balloon over his head that said, "Ladies and gentlemen, the magnificent Abby the Helldog will now be shot from a cannon into a pile of strawberry jam!" In the lower left corner of the paper was a gooey red mass with a signboard reading "So long, overbearing unquenchable idealistic conscientious dreams!"

Sometimes she'd call, "just to hear your voice." She once told me that she'd phoned so she could sit on her front porch and tell me about the fireflies, and for my birthday she sent me a brightly colored, tentacled flower-alien thing she'd made out of Sculpey. It was improbable, funny, odd, and beautiful, like Abby.

The Call the Publicist Never Forgot

The morning after my return from San Francisco, Tim and I sat in our back yard, smoking and drinking coffee. My father suddenly appeared at our fence.

"I'm having a heart attack!" he announced in a metallic voice.

Tim jumped up and ran into our house to change. He'd drive my parents to the emergency room because my mother had trouble with her hips at the time. My father turned and headed for his car. I followed, and as we passed my Aunt Marion's house, Marion's housekeeper poked her head out the back door and called, "Say, Ed! Do ya have any garbage bags I can borrow?"

My father shouted, "Can't talk now! I'm having a heart attack!"

The housekeeper withdrew and closed the door like a cuckoo going back into its clock. My father sat in the front passenger seat of his car as my mother came limping out of her house.

"Did you get my message?" she asked sweetly.

"Let's go! Let's go!" my father yelled, so I got behind the wheel, unbathed and in my flannel pajama-pants, with no driver's license, but Tim raced up and took my place. He and my parents sped off to the hospital and I went home to check the answering machine.

"*Wake up! Wake up!*" my mother's voice yelled. "*Pick up the phone! We need you! Where are you? Isn't anybody there?*" A tsunami of guilt, enough to wash away an entire nation, swept through me. I sat by the phone, and after an hour it rang. It was a publicist I knew pretty well.

"Hey, Tom," he said, "I'd like to toss a couple of ideas your way."

"Well, see, my father's had a heart attack and he's been rushed to the hospital, and I'm waiting to see if he's still alive, so can I call you later?"

"Ah. Well. How is he?"

"That's what I'm waiting to find out. Can I call you later?"

"Sure. Um, goodbye." *Click.*

After a couple hours, I got word that my father hadn't actually had a heart attack but suffered from massively occluded coronary arteries. Two were completely blocked and two were operating at 20 percent capacity. A quadruple bypass fixed Dad right up. I later phoned the publicist, but he wouldn't take my call. It was months before he worked with me again. When I told Tim, he said that I now represented such a horrific memory to the guy, like someone cut in half who was still alive and talking, that he had no idea what to say to me. I still feel bad about it.

I'm sorry, Mr. Publicist. But you do have to admit it's kind of funny now.

The First Ghost Speaks

In August of 1999, I came home and found a message on my answering machine.

> Hey, Tom Wictor. This is unbelievable! This is Brigitte Cardei! I just got your number from this other [withheld] girl that you met at a party last March, and I

can't believe it! I can't believe that you're here! [Laughs.] I haven't talked to you in twenty, twenty-three years or something. I'm so glad to get your number. So give me a call! I'm in [withheld], in the Valley. My number is [withheld]. I even called my sister this morning to tell her! And she was like, 'Oh my God!' She was just thinking about you! So we have a lot of catching up to do. So call me, okay? It's Sunday, eleven o'clock. Can't wait to hear from you. Hope everything is well! Take care. Bye!

Her voice sounded the same as when we were thirteen, but her native-language accent seemed slightly stronger. I called, and we had a nice chat about what we'd been doing since 1977, filling each other in on our families. Though she was super busy, we arranged to meet at a cultural function for people of her nationality in a few weeks. I was blown away, my head filled with the image of her outline fading into the fog in the Netherlands as she walked out of my life twenty-two years earlier, and now we were going to meet. I was indebted to Scott Thunes, in whose house I found the magazine that alerted me to her presence in Los Angeles.

Exit Plan B

August of 1999 brought with it the reintroduction of my first ghost and the destruction of my fallback plan for what to do if – now *when* – my career in music journalism didn't work out. Since 1992 my skills as a model maker had steadily improved until I'd become what is referred to as a "master modeler," a term dating back to the days when model makers built for governments. I'd published dozens of articles in prestigious British and American periodicals. My plan was to offer my services to museums, which are always in need of dioramas and models. I could also tap into the network of collectors who pay handsomely for others to assemble and paint cars, ships, aircraft, military vehicles, and figures. I'd bought a 35 mm camera with a macro lens, built a lighting setup, and learned how to photograph my work.

One night in August, when I sat down to continue painting a face the size of a pea, I found I couldn't focus on it. My painting technique required that I bring these pieces to within about four inches of my eyes, but for some reason I couldn't focus on anything closer than about sixteen inches. I went to my eye doctor and told him what the problem was. We did some tests, and his conclusion: "Welcome to middle age." I got my first set of bifocals, but they didn't help. Magnifying rings or visors didn't work, either, because of the inherent depth-perception problem. They made it impossible to judge when the tiny paintbrush was actually about to come into contact with the figure's surface. My painting technique of layering with acrylic washes required absolute precision and a delicate touch. I simply couldn't do it anymore. At the end of 1999 I stopped building models and painting figures.

In Cold Sweat

August of 1999 was an eventful month. I began shopping around a book I titled *In Cold Sweat: Interviews with Really Scary Musicians*. It was unexpurgated interviews with Gene Simmons, Peter Hook of New Order, Jerry Casale of Devo, and Scott Thunes. Each section of the book consisted of an introduction, the interview, and a conclusion. I queried dozens of literary agents with no success. I then moved on to publishing houses that accepted unagented submissions. I'd written the whole book before I made my queries, which you're not supposed to do with nonfiction, but I didn't care. Following the rules hadn't worked at any time in my life, so I decided to start doing things my way.

The Return and Exit of the First Ghost

I met Brigitte at her cultural function. She was a ravishing adult woman now. We hugged and she teared up momentarily, but she couldn't talk much. The second or third thing she said was, "I'm leaving L.A." After we met that one time, we spoke occasionally by phone. Finally, on a Thursday in March of 2000, I drove out to her home in the Valley and helped her pack. Actually, I did almost all the packing while she fielded an endless stream of phone calls from close friends, none of whom, she informed me, had offered to give her a hand. She'd pick up the phone and unleash a torrent of her native language, in the midst of which I'd hear, "Tom Wictor." And once or twice she'd switch to English and say something like, "Yeah, my friend Tom Wictor, who I haven't seen in twenty-five years, came over to make sure I hadn't cut my throat. He went through a lot of trouble to find me, but I was too fucked up to see him. Now he's packing my things. This is the only chance we've had to talk."

And talk we did. We spent about ten hours together, discussing pretty much everything but initially avoiding our time in Holland. She was beyond caring about anything. Her physical and emotional exhaustion made it the most candid conversation I've had in my life. Her frankness rubbed off on me, and I joined right in. We talked about our families, what failures we were in so many arenas, our lack of judgment in personal and professional relationships, the first time we were kissed, the first time we had sex, and how we'd both felt like Martians all our lives no matter where we were or who we were with. It was a marathon of self-revelation, no holds barred.

As I helped her move out of my life again, I discovered that she was frighteningly intelligent and extremely funny, my two favorite attributes in women. I didn't remember her being so funny when we were kids, but she was like a standup comedian, all of it in her second language. At one point, she showed me a photo taken on her parents' farm and said, "Here I am milking a goat. The goat is the one facing to the right," which was hilarious because she actually *did* look exactly like a goat in that picture. A thin, wild-haired, stressed-out nanny goat.

Her situation was so over the top, we couldn't stop laughing. Her business had failed even though she'd had a list of very high-end Hollywood clients. She was flat broke, on the verge of another breakdown, and felt completely alone despite her 50,000 good friends. She'd had an absolutely horrible life. The more she told me, the more we'd laugh. No one would ever believe it. Just a week after the photo shoot for the magazine I'd seen, she'd had to start a six-month chemotherapy regimen, so by the time the magazine hit the stands, she was too sick to take advantage of the publicity. After she related a litany of total disaster – an unending stream of health crises, business crises, relationship crises, family crises, crime crises, pet crises, and car crises – she yelled, "So what do you think, Tom? Should I kill myself or go to Bali? Which do you suggest?"

"Try Bali first," I said.

She had two black cats. I asked her why she preferred black cats.

"Because I'm a *witch*," she said, grinning. "Didn't you know that?"

We talked about our mutual interest in witchcraft and agreed that we tried to live by the Wiccan rede, "An' it harm none, do what ye will." Later, when Holland did come up, I told her I always thought she was part of the in-crowd because she was a cheerleader and seemed really popular.

She shouted, "Don't say that! I *hate* the in-crowd!"

It turned out she didn't have as many friends in high school as I'd thought. She was lonely a lot of the time, her aloofness masking her lack of confidence. The foreign population of our neighborhood in Holland consisted entirely of NATO and oil families, entire clans of maniacs. Even the infants were deranged.

"You know what's so pathetic?" she said. "You and I were the most normal people there! *You. And. I!*" She was right; it was a joke. We doubled over, howling. I then found a plastic container of catnip in her cupboard, left by the previous tenant. Since she'd never seen cats do this particular herb, we spread some out on a towel and watched her kitties get very mellow. She was fascinated and sat on the kitchen floor observing them for fifteen minutes, shaking her head and whispering, "*Look* at that! *Look* at it! They're completely *wasted*. You don't think it'll hurt them, do you? Oh my God, I've turned them into *drug addicts!*"

We broke for lunch at a Pollo Loco, and found a real difference in our personalities. Moving around a lot as a child can have one of two effects on you: Either it makes it easier for you to haul up stakes and start over, or it makes it impossible for you to say goodbye. She was in the first camp, and I'm definitely in the second. I've gotten myself in a lot of trouble because of my inability to let go.

"I *do* care about people; I really do," she said, picking at her chicken salad, "but it's just not that big a deal for me to leave them if I have to. It's painful, but I can do it. I don't agonize over it."

"Has every person you've ever met wanted something from you?" I asked.

"Yes," she said, and told me how her landlord came over once to do some work on the house, and she offered him a glass of wine because she was going to have one. The next day, he showed up unannounced with his own bottle of wine. His attentions got more and more intrusive until she had to speak sharply to him. After that he wouldn't come out and make repairs anymore. She'd also told me her ex-boyfriend Nelson was so angry with her for leaving that he refused to see her off. He'd called soon after I'd arrived at her house, and she'd spoken to him very soothingly. After a few minutes, she'd put the receiver against her chest and smiled at me, saying, "He's being a real asshole."

We went back to work packing, and she asked over and over, "This isn't so awful, is it? You're having fun, aren't you?" While we talked, she threw her life away, bit by bit. She filled a huge trash container and gave me what remained: ceramic planters, a shopping bag full of new pens, a poster, books, a camera, a CD player, lanterns, a Palm Pilot, even her pager. "Just take it. I don't care!" She was in a fugue state, sleepwalking through this latest upheaval, telling me, "I can do it because I'm numb. I don't feel a thing." The saddest part was watching her dump an entire box of business cards, a thousand of them. She offered me one as a keepsake. In her office, she showed me what she'd done for her A-list Hollywood customers. I guess she really must've been the terrible businesswoman she said she was because she should've made millions. I told her I thought her ideas were brilliant.

"I hate it all," she said. "I'm sick of it. I can't stand it anymore."

I returned to the living room, and she came and got me twice because she found spiders in her office. They turned out to be black widows. I caught them in paper towels and released them outside while she stood by, shuddering. I was surprised that after all she'd been through, something as innocuous as a black widow could scare her like that. We finally called it quits when I'd packed everything except her business records. There was nothing more I could do for her. She broke it to me gently, explaining that she had to go through her records herself. What she wanted to do was to take them all into the back yard and burn them.

"Aren't bonfires an old tradition in your culture?" I asked.

"You've been around me too long," she said. "You're starting to sound like me." She apologized for everything, told me I looked very tired and depressed, and said I should go. I wanted to stay because I knew this would be our last time alone together, but she said she was going to shower and go right to sleep.

We met the next night at a Mexican restaurant in Long Beach, owned by her best friends. It was another of her many goodbye parties. At her house, she'd shown me a hideous scrapbook another group of friends had made for her at the last party. Everyone had been divided into four teams that had to come up with the best Brigitte jokes and stories. She was the judge, and the questions were on the order of, "Is Brigitte more likely to have sex with one man seventeen times in a row, or seventeen different men one time each?" The questions, stories, and dozens of grotesque Polaroids were pasted into the book and bordered with brightly colored kindergarten stickers that said, "Terrific!" and "Fantastic!" and "Great!"

At the restaurant, I met "Anton," Brigitte's younger brother, whom I hadn't seen since he was eleven years old. He was now a gigantic, weathered civil servant living near the Canadian border, very bland and preoccupied the way I remember his father being. All he wanted to talk about was Holland. He'd thought about my family a lot over the years; "You guys had the neatest toys," he said. There was a battery-operated plastic helicopter that had made a lasting impression on him, so we reminisced about that while he drank gin and tonics. Brigitte and I didn't speak much because she had to talk with her friends, the ones who hadn't helped her move. Occasionally, she'd share a few words with me, but after a few seconds, she'd break off and croon, "Ohhh! *Hi!* How *are* you?" to someone behind me. I left at midnight.

On Sunday, Tim came along to help load the Ryder truck that would take Brigitte's things to her sister's home in another state. At Brigitte's house, we met her ex-boyfriend Nelson, who'd showed up after all. He was an aspiring country singer and told my brother and me right before he left that we had just met the next Kenny Loggins. After he was gone, Brigitte said, "One down..." and rolled her eyes.

Tim, Anton, and I loaded the Ryder while Brigitte dismantled her office. As I carried her pillows and bedclothes to the truck, they brushed my face, and I finally figured out what her scent was like: peaches. She smelled just like fresh peaches. Everything was finished by four, so we went to El Torito for even more Mexican food. Then it was time to say goodbye. We all hugged and promised to write, and then Brigitte folded her arms and went into the house, slipping out of sight exactly the way she'd vanished into the fog twenty-three years earlier.

A Tiny Publisher Takes a Chance

In March of 2000, I submitted a query for *In Cold Sweat* to a small publishing house that specialized in books about entertainment, and I received a positive but strange reply. The publisher – a New Yorker – said he'd be in Los Angeles in a week. Would I mind bringing him the manuscript? I agreed. My friends Roger and Dolores said that his hotel was a notorious dump full of crackheads and whores. Of course, I thought. Who but a crackhead or a whore would be interested in my work?

But the hotel was actually a beautiful, very exclusive little place, which matched the publisher, Mel Zerman. He was small, elderly, and very self-possessed. I handed him my manuscript and we talked for about half an hour. He promised nothing and we parted on friendly terms. By the end of the month, Mel sent me a contract, which I had a literary lawyer look over. She was nice and straightforward, but she had a habit of waiting several seconds before answering each of my questions. Since she billed me by the hour, I wondered if it was a way to stretch out the consultation. She said the contract was reasonable, except that I should be getting more of the foreign-distribution rights. After telling me what she thought was a reasonable percentage, she offered to negotiate for me. I told her I wanted to do it myself for the experience.

I called Mel, and we had a nice preliminary chat. The first part of our discussion of the contract went fine, but when we got to the foreign-distribution rights and I told him I wanted a higher percentage, he began shouting that my demands were completely unreasonable. It was one of the most stressful twenty-minute periods of my life. "I have to make *some* money, don't I?" he yelled. "Or maybe you think I don't deserve to? *Well?*" All I could think of was the endless fights with Carmen, when she'd attack me in ways she knew would cause the most pain. I kept telling myself that this was just an old trick that Louis B. Mayer used, and I held firm. Eventually, Mel agreed, and then he was affable again. He seemed completely unperturbed that I hadn't given an inch. I signed the contract in August of 2000, and the manuscript was copyedited by December.

The only thing that bothered me was that Roger and Dolores had told me that Mel's hotel was a dump. In retrospect, it seemed that all along the process of me landing my first book deal, they'd done everything they could to denigrate it and discourage me. They – like so many people in Hollywood – were of the same mindset as Gore Vidal, who said, "Whenever a friend succeeds, a little something in me dies."[4]

Roger and Dolores also played a practical joke on me that I never really got over.

My First Blind Date

She was perfect for me, my friends said. Smart, funny, unconventional, and voluptuous. I'll call her Tarynn. She was Armenian, and she worked in the music department of a film studio. We'd therefore have something in common. After weeks of Roger and Dolores's badgering, I finally agreed to e-mail Tarynn despite my doubts. Dolores gave me her e-mail address and I sent her an introduction: "Hi. You don't know me, but my name is Tom, and I got your e-mail address from Dolores, the original Goddess Pomona herself, and – " It was a terrible first contact that reeked of fear, but she wrote back a couple of days later. Suddenly, I was in the middle of a sexy and mysterious exploit.

In her fourth e-mail, she told me she was an actor, which chilled my blood. Actors are dangerous. I'd enjoyed our exchanges, though. In the same message, she said, "We must meet! The suspense is killing me!" So, actor or not, I sent her my phone number, and she called the next night. We had a fun, hour-long conversation about New York, cigarettes, traveling, movies, food, and Europe. She seemed slightly shy, in that there were a lot of extended silences, or the beginnings of extended silences, I mean, because I immediately filled them with babble. I loved her deep voice, and she had a humorous flustered quality, like Joan Rivers. By the end of the call, I really liked her. She was very bright, and she said her e-mails to me hadn't been very long because she couldn't compete; I was just too funny. I blew a raspberry, and she blew it right back. That told me we just might click.

I'd said in my e-mails that my only requirement was that she be brutally honest. If she didn't think things were working out, she should just tell me. She shouldn't try to cushion the blow. I'd never been on a blind date and didn't know the rules, so I wanted to make my own: Let's just be honest. The original plan was to meet for coffee, but after the e-mails and phone conversation, we agreed to make it a dinner date because we were already getting along so well.

After the phone call, I looked her up on the Internet and found a site with her photo. She was beautiful, with long dark hair and strong features. Having recently finished graduate school, she lived with her mother and grandmother so she wouldn't have to pay rent and could pursue her art. Just like me. Roger and Dolores again swore we were a perfect match. I'd called to complain that they hadn't told me she was an actor, but they said she was very down-to-earth, completely unactorish. "All she cares about is if you're a nice guy," Dolores said. "She's had it with L.A. guys and their Palm Pilots and big talk."

That was apparently the truth because I'd told her in my e-mails that since I was a struggling, would-be, emerging, incipient writer, I wouldn't be able to wine and dine her the way other men could. She wrote back, "A lot of women think money's important. I'm not one of them."

I prepared for the date by buying a new jacket. I'd lost a lot of weight recently and shaved off my goatee, and I brimmed with newfound confidence. Also, I told myself I wouldn't care if it didn't work out. It would just be an adventure.

The traffic on the way to West Hollywood was horrendous, making me almost ten minutes late. I arrived at the coffee shop where we'd arranged to meet and parked in the 7-Eleven lot next door so I could run in, find her, and apologize. The second I saw her, I knew it wouldn't work. She had that horrible Los Angeles-actor look. When she saw me, she smiled a glittering stage smile and swooshed forward, leaning back with her hand out, like, "*Darling!*" I wanted to go right home. But I didn't. We got in my car and drove to the Mexican restaurant she'd picked out. On the way, she sat sideways in the seat and stared at me. And stared at me. And stared at me. She never took her eyes off me. I don't remember what we talked about in the car. What was I doing with an actor? It was crazy. She was nothing like the way she'd been on the phone, her fluster replaced by a TV commercial for soothing lotion.

At the restaurant, we talked almost entirely about acting, with a few detours every now and then into other subjects. There was a lot of dead air that I had to fill because she didn't seem capable. I wracked my brains for acting-related things to talk about, like training methods I half-remembered from a biography of Brando. It was exhausting. I hadn't had to work so hard with someone in a long, long time, especially not in a situation I'd volunteered for. She was emotionally sealed off, as though she were auditioning. Plus, she would *not* break eye contact. It made me so self-conscious I had to take off my glasses. She had a chicken enchilada and I had a beef burrito. We each had a taste of the other's food, which was a strange thing to do.

Her main philosophy in life was that if you were a good person, you should be rewarded with success, happiness, a meaningful relationship, etc. She was bitter that so many of her peers landed great acting jobs when they didn't deserve them. It made her feel there was no justice in the world. "This is my major problem," she said. "I'm bitter and angry sometimes. A *lot* of the time." I told her that while I had my own problems with anger, bitterness, and injustice, other people's situations were irrelevant to me. I could only worry about my own life because whether Bill Gates had eighty, ninety, or 100 billion dollars, it had no effect on me. She disagreed, so we dropped it and went back to acting.

After dinner we took a long walk, talking about acting, poetry, and some of my writing. She seemed to relax somewhat and became less distant. I thought that maybe I was being unrealistic. No doubt I'd wanted an explosion of instant attraction, a lightning bolt, the way it'd been with Carmen, and when that didn't happen, I was upset. Maybe Carmen had ruined everyone for me. Just to see how I felt about it, I imagined going to bed with Tarynn. I pictured her naked, but I didn't know how I felt about it. Even though she was very voluptuous, I just didn't have much of a physical attraction to her. I couldn't get a sense of her personality because she hid behind her craft, which blunted my interest in her.

Still, there was a growing sense of... something. It came out only in our last few minutes together, when we laughed about the acting roles she was offered. She's not a tall, thin, blonde girlie-girl, so she's not much in demand. We described our exercise programs, and she said she didn't lift weights because it would make her look even wider. She slapped her rather large rear and said, "That's me, man. The stocky Mediterranean type." I started to like her a lot more. The person she'd been on the phone had reemerged. As I drove her back to where she'd parked, she said, "Well, this wasn't a disaster after all, was it?" I agreed it wasn't.

"The question is, should I call you again?" I asked lightly, fully expecting her to say, "Of course!"

"Well, I don't know," she answered. "There're no real sparks, are there? I mean, I had fun, but there's no real attraction here. Some people think it's a waste of time to keep trying when there's no initial attraction." She said more, but I don't remember any of it. I just have a memory of her in my car, her mouth moving. She finished with, "Um... I hope I haven't hurt your feelings." I assured her she hadn't, and we parted on a note of, "Maybe we can be friends. We had a nice time, so maybe we'll catch a movie sometime." I offered to shake her hand, but she hugged me instead, with sympathy, it seemed, and I got into my car and drove away.

On the way home, I became depressed almost to the point of tears. I have an idea why. It wasn't just the roller-coaster quality of the evening, with its initial shock, subsequent hard work, gradual recovery, and unexpected deathblow. It was something else entirely. I'd trusted my friends, and they'd deliberately set me up with someone they had to know wouldn't find me attractive. They'd played a joke on me to hurt me. It was pure lookism on her part. My e-mails were great, my phone technique was terrific, and yet when we met face to face, she lost interest. It was too bad; in the waning moments, I'd really started to like her again, her and her big ass. I liked the way she slapped it. A couple hours after I got home, I learned the burrito had given me food poisoning. Or maybe it was the bite of her enchilada. Anyway, I was sick as a dog for three days.

By the end of my relationship with Roger and Dolores, they were openly hostile toward me.

Exorcising the Mailman

The most frightening assassin in cinematic history is Gunnery Sergeant William Lloyd, the Mailman in *Three Days of the Condor.* Anton Chigurh of *No Country for Old Men* can't even begin to compare to the Mailman. Chigurh is contrived and chews the scenery, while the Mailman is horrifyingly realistic. The first time I saw *Three Days of the Condor,* the brutality and impersonal mercilessness of the killings and attempted killings by the Mailman upset me greatly. I couldn't get over the injustice of gunning down helpless, cornered, pleading, terrified, and unarmed innocents.

For me the Mailman took on a special significance after the 101 California Street shootings of July 1, 1993. A fat, aging screwup took two TEC-9 assault pistols to the law firm of Petit and Martin and murdered eight people. It was one of the reasons I left San Francisco; my document-retrieval company regularly did work in that building, and I'd been there myself. The fat, dead screwup's hands were cut to ribbons when the cops found him because the guns kept jamming and he had to clear the stoppages by hitting the sharp bolt handles. That notorious jamming issue was probably what'd saved Tim and me on December 28, 1995, the night a jolly would-be killer attacked us with the same weapon and I begged him for my life.

The sheer evil of office massacres and other mass shootings has always enraged me. In the spring of 2000 I met Hank Garrett, the actor who played the Mailman in *Three Days of the Condor.* He couldn't have been nicer, and when I told him that his character had haunted me for twenty years, he apologized. I shook his hand and he autographed a photo of the Mailman for me. It's from the fight scene in Faye Dunaway's apartment, one of the most chilling confrontations ever staged. Hank's is the only autographed photo of an entertainer I own. His friendliness and concern helped me put a few of my long-standing issues to rest.

Thank you, Hank. I'm not afraid anymore.

Publicists Lead Interesting Lives

I interviewed a young musician whose publicist sat next to him, clarifying everything he said: "Actually, what [withheld] means is – " After the interview, I served as the stand-in while the photographer took Polaroids. The photographer was interested in cloning; he mentioned Dolly the Scottish sheep.

"Was it a sheep or a goat, though?" he asked me.

Before I could answer, the musician let out a huge sigh and said, "It was a *ewe.*" He sat slumped on the sofa, his arms folded across his chest. His head rested on the back of the sofa, and his eyes were closed. He spoke with an exhausted, blaring emphasis. "That's E-W-E. It's a female *sheep.* Female *sheep* are called *ewe.*"

The publicist just sat there, examining the backs of her hands.

Every publicist who opened up to me on a personal basis – because I'm a nosy bastard and wanted to know everything about their business – told me the same thing: To keep on top in the Industry, you had to know what was going on at all times, so you had to hang with producers, agents, and publicists. You worked from at least eight in the morning to eight at night, then you went to the gym for an hour. All you ate was restaurant food or takeout. You never cooked. At that time everyone used pagers, voice mail, and faxes, so you had to keep going back to your office to send someone a fax. Everybody worked the same insane hours, and if someone mentioned they'd invited the latest stud actor or latest babe actress to a party, nobody got hysterical the way civilians would. Other people in the Industry wouldn't beg to meet the star or interrogate you about what the evening was like. People in the Industry never dated civilians.

I got to know one relatively high-ranking publicist well enough that she once invited me to her apartment after a concert by a band she wanted me to write about. As we sat on the sofa talking, she asked me to describe my most audacious sexual exploit. I told her, and she laughed. She got up, went to her closet, pulled out a black plastic garbage bag, and dumped the contents on the sofa. It was full of envelopes. She handed me one; when I opened it, I saw that it was full of photos of her naked.

Not knowing what else to do, I went through them as she sat and watched me closely. The pictures had been taken on someone's front lawn in broad daylight, a house clearly visible in the background. There she was, without a stitch, assuming various classic porn poses: standing with her hands in her hair, her hips thrust forward; facing away from the camera and looking back over her shoulder; on her knees, facing the camera and leaning forward; on all fours, facing away, her back arched and her rear in the air; cupping her breasts; and spreading her buttocks or labia. In every shot where her face was visible, she had the same expression: arch, passive, and smug, all at the same time.

In the last shot, she stood with her back to the camera, looking over her left shoulder at the photographer. Her legs were spread and her hands were out of sight in front of her, as though she were opening her lips again. She probably was, because in this photo a man lay on the grass in front of her, aiming a camera up at her crotch.

I studied her face in the image. She had the same placid, defiant contentment as in the others, but she'd added a tiny, secret smile, sharing something with the photographer who'd taken the rest of the roll. The smile said, *You and I are the only ones who understand.*

"So who took these?" I asked.

She shrugged. "Just a guy I know."

"Who's this other guy in the last shot?"

She smiled. "I don't know."

"You don't know?"

"Nope. He was walking by while we took the pictures, and he just ran up and started taking some himself. I have no idea who he was. When he was done, he just left. We didn't say anything to him, and he didn't say anything to us. I never saw him again." She gave me the arch, docile look she had in the photos.

"So you posed naked on someone's lawn in the middle of the day, and when a complete stranger showed up and started taking his own pictures, you posed for him, too."

"Yup." She nodded and said nothing else.

"Why'd you do it?"

She frowned and pulled in her chin, a comic expression of confusion. "Because they wanted *pictures!*" She laughed. "They wanted pictures of me naked."

"But you didn't even know this second guy. You didn't know what he'd do with those pictures."

"So?"

"Well, what if he's a stalker or tries to blackmail you? Didn't you think it was dangerous?"

The Wictor family, December 4, 1970. From the left: Thomas, Tim, Cecilia, Paul, Pat, Edward, and Carrie. Portrait by Foto Studio Girone, Ciudad Ojeda, Venezuela.

Me in the Netherlands in 1976, fourteen years old and in dire need of a personal stylist. Although I listened to Led Zeppelin at the time, it didn't take. My brother Paul — whose broad, square shoulder is seen on the left — was a Pink Floyd devotee who modeled himself on Roger Waters. Nobody ever mistook him for a middle-aged Latvian spinster.

Tim (right) and me, Stavanger, Norway, summer of 1981; I'm cutting the grass with a reel mower. This is the only photo of me as an adult I ever allowed to be taken when I was shirtless. I was very proud of my physique, honed through backbreaking labor at a shore-support base supplying oil platforms. Tim calls this his "ELO Period," even though he never liked the band. In 1981 I took up the bass guitar.

Joe Cady, my punk roommate in college from 1981 to 1983. He introduced me to great music that I still love, and we've been friends for over thirty years. Neither of us knows what was going on in this photo. Whose legs are those on the floor to the left?

Joe's drawing of me with my upside-down Fender Musicmaster. A comparison with my college I.D. photo from the time (inset) reveals how Joe perfectly captured the sheepish fright that characterized my existence. In the drawing note my tongue protruding as I labor to play. Joe remembers this as my "John Lennon-chewing-tobacco" phase, because of my hair and brief addiction to Copenhagen dip that ended when an unfortunate floor mate confused his beer bottle for the one I used as a you-know-what.

Ray Shulman of Gentle Giant, my bass idol. In the background is drummer John Weathers. My goal – never achieved – was to duplicate the bass line of Gentle Giant's live version of "Free Hand" note for note. Courtesy Alucard.

"Nakamura," the Cat-faced Ghost in the Rising Sun, on one of our photo excursions in Tokyo, 1986. Though a skilled photographer, she — like all the women who've haunted me — hated having her own picture taken. To coax this smile from her, I talked dirty and promised to use a long exposure time.

A Window, March of 1988. I'm on the left; Tom Hojinacki is on drums; and the late Steiv Dixon — the First Ghost Who Released Me — plays guitar on the right. All three of us were left-handed Catholics. Steiv was six feet, five inches tall and one of the handsomest men I've ever met. He also had the ability to make me laugh myself sick.

Me playing bass with A Window in April of 1988. I was so crippled by stage fright I often took off my glasses to dissolve the audience into a comforting blur. Lots of beer helped, too, which gave me the shiny fleshiness apparent in this photo.

"Carmen," the Cardinal Ghost, performing one of her signature walkovers.

Carmen and me in Tokyo, January of 1988. When we met a couple of months before we took this photo, I recognized her and knew instantly we were supposed to be together. That had never happened before and has never happened since.

Carmen's photo of me in Tokyo, 1990, during the happiest extended period of my life. I'm surrounded by my interests and pleasures: Carmen; the sweet cat with the hilarious name that Carmen gave her; Carmen's recording equipment in the background; and a video guide for choosing the night's entertainment.

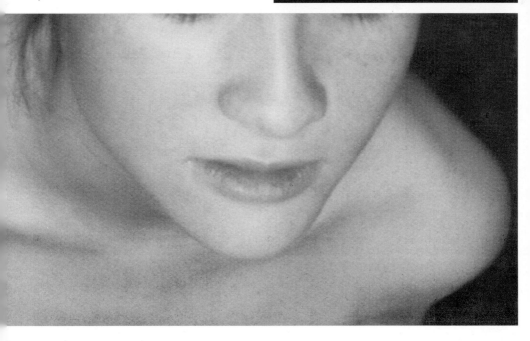

The Carmen bass, a MusicMan Sting Ray she bought me in Tokyo. A right-handed instrument, it had a left-handed body crafted by Japanese luthiers. The face under the clear plexiglass pick guard is Billy Graham, chosen simply for the reason that it was life sized and I wanted it to look like a man stared out of a portal in my abdomen as I played. Photo by Tim Wictor.

Listening to the foghorns at night, after collecting sea glass and polished stones at the beach, 1991. The pinnacle.

Carmen in San Francisco, 1992, near the end of our happiness together.

One of Carmen's self-portraits, executed in acrylic. She has no formal training in art. This painting dates from soon after August of 1992.

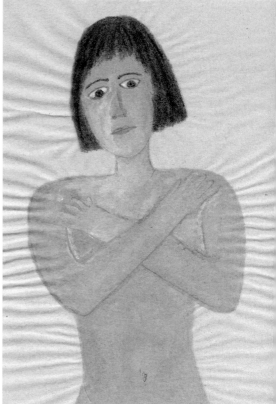

Carmen playing her MusicMan Sting Ray bass, a birthday present I bought as a last-ditch effort to save our relationship. She laughed, cried, and hugged me, the last time I felt her touch. Her positive feelings toward me lasted two days; I took this photo after she'd had the bass about a week.

The daring young hang-gliding stud who performed aerobatics for Carmen as we walked along the cliff in San Francisco. He then landed at her feet like James Bond. It was the final moment of beauty and romance we shared.

John Taylor of Duran Duran, a fantastic player, artist, and person. Another of my bass heroes, whom I had the great privilege of interviewing twice. Photo by Jay Blakesberg.

Tim preparing to murder a cake. Though the blunt-ended knife in his hand doesn't appear to be much of a weapon, Tim could actually ram a spoon through a telephone pole.

Me at my fattest, tipping the scales at 275 pounds in the summer of 1995. After breaking up with Carmen, I didn't go back to drinking and getting high. Instead, I spent a year eating fast-food cheeseburgers and fries. In the background is Eric Wictor, my youngest brother, today an engineer in the Netherlands. Photo by Tim Wictor.

"Dolores" and "Roger," my guides in Hollywood from 1995 to 2004. Photocollage by Tim Wictor.

Andy West (left), the Ghost who Never Was, and Steve Morse of the Dixie Dregs. Andy is one of the most innovative, technically gifted bassists in the world, and he set a fantastic example for me through his ability to surmount setbacks with good cheer. He also holds the distinction of being the last musician I interviewed. Photo by Jon Seivert.

My nephew Hunter James Gonzales and me in the summer of 1996. He was two and fascinated by water. I'm filling a plastic bottle for him to pour back into the wading pool. By this time I'd lost about fifty of the nearly sixty pounds I put on after I left San Francisco. However, I didn't cut my hair for three years.

Gene Simmons of Kiss, performance artist and man of great perception. He gave me one of the two best interviews of my career, without preconditions, and he blessed me and wished me well. It took years, but the most important of his wishes for me finally came true. Photo by Jill Furmanovsky.

Guitarist-keyboardist Mike Keneally, Zappa alumnus and solo artist who's played with Steve Vai, Joe Satriani, Metropole Orkest, Beer for Dolphins, the Mistakes, Marco Minnemann, and Dethklok. He negotiated my interview with Scott Thunes and was always there to help when I asked. Photo by Kevin Scherer.

Scott Thunes, the Collateral Ghost, almost-smiling in his 1987 Carvin advertisement.

Ray Shulman of Gentle Giant. I fulfilled a lifetime ambition by interviewing him, only to have my new editor kill the article as "yesterday's news." Photo by Ueli Frey.

Me wearing one of "Noreen's" midi skirts, back when she was a family friend instead of whatever it was she became in 1996. It may be a stretch, but I think this could have something to do with why I'm attracted to butch women and vice versa.

The Ghost in the Miniskirt, bassist Anne Kadrovich (left) of Sissy Bar, seen here with lead singer Joy Ray. Anne's treatment by my magazine was so unjust that it still pains me. Photo by Al Seib, copyright © 1997. Los Angeles Times. Reprinted with Permission.

Curt Smith of Tears for Fears, a great musician, incredible bassist, and a terrific inspiration for the way he never succumbed to anger and bitterness. Photo by Jay Blakesberg.

A model of a Senegalese infantryman of World War I, which I converted from a commercial figure and painted with acrylics. The figure is about two inches tall. In August of 1999 I lost the ability to build models to this standard, due to failing eyesight.

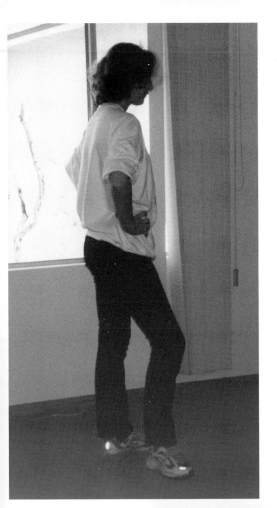

"Brigitte," the First Ghost, on the day I helped her begin the move back to her home country. I hadn't seen her in twenty-three years. We had a ten-hour conversation that was the most candid of my life. I've achieved that level of intimacy with a woman only twice, and this time it lasted less than half a day.

The "Mailman," Gunnery Sergeant William Lloyd. A merciless assassin in Three Days of the Condor, actor Hank Garrett played him. Meeting Hank and having him autograph this photo allowed me to put a few major post-traumatic issues behind me.

Scott, Hazle, and Georgia Thunes, September 16, 2000. We all had a terrific, low-key time. Hazle was the most articulate baby I've ever met. When she said, "Hi, Tom," she sounded like a senior in high school. Today she's six feet tall and projects like a twenty-seven-year-old.

Photo of me taken by Scott Thunes on September 16, 2000, about two seconds after he showed me a picture of himself. That which is seen can never be unseen.

November 28, 2000, the day I left New England after my disastrous, madness-inducing visit with my doomed friend Abby.

Me performing a reading of In Cold Sweat: Interviews with Really Scary Musicians, accompanied by Ak & Zuie. Pete Gallagher is on percussion and Stephen Jay is on the bass. Stephen is easily one of the most technically accomplished yet thoroughly artistic bassists and composers of all time. His main gig is bass player for "Weird Al" Yankovic, but his solo material is unbelievable.

The bassist I cut out of a Carvin ad in Guitar Player and glued to a piece of poster board for my memory box in 1985. I had no idea who he was. It was only in 2006 that I discovered he was Scott Thunes, a bassist whose name and music I didn't know at all when I built the box.

German portable-flamethrower squad of World War I. Without intending to, I became the planet's greatest expert on World War I flamethrowers, which is akin to being the planet's greatest expert on pencil erasers or plastic bread-bag tabs.

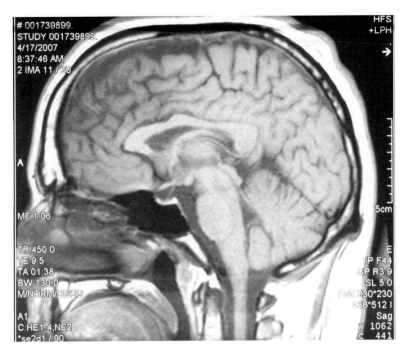

Portrait of my brain, taken during the First Really Weird Disease. The near-perfect flatness of the top of my skull always bothered me. I once considered having a domed plastic implant custom made and installed, but now I don't care. Even if I were given the convex crown I wanted, it wouldn't do anything about my wide hips and narrow shoulders.

Ventsislav Gramatski (right) and Anna Dyulgerova, Senior Expert of the Directorate of Funds, Restoration, and Military Monuments, National Museum of Military History, in Sofia, Bulgaria. They hold my book Flamethrower Troops of World War I, which Ventsislav helped me research by conducting interviews with museum staffers. I donated a copy of the finished book to the institution, which commemorated the occasion with this gorgeous photo.

Colonel of the Reserves Mikhail Vasilyevich Supotnitskiy, M.D., Army of the Russian Federation. He's a microbiologist, an expert in plagues, and a lover of art and whimsy. Our cooperation on my second flamethrower book led to a friendship. Someday I hope to meet him in person. His favorite movie is Apocalypse Now; he says that the famous line about loving the smell of napalm in the morning is a healthy reaction by a military man after destroying the enemy. Photo by Nadezhda Supotnitskiy.

Stephen Jay — composer, songwriter, vocalist, bassist, and master of presque vu — demonstrating the amazing thumb-slapping technique that allows him to play rhythm and lead at the same time. His "polymetric funk" is mesmerizing, and his lyrics are otherworldly.

Deep Thoughts of a Pilot, by Leslie Ditto, the only piece of original art I own. The second I saw it, I had to have it. This painting played a significant part in my un-haunting. Photo by Tim Wictor.

My brother Tim, the reason I don't worry about stalkers. In fact, stalkers really should worry about Tim. Photo by Tim Wictor.

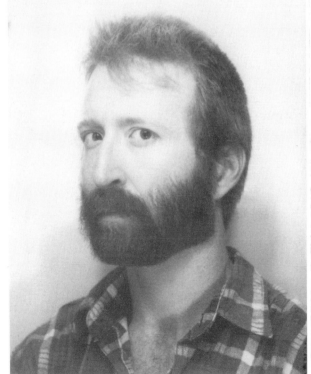

Syd the Second, who adopted us on August 22, 2010, and left us August 22, 2011. He lies in the Angry Chair outside my back door. His terrifying claws did the damage to the wood. I have scars on my hands as a testament to his demons, which he finally cast out through sheer willpower and force of character. Photo by Tim Wictor

Major Bernhard Reddemann (left), commander of the German flamethrower regiment in World War I. Only after publishing three books in whole or in part about him did I realize that he was another ghost, warning me of the fate that awaited me unless I made drastic changes.

Bryan Beller, bassist at various times with Steve Vai, Dethklok, The Aristocrats, Mike Keneally, Dweezil Zappa, Wayne Kramer, and James LaBrie. He's also my official hands, playing bass for me because I can't anymore. That means I'm now a musical genius. Photo by Rob Olewinski.

Scott Thunes with the Mother Hips in 2012. Thunes's live performances as bassist for this band are likely his best playing ever, eclipsing even his stellar work with Frank Zappa in 1988. Photo by Jay Blakesberg.

Scott Thunes with Mother Hips guitarist-vocalist Tim Bluhm and drummer John Hofer, 2012. Photo by Jay Blakesberg.

Private F. Eger, a soldier of the Russian Expeditionary Force, in a postcard he sent from France to his friend Frida on June 12, 1916. The message he wrote on it condensed my entire memoir into one paragraph. Finding this card, as well as the timing and manner thereof, affirmed my belief that our existence has meaning.

A triptych I did of Carmen and me in Tokyo, January of 1988. Even back then, she'd mastered the art of not-smiling for photos. Me, not so much, especially when she sat on my lap. I loved the way her smile utterly transformed her face. It was an act of magic she could perform at will.

Carmen, July of 2012.

Deep Thoughts of Carmen, 2012.

The Carmen bass and me, August 26, 2012. Though I told Carmen I'd sold it because at the time I honestly thought that was the only way for me to achieve peace of mind, I now realize I was wrong. It's beautiful and I love it. I've kept it to remind me not of all that I lost, but of everything I once had. Photo by Tim Wictor.

Carmen performing live in late 2011. Until she sent me this photo, I didn't know she'd begun playing again.

Scott Thunes and me before a Mother Hips show at Saint Rocke in Hermosa Beach, California, on September 7, 2012. It was the first time I'd seen him in twelve years and the first time I saw him play in person. Photo by Jay Blakesberg.

Carmen in 2012 at our favorite place, a cold, gray, cloudy beach. I hope she finds all the sea glass and polished stones she ever wanted, and I hope all the rest of her lives are full of unexpected beauty and surprises, like an endless stream of daring young hang gliders landing at her feet.

Goodbye, J., and thank you for the chance.

The elusive *retunsus risu,* only two photographs of which are known to exist. Xenologists have dubbed this 1992 image the "Bat Lady of San Francisco," while the second photo is the "Tokyo Grace" of 1988. The *retunsus risu* was once plentiful in both cities. Though its current whereabouts and outlook are unknown, the species is possessed of hardiness and resilience that have no doubt ensured its survival.

"No."

I stacked the photos, put them in their envelope, and handed it to her. She seemed hurt.

"I thought you'd like them," she said.

I shrugged, at a complete loss.

"Well, I want you to have them, Tom. I have lots of copies."

"Why do you want me to have them?"

"Because they're *sexy!* I fulfilled a fantasy! I had a good time. I wanted to share that with you."

"Oh. Okay, sure," I said.

She hugged her knees against her chest. "There's lots more I'd like to share with you, Tom. An *awful* lot. Those pictures are nothing. I trust you now. I'd like to show you some more things one of these days." Her eyes glittered above her little smile.

I burned the photos she gave me. We never worked together on anything. I have no idea what happened to her because I never heard from her after she gave me the photos. Though I could easily look her up on the Internet, I won't.

How to Win Over an Interviewee

I liked Lynn Keller when I met her. Not surprisingly, she was suspicious of me. Over the course of my career I'd discovered that there was genuine prejudice in the music industry against women who play the bass, just as there is in the entertainment business against female standup comedians and comedy writers. "Women aren't as funny as men" is one of the stupidest statements ever uttered, but "Women can't play the bass" is just as idiotic. I'd seen the way the music press treats women bassists, so I understood Keller's wariness. Women who play the bass are always called "female bassists" instead of just bassists. Though Keller was pleasant during our pre-interview chat at the outdoor café in Pasadena, she was a bit too standoffish for me to perceive how best to engage her.

My goal was to make her feel at ease. Almost immediately, nature came along and lent me a hand. Well, okay, not a *hand*. At any rate, it made Lynn relax and give me a great interview.

Could you tell me a little bit about your musical background?
I was raised by two musicians, so I kind of grew up in music, starting with piano at a very early age, when I was seven, and ended up with the flute as my main instrument for the early portion of my life. I was a flute major. Went to the University of Illinois in Champaign as a flute major on scholarship there. Studied there a couple years on flute. Really didn't like it. Found there was just a lack of inspiration from the teacher I was with, the professor I was with. Kind of just lost my zest for it, and during that time, I was sort of prompted to begin playing bass by a friend of mine who was in a rock band back in the seventies.

Actually, it was a woman friend of mine, and I was playing keyboards in the band, and she said, "Well, we need a bass player. Do you want to learn?" So every day, her boyfriend would bring a different bass. He was a guitar player, but he'd bring a different bass every single day to rehearsal. I picked it up, and I never put it down, and it was 1976. So by the time – [Laughs.] By the time I left Champaign – [Laughs again.]

Perfect.
[Laughing.] Ah. Oh. Um, should we find you a napkin?

Yeah. I've got one here in the bag.
Wow.

As long as it doesn't happen on my head, I'm okay.
Wow. I can't believe that. I've never seen that happen, like, in person.

Not in real life. Yeah.
No!

And now it's on tape, too!
[Laughs heartily.]

For the benefit of the tape, I just got crapped on by a pigeon.
Yeah. Gotta love *that!*

[Wiping my leg.] Okay! So...
So shortly after starting bass, I ended up moving to Austin, Texas, because I heard they had a great music scene. So I moved there and began playing bass professionally...

Thank you, pigeon, for breaking the ice.

Money is for Idiots

I tried for months in the pre-Internet days to track down a bass legend. Here's the query letter I wrote to the record label that released his two solo albums.

> Dear Mr. [Smith]:
> I am a Contributing Editor at *Bass Player,* and I'm trying to locate [a bassist], formerly of [a huge band] and creator of two solo albums, [title one] and [title two], both on your label. I'd like to do a feature-length article on [the bassist] in response to the many letters the magazine gets asking why he's never been covered.
> I've been trying for several weeks to obtain information from [your label], but nobody ever returns my calls or answers my queries. In addition, the switchboard operator there in New York wouldn't tell me the name of anyone in Publicity. I got your name from an anonymous switchboard operator in Los Angeles, so I hope you're the right person. I spoke on the phone to your assistant [Ms. Jones] a week or so ago, but again, I've gotten no response.
> Since the two solo albums by [the bassist] are still in print, [your label] must be sending him royalty checks, which means you have an address on file somewhere. Could you let me know one way or another if [your label] plans to help me out here? I want to write a long, in-depth article, and the magazine has an extremely large circulation. This is a pretty decent opportunity to garner widespread exposure. If you don't have or can't get an address or number for [the bassist's] management or publicity, could you let me know so that I can look somewhere else?
> Thanks for your cooperation, and I look forward to hearing from you soon.
> Sincerely,
> Thomas Wictor

My letter was sent back to me with the scrawled, handwritten note at the bottom, "No forwarding address or phone # for [the bassist] at this time."

I guess they didn't bother sending residual checks, and the bassist wasn't upset that he received none of the substantial money generated by the sales of his two highly successful albums. Everything was cool, and I never got to interview him.

A Nice Time with the Collateral Ghost

On September 16, 2000, I paid a visit to the Thunes household, since I was in the Bay Area to look in on other friends. I also needed to pick up photos of Scott for *In Cold Sweat*. We had a terrific afternoon and early evening together. I met Scott and Georgia's new baby Hazle Nova, who greeted me in crystal-clear, perfectly articulated English, even though she was still an infant and preferred scooting around on her seat instead of walking. Scott and Georgia told me that many of their acquaintances worried that Hazle would suffer from stunted development if she were allowed to continue her preferred mode of locomotion. The Thuneses disagreed, telling me that their daughter would decide for herself when she was ready to walk.

In March of 2012, I watched a YouTube video by Hazle, in which she sang an original song titled "City Love," accompanying herself on the piano. The video becomes astonishing in its presentation of a fully formed, utterly authentic talent after the viewer learns that Hazle was twelve when she performed it. She's also nearly six feet tall. The Thuneses had her number from day one, a skill so rare among parents that it often seems nonexistent. Yet here was the proof that good, supportive, deeply engaged parents do walk among us.

During that visit in 2000, I begged Scott again to let me ghostwrite his memoirs, and he again refused. This time, however, I stayed for dinner and left at a reasonable hour instead of fleeing at 11:00 P.M. After dinner Scott surprised me by taking my picture with a Polaroid. Although my face is that of a man preparing for his execution by firing squad, I actually enjoyed myself immensely with the Thuneses and was grateful for the time I spent with them. My expression was due to a photo Scott had just shown me of the worst sunburn he'd gotten in his life. It was a nude photo.

You'll thank me for not describing it to you and not including it in my book, as Scott suggested.

King Mensch

After Mel Zerman decided to publish *In Cold Sweat,* he changed his mind about it being mostly text and said it should be lavishly illustrated with photos. I set about trying to collect them. All the photographers were given the deadline, and most sent me what they had far ahead of time. Two of the giants in the rock-and-roll photo industry, Jill Furmanovsky and Neil Zlozower, were the most helpful, offering some of the best images in the book for very reasonable rates. One big-named guy, however, simply did not follow through. I'd call, write, fax – no response, or "They're on their way." Three days before the deadline, in desperation I went to Neil Zlozower's studio and begged him to look through his collection to see if he had any more of the musicians I needed.

"Who's the photographer you're waiting for?" Neil asked in his unique voice, which makes him sound like a hit man. If you heard that voice coming out of the darkness in your apartment at night, you'd fall right over dead. You'd instantly give up the ghost. I identified the photographer, and Neil said, "I know him. Let me give him a call." So he did, and he asked in a jovial, menacing way what the holdup was, because he had the writer sitting right there with him, freaking out, and the deadline was only three days away. What was the deal?

I heard the guy whine something, and then Neil thanked him and hung up. "He said you didn't give him a *drop-dead* deadline, so he thought he had more time." Then Neil Zlozower did something that showed the sort of person he is: He gave me original, irreplaceable negatives and let me take them to a local photo lab, where – since he's a legend in the industry and he'd called ahead – they made prints immediately, on the spot, and I brought Neil back his negatives an hour later. I then FedExed everything to Mel and made the deadline with a day to spare.

Neil saved my bacon. He had no reason to do so, and he risked negatives that are worth thousands because they're part of his decades-long body of work. He did it purely to help me.

Thank you, Neil. I've never forgotten it.

Once a Nymph; Soon to be a Ghost

After we shared eighteen months of correspondence and phone calls, my little hippie-friend Abby invited me to New England for Thanksgiving. I decided to drive, since I'd never crossed the country by car. The closer I got to my destination, the happier I became. When I arrived in her hometown, I found a motel and then went to where she worked to surprise her. I came up behind her and said, "Excuse me, miss," in a nasal tone, and when she turned around, she fell back against the counter and then lunged at me and gave me a hug that almost broke my spine, laughing and crying exactly like Carmen had done when we'd reunited in July of 1989 and when I'd phoned her in June of 1996. "Oh, my *God,* it's so good to *see* you!" she gasped. She still had an hour and a half left before she got off work, so I went next door to a Bed Bath and Beyond and mooned around, floating several inches off the floor. It was the second-happiest moment of my life. To be greeted that way is something everyone should be lucky enough to experience at least once. It does wonders for your psyche.

When Abby and I met up ninety minutes later, she'd changed. She was aloof, munching on a sandwich. I said, "I thought we were going to have dinner together."

She shrugged. "You didn't say anything about dinner. I always have a sandwich after I get off work."

At her insistence, we went to a Thai restaurant, where I had an order of chicken Pad Thai and she sat there fidgeting and rebuffing all my attempts at conversation. I took a photo of us by holding my camera at arm's length; it's a remarkable image I didn't see until I had it developed a month later. She leans forward with her elbows on the table, her right hand clenched in a fist against her cheek and dragging down the corner of her open mouth. Her expression is appalling, a wide-eyed, childlike gape of terror. She looks like a little girl who's either been kidnapped or caught doing something she knows she shouldn't and now faces draconian punishment. I missed this because I was busy grinning in complacent obliviousness at the camera.

Over the next three weeks, we got together twice. My motel was amazing, a perfectly preserved relic from about 1946, with dark wood-paneled walls, steam radiators, and mid-century modern furniture. It was like a set from a film noir, which was appropriate. In the mornings I'd lie in my sagging, steel-springed mattress and listen to the hunters shooting deer in the woods. Those .30-06 bullets could travel miles and penetrate everything except steel plate, I knew. Soon after I arrived, Abby told me to go to her parents' house to meet her wonderful father. I did so and hated him on sight. He was simply *off,* like a more subdued, white-bearded version of Pee-Wee Herman. We sat in the living room and talked. He kept making strange faces at what I said, as though amused and mystified at my thought processes. There were easily a hundred framed photos of Abby hanging on all four walls and propped on the fireplace mantel. The largest showed her doing the splits with a docile, sheepish, yet arch expression. After a couple hours of conversation he abruptly stood and told me I had to go because he had work to do.

Each time I called Abby, she said she was too busy to see me, but then she told me that she was going skiing in another state with friends for a few days. I stayed and kept trying to meet up with her because as is my pattern, I refused to accept what my eyes, ears, and brain told me. It simply wasn't possible that this was happening. My friend wouldn't do this to me.

Goulash with my Deranged Future Self

Abby's father told me I should have dinner with a pal of his, a writer like me. He said we'd get along great. Since Abby was unavailable, I went to this guy's house. He was the most annoying and worthless person to whom I've donated irreplaceable hours of my existence. The high point of his life was the graduate work he did in Hungary in the sixties. It was all he talked about the whole evening. It was a kind of seminar that he assumed I was happy to attend because of course I shared his fascination with all things Hungarian. He made us goulash from scratch, with giant wads of fatty meat and so much paprika that it looked like a pot of blood. Abby's father said he was a writer, and he was. He wrote in notebooks. About Hungary. I have no idea if he had a job or was some kind of ward of the state. His incontinent jabbering, monomania, and hunched posture would seem to preclude employment anywhere except maybe as a university professor.

It was clear that Abby's father didn't like me any more than I liked him. His assertion that I had a lot in common with this maniac was about as unambiguous an insult as he could deliver without coming right out and telling me to fuck off. It was also deeply painful because I could indeed see a lot of myself in this poor shut-in. He was a failure and didn't know how foolish he was. Blind to the contempt shown to him by people he thought were his friends, he was an incompetent, obsessive blockhead who'd spun his wheels for decades and learned nothing. He spent all his time living in the past, reveling in his memories because he was incapable of moving forward. Abby's father was a very perceptive man.

That was the first time I had Hungarian goulash. It tasted like spicy, dirty hair.

Surprise! Not Really

I went to Abby's parents' house for Thanksgiving dinner on November 23. Her mother was an obese hysteric who never stopped talking. Abby didn't come downstairs until right before dinner was served. She'd squeezed into skintight jeans with giant holes ripped in the seat. Her round dancer's bottom was magnificent, which I hadn't known because she'd always worn loose trousers in San Francisco. Before she sat down, she touched her toes several times, bending over in front of her father, who crossed his legs and stared intently at the black underwear exposed by the tears in her pants. She said nothing to me the entire meal, while her mother gushed nonstop and her father strutted like a peacock even though he remained seated. After dinner Abby left to go out with a friend. "He's my other friend who's a lot older than me," she said as she put on her jacket. I helped the mother wash the dishes and then bade her and her evil husband farewell. On second thought, they're both evil. The mother's obesity and hysteria don't make up for what she'd allowed. I spent four days in a fugue state, driving aimlessly through the countryside and taking photos. On November 27 I called Abby and told her I was leaving in the morning. She was indifferent.

"Hey, you gotta do what you gotta do," she said. "Whatever."

I drove back to California – all 3000 miles – in seventy-two hours, stopping only to refill my tank and grab convenience-store sandwiches. In Tyler, Texas, I mailed Abby a letter excoriating her for her treatment of me. Of course I shouldn't have done it, given the other burdens she already carried, but I was pretty much out of my mind with grief and horror. I then went and found my childhood home and took photos of it. Since there were no shoulders on the road – a fact I'd forgotten – I parked in the middle of the right-hand lane and got out with my camera, not caring if someone ran me over or hit my car. Somewhere in Arizona I pulled off the freeway at three in the morning to urinate. The exit ramp went into the desert for about a hundred feet and then the paving ended. I got out and marveled at the brightness of the moonlight; I could actually read my copy of *The Far Arena* by it. The Saguaro cacti all held up their arms in surrender, the blue landscape silent as a tomb. When I yelled, *"Pumpernickel!"* as loudly as I could, the deep-space vacuum made me sound stranded and puny. I thought I might be dead, but that didn't really bother me.

By the time I arrived in Los Angeles, everything looked two-dimensional, as though projected on three screens: one in front and one on each side. Sitting in my car was like being in a simulator. It was genuinely fascinating and made me wonder if I'd given myself brain damage by combining marathon driving with infinite sorrow. Tim was furious at me and called it a suicide attempt.

"Don't you *ever* do anything that stupid again!" he said. "Do you hear me?"

I thought that was funny. It went without saying that I had ahead of me at least two or three more decades of doing stupid things, assuming I lived that long. Abby sent a reply to my letter, saying it was the worst thing she'd ever read in her life and that she had to regretfully cut off contact with me. As for her treatment of me, she didn't agree that it was selfish. To her, it was simply how she had to live.

"I have to be nice to myself," she wrote, "because I'm the only person I know for sure will be spending the rest of my life with me."

Actually, I had a hunch there was another person she'd be spending the rest of her life with. I looked her up on the Internet in 2012: Yup. At thirty-two she runs her business out of his house. What still saddens me is that she seemed so normal in San Francisco. I can't help but wonder how her life would've turned out if she'd stayed there. One of her letters refers to her time in the Bay Area as her "selfish escape from reality." Tim tells me that she would've been inevitably drawn back to New England, like a moth to the flame. She does look burned in her present-day photos. Soul-burned.

I'm sorry, Abby. Despite your fate, you gave me almost two years of happiness. And thank you for the flower-alien.

My First Book Hits the Stores

In Cold Sweat was published in July of 2001. To market it, I put up a Web site designed by Georgia Thunes, Scott's wife. I read several positive reviews, including this one by Ben Watson of *The Wire*.

> Although the title looks daft, it turns out to be an excellent premise. Thomas Wictor taped these interviews for Bass Player magazine, and bringing himself and his anxieties into the picture – the fan faces the wildman – makes for a dramatic and entertaining read. Details which editors prefer to glide over become part of the story. The bassists he interviews are Gene Simmons from Kiss, Peter Hook from New Order, Jerry Casale from Devo, and Scott Thunes from Frank Zappa's group.
>
> True to form, Gene Simmons is the most objectionable, refusing to talk unless his face goes on the cover of the magazine, declaring that women have no affinity for lower sonorities. Simmons spouts bar-room political banalities like they're lessons in life. However, he explodes when Wictor mentions that the 'SS' in Kiss's logo resembles the lightning bolts Hitler's Schützstaffeln wore on their

collars. He's Jewish, born in Israel, and once rejected the album title *Gas Chamber Music* because it would be "insensitive to what went on in World War II." As one might guess, Simmons is more intelligent on comics than genocide, claiming that Marvel heroes got popular, not because they were Nietzchean Übermenschen, but "scary, mixed-up people" like Spider Man.

Devo's reputation for cynicism and stunts is explained as the rock press's inability to grasp satire by some extremely concerned minds. Jerry Casale is analytic and cute, talking about learning to fit together Trout Mask Replica's parts and playing 16th notes on bass. He defines Devo's amazing cover of "Satisfaction" as a "Jamaican sort of polka." He's still bitter about the press treatment of Devo. Despite their differences, Simmons and Hook are happy with their places in pop music history, a satisfaction which makes them seem rather uncritical and complacent. Casale, in contrast, wants to re-form Devo and show Nine Inch Nails, Prodigy and the Chemical Brothers how the modern equipment they're using could be used.

Half of Wictor's book is devoted to Scott Thunes. It takes Thunes much effort, but he finally manages to explain to Wictor that despite being the toast of rock bass players – Zappa's music gave virtuosi a chance to shine that is rare outside jazz – he's today much happier out of the industry, jamming occasionally with friends. Originally a fan of Bartók, Stravinsky and the second Viennese School, he played jazz on bass until he heard Devo's "Mongoloid" and "gave it up immediately, lost all my friends." Thunes was Zappa's bass anchor throughput the 80s, up until Zappa's last tour in 1988, and then played bass for Zappa's son Dweezil. His turn against Dweezil's metal – he complains that their original 'anti-rock' became straight – is fascinatingly described, as is his subsequent involvement with the punk group Fear: "complicated, hard-edged, fast music that people can actually dance and pogo and freak out to, instead of this analytical hard-rock stuff, which only goes to the front of the stage and then stops, energy-wise."

There are some tantalizing technical discussions of little understood Papa Zappa's compositions like "Mo 'N Herb's Vacation" and of stacked fifths in Zappa's guitar solos, but these are eclipsed by the explosive, painful conflicts of the 1988 tour. Thunes was straw boss and the group mutinied. What emerges is the kind of larger than life, integrity driven, musically literate character required to play Zappa's genre-defying music: "if you want to look at me and what I deserve, I don't deserve anything because I'm a fucking asshole. But I'd rather be a fucking asshole who can express himself whenever I want to." It's not easy to get a sense of the people behind a music as glassy, complex and deliberate as 80s Zappa. Thomas Wictor's courage in facing this 'scary' bassist was rewarded with a revelatory interview.[5]

One correction to this otherwise very fair and insightful review: As is clear in the book, Simmons actually consented to the interview not knowing if he'd get the cover or not. He took a huge professional risk, for which I'm forever grateful.

That's pretty much how every review I read of the book went, and then I saw the review in the *Chicago Sun-Times*. I don't remember it word for word, nor do I remember the reviewer's name, but this is a pretty accurate paraphrase.

A much less useful book is *In Cold Sweat: Interviews with Really Scary Musicians,* by Thomas Wictor. Apparently, the author simply had some transcripts lying around in his desk drawer and tried to figure out a way to make money off them. Save *your* money. Not worth anything.

That review was astonishingly painful: not in a personal sense, but because a big, reputable publication with thousands of readers dismissed my labor of love with such offhand contempt. There's no doubt in my mind that the reviewer didn't even read the book. He just flipped through it, like he was shuffling a deck of cards – *frrrrrrrrrrrp* – wrote the review in five seconds, tossed the book in the trash, and went on to the next one. That old rage at injustice flared right up and consumed me again.

I've never read another review of anything I've written. It's a good policy for me. This memoir is my fifth published book, but I won't read a thing about it. The work is finished and has to stand or fall on its own. And with such wildly divergent assessments from the reviewing class, I've realized that most critiques aren't worth any more than my own opinions. But I do thank Ben Watson for his careful, literate analysis of my book. Though it wasn't in actual fact the last review of my work I ever read, I've deemed it so. It's a perfect end piece.

A Little Help from Your Friends

Bass Player refused to promote or review *In Cold Sweat*. I never understood why, since the interviews were all conducted while I worked for the magazine. You'd think that the publication would want to hype a book of its more memorable interviews, but you'd be wrong. In 2001 the editor who'd destroyed my career was sent packing. The new editor regarded me as a total nonentity. I simply didn't exist for him. After he rejected something like ten of my proposed interviews, I told him in January of 2002 to take my name off the masthead. He cheerily complied. In desperation, I bought an ad for the book in the back of the magazine. It ran on page seventy-eight of the February 2002 issue and cost hundreds of dollars.

I invited the entire *Bass Player* staff to come to a reading for *In Cold Sweat* not far from the magazine headquarters. It was free, of course, and Scott Thunes appeared with me. Thunes did it as a favor. It was a hugely generous gesture on his part that was surely hard for him to do, but he suggested it himself. He volunteered to do it out of respect for me.

Not one person from *Bass Player* showed up.

My Fans

At every reading I did, there was always one jabbering, deranged person; one person who did nothing but insult me; and one person who sat in front of me reading a different book and ignoring me. It was 100 percent consistent. And they were always different individuals. It felt as though I were in some special hell for failed writers, condemned to eternal driveling, derision, and disregard. Who goes to book readings to ignore or insult the author?

At the reading Scott Thunes attended with me in the Bay Area, we offered to take questions. A fat, bearded oaf immediately raised his hand and said, "Yeah, *I* gotta question! Whadja do, just take the transcripts of your interviews and publish them? Pretty easy way to write a book if you ask me!"

I said, "Well, try it sometime." What I actually wanted to do was pick up Scott's bass, plug it in, crown the guy with it multiple times – *ba-wahng, ba-wahng, ba-wahng* – and then say to the crowd, "So: Any more questions?"

My publisher arranged for me to go to a Zappa convention, where I set up a kiosk with piles of *In Cold Sweat*. The convention lasted about five hours. I didn't sell a single copy, even though I'd made a big poster indicating that fully half of it was Scott Thunes talking behind-the-scenes stuff about his years with Zappa. Nobody even stopped to ask anything about it. It was as though I'd been cursed by a Hopi shaman and made invisible.

Near the end of the evening, a man finally addressed me. He was so obese that he had a 150-inch waist. Not wanting to call attention to his massive paunch by letting it hang over his belt and framing it with suspenders, he wore the top of his pants at waist level. Since the waist size was 150 inches, the pants legs were gigantic but with cuffs of normal size.

The pants legs were therefore tapered; they were funnel shaped, wide at the top and narrow at the bottom. Being dress pants, they had sharp creases on the fronts of the legs. The way dress pants are made, the creases go all the way up to the belt line. On these huge, funnel-shaped pants legs the creases were diagonal. The man's pants looked like the prows of two approaching ocean liners. His shoes seemed tiny, as though his feet were bound in the ancient Chinese style.

He wanted me to give a message to Zappa's wife Gail, whom I don't know and have never met. I explained to him that there was no way I could accommodate him, and he said, "Do you know who I am? I'm [withheld], creator of [a hugely popular TV show]!" I told him that wouldn't help me pass his message along to an inaccessible stranger. He steamed off in his ocean-liner pants, indignant that he'd been unable to turn a struggling writer into an errand boy.

When the convention was over, I loaded up all my unsold books and punched my foam-board poster into a trash can. As I left, one of the cooking staff – a kid in his early twenties – walked out with me. He said, "What's your book about, man?"

"Really scary bass players."

"Far out! How about giving me a copy?"

"Well," I said, "I'm actually trying to sell them."

He laughed. "Yeah, you didn't do all that hot tonight, though, did you? I saw. So how good could it be? C'mon, man, how about a copy?"

I thought, Why the hell not? He was the only person that whole night who walked away with a copy, after telling me he wanted it only if he could pay what he thought it was worth.

At one of my readings, I raffled off a copy of the book by putting a large plastic jug with a stack of pale-green fliers next to it on the table. I told people to write their names on a flier and I'd choose one. The jug was filled, and a man in a down hunter's vest was the winner. I took the jug home and in the process of emptying it a piece of white paper fluttered out among the green. It had a message for me.

> Mental illness
> I can't think!
> for myself – Because of you controlling my thoughts with cigarettes, I do what I wanted to do in public; eyes! Because of your doing, guy!
> I can't talk one on one personal because you talk for me, which I would like to talk on my own – without control, but you don't like me to talk! Because of others who smoke, with the audio tape on! Even if you're made to write; because of them who have home broken, my self from talking to others! In time I was in Shetten and the lies of like they kids, who talk in Spanish – why they are? There's no pain in my side!
> When others say you're in there recording, they are eat.
> Martinez! But why?

I wondered which one of them had written that and then sat there the whole time, watching me.

A Message from the Cardinal Ghost

In March of 2002, I got an e-mail from Carmen, congratulating me on my book. Instead of being moved that she'd obviously been following my career and had cared enough to contact me after almost two years, I immediately wrote her back that I couldn't bear to hear from her. All I could think about was that we were supposed to be together and we'd fucked it up. We'd never walk on the beach, have dinner, or see a movie together again. We'd never even laugh together again. I was glad she was happy, but there was just no way we could talk because the further away we got from each other, the worse it became for me. I was even more crippled and fragmented by our breakup ten years later than I was the day it happened, and I'd faked all the friendly correspondence we'd had about music. Though it wasn't her fault, it just wouldn't be possible for us to have anything to do with each other. Being without her was living death, while platonic, superficial contact with her was unspeakable torture. I had to choose death over torture that would never end.

Eventually, she replied.

> Tom:
> I took several days to try and think of a response, but I couldn't come up with anything except I'm sorry. I hope you can find happiness someday. Please take care of yourself.
> Carmen

The Re-return and Re-exit of the First Ghost

In 2002 Brigitte contacted me and told me she'd moved back to L.A. I was overjoyed. We got together and had a fun dinner. She'd started up her business again, this time with a partner, and she said everything would be different. She found an apartment in a beach community, and we had dinner there a few times. I was unnerved at the massive amounts of wine she drank, sometimes two bottles at one meal.

Soon her business began having the same problems as before. After a few months she told me that she was about to be evicted because she was broke. I lent her $1500, and she wrote out a receipt, promising to repay it. A couple of weeks later, she asked me if I could drive her to the Bay Area for a promotional event for her business. She'd pay for the gas and the accommodations. None of her friends would do this, and she couldn't fly because she had to carry so much stuff. I agreed. When we arrived, her credit card was rejected, so I paid the $500 for the room we shared. We watched an episode of *Six Feet Under,* and then she went to sleep. She slept on her back, arms folded on her chest, and didn't move or make a sound all night.

After we got back from the Bay Area, she disappeared. A week later I received an e-mail from her.

> Hi, Tom.
> I'm writing from Milan! I just had to get out of L.A. for a while.
> Talk to you soon!
> Brigitte

Over the next five months, she'd call about once a week and monologue for two or three hours, drunk. It was the same litany of disaster she'd spooled out when I'd helped her move in 2000. After a while, I began telling Tim – with whom I still lived at the time – that I wasn't home. One night Brigitte left a message saying it was a shame we'd fallen out of contact. That was the last I heard from her. She never offered to repay the more than $2000 she owed me.

The Advantage of DVDs: No Manimals

Roger got us free tickets to see the remake of *Shaft,* starring Samuel L. Jackson. I didn't want to go, because I utterly despise Jackson on every possible level: professional, personal, aural, visual, aesthetic, spiritual, physical, social, philosophical, human – you name it. He gives me skittering, nauseous chills at how low a person can go. The only performance of his that I enjoy is the two seconds that follow his canned fuckity-fuckin'-motherfuckin'-fucked-up-fuck speech in *Deep Blue Sea.* I'd love to see those two seconds expanded into a feature-length film. Otherwise, I can't bear to contemplate him.

Shaft was garbage. It stank of decay and rancid cynicism. There were only two notable aspects about the movie. The first was that one of the middle-aged character actors had recently gotten a facelift, which was inexplicable since his main asset was his craggy, Mafioso's mug. On the giant screen, you could see a perfect black line all the way around the perimeter of his face; it was as though he wore a mask that could be detached, like the robots undergoing maintenance in *Westworld.* The facelift just made him look strange, not young. His new smoothness came at the price of an unnaturally wide mouth and the loss of the only real tool actors have: expressiveness. An analogy would be a professional concert pianist having his hands amputated and replaced with those of a department-store mannequin.

The second thing worth mentioning about seeing *Shaft* was that there were only four people in the theater: Roger, a couple in their thirties, and me. The whole time we were there, the man kept up a monologue at the level of someone talking with friends at a sports bar. He sat in the back row, but his deep, thick voice actually made it hard to catch the dialogue. The sound was like a slowed-down turboprop engine: *wob wob-wob wob wob-wob-wob wob wob wob-wob wob wob-wob-wob wob.*

Though I hated the film, the turboprop noise worsened it, the same way that carsickness can be made vastly more intolerable by an attack of diarrhea. After half an hour, I turned around and called, "Could you please stop talking? We can't hear the movie."

The guy shouted, "Hey! I'll talk as *loud* as I want, *when* I want, *where* I want, and as *long* as I want. Got it?"

That's what he said in English, but phonetically it sounded like, "*Huy! Ull tuk uz* lud *uz uh wun,* wun *uh wun,* wuh *uh wun, uhn uz* lung *uz uh wun. Guh ih?*"

I had no response.

Roger loved debauchery, debasement, and devolution. He snorted and said, "White men can't jump; black men can't act; and manimals can't speak."

We left about three minutes later. The only exit was right beside the manimal. He was a muscular Caucasian fellow with an afro and a huge, black mustache; maybe his voice resulted from hair growing inside his mouth and throat. Maybe he was semiaquatic, a filter feeder with baleen instead of teeth. As we walked past him, he fixed us with a proud stare. His ladyfriend appeared to be a two-dollar Vietnamese hooker.

The horrible movie, horrible Samuel L. Jackson, horrible facelift, and horrible manimal put Roger in such a good mood that he bought me a vast, expensive dinner at Musso and Frank Grill and kept cracking up for the next three hours.

Shaft was the second-to-last movie I saw in a theater. The last was *Signs,* in 2002, to which I went with Tim. All around us people had high-volume conversations on cell phones, ran up and down the aisles, crashed in and out of the doors every three seconds, talked constantly, threw things, spilled things, belched, and yelled to each other, "Get me a hot dog, some popcorn, a Snickers, and a coke, okay? How much should I give you? Twenty-five bucks? Fuck me, is it really that expensive? Holy *shit!*"

Tim and I should've taken Roger. After the show, he would've bought us each a Mercedes.

Another Ghost; Another Failed Literary Excursion

In 2002 I completed a novel about the suicide of my best friend. He'd talked about ending his life for the many years I'd known him, since he suffered from an incurable condition that left him in chronic, agonizing pain. In retrospect he said goodbye the afternoon of the night he did it, using nearly the same farewell Steiv Dixon gave me: "It's been pretty damn good knowing you." I thought it was just a compliment, because my friend gave me lots of them. He always told me quite brusquely that I was nowhere near the failure I thought. The next day, I realized I didn't have a photo of him. I took my camera out to where we met every afternoon, but when I came up over the hill and saw our spot, he wasn't there. In his place was what looked like a medieval roadside shrine, a beautiful little wooden structure with a roof. The second I laid eyes on it, I knew he was gone. I was one day too late to capture him on film. The memorial had a wooden placard with a picture of him, his name, and the phrase "Rest in Peace" painted in black. Surrounding it on the sidewalk were bouquets and dozens of lit votive candles, their flames protected by glass and metal holders.

Though I knew he'd kill himself when he could no longer tolerate his circumstances, I had no idea I'd react to his choice with stupefied shock and almost unendurable sadness. As in the case of Steiv, I missed my chance to tell him how much he meant to me. To banish the pain, I wrote what I described as "a black comedy about love and suicide in wartime America." It blended the story of my friend, my interest in current events, and the saga of a man haunted by his traumatic past and who couldn't accept losing the woman he'd thought was destined to be with him forever. Like this memoir, my novel included as much humor as possible to offset the dark themes.

I sent out queries to literary agents again, and again received nothing but rejections. Some agents were themselves quite funny in their unnecessary cruelty. One scrawled, "No thanks" in blue felt tip on my query letter and sent it back, while another put a pretty lime-green sticker on my letter that said, "Sorry. Not Our Market." I gave up quickly. Writing the novel hadn't made me feel better, and having my friend's tragedy dismissed so impersonally just added to my steadily increasing rage.

My Last Two Interviews

The next-to-last was with one of the most phenomenal bassists I've ever met. Even though the interview was one of two that my final editor approved, the article was never published. The bassist told me a story that made my blood boil, about his audition for a godlike legend whose musical prowess was eclipsed by his gleeful sadism.

> He sat through two sets of our show, paid us some great compliments. I said, "If you're ever looking for a bass player, give me a call." A few weeks later, he called me up and said for me to come out to Los Angeles. When I went for the audition I set everything up while all these people sat there and watched, and then my amp didn't work. I was frantically checking everything, and [the legend] said, "What kind of idiot brings a broken amp to an audition?" I apologized and told him it worked before I came to his house, and then one of his crew came out from behind my amp and held up the plug. "I unplugged it!" he said, and everyone laughed. And then [the legend] gave me [a famous piece], much to my amazement. As a great fan his, I had read about [this piece] it seemed like all my life. It was this incredibly, complexly notated piece of music that no one could possibly ever read, I guess designed to put musicians in their place or something.

And when he put it in front of me, I was kind of shocked because I assumed that we were all, you know, people who wanted to play music and weren't trying to be one up on each other. And I really didn't think he was serious.

Then I realized he was. He actually wanted me to read that, and that was how he was going to evaluate my playing. I don't do too well eleven ledger lines above the bass clef, you know, with a seventh-note figure above it, so I just told him I'd have to work on it a little bit, and he told me, "Well, we need somebody who can read fast. Next!" So I didn't even get to play. And that was after driving all the way across the country to L.A. I like to think the best about a great musician like [withheld], but it was as if I were brought out there to be embarrassed. And hell, I'm cool with that. I'm easy to embarrass, you know. I'm not proud. If somebody wants to do that, they have my blessings. But I was under the impression that he wanted to hear me play, so that was a real heartbreaker. [Laughs.] Tears ran down my cheeks.

This bassist is hugely successful and a composer himself. His songs and pieces have only a billion times more listenability, beauty, emotion, and – most importantly for me – humanity than the legend's work.

The final interview I conducted took place on May 22, 2002, with Andy West. We spoke about his solo album, *Rama 1,* which included drummers Rod Morgenstein, Jonathan Mover, and Mike Portnoy; guitarists Toshi Iseda and Mike Keneally; and keyboardists Jens Johansson, T. Lavitz, and Kit Watkins. Andy played guitar and keyboards along with the bass; he told me that the music on the album was influenced by "heavy, industrial, apocalyptic rock" such as that produced by Ministry, but "tweaked and skewed into something else." This article was never published, either. On May 13, 2012, I found it on a Web site advertising Andy's album. It's not credited to me, and neither Andy nor I can remember how it got there.

However, I'm honored that Andy West was my final interviewee. It's fitting, since he set such a great example of how to handle adversity without descending into bitterness.

Death of a Music Journalist

I hadn't had anything of consequence published in *Bass Player* for two years, but in 2003 the editor who generally ignored me asked me to write an op-ed for the "Soapbox," the last page of the magazine, where they let staffers and musicians talk about music topics not confined to the bass. I submitted a piece called "Shut Up and Play," about how I was tired of musicians expressing their opinions on geopolitics and social issues. After I was told the magazine wouldn't run it, I finally accepted that ten years of my life had come to exactly nothing.

Soon afterward, the Internet service provider took down my Web site because my credit card was cancelled after being stolen. I was assured that the site would be put back up as soon as I provided a new credit-card number. It was too funny. Why would I want a Web site reminding me daily of my failed career and failed book? I declined the offer and wrote an e-mail to Georgia Thunes thanking her for her help. She sent a gracious reply.

The same day, I got an e-mail from Scott Thunes that said, "If you wanted to get rid of us, there were less drastic ways, you know."

Scott always unerringly perceived my actual motivations. However, he had it reversed in this case: I didn't want to get rid of *them;* I wanted to get rid of *me.* It was necessary for me to remove myself from their lives to spare them further embarrassment and the chore of having to tolerate my insurmountable loserdom and triviality.

We had no more contact after 2003, except for one or two brief messages.

Saying Goodbye to the Woman who Made it Bearable

Every time I went to West Hollywood, I visited Tower Records and the bookstore across from it on West Sunset Boulevard. I'd park in a nearby lot and walk a couple of blocks to my destinations. Being both a music journalist and friends with Roger and Dolores meant that I went to West Hollywood at least once a week. To get to the bookstore and Tower, I walked past a restaurant with outdoor tables. For the final year of my stint in music journalism, the hostess who greeted customers at a little podium on the sidewalk was a beautiful young blonde woman who wore her hair in a loose bun, tendrils hanging down on both sides of her face. Whenever I walked past, she smiled and said hello, even though I never ate at her restaurant. We greeted each other almost once a week for a year. She could've been a model, but she was so un-L.A. that she stood out from a hundred feet away. You could instantly see that she was different.

After it was clear that I wouldn't be going to West Hollywood anymore because I'd failed as a music journalist and my friendship with Roger and Dolores was just about dead, I drove to my usual parking lot one last time. Instead of using the regular crosswalk so the friendly hostess and I could say hello, I stayed on the Tower side of Sunset, bypassing the restaurant. The hostess had her back to the traffic, so she didn't see me. One intersection up, I crossed the street and went to the bookstore, where I bought a tiny volume of humorous advice, I think, on how to live in L.A. It was a hardback only about two inches by three. The clerk gift wrapped it and put it in a little paper bag with stiff twine handles.

I then walked to the restaurant from the other direction than I usually did. The hostess looked up and said, "Hi! Nice to see you again! How've you been doing?" with her usual warmth.

"Just great," I said. "You've always been such a nice person that I wanted you to have this." I held out the little bag. She hesitated for a second and then took it. I smiled and walked back to my car.

Thank you, young lady. Whenever I think of West Hollywood, I think of you and your kindness instead of everything else. I hope you've found total fulfillment, success, and happiness.

Endnotes
    [1] "Ray Shulman Interview by Thomas Wictor," http://www.blazemonger.com/GG/Ray_Shulman_interview_by_Thomas_Wictor (accessed May 3, 2012).
    [2] Neil Zlozower, interview with the author, October 23, 1997.
    [3] Anne Kadrovich, interview with the author, November 20, 1997.
    [4] "Gore Vidal Quotes on Gore Vidal," *The Gore Vidal Pages,* http://www.gorevidalpages.com/2011/01/gore-vidal-quotes-on-gore-vidal.html (accessed August 3, 2012).
    [5] Ben Watson, review of *In Cold Sweat: Interviews with Really Scary Musicians,* by Thomas Wictor, *The Wire,* September 2001, 83.

Interlude with Scott Thunes
Communication

When I was a kid, I didn't know what kind of communication I was looking for. I didn't know what I had. I didn't know where I was going. I went to college in Marin; I did a bunch of stuff. I hung out with and saw adults all day long. I didn't see much difference between them and the high-school people that I'd been hanging out with. They were just older. They were still goofballs. I played in a couple of bands with really cool people, really smart people. I got a sense of "brains are not just for personal experience. They're for talking to another person and finding out what's going on," and with those bands I was very much aware that these people were thinking a lot of things that didn't immediately have to do with themselves alone. All the things that I did in my life before were instant-gratificatorally motivated, and just the kind of rock that these people were thinking about, the kind of rock they were doing, was different. I was listening to good music, and I was hanging out with good people, and I knew the difference between a jazzbo who was trying to be a jazz Nazi and tell me how to play and a bunch of other people who were all interested in expressing themselves as much as they possibly could through their instruments. I didn't worry about talking. I didn't think about communication at all because now it was happening.

The two lowest types of communication are stories and jokes. The jokes come out almost immediately. It's nice to have a good joke, but I read once a long time ago that the lowest form of conversation is telling jokes. After everything's been exhausted, you just sit around and tell jokes. But one level above that is storytelling. It's just another kind of joke. And depending on how good you are of a storyteller, you can keep people's interest. But it's a form of performance, not a form of interaction. The next level above that is people talking *at* each other and not transforming or being transformed because of the conversation. The next level above that, of course, is true intercommunication, where you learn something; you take something away. You're able to communicate with the person who's telling you that stuff; you have learned; your life has changed; and you can move on. Even if it's only one of the two of you, that's pretty good. It's better when it's both of you. As far as I can tell, that form of conversation is the ultimate form of expression.

You don't want to be didactic. You don't want to sit around and tell people stuff all the time. You want it to be juicy as hell for both of you. You both want to learn something, but 98 percent of all conversations is storytelling, and as soon as somebody starts telling a story, I pull back. I go, "I don't have to be here." I've heard stories. I've experienced them. I've made them. I've invented them. It's fun to tell my story. I enjoy it. I enjoy listening to other people's stories, but for me to get excited I have to live in New York because those are the kind of conversations you have. Every single conversation you have with somebody in New York is a fucking intense experience at that moment. The conversation is an intense experience, and you don't get that here. You certainly don't get it in Los Angeles, so you get trained to be dumb.

I think a normal human is adaptable. And most people are not. They're very much animals. They do what they do, and they say what they say, and that's about all you can get out of them. I try and keep my ears open, and my heart open because I work in an office, and that is the first bastion of retardation, emotional and otherwise. Somehow I fucking work at this company where the people in general are really delightful, and in my immediate environs, of the twelve or eleven people that work in tech support, four of them are really cool people. They're weirdos; they're freaks. Freaks get to enter into the office environment by the back door of software because software's such a weird area anyway. You can be a complete and utter Nazi freak and write software and present it to the world. People have written Nazi games. You can be a fascist and write software. But you can also be a complete and utter hippie freak and do things that you think are going to make the world better. Most of that stuff doesn't end up getting out into the real world because of the way finances work.

This company is run by some pretty scary South African people, whose real values we don't really know, but *they* pretty much don't know what's going on here, on the bottom half. My supervisor is a woman who scared me, just because of the mere fact that she has worked twelve years in an office environment. You have to find a place to work, you know? You gotta find out what you're doing. I spent most of my life being a musician so that I wouldn't have to work in an office. I didn't know that it was such a bad thing to work in an office. I knew that there's a very good chance that if I *did* work in an office, I'd have to cut my hair and I'd have to act normal. I'd have to, you know, goose step in and out of work every day.

This job is the exact opposite. I can wear pretty much whatever I want. I wear my Joykiller T-shirt with the cartoon of a guy with a fucking bloody axe – serial murderer guy with a clown hat on. I wear him to work; nobody even blinks. They go, "Huh, Joykiller!" I've got some normal people that hang out, and the rest of them are freaks. Almost everybody at work has a pierced tongue, ear, and massive amounts of tattoos. I work with a bunch of freaks. So I don't have to worry about communication, very specifically because I find the people that I'm working with right now – not because of the goatees, and not because of the tattoos and the piercings – I find them in general to be way cooler than almost anybody I ever worked with in music.

At my company, the people are semi-mercurial, can go with my humor, enjoy my humor, give me tons of glory, and I don't short them on the glory either. I give everybody at work tons of glory all day long. We're all totally intercommunicative. They're all really nice, and none of them are stupid. They can talk. They can listen; that's the important thing. They sit around and they listen to you, like they're actually interested in what you have to say. Everybody in rock has to get their piece in because they're all trying to climb some little ladder. If anybody could meet the bigger rock star and get in that $5000-a-week gig, they'll do anything to do that. Nothing else matters. They don't know how to communicate in any other way except, "I really need something better than this, and I'm going to get it."

In music, where I got my own glory was knowing that what I was playing sounded really fucking good to me. That's all that mattered. Didn't really matter what happened elsewhere. I knew what was going on musically, and I knew that Frank liked it, and it sounded good to me. What prevented me from getting my glory came from two different areas: the audience, and the band members. Band members hated me and even if they didn't hate me, they were too new and too ineffectual as communicants to inform me with the necessary passion, to allay my fears, and to get me out of my doldrums. The audience was different, because unless you're a real fucking egomaniac, there's no reason to go out and try and search for that kind of information. "How was I tonight?" You stand by the door after the concert, and as people walk by, they go, "Hey, Scott! You were great." You know? That was one thing. But "Hey, Scott, you were great. Uh, do you have one of Frank's picks I could have?" That's another thing.

Things go over their heads. You don't search for audience accolades. The only thing I noticed in 1988 was that nobody ever kept their eyes on me. I would stand there, and I would play, and I would do my stuff, and I didn't see any immediate audience recognition. There's so much energy in the place, and all of it goes to Frank. If you needed energy, you would get it from the audience. And since I wasn't getting it there, I decided not to play at all to any audience members. I couldn't turn around and play to my band members because they either burned me on purpose or were such ineffectual communicants that I didn't get any energy from them. I wasn't about to pay them back. So the pain, specifically, was in not being visually recognized on stage.

Looking at every single person in that audience – every single audience member, every single night – and seeing that every single one of them was looking only at Frank, knowing this was going to be his last tour, knowing that it's the twenty-fifth anniversary of his first concert, and knowing that this is a very special occasion. They wanted to get as much of him as they possibly could. There wasn't any time for me. None. So I felt bad, for three or four different reasons: Mostly, I'm alone. Secondly, I don't think I'm a great bass player anyway, so I'm not expecting anybody else to think I'm a great bass player, but if I am going to be on stage, playing for these people, I want a little recognition. The only way you can get it is visually. I didn't get anything. What kind of bad do you want to hear about? What kind of negative feelings are there, besides, "This really sucks"? There were so many other sucky things going on at the same time. I think, for those people who may be reading at any point in time a book about a bass player and wondering why he feels bad, it's just the lack of communication. It has nothing to do with humility; it has nothing to do with anything except communication.

I don't know what you mean that any of this was satisfying. What do you mean by romantic? When I was thirty years old and playing with a kid who was exactly ten years my junior, playing for hardly any money but that person was a millionaire, there was nothing romantic about it at all. I am struggling with demons inside myself that are winning, and that's a bit different than somebody like you deciding, "I am going to do my art, and this art isn't killing me." You're not dead. You're healthy. You've got your brain intact. Your heart is still even intact, and the most important thing is you getting your art done.

If you had a straight job, it would be much more difficult for you to get any writing done. So there's nothing romantic about that to me. You're really just opting to have a certain kind of reality that most people would be very willing to have. Most people would much rather produce something. But most people don't have anything to produce. Ninety-eight percent of the people on the face of the planet do not have anything to produce, and artists are more of a liability than anything else. There's nothing great about being an artist. There's something great about producing art, and that's what you're doing. That's why it's so easy for you to make that decision. Why would you want to do anything else?

• • •

The 1988 Zappa tour was over, I'd been sitting around spending my money and being morose after the loss of my girlfriend (who dumped me when I told her that a piece of music I was working on was more important than her... Don't ask. I was wrong. Well, maybe...) and lack of gigs (even though I'd just done 6 months with Frank).

During an earlier tour (1984?) I met a German man who later became a "friend" of mine. He worked as a caterer on this tour but later used his powers of people-pleasing to work for Warwick Basses as an A&R guy. He called me up one day and told me A) I should be playing a Warwick. I'll get you one and B) I should come out to the Musik Messe (Europe's equivalent of the NAMM show) on their dime.

"Sure," I said, and asked for $50 so I could get my passport updated. They sent me a ticket, and I flew out to Germany with a single dollar in my pocket. I sat next to Jimmy Earl on the plane and we talked bass for a few hours. It was nice. I spent a week being wined, dined, interviewed, and getting to share a table with John Entwistle, Doug Wimbish and a couple of other bassists. I also met the woman who would become my first wife, but that's a different story.

Doug came up to me and asked me about my "career." I told him how difficult it was to get gigs based on my particular skill-set, and how insular the Zappa world was and how they weren't really all that gung-ho on getting their "people" gigs in the outside world (except for that one time that Frank actually invited an oboist he knew up to the house to meet me [he was a orchestral union-leader who got people gigs all the freaking time]). Doug told me in response that he had a manager and that she was great and she should meet me so she could give me pointers on what to do about my stalled career.

That night, after another day on the floor of the Musik Messe (where I sat at a wet-bar all day drinking free beer and staring into the pretty eyes of the blonde German woman who would later become my first wife, but that's another story) I found myself at a restaurant with Doug, his manager, and several other bassists, all having just eaten with the owner of Warwick basses on his dime and being served ice cold German beer and having pretty much a grand old time.

One of the things I liked to do when I went to Europe was pick up a bunch of Swiss Army knives (they were cheaper than in the US and in the 80s were starting to come out in other colors than red, such as white and black and green. Very sexy.) and Mont Blanc pens. Mont Blanc is famous for their super-expensive pens, but they also make cheaper, normal pens. These pens were beautiful, and I used to get a handful of them as well, bringing them home to give away and keep as many as I could. I liked these pens so much that I used to talk about them to people. Why? 'Cause I love pens and these were good pens.

So I'm standing next to Doug Wimbish's manager and a French bassist named Pascal and I don't know what I'm supposed to say to this woman, this beautiful African-American woman in a place of power over me, who could control my very existence by her getting me gigs that could change my life, make me rich, make me famous like Doug Wimbish. So I pull out one of my pens, and I proudly hold it aloft – like the Lion King – and I say "Is it sick to love a pen?"

This angel, this woman – this woman who is probably so interesting in her own life that she tries spending time with us lesser mortals to keep herself humble – turns to the French bassist and says – more to the rest of the world than to either of us – and says, right as I'm kicking into my speech about how awesome this pen is: "What the hell am I listening to?" as she turns on her heels and walks away. I never saw her again, and Doug and I never spoke after that.

For me, that was one of many formative experiences in the music world. Cutting off my own nose to spite my face, killing my career over a pen. But more importantly, I learned the necessity of having a good "story" at hand to tell people you don't know. I am full of "interesting'" stories, and this is why I will never write a book about my life.[1]

Endnotes
[1] "Interviewing Bassist Stories," http://www.talkbass.com/forum/f32/interviewing-bassist-stories-866617/ (accessed May 19, 2012).

Anthology Six
Abyss
2003-2011

In the desert
I saw a creature, naked, bestial,
Who, squatting upon the ground,
Held his heart in his hands,
And ate of it.
I said, "Is it good, friend?"
"It is bitter – bitter," he answered;
"But I like it
Because it is bitter
And because it is my heart."

I Know: Flamethrowers!

After I involuntarily resigned from music journalism, I had no idea what to do – except begin buying postcards of World War I flamethrowers on eBay. For some reason I'd always been interested in those weapons, but only from that era. It all started in 1969, when my father bought me a set of tiny plastic World War I German soldiers at the Orange Blossom Hobby Shop in Miami, Florida. The two flamethrower operators were my favorite. I spent hours looking at them and playing with them. They seemed oddly familiar.

The problem with buying World War I flamethrower postcards on eBay was that another bidder would double or triple the price at the last second. It was always the same person. After this happened a handful of times, he sent me a message through eBay asking if I was a historian or some kind of expert on the devices from the period. He himself was interested because his father had been a member of the German flamethrower regiment during the war.

I figured he therefore had to be at least eighty, but he turned out to be a spry sixty-five. I'll call him Lew. We corresponded back and forth, and I liked his quirky sense of humor. Eventually, he raised the possibility of he and I coauthoring a book on German flamethrowers of World War I. The information out there was terribly inaccurate, we both knew. This would be a great opportunity for us to set the record straight. I demurred, having no desire to write another failed book. I also didn't want to rely on others again, the way I had for *In Cold Sweat*. Lew was persistent, however. It was his life's ambition to author such a book. He said he'd write the text, and I'd provide the photos and do drawings of the weapons.

After extracting written promises from him on five occasions that he'd fulfill his end of the bargain, I pitched the idea to a publisher, and in January of 2004, Lew and I signed a contract to write a book titled *German Flamethrower Pioneers of World War I*. We were given a year to complete the work. Since I already had an extensive collection of photos, I spent months doing drawings of the weapons, piecing together details from as many as a dozen different images each and estimating dimensions based on the known size of equipment worn by soldiers carrying the apparatuses.

Four months into the project, Lew hadn't produced a single paragraph. I began to get nervous, but he assured me that he was still gathering information and would throw everything together lickety split when he was done with his research. He then embarked on the first of two European vacations that he took during the year we worked on our project.

The Chicken-Voiced Fabulist

After six months, I asked Lew to show me what he had. Still nothing, but it would flow out of him at any moment, he said. I called him and discovered that he had a high-pitched, gabbling chicken-voice, his words all rushing into each other amid the sound of saliva spraying uncontrollably. He affected a Hitlerian German pronunciation for the names of units, weapons, and equipment, violently rolling the *r* and barking the vowels. His life was one of swashbuckling adventure, romance, travel, wealth, and bringing down those who had wronged him.

There was only one conceivable conclusion to this escapade, so what I did over a period of months was casually ask Lew to send me photocopies of the material he'd gathered. When we were down to the last few weeks, all I could do was wait. The day of the deadline, Lew wrote me an e-mail filled with cheery prattling about how the march continued onward and upward. He made no reference to not having fulfilled his contractual obligations. I replied that I wanted no more contact with him and then informed the publisher that the book would not be written. The response was a "Thank you for letting us know" e-mail. They probably get plenty such notifications; I've read that only 5 percent of first-time authors ever finish the initial draft.

It was fitting that after my failure in music journalism, my first venture in military history would be a ludicrous nosedive into an empty swimming pool with a blathering, Hitler-voiced chicken riding on my back.

Saying Goodbye to My Guides

August of 2004 was the last time I saw Roger and Dolores. They'd begun shunning and denigrating me over the previous two years, actions certainly not coincidental to my steady collapse in music journalism. In L.A., you don't tether yourself to a rotting corpse. The two of them fought constantly, and at one point, during dinner at their house, I simply got up and walked out while they were in the kitchen. They came back in to find an empty chair. They never forgot the insult. On another occasion Dolores became furious with me for saying that the comedienne Margaret Cho struck me as vulnerable.

"*Vulnerable?* What the *fuck?*" Dolores shouted. "She's hard as nails! *Vulnerable?* Do you know how stupid you sound?"

Roger once asked Tim and me to help him on a home-improvement project. We agreed, thinking we'd be laborers to his supervisor, but his actual plan was for us to do the entire project ourselves while he absented himself. "You'd really be helping me out," he said, so Tim and I dutifully spent the entire day going back and forth to Home Depot, buying sheets of plywood, measuring, sawing, hammering, screwing together, until the project was finished. It took about seven hours. When Roger came back, he said, "You know, that's not exactly what I had in mind." I was so ashamed that I'd dragooned my brother into being used as a slave that I blew up. Roger quickly invited us out to dinner, during which Dolores got plastered, draped herself all over Tim, and rested her chin on his shoulder, slurring, "You look just like Tom. He's just the puffed-up version of you."

Both my friends taunted me sexually. Once, as I walked up a flight of stairs behind Dolores, she looked back over her shoulder, smiled, and said, "You're thinking about fucking me in the ass, aren't you? Well, you can't. My asshole is too small." As I helped them move from one house into two when they separated, a photo dropped out of a box Roger carried. I picked it up; it showed a young woman in a short skirt and sunglasses, standing knock-kneed, her panties around her ankles. "That's Roger's sister," Dolores said. "He fucked her because they thought it would be fun." When Dolores sat in front of me in her kitchen, she often spread her legs like a drafting tool, putting one foot on the table and one on an adjacent chair, daring me to look at her plump, blue-jeaned camel toe. She bragged about her affair with a washed-up, bloated TV actor who had a sick wife.

"He's a lot more handsome in real life than he looks on TV, and he spends all his money on me. He's in *love* with me!"

At a restaurant one night they regaled me with a very dirty, very funny story that made us all laugh, and in return I told them about having roast-beef sandwiches with a girlfriend. We were both drunk and high. Sitting Indian style on the floor, she ate her sandwich in a happy daze as pieces of roast beef fell into her lap. Every now and then she'd peer down, carefully retrieve the scraps of meat, and eat them. She wore leotards and no underwear; she also had very large labia. When she changed positions and raised her right knee to pull her thigh against her chest in the yogic posture she favored, one of her labia poked through a hole in the crotch of her leotards. She noticed and yanked at it, thinking it was roast beef. Her scream of horror made me drop my sandwich, and then we almost died laughing. The total Dadaism of the scene still makes me smile. Roger and Dolores, however, stared at me in silence, as though I'd broken some ironclad social taboo. After a few seconds they started talking about something else entirely. They liked making me feel stupid.

Yet they also bought me stylish clothes for no reason, invited me to dinner and paid for it hundreds of times, and told me I was incredibly lucky to have had the experience of recognizing Carmen the first time I saw her and knowing instantly we were supposed to be together.

"I've never had that happen," Dolores said. "You haven't either, have you, Rog?"

He shook his head.

Dolores smiled at me and said, "The only reason we're together is because we're too sick for everybody else. That smart, funny, talented, beautiful woman had to be with you at all costs. I'm really jealous. Nobody's ever felt that way about me."

There were also moments of true fun and hilarity. We saw *Titanic* together, and during the scene where Kate Winslet takes the fire axe and chops Leonardo DiCaprio free of his handcuffs, I couldn't stand it anymore and shouted, "I *hate* this movie!" Everyone around me gasped, stared, and shushed, but Dolores leaned forward, her shoulders shaking as though she were silently sobbing, took a deep breath, and let out the most gratifying scream of laughter I've yet heard. And when I gave her a figurine of a soldier I'd painted, she said it was the best birthday gift she'd ever received. She was genuinely moved. Both Roger and Dolores sent me wonderful homemade birthday and Christmas cards that I still have.

Driving on the freeway in my car with Roger, I was tailgated by a black BMW tucked so close behind me I couldn't see the headlights in the rearview mirror. After a quarter-mile or so, the driver – a lantern-jawed exec in a white shirt and sunglasses – lost patience, changed lanes, floored it, and roared past me. He cut me off with inches to spare, slammed on his brakes so that I had to stand on mine, turned completely around in his seat, and shot me the finger, his giant chin flapping and his beautiful white teeth like halogen lights as his mouth formed the words *Fuck you, asshole!* Then he rocketed off.

I said, "With all the psychotically aggressive driving here, I've never understood why they call it La-la Land."

Roger said, "Because compared to everywhere else, this *is* La-la Land. Back east they don't even drive in their own lanes. They straddle them and lean on their horns and scream, '*What's wrong witchoo?*' out their windows. New Yorkers are moved to tears by how polite and considerate the drivers are here. In the Midwest you have Camaros, Trans Ams, and Firebirds drag racing on every street, and they give fourteen-year-olds driving permits. The South has the highest death rate from drunk driving. You went to school in the Pacific

Northwest; ever see a logging truck that wasn't doing at least eighty-five on those mountain roads? Go to Montana sometime. Every single road sign has bullet holes in it, some of them three or four inches wide. What makes a bullet hole four inches wide? A cannon? How'd you like to share the road with people who have cannons in their cars? No, we're lucky. The driving here is just fine."

It was a lesson in perspective I never forgot.

The last time I saw Roger and Dolores, they were in the middle of a project. They both smiled too widely when they saw me. We hadn't gotten together since I'd informed them of my official death in music journalism several months earlier.

Dolores called, "Tom! Wow! How've you *been?*"

"We're really busy now!" Roger said. "Can't really talk right now!"

"Oh, okay," I said. "Sure. I just wanted to drop by, since I hadn't seen you for so long."

"We'll call you!" Dolores said.

I waved and walked off. Our final encounter lasted about seven seconds. Nine years' worth of shared history ended in a seven-second goodbye. Still, I do have good memories, so as my tribute to Roger and Dolores, I present my favorite episode with them.

My Dinner with Nicholas

The biggest problem Roger and Dolores had was their refusal to communicate. Roger once invited me over for dinner on the same night Dolores had made plans for them to go out with their new friend, an astonishingly handsome actor who'd once had a popular TV show. I'll call him Nicholas. My arrival touched off a violent squabble, my two friends each blaming the other for the screw-up. I offered to leave, but neither found that acceptable. The solution, they said, was for all of us to have dinner together. I agreed. Nicholas, however, unexpectedly showed up with two of *his* friends, a producer at a major studio and a senior editor from a famous trade magazine. They'd just attended a wake for a friend who'd dropped dead at thirty-five two days before, the second such tragedy they'd endured that year.

This was the cast: a raggedy, marginalized writer; an unhappy married couple in the second tier of the Industry; and three Players who'd already made it. The setting was a Chinese restaurant in West Hollywood. Roger and I went in my Blazer and Nicholas drove Dolores and his friends in his BMW.

"That's a gorgeous car," I told him before we set out.

Instead of "Thank you," Nicholas nearly screamed, "It cost $100,000 and has a voice-activated, hands-off phone!"

Roger and I arrived at the restaurant first. When our companions walked in, Dolores was in front, rolling her eyes and mouthing silent obscenities at the other three behind her. She later informed me that in the twenty-minute ride from their house, nobody said a single word.

My experience as an interviewer had honed my schmoozing skills, so I led where I could, put at ease where I could, and let myself be ignored where I could. Both the editor and the producer were conversational Black Holes; everything I said to them was sucked up and disappeared without a trace. They sat and stared at me in silence most of the time. I would've been happy to just sit and stare, too. We could've had a staring contest like back in elementary school, where the winner got to punch the loser on the arm: "You blinked!" *Bam.* But since Dolores needed constant chatter, for her sake I kept up my monologue. Afraid I was running out of material, I asked the three Hollywoodians about their dead friend.

"He was the rudest, most self-centered person I ever met, but so lovable," sighed the editor.

"He was always talking, never listening, but just the sweetest guy," recalled Nicholas.

"When his wife found him on the kitchen floor, she thought it was just one of his practical jokes," related the producer.

I could just imagine: "Look, honey, I'm dead! Ha-ha! Gotcha again! Hey, what the – Ow! My heart! Ook! Umph! Gaaaaah..." *Clunk.*

"Aw, come on, sweetie. Quit fooling around. Honey? Poopykins?"

We eventually settled on the topic of film and television, of course, which allowed everyone to babble on with relief while I took a breather. Nicholas was obviously infatuated with the lovely Dolores, so much so that he lost control. Somehow the two other Hollywoodians got on the topic of an ancient Chinese military hero called General Tripod because of his purported three-foot *Schwanz.* That led to the editor revealing that her last boyfriend had been a porn addict, and they once watched a movie with an actor who had his own three-foot organ.

"It looked like an anteater's head, and he wore a special harness around his waist to hold it up. It was as big around as Ahnold's forearm."

"Where did he keep it?" Dolores asked. "I mean, did he wrap it around his waist?"

The producer looked up. "Obviously, he'd have to stuff it down his pants leg."

Nicholas began whinnying and stomping his foot, screaming, "Could you imagine if he was walking down the street and saw a *pretty girl* and got *turned on?*"

He leaped up in the middle of this crowded restaurant full of grim-faced, elderly Chinese, ran about fifteen feet from the table, turned around, pointed his right leg straight out in front of him at waist level, and hopped back to us on one foot, waving his arms and yelling, "Aaargh! Aaah! Eeyaa!" He sat back down, panting but completely at ease. Dead silence had descended over the entire restaurant.

Without missing a beat, the producer mentioned that Nicholas had recently made several guest appearances on a prime-time series that I loved. I asked Nicholas which character he'd played. He ignored me. I asked again, more loudly. He pulled his head down into his shoulders, readjusting his grip on his beer bottle. I tried a third time. He squinted his eyes, clamped his lips shut, and leaned forward as if into a gale-force wind. I began asking him over and over, like a parrot: "So whodja play? So whodja play? So whodja play?" He never answered my question, and I ceased to exist for everyone at the table until I stopped pestering him.

Later, I spoke with the editor about a famous writer-director. She asked me if I'd seen his latest movie.

"I never see his films," I said. "I hate him and his work. He's horrific in interviews; he's a fraud; he's an arrogant creep; and I don't want to support his work."

The producer blinked. "I hate him, too! I think he's a disgrace! You're the only person I've ever met who agrees with me!"

I said, "I can't even look at him. He looks like a Punch puppet. He looks like a troglodyte," and the editor shocked herself by laughing. She examined me closely, trying to see my face under my beard and glasses. Nicholas interrupted from across the table.

"Ex*cuse* me. The word is *troglyte*." He winced at me in commiseration. I didn't know what to say, so I told him I was pretty sure it was troglodyte.

"No." He shook his head. "You're talking about a cave dweller?"

I nodded.

"A spelunker?"

"Uh... maybe not."

He scooted forward in his seat, dipping his head in gracious apology. "The word you're trying to think of is troglyte. My economics professor used it all the time."

There was a caesura, uncomfortable for all, so I said, "Actually, a Trog Light is a low-calorie Norwegian beer." Nicholas glared at me for a full three seconds, then he threw back his head and went, "Ah-HAAaa. HAAaa. HAAaa," at the ceiling. Everyone else laughed, and I stole a glance at Dolores, who gazed at me with a cocked eyebrow and her ferocious little kitty-cat smile. I knew she was thinking, "You're the coolest guy at this table." She was also comparing my tattered K-Mart Velcro watchstrap to Nicholas's gold Rolly and thinking, "Too damn bad."

When it was time to leave, Nicholas smashed my hand in his weightlifter's grip. "Hope to see you again," he lied. I silently thanked him for some great material. Earlier in the evening, when I'd asked him his life's ambition, he said, "I wanna fuck Winona Ryder! She's got a great rack!"

"What's a rack?" I asked, since even that late in life I'd never heard the term.

He hunched over, cupped his hands in front of his chest, and chuffed out the word, "*Tits.*"

To achieve his pronunciation, you have to clench your teeth, open your lips, pull the corners of your mouth down, tuck your chin into your neck, raise your eyebrows as high as you can, and say it with lots of saliva. Then wipe your chin, something Nicholas didn't do.

Flashback: Think Globally, Act Locally, and Gimmie

I'd developed a close working relationship with an independent publicity firm in L.A. that no longer exists. One time they invited me to a show by a band that also no longer exists. It was held at the House of Blues on Sunset Boulevard. I was given two all-access passes, which allowed me entrance into the VIP room of the club, where all the celebrities hung out. I took a photographer I knew because he loved observing ostentatious Hollywood show-offery, and he'd probably be the guy who'd photograph the bassist if the magazine okayed the interview.

In the VIP room, they had massive amounts of free food and free booze. There were tubs of fried chicken and fried catfish, gumbo, Cajun rice, crawfish, shrimp Creole, bananas Foster, beignets, and whatever other cuisine Louisiana is famous for, because the band was from the Pelican State. I had some chicken and gumbo and a Diet Coke. All around me were famous actors, singers, and standup comedians, cramming their gobs with food and swamping the bars with their demands for booze. As I got my chicken, a voice behind me said, "The best food is free food!"

I turned and saw a household-name actor, a guy long past his prime but still immensely famous, grinning like a happy baby and clutching a plate piled high with grub. I was amazed that such a wealthy person would even think twice about the cost of one meal, of all things. When I later told that story to Gene Simmons, I asked, "Why would such a rich guy care about how much one meal costs?"

"That's how he got to be rich," Simmons said deadpan, although there was an unmistakable "Good for you!" in his eyes as he spoke.

When the band began performing, my photographer and I went out onto the large balcony overlooking the stage. The music was horrible. It was some kind of zydeco-rock that just didn't work. The bassist was about eight feet tall, with a massive beer belly. He played his bass below his gut at arms' length, and he looked just like Joey Buttafuoco with a spectacular curly blonde mullet – a Kentucky waterfall, as it's known. It appeared to have been doused in baby oil, because it glittered with a million points of light. My usually restrained photographer gaped and said, "That? *That?* No. Absolutely not. I'm sorry. There isn't a *thing* I can do with that."

He shouldn't have worried. The band went over like some tedious Bulgarian performance-art troupe. The lead singer couldn't sing and was far too old to be sporting her tattoos, bracelets, and Mardi Gras beads. She was in love with the phrase "what the fuck," and she would not shut up, apparently believing that because she was onstage we all wanted to know her every thought.

"I wrote this one last year, when I was goin' through some pretty tough times, like we all do from time to time. What the fuck, man, it's called 'So Alone,' and I hope you like it, man, 'cause it meant a lot to me, I can tell you, to be able to express exactly what I was goin' through, to share what I was feelin' and shit. Like, it was really not the best fuckin' time of my life, I guess you could say, what with all the shit I was goin' through, so what the fuck, man, let's do it!"

Back in the VIP room, we witnessed the arrival of an ancient pornographer and his two twenty-three-year-old blonde girlfriends. The staff and other celebs welcomed this ghastly trio like royalty. Both women had the eerie calm of robots or heavily sedated psychiatric patients, and their boss-boyfriend's teeth were black, as though he'd been chewing on charcoal. Maybe he had; it's an old folk remedy for settling an upset stomach.

We stayed and watched the notables drink and eat until two in the morning. By the end, there were unconscious people being carried away by staffers. I met a filmmaker who was just starting out; he was a really nice, down-to-earth young guy as disgusted by everything as I was. He's become a successful producer, so God bless him. I can take a little credit for his artistic growth because we had a long conversation about theatrical portrayals of the Angel of Death, and I told him that one of the best was Robert Redford in a *Twilight Zone* episode called "Nothing in the Dark," which the filmmaker had never seen.

"The key is the ambiguity," I said. "He's compassionate yet dispassionate. The Angel of Death should be caring but businesslike, understanding but undeterred and not subject to influence by any argument or pleading from the person about to die." I later saw a movie this guy did before he became a producer, and he captured the ambiguity of the main character perfectly. This filmmaker was another respectful, intelligent, funny person who actually listened, which is so rare in Los Angeles it can overcome you with emotion. You fall in love and want such relics of a bygone era to never leave you.

I reported to my boss that the band was garbage, and no article was written. The publicists understood. I think some A&R heads rolled after that debacle. For my part I got to witness firsthand the fabulously wealthy and famous at play in their element. I have nothing against fantastically rich people; I met some really wonderful and responsible ones who were grateful for their fortunes and used them to do a lot of good. But that night torments me. I try not to think about all the food they threw out after the celebrities were done gorging. The staff had already begun tossing it into dumpsters as I left.

The First and Last Writers' Conference

In the summer of 2006 I drove up to Portland, Oregon, to attend my first writers' conference. I was conflicted: I knew I wanted to write, but my problem was that I couldn't seem to find a way to break through to a fully formed style that allowed me to express everything I wanted without being derivative, hackneyed, or just embarrassing. Music journalism had been the ideal vehicle for me because the interviewee had done all the talking.

I was leery about the publishing industry. At a reading for *In Cold Sweat*, I met a young novelist who quizzed me about my promotion efforts. He shook his head and laughed, saying, "You mean your publisher hasn't – ?" and then rattled off a series of things I didn't understand. He could barely conceal his pity for my amateur-hour idiocy. His own novel was in its second printing, and his book tour had been a huge success. He had blurbs from some of the most famous writers in the nation, all praising him for being an astounding new voice in fiction.

After talking with him for a while, he admitted that his literary agent only took him on as a favor. This new voice in fiction also said that he'd paid for the second print run himself. I bought the book, and it was unreadable. Some of the pages were piebald, sporting large irregularly shaped white patches with no text in them, as though leaves or scraps of cloth had somehow fallen into the printing press. The novel was so awful that it left me disoriented.

What am I missing? I asked myself. Did he buy the blurbs, too? Is every opinion, review, and critique for sale now? I couldn't read more than fifty pages of the novel because I felt as though I were going insane. I was in Opposite World, where horrible was great, lies were truth, and white patches of paper contained great prose. That experience dejected me so thoroughly that I thought I had no chance whatsoever in fiction. It was all about who you knew and how much you were willing to pay.

At the writers' conference, I attended a few seminars, which weren't particularly useful. I learned how to pitch my novel about the suicide of my best friend and got cards from dozens of agents. One young writer recommended his editor, who had completely rewritten his book. He gave me her contact information. When I returned to Los Angeles, I sent her the manuscript, which she immediately rejected. That was enough. I gave up on fiction.

Flamethrowers a Second Time Around

The rage and humiliation I felt at having failed to provide my publisher with a book on German World War I flamethrowers ate at me, but I didn't know what to do about it. Finally, I crammed down all my feelings and e-mailed the editor, asking him if I could write the book myself to make amends for letting them down. To my surprise he agreed, and I signed a contract in October of 2006. Since I already had the photos and drawings, it was just a matter of writing the text, which took months to research and then months to write. I turned in the manuscript long before the deadline. It didn't give me any sense of achievement; the squawking of that Hitler-chicken was in my ears the entire time I worked on the book.

Dismantling the Memory Box

My great-aunt Marion died in January of 2006, and I moved into her house. My parents, Tim, and I now live in a three-house compound of sorts, like the Kennedys. Tim and I were finally out of each other's hair, and I could continue living rent free as I tried to do something – *anything* – with writing. Remember, I told myself, Grandma Moses started her painting career in her late seventies. I gradually cleared my possessions out of Tim's house. One of the last things I discovered in my closet was the memory box I'd made in 1985 after I graduated from college. My accomplishments, goals, and dreams seemed really silly now, so I dismantled the box and put all the mementos in a little plastic tub I could tuck away out of sight. In the lower right-hand corner of the box was the bassist I'd cut out of a Carvin ad in a *Guitar Player* and glued to a piece of poster board. I wanted him only because he had the same model of bass I had. His identity was totally unknown to me at the time.

I broke him off his little wooden peg and examined him before I was about to put him in the plastic tub.

It was Scott Thunes.

The Best Editor in the World

In March of 2007, I was contacted by an editor named Jason S. Sitzes, who had without my knowledge gotten a hold of the manuscript for my novel about the suicide of my best friend. The editor who'd rejected it had given it to Jason. He asked if I wanted him to edit it. I didn't, really, because I was sure I sucked as a novelist, but I figured that it wouldn't hurt. Almost everything else I'd tried hadn't taught me anything. I researched Jason and found he had an amazing reputation, so I agreed.

It was expensive and quite humbling – mortifying, actually – to have my work gone over by a consummate professional, but it was the key I'd been looking for ever since I sold my first article in 1992. I learned more from that experience than I learned from the dozens of classes I took on writing, the books I read on writing, the writers' conference, and the advice from other writers. None of it even began to compare to having a real pro tell me exactly what was wrong with my writing.

Allowing a great editor to remake your book is not for the faint of heart, and unless you're willing to do what the editor says, it's a waste of everybody's time. There's a novelist who reissued his best work after he became a global phenomenon. He put back in everything the editor had taken out. The reissued version of the book is remarkable because there's a flatulence, urination, or defecation reference on almost every page. It's an absolute frenzy of toilet-obsession. When I read it, I thought, *This* is what bugged him for all those years? The fact that he couldn't talk freely about elimination?

Ultimately, the novel that Jason helped me produce was an order of magnitude better than the one he'd first received, and I hope to have it published someday. Does that mean that he diluted my "purity of vision"? No, it means he taught me how to articulate what I wanted to say all along. He showed me what worked and what didn't, and now I can do it much more easily on my own. I'm interested only in results.

Jason taught me several tricks of the trade that I won't reveal because that wouldn't be right. If you want to learn them, you need to hire him. That's how he makes his living. But everything you're reading in this memoir, I owe to Jason S. Sitzes. He fixed me, and for that I'll be forever grateful.

Thank you, Jason.

The First Really Weird Disease

Beginning in the spring of 2007, I started seeing perfect circles of flashing light in the corners of my eyes, and my vision would darken from the outside in. It was exactly like when you stand up too quickly, but it began happening all the time. I went to my eye doctor; he told me that my optic nerves were swollen. I asked him what that meant, and he hesitated.

"Doctor, just tell me," I said. "Worst-case scenario. I can take it." In reality I didn't know if I *could* take it. But I had to know.

"All right," he said. "It could be a brain tumor, or it could be the first sign of multiple sclerosis." He flapped both arms in a giant shrug.

Brain tumors and wasting diseases were my biggest health fears. With my luck, I'd have both. My doctor's receptionist made an appointment for me with a specialist, and then I went out and sat in my car in the parking lot. After a while, I thought, Why not me? People get terminal diagnoses every day. What makes me so special? If it's death, it's death, and I'll deal with it. I took solace from Elizabethan playwright Thomas Nashe, whose poem "A Litany in Time of Plague," written in 1592, reminded me that I had a lot of company in what I faced.

> *Adieu, farewell earths blisse,*
> *This world uncertaine is:*
> *Fond are lifes lustful joyes,*
> *Death proves them all but toyes.*
> *None from his darts can flye:*
> *I am sick, I must dye.*
> *Lord, have mercy on us!*

Nashe himself died at thirty-four. I prayed to Whomever might be up or out there, asking for strength instead of mercy. Then I went home and told Tim, who was more upset than I was.

I underwent a series of bizarre tests at two specialists. One consisted of me staring into a machine that assaulted my eyes with blinding flashes. It was like facing a million paparazzi. Another test was some kind of dye injection that flooded my mouth with the taste of iodine and made me feel as hot as a furnace. These were followed by MRIs of my head. When they were inconclusive, I was given my MRIs and told to go to the Doheny Eye Institute at the University of Southern California. After I was shown into a consulting room, a doctor put my MRIs up on a light board in the hall for his flock of medical students to examine. He told them – as I sat there six feet away, listening – that the doctor at the imaging center had noted the atrophy of my frontal lobes. That would explain a lot: The frontal lobes control planning and motivation. My entire life wasn't my fault!

A few minutes later, the most intelligent-looking man I've ever seen walked in. He had blue eyes that gave off a stunning electricity, and he calmed me immediately. His demeanor was perfect: compassionate dispassion. He was like one of the angels in Wim Wenders's *Wings of Desire*. Or like Robert Redford as the Angel of Death in the *Twilight Zone* episode "Nothing in the Dark." Either was fine with me. What would be, would be.

He told me he was certain I had pseudotumor cerebri, a condition I didn't know existed until he mentioned it. The cause is unknown, but suddenly your brain starts manufacturing too much cerebrospinal fluid. Since it's a closed system, the pressure builds up, and your optic nerves are affected. It's absolutely curable. I asked him if he was sure it was pseudotumor cerebri and not MS, and he said, "I'm 99.99 percent sure." Then he smiled.

"Are my frontal lobes atrophied?" I asked. He glanced at my MRIs. "Not in the least. They're perfectly normal."

The only sure way to confirm the diagnosis of pseudotumor cerebri is with a spinal tap. The needle is inserted through the spinal meninges or coverings that surround the canal, and the rate at which the cerebrospinal fluid sprays into the body of the syringe allows measurement of the pressure. This test was scheduled, and it turned out to be the most intense physical agony of my life. As I lay shirtless on my stomach, a thick-accented doctor from a nation not known for valuing human life thrust the needle into my back after applying a topical anesthesia that did nothing. The spinal tap took fifteen minutes and felt like a pair of fingers jamming in between my vertebrae, trying to yank them apart. Ten minutes into it I told the doctor we had to stop; I simply couldn't take it anymore because it hurt too much. Forty-five years old, I blubbered like a kindergartener. The doctor said "we" were more than halfway there, and if "we" stopped now, "we'd" just have to start all over again. Five interminable minutes later, the needle punctured the three tough membranes; the fluid jetted out; and the diagnosis was verified.

What followed was eight months of acetazolamide, which indeed cured me. The only aftereffect was gray spots in my vision that look like cute little dust bunnies. I asked the blue-eyed angel-doctor if they were permanent, and without hesitation he said yes, because the swelling of the optic nerves created damage that can't be repaired. My optic nerves are now irregular in cross section instead of circular.

Although having this odd, to me unheard-of disease did change my appreciation of life, it wasn't by much. I hadn't yet lost enough for reality to be pounded through the thick skull housing my overzealously fluid-producing brain.

Flamethrowers *Burn!*

My book *German Flamethrower Pioneers of World War I* was published in October of 2007, and I had the marvelous luck of observing in real time as my bogus, self-described cowriter Lew learned of it. I never told him that I'd gone ahead with the project. As I lurked on a discussion forum, someone called Lew's attention to a newly released title on German flamethrowers, which looked amazing. The commenter asked Lew if he'd heard of the author, Thomas Wictor.

Lew completely lost it and became hysterical, writing that he had to do some emergency checking because it appeared that his work had been stolen. A few minutes later he came back and immediately began a years' long campaign of accusing me on World War I discussion forums of having poached his research and refusing to credit him for it. To address this ridiculous allegation, let me point out that he never wrote a word. Unless he believed I'd somehow entered his mind through remote viewing or astral projection and sucked out his knowledge with some kind of psychic vacuum cleaner, there's no way I "stole" his research. My book is extensively footnoted. In addition, I thanked him in the acknowledgements.

He apparently revised the history of our agreement into an arrangement in which he provided the research and I wrote the whole thing but shared authorship with him because... Why? I have a pathological need to write gigantic tomes by myself and then share the credit with Hitler-voiced chickens? The reality is that he never provided me with any research other than the titles of three books I would've found on my own. Within two years of meeting him I knew more about the topic than he did.

But Lew had a lot of credibility in the World War I history-buff community. He belonged to the tribe, while I was a newbie with no connections. Branded a dishonest, conniving backstabber, I found that my reputation – and likely my sales – suffered.

Flashback: Don't Make Assumptions

A band that'd recently signed a record deal invited me to one of their shows. The bassist wanted me to arrive the same time the band did, so I could see what they went through when setting up. We all gathered outside the club on Hollywood Boulevard, waiting for the staff to let us in. As the bassist and I stood on the sidewalk talking, he elbowed me and pointed. "Whoa! Check it out!"

Across the street was a line of apartments. One of the windows was brightly lit; it was fitted with semi-opaque frosted glass, but we could see a perfect silhouette of a naked woman sitting in front of a mirror applying makeup. She got up and pirouetted, examined her front and back, weighed her breasts in her hands, sat down, and painted her face some more. After a few seconds she stood and hopped slightly to make her breasts bounce, then she turned around and did it again, peering over her shoulder to watch her buttocks bounce. From all the spinning, we saw that she had a long sinewy back, broad shoulders, and narrow hips. Her silhouette was so clear and her performance so mannered I wondered if they were filming a movie.

The bassist leered. "Is she totally fuckin' hot or what?"

I said, "Don't you know where we are? How do you know that's a she?"

"*Oh, my God!*" he shrieked. He turned and literally ran over to his band mates, huddling in their midst like a child who'd just been told a terrifying story about monsters in the woods.

Flamethrowers, Flamethrowers, and More Flamethrowers

Despite the indifferent or hostile reception of my first flamethrower book, in April of 2008 I enthusiastically agreed to write a second volume, this time about the flame troops of all the nations that fought in World War I. I reached out to enthusiasts in Britain, France, Italy, Germany, Bulgaria, Russia, and Turkey, all of whom were happy and excited to be involved. Even with the Internet, research was incredibly hard to carry out because many of the records are located in former Eastern-bloc nations whose governments and institutions retain the traditional suspicions that characterized them during the Cold War. I was told that museums and archives never answer their phones and never respond to e-mails or letters. The way to proceed was by making personal contacts, two of the most remarkable being the following.

Are All Bulgarians This Nice?

Ventsislav Gramatski – Ventsi to his friends – is a young Bulgarian man who speaks perfect, colloquial English. When I met him on an English-language history forum, he was a college student studying international relations. In response to my request for any tips on researching the Bulgarian army flamethrower effort during World War I, he immediately offered to take a bus to the National Museum of Military History in Sofia to ask questions. He refused all offers of compensation and conducted an interview with a museum staffer that provided most of the information I needed.

I almost had to force him to accept a copy of the first flamethrower book and a copy of the second when it was published. He's a remarkable guy whose contributions to my project were vital. And he did it simply for the love of knowledge and as a favor. When I donated a copy of my second book to the National Museum of Military History, the staff commemorated the moment with one of the greatest photos I've ever seen: giant Ventsi and a Bulgarian knockout, Ms. Anna Dyulgerova, Senior Expert of the museum's Directorate of Funds, Restoration, and Military Monuments, holding my book. It's a truly fantastic image because of its glorious improbability and touching combination of pride, gratitude, friendship, and eastern European formality.

At the time of this writing Ventsi was a Junior Expert at the Bulgarian National Commission for Combating Trafficking in Human Beings. He developed policy for fighting organized crime, worked on international anticrime projects, and was responsible for identifying victims of human trafficking and ensuring that they were returned safely from abroad. All this while studying for a master's degree in International Security.

Thank you, Ventsi. You'll go even further than you already have.

An Authority on Plagues; a Lover of Beauty

In June of 2008, I found a Russian-language Web site that contained the text of a Soviet-era book on chemical warfare of World War I.[1] The Web site owner was a Russian Colonel of the Reserves, microbiologist Mikhail Vasilyevich Supotnitskiy, M.D. I wrote to him in Russian, using Babelfish to translate my letter. He responded in Russian, telling me that he read and understood English. I could write to him in English, but he'd answer in Russian to avoid misunderstandings.

Colonel Supotnitskiy, too, was vital to my project. After the book was finished, we continued to correspond, and gradually we developed a friendship, even though we've never met in person and despite the fact that machine translation from Russian to English often creates sentences diametrically opposed to the meaning that the colonel tries to get across. For example, he once told me, "I'm offended by you." I asked him what I'd done to offend him, and it turned out that he'd written "I'm offended *for* you," a sentiment he'd expressed after reading a newspaper article about a case of American political corruption.

The colonel is a political junkie, and we likely disagree on most geopolitics. However, we don't spend much of our time debating the state of the world and who's responsible. We've had our little spats about Iraq and Afghanistan, but mostly we discuss music, art, and absurdity. The Anna Chapman spy caper enthralled him; in order for him to be on the lookout for this dangerous agent, I sent him updates that included photos of her barely clothed. For his part, he e-mails me his beautiful photos of the woods, Orthodox churches with golden domes, old barns, vacation spas, rocky beaches, and his family. An accomplished photographer and connoisseur of literature, poetry, and paintings, he introduced me to Alexei Savrasov; I reciprocated with Maxfield Parrish, whom the colonel instantly loved.

His sense of humor is on the bizarre side, which I always like. He e-mailed me a photo of his infant grandson Peter cavorting to a YouTube video I'd sent of Cleary & Harding doing the hand-dancing routine they choreographed for "We No Speak Americano." The baby wore an orange T-shirt with a green ribcage on it. I asked the colonel what in God's name *was* that, and he said it was a radioactive cancer-shirt. When I told him Orwell's aphorism, "At age fifty, every man has the face he deserves," he wrote back, "I often think of that when riding the trains and subways." His response – in Cyrillic – to my story of how my first ghost Brigitte took me for $2000 was only one word: "*Suka!*" I laughed even before I translated it because I knew what it surely meant.

I told the colonel that I sometimes contemplated immigrating to Russia and working at his think tank as a sweeper. He said, "We already have a sweeper. She sweeps in the Kazakh style, which is very attractive. However, maybe you can introduce the American style of sweeping to the rest of the Russian Federation. Vladimir Putin will present you with the Order of the Golden Broom, and I – because of the glory reflected from you – will be promoted in the Defense Ministry to head the Directorate of Bribes."

I also enjoy his ambiguity. His reply to a message about my father was, "The Russian poet Vladimir Mayakovsky said about your father: 'Make nails of these people; in the world of nails there would never be any stronger!'"

He recently wrote me, "Your destiny mirrors that of Mark Twain. You were created specifically to do what you are doing – professional writing. All the previous kinds of work you did were an accident. You pushed yourself into precisely the sorts of situations and activities that would allow you to show the strongest part of your character. When I read your books, I see all the careful work you put into them; most importantly, you love your work, as I love mine. Otherwise you would not have so thoroughly studied the illustrative material, not gone digging for old patents (something that except for you and I very few people do), and not so carefully listed your bibliographic sources. The subjects of your books are original. So take chances, cheerfully and without fear! In Russia after the war ended, there was a saying: 'Relax; this is no longer 1941.'"

Thank you, Colonel. I'm taking chances now, cheerfully and without fear.

Flashback: A Druid in Los Angeles

Stephen Jay has been "Weird Al" Yankovic's bassist for over thirty years. However, he's also a multi-instrumentalist, vocalist, lyricist, and classically trained composer who studied with John Cage, Lukas Foss, Max Neuhaus, and Charles Wuorinen; in addition, he's a music ethnographer who's traveled the world playing with and recording folk musicians from multiple cultures. Finally, he's one of the most technically skilled, innovative, and melodic bassists alive. The music of his film and TV scores and his solo albums is genuinely astonishing. He's developed a hybrid picking-slapping technique like nothing I've ever seen. It allows him to play rhythm and lead at the same time, as well as superimposing different meters on the same pattern, a technique he describes as "polymetric triangulation."

"That's the way I think of focusing on the groove. You use two meters at once. If you're playing in 4/4, you can nail your groove and feel the inertia, but as soon as somebody starts playing a three-figure against that, all of a sudden the groove locks. It works the same way as a sextant or a global-positioning system by having two fixed points of reference and your own position, creating a triangle that allows you to determine exactly where you are. The way it works in music, it's focusing time to determine more closely where 'now' is, and the groove is basically all about 'now,' the source, where things comes from. It's the edge of creation, where that which didn't exist before suddenly does and then doesn't again. That's the essence of the groove. By staying closer to that origin, the source-point of 'now,' we can ride along right on the edge. It's always going to be two against three, or four against six, or eight against five. You and another musician can play different meters, or you can play different meters in your own part.

"Let's say you're playing eighth notes, alternating between a loud and a soft. You're going up and down with your thumb, an upstroke and a downstroke. Then you can switch from accenting every other note – a straight two – and you start accenting every third one. Rather than changing your technique to produce a three-pattern, such as two strokes down and one up, or one down and two up, you keep that two-pattern as your technique but superimpose accents in alternating positions along the pattern. You've got a really nice two-pattern going, and you superimpose the three on top of it, producing the same triangulating effect as a sextant, pointing you to where the 'now' is. It can get really complex. This happens spontaneously as you play, as opposed to it being something you've rehearsed beforehand."

He slaps eight- and twelve-string basses in a way that makes him sound like an entire band. Discovering Jay's incredible talent was like finding a chest of gold doubloons in a lagoon where you thought you'd be lucky to pick up a few pretty shells. He's the only bassist with superhuman technical skill I ever saw whose chops never overwhelmed the music and actually created deep emotional resonance.

When I attended shows put on by Ak & Zuie, a duo consisting of Stephen and drummer Pete Gallagher, I was transported into an entirely different plane of perception, due to the intricate interplay of the bass and drums. Stephen told me it's based on decades of studying how rhythm and melody can change brain chemistry and make you feel good. The overtones and polyrhythms interact in such a way as to make you think you're hearing an entire ensemble. Jay calls the invention "polymetric funk." He also uses his Theory of Harmonic Rhythm,[2] his discovery that a consonant harmonic interval produces a consonant regularly rhythmic interval, creating a "universal substance" between harmony and rhythm. A player can create a kind of musical sympathy by being aware of the symmetry between harmony and rhythm and understanding how the two elements focus in terms of delicacy and scale.

As Jay told me, "A simple example would be if you were going to write a song in A, and you're tuned to 440, and you make your song tempo 109. Every time you start a cycle in an A 440 – let's imagine that you can be mathematically perfect in your beginnings – if your tempo is 109, that waveform would always be chopped off before it completed itself because the tempo isn't 110, a subdivision of 440. So by simply synching up the tempo to the pitch, you create complete waveforms rather than incomplete waveforms. They're broken up evenly. When little things like that are expanded out to the scale of how each individual note in a chord works in relation to the other notes in the chord, it becomes an equation that's so immensely complex that it seems to me like it would be incalculable, and that's what makes music magic."

Some scientists believe Stonehenge was built to enhance the experience of the drumming and chanting rituals performed by the druids. When I attended Ak & Zuie concerts, the polymetric triangulation, polymetric funk, and Theory of Harmonic Rhythm combined to create moments when I entered a trancelike state, and I had to ask myself, What's going on here? It was the only time in my ten-year career that music did that to me. I suddenly understood the true power of this art form and its ability to induce euphoria. Ak & Zuie backed me up at some of my readings for *In Cold Sweat,* a surreal and magical escapade.

I fell deeply in love with an instrumental Stephen played for me that he said might go on a future album. That composition stayed in my head for years, though I couldn't remember the title. I didn't want to contact Stephen because of the shame and humiliation I felt over the collapse of my career in music journalism. He told me the title of the piece on April 15, 2012; "Telenergy," on his CD *Tangled Strings*. It was a great relief to rediscover it. Stephen writes far too many brilliant songs for me to list, but some of the standouts on his many solo albums are "Big Shoes," "Go Like This," "Deny the Accuser," "Tangled Strings," "Suva," "Self Avoiding Random Walk," "The Mistake," "What the Voodoo Became," "Underwater," "What They Say," and "Hungry Target." All are dumbfounding confluences of musicality, lyricism, vocal skills, and – above all – effortless bass prowess that never distracts. Perfect Stephen Jay samplers are his albums *Sea Never Dry* and *Self Avoiding Random Walk*, both on the Ayarou Music label and available on his Web site. They contain songs that you can sing or hum after just one listening, despite their devilish complexity.

A tremendously original song from the album *Physical Answer* is "Bailed Outside," on which Jay uses a Moroccan *gimbri* – a boat-shaped instrument with a fretless neck like a broomstick and a skin top – which he converted by adding electric-bass strings, tuners, and a pickup. The resulting creation sounds exactly like a hybrid electric-standup bass. Stephen also played his father's old bugle in one of the most haunting horn passages I've ever heard.

My favorite track on *Sea Never Dry* is "Trouble," a traditional Turkish song that Stephen adapted, writing his own lyrics.

> *Ashram in the bedroom*
> *Solemn like soldiers*
> *Happiness in hell fire*
> *Sadness in heaven*
>
> *Who called this meeting*
> *Who knows the reason*
> *Who are all of these people*
> *Happy like children*
> *Empty like cauldrons*
> *Happy to be here*
> *Swallowed not eaten*
> *Taken not bitten*
>
> *Who made them lay down*
> *Jah must have made them*
> *Ghost made them play dumb*
> *Saved for no ending*

The combination of the middle-eastern melody and instrumentation, the passion of the singing, and the ambiguity of the lyrics makes this one of Stephen's most memorable efforts. Tim told me that his art teacher in college said, "Great art asks more questions than it answers." That's my position, too. I don't know what these lyrics mean, which is why I like them. According to Francis Bacon – another painter I revere – the job of the artist is to always deepen the mystery. It's an approach Stephen Jay has taken to heart.

Ak & Zuie even do something indescribable to cover songs. Their versions of "Cinnamon Girl" by Neil Young and "Rock On" by David Essex are unforgettable and immensely moving. Listening to Stephen Jay was one of the rare times as a music journalist that I felt privileged to be in the presence of such greatness. In my career Scott Thunes, Gene Simmons, John Taylor, Andy West, Bryan Beller, and Stephen Jay made the most lasting impressions on me as both accomplished artists and people. The music that entered my very being – separately from its creators – and made a permanent change was the work of Ray Shulman, Scott Thunes, and Stephen Jay.

The Second Really Weird Disease

One night in August of 2009, my abdomen began to ache. The pain grew and grew until it felt as though I'd swallowed a bayonet. After a few hours of this, I suddenly threw up violently several times, my entire body clenched as tightly as a fist. I had Tim drive me to the emergency room. Once I was admitted, they gave me morphine and took a urine sample. It was coffee colored. The doctor asked, "Is your urine always this dark?"

It seemed like such an absurd question. Was any living person's urine ever that dark? It was like pee from one of those 2000-year-old Danish bog mummies. I wanted to answer, "Actually, my urine is usually pitch black. It's much lighter tonight," but I said no. They took my coffee off to test, and then the doctor came back after about twenty minutes. He seemed nervous.

"Just tell me what you think is happening," I said. I wasn't afraid at all, because I already knew my body had gone utterly haywire, probably fatally so.

"Well, it appears that your liver has failed," he said. "You may have picked up hepatitis somewhere, maybe at a fast-food restaurant where someone didn't wash their hands, but we think you're in total hepatic failure. I'm surprised you're not jaundiced."

As far as I knew, liver failure meant death, unless you were lucky enough to get a transplant, but I was very calm. They let Tim in.

"So what's happening?" he asked.

I said, "Well, you need to brace yourself. It appears to be very bad news. They tell me that they think my liver has failed."

He went completely white. I felt terrible for him. "Are they going to do more tests?" he asked shakily.

"Yeah. The fact that I'm not jaundiced might mean that it's not complete liver failure, but they're testing my blood, looking for hepatitis C. It's not certain yet, so let's just wait and see." I figured I was done for, and I'd accepted it. It just didn't scare me at all. I was sad but not afraid. Poor Tim seemed to be having trouble containing himself.

Eventually, the tests all came back negative, and since I wasn't jaundiced, the doctors released me, but I had to make an appointment with a liver specialist immediately. I went home and the next day called my doctor, who gave me a referral. The specialist couldn't see me for three days. I made the appointment, and in the afternoon I went out behind my house to talk to Tim. He took one look at me and said, "Tom, you're yellow."

I went into the bathroom and looked in the mirror, and sure enough, I appeared to have been lightly dusted with pollen. My eyes were yellow, too, like a cat's. I called my doctor, and he told me to get to the emergency room right away. So back we went, less than twenty-four hours after we left the first time.

They admitted me again, and in an hour or so, I was as yellow as a lemon. Tim was extremely upset but doing his best to not show it. I still wasn't afraid. When I'd returned from Japan in 1990, I sat next to a laconic Asian man. The 747 careened all over the sky and the engines howled desperately as we approached the runway at LAX. It was some kind of crosswind or microburst. I was so terrified I was almost in tears.

"This pilot's fucked up," my seatmate mumbled.

Conversation! It would distract me. "What do you mean?" I asked. "How do you know?"

"'Cause I'm a pilot in the Singapore Air Force," he said. "I fly an F-16. We're gonna crash."

"*Don't say that!*" I screamed.

He lazily glanced over at me. "Why get upset? You can't fight it. When it's your time, it's your time. There's nothing you can do about it, so you might as well relax."

Now, almost twenty years later, I finally understood that sleepy pilot's attitude. I couldn't fight liver failure. If it was my time, it was my time. After a while, a paramedic came in and said he was in training to be a doctor. He asked questions about my pain and when I'd started to turn yellow. I told him they'd said that as long as I wasn't jaundiced, it might not be serious, but now that I was yellow, it looked like it was.

He nodded vigorously. "Oh, yeah. It's liver failure, all right. You're gettin' yellower as I talk to you. I can see it happenin'." He patted my shoulder.

Tim snapped, "For fuck's sake!"

I just laughed and said to the paramedic, "Man, you really need to work on your bedside manner."

The paramedic nodded rapidly again and said, "Yeah, I do," and kept taking notes. He stayed for a while and told us about all the people he'd seen die from rapid liver failure. By the time he left, Tim was purple.

"That asshole's like a talking dog," he said. "He's like a German shepherd in a paramedic's uniform. I kept expecting him to scratch his ear with his foot. The way he was going, 'Yeah-yeah-yeah-yeah-yeah,' he was just like a panting, cartoon dog." Tim despises dogs.

Nobody seemed to know what to do with me. My doctor showed up and had a vigorous discussion with the ER doctor, demanding several tests be done on me. I really like my doctor. He's Taiwanese, very businesslike but personally enigmatic. It's a quality to which I respond well. He reminds me of a sorcerer; I can easily see him casting spells. As he and the ER doctor argued, something odd happened: My jaundice began to disappear. Within a couple of hours, I was completely normal again. Nobody could explain it. My urine reverted to urine-color, and all my tests came back negative. I was released.

Over the next few weeks, I was tested for everything, including gallstones, liver cancer, pancreatic cancer, cirrhosis, sclerosing cholanitis, and Gilbert's syndrome. I was given MRIs and ultrasounds. Nothing was ever found. I seemed to have recovered completely. None of my doctors had ever seen someone turn lemon yellow and then shake it off in two hours.

I wondered if that idiot paramedic had somehow cured me. Maybe he was a miracle worker who only pretended to be an insensitive clod. Or maybe he didn't even know he could cure people with his doglike self. On the other hand, it could be that my ambiguous Taiwanese doctor *is* a sorcerer after all and cast a spell to heal me. He and I get along because I'm his best patient. He says I'm the only one who follows his orders. I also knew about stinky tofu, which made him laugh. He almost never laughs.

Tim may have cured me, too. Three years later, Tim had an outpatient procedure to repair an umbilical hernia. That afternoon I took him to the emergency room when he began to experience agonizing abdominal pain. We had to wait for six hours – Tim doubled over and breathless – while people who couldn't speak English and who had headaches and sniffles were admitted. Finally, I told Tim to prepare himself because I was about to start smashing up the nurses' stations, and at that precise second we were called in. They discovered the doctor had punctured his bowel during the hernia operation. Tim had a systemic infection and was about an hour from death. He needed emergency surgery and a stay in the hospital, where they tried every known antibiotic. All were failures except for the one of final resort. I visited Tim once or twice a day; the first night, high on morphine and fever, he told me that famous radio talk-show hosts and chefs from the Food Network had recorded shows in the hallway, protected by army canine units with rifles. After two weeks he recovered. He said my visits saved his life.

Following my own recovery from my mystery pain and jaundice, I went back to my old ways of letting myself become consumed by anger. The only change was I'd outgrown my fear of death. I wasn't afraid at all the entire time I was yellow. Though I didn't want to die, if it was my time, it was my time.

Thank you, laconic Singaporean fighter pilot. You were right.

Flamethrowers Aren't the Answer After All

By the time I finished my second military-history book, *Flamethrower Troops of World War I: The Central and Allied Powers,* I'd completely lost interest in writing for the sort of people who'd buy it. I'd discovered that the vast majority of them were like the *Bass Player* editor who killed my career in music journalism. There was simply no way to reach them. New or different ideas were anathema, to be ignored or mocked. Since nobody had ever written books about flamethrowers of World War I, there obviously had never been a need for such compendia. They were therefore clearly worthless and ought to be scorned.

Posting my views on discussion forums was exactly like the endless arguments I'd had with my editor. The dynamic was identical: Once again I persisted in bringing my own approach to the field while being told in plain English that my contributions were not wanted. Yet instead of simply saying, "Okay, goodbye," I again allowed myself to be consumed with rage at the injustice of it and tried endlessly to argue or convince. This time, instead of fighting with an editor, I fought with famous historians and dozens of people on several forums.

A perfect example was the day I posted a beautiful image of a German flamethrower squad running through barbed wire. It was a genuine combat photo, an extremely rare find. The same photographer who took it also produced a well-known image at the same location, which is in the collections of several national archives and commercial photo libraries. My photo was unknown before I bought it on eBay. The two images were taken on February 21, 1916, the opening day of the Battle of Verdun. What makes my photo historically significant is that the photographer identified the exact place and time of day on the glass-plate negative. Also, the equipment of the flamethrower squad was clearly shown. Most importantly for historians and uniform buffs, the photo showed that the lance operator wore a spiked helmet, while the flamethrower carrier had a steel helmet, the familiar German coalscuttle model.

This photo had never been published before. I posted it in response to a comment by one of Britain's more respected military writers, an expert on the Battle of Verdun. I pointed out the weapons, the equipment, the white brassards used as identification, and lastly, the two differing helmets, which was very unusual.

The writer wrote, "Sorry. Don't see it."

I'd expected, "That's great! Thanks for posting it!" The response I got was horrifying, inexplicable, and infuriating. A person who'd written several books on this major battle was not even slightly interested in a dated photo that depicted the exact place and time of day that part of the initial assault took place. The thoughtless, rude comment was absolutely stunning to me. I outlined the helmets with black, enlarged the photo, and reposted it.

"Nope. Still don't see it."

And that was the end of the conversation. After a couple of years on these forums, I'd dubbed myself the Great Thread Killer because any time I posted one of my photos or comments, everyone would flee. There was almost never a discussion of ideas that didn't fit into preconceived notions or didn't come from either pedigreed experts or recognizable members of the tribe. A few European enthusiasts valued my work, but the vast majority of British and American historians ignored it or actively denigrated it. I don't mean in reviews; I'm fairly sure none of my military-history titles have been reviewed. Though I don't read my reviews, I came to this conclusion from discovering that nobody in the World War I field has heard of my books. I'm talking about when I expressed my views and shared new information on Internet forums, which is where most of the action takes place. Regarding institutions and academia, I haven't even bothered to check how my books have been received. Anything that isn't produced by an accredited scholar doesn't exist.

This scathing, near-universal rejection made me as angry as I'd ever been during the worst period at *Bass Player.* Despite my rage, I was still too afraid to try selling the novel

I'd had edited, and even though I didn't want to write any more books on military history, I still felt the need to stay and try to convince people that they'd completely misunderstood me. I *knew* I could reach them, if I just tried hard enough. It was beyond that, actually: I *had* to reach them. It became an imperative, as it was with Carmen and my indifferent editor at *Bass Player*. I'd put so much of *me* into this, so much effort and care, so much thought, that I *had* to make them see.

Deep Thoughts of a Pilot

One night in December of 2009, I came across a Web site touting new artists. The work of one, Leslie Ditto of Memphis, Tennessee, attracted me. I found her own Web site[3] and looked through her online portfolio. Her paintings were terrific, both humorous and disturbing. She has a completely original style and works in oils. Her art captures dream imagery in a stylized yet completely realistic way; she does many portraits of what appear to be doll-like or animated characters rendered in three-dimensional flesh. Ditto's paintings are also stuffed with allegorical references and symbols.

I found her work mesmerizing and spent an hour studying it. While examining her portfolio, a painting leaped out at me. It was titled *Deep Thoughts of a Pilot* and depicted a young, dark-haired, tattooed woman sitting in a canyon of jagged peaks. She wears an old-fashioned, leather flying helmet; a fur-lined, buckled jerkin; a scarf; and cargo pants. Her helmet has two birds' wings on the top, like those worn by the Greek god Mercury, but these are actual wings, with feathers. It isn't clear if they're attached to the flying helmet or grow out of the young woman's head. Perched on the pilot's shoulder is an owl.

What drew me is the pilot's expression. It's deeply, horribly sad, her eyes haunted and her downturned mouth almost trembling with misery, and yet she also projects gallant strength and resolution. Her posture is one of exhaustion, her forearms braced on her thighs and her gloved hands dangling limply between her knees. She's accomplished much, but she's in mourning for all that's happened to her. Despite the pain and anguish radiating from her face, she presents herself to you without apology, rejecting your pity even though her eyes are filled with tears and appear ready to spill over.

It was one of the most compelling images I'd ever seen. It spoke to me like nothing had in years. I saw with excitement that it was for sale. For the first time in my life, I bought a piece of original art. My plan was to someday hang it where I could gaze at it as I wrote, the way I listen to Suzanne Vega when I write.

When the painting arrived, it was so new it still had that turpentiney smell. Owning it calmed me, as though a missing piece had been returned to me. I felt relief having it in my hands.

Flashback: How to Shock People into Speechlessness

When researching my failed novel, *The Mermaid Lamp*, I contacted an unsigned band and arranged to observe them for an entire night. The club where they played was a nightmarish den painted black and red on the inside, with a sort of Gothic Mardi Gras theme complete with Gigerish stools, chairs, and tables that were bonelike and creepily erotic. Since the stage was on the second floor, you had to walk up a flight of narrow, black-painted stairs enclosed by red, smeary, visceral-looking walls. It was like being inside the dissected thorax of a giant animal. Blinding white spotlights illuminated the tiny raised stage, giving the stark, black-painted upper level a sinister documentary-like feel, the ideal setting for a snuff film.

As the band set up, I listened to them chat.

"Aw, I forgot to bring my cool strap," bassist said. "And I wanted to wear different shoes. Dammit! I wanted to be vampier." She wore a black suit jacket and miniskirt, a purple blouse, black tights, and black stack-heeled pumps.

"You're vampy," the guitarist assured her.

"*Damn* vampy," said the drummer.

The drummer and the guitarist sat at a table to write out the guest list for the doorman. I joined them to listen. The guitarist said, "I had a friend who smoked a frog. Really. He got sent to Southwest Africa by *Details* magazine, I think. He had his picture taken smoking this frog. He showed me the picture. They'd dried the frog and ground it into powder, and then he smoked it in a pipe just like weed."

The drummer said, "I've heard of people licking frogs but never smoking them."

"Well, he smoked it, all right."

"Did he get high?"

"Oh yeah. He had wicked hallucinations for about twelve hours."

The drummer shook his head. "Wow. Was he okay after he smoked it?"

"Nah. It fucked him up."

"Really? What, for good?"

The guitarist nodded. "For good. Yup. Permanently. The right side of his face was paralyzed when I saw him, and he couldn't really talk all that well. And he used to be really smart before, but he couldn't really keep track of his thoughts any more. He couldn't write the article he'd been assigned about smoking frogs, and he didn't know what he was going to do. Yeah, it really fucked him up, but good."

I told them about a guy I met in college, who had two criteria for every substance he came across. One, did it burn? And two, could you get high on it? He'd smoked plastic, cotton, oak leaves, vitamin pills, and horsehair. He'd once tried to smoke the British yeast extract Marmite. He was nineteen and looked to be about fifty, with an oily, deeply wrinkled face and a croaking, phlegmy voice. His entire life, he said, would be devoted to seeing what he could smoke to get high.

The guitarist and drummer looked at me as though I were completely unhinged. After several seconds, the guitarist said, "That's *just* not *good*," in a sarcastic, schoolmarmish tone, glancing at the drummer. Neither said anything else after that. I'd killed the conversation.

The Family That Set a Trap for Me

I knew a family for nine years. When I first met them, their daughter – whom I'll call Leni – was three. The parents were both recovering alcoholics and drug addicts who spent much of their time in group therapy, encounter sessions, drumming circles, and so on. I felt a kinship for them due to my own drug and alcohol issues, but they embraced the recovery culture more rabidly than any people I've ever known. It was almost the sole topic of their conversation.

"Charles" had the wacky sense of humor I like. I've never laughed hearing someone describe how his teeth fell out from meth addiction, but Charles made it sound like a *Fawlty Towers* episode. He once said he considered me his brother, which was extremely flattering. His wife "Astrid" was much more high strung. She'd learned how to be an "active listener," which meant that when you spoke to her, she'd go, "Uh-huh. Uh-huh. Uh-huh. Huh! Wow. Uh-huh. Hah!" every few words, to show you that she was engaged. They rejected the real powerhouse in the recovery world, the Swiss psychiatrist Dr. Alice Miller, preferring the likes of M. Scott Peck and Robert Bly.

Leni was one of the most anxious, neurotic, badly behaved children I've encountered. My view is that the parents were terminally damaged by their horrendous upbringings and their drug and alcohol abuse. In addition, the heavy psychotropic medications they'd been on for years and continued to take after Leni was born produced in them a flatness of affect that their child perceived from infancy but of course couldn't understand. All she knew was that Mom and Dad didn't connect with her. Soon, she discovered that acting out made her parents wake up for a while to scold and punish her, which inevitably led to her associating negative attention with love. The same story has been told only about a billion times by now.

Leni and I always got along. I felt bad for her because I believed that her parents should never have reproduced. They were simply unfit, regardless of how devoted they were to recovery. Despite her problems, Leni had a goofy sense of humor and loved to laugh. She was very physically affectionate with me, which her parents said was utterly anomalous. With everyone else, she was standoffish. She liked to sit next to me on the sofa with her arm around my shoulder as I read to her, or sometimes she'd sit on my lap when we watched TV.

When Leni turned eleven, her parents abruptly prohibited her from having physical contact with me. They gave her lectures – in front of me – about how now it was unacceptable for her to show such affection to a man. She was too big to do that anymore. I understand the trickiness here; nobody wants their teenaged daughter sitting on the lap of the middle-aged, male family friend. But I'm convinced that these things tend to sort themselves out. Generally, as girls get older, they taper off physical contact with older men on their own initiative, I think. If they've been raised properly, they know what's appropriate.

What resulted in this situation – after physical contact was allowed on one day and banned the next – was just the opposite of what Charles and Astrid intended: Leni began surreptitiously touching me when her parents were out of the room. It started with just brief strokes on the head or shoulders, and then it escalated into her rubbing her chest or bottom on me by the time she was twelve. She kissed me on the cheeks and tried to go for my mouth, though I always turned my head in time. Once she raised her shirt and flashed me, coolly gauging my reaction. Another time she sat in the chair across from me in jeans, spread her legs, and rubbed herself with a creepy, artificial, come-hither smile. I sometimes spent the night with the family on an inflatable mattress in the living room; that ended when I woke up to find Leni trying to crawl into bed with me. I sent her back to her room and stayed up reading until dawn.

Concurrent with her advances toward me, Leni began ostentatiously telling her parents how much she loved them. "I *love* you, Mommy!" she'd coo. Astrid would beam at me in self-satisfaction. "We've really changed the road she was on," she'd say. To me, Leni's manipulation was as subtle as a whack on the noggin with a golf club, but her mother and father were desperate to believe that they hadn't ruined their daughter.

It was much more ominous when Leni started to slap, punch, and kick me, accusing me of having hit her first. I'd hear her whispering to her parents in the kitchen, "But it's *true!* He *hit* me! He *kicked* me! He's *lying* about it!" After each visit, she'd send me a letter apologizing and promising she wouldn't do it again.

Charles once took me aside and said, "Sometimes I feel like I have two children, Tom."

"So you honestly think I'm hitting and kicking Leni behind your backs and lying about it?" I asked.

He looked miserable. "I... I don't know *what's* going on. It's just getting out of control is all I'm saying."

It was. One evening as I sat on the sofa, Leni came to me on all fours. In a chilling, unconscious imitation of Nakamura, the Cat-faced Ghost in the Rising Sun, who liked to scamper over on her hands and knees and wag her round bottom like a dog's tail as she asked for sex, Leni turned and brushed her rear against my shin several times, peering back at me with her sunny, completely fake smile.

My refusal to acknowledge the danger I was in can be partly explained by both the nine-year history I had with these people and the old, familiar sense of outrage and injustice that induced me to stay and try to rectify the situation. More importantly, I simply didn't know how to broach the topic. Not only was this an emotional powder keg for me, I worried that given her parents' ham-fisted, oblivious approach to raising their child, exposing her actions would saddle Leni with a lifelong sense of being dirty and worthless.

The last time I saw the family was on a Sunday. Charles and Astrid invited me over for breakfast and then suddenly announced that they were going to church. Since they were generally antireligious, I was very surprised. They asked if I'd stay and babysit Leni. I reluctantly agreed. After Charles and Astrid left, Leni immediately said that she was going to take a shower. I didn't respond. She went into the bathroom and closed the door, and I heard the water run for fifteen minutes or so. She then emerged wet haired in a bathrobe and ambled toward me, playing with the belt and smiling.

I knew just as surely as I knew the sun rises in the east that she was about to drop the robe, so I said, "Go get dressed now, kiddo."

"Why?" she asked saucily.

"Because it's what civilized people do." I reached out, gripped her shoulders, spun her around, and propelled her forward. She leaned back against me, but she was only twelve, so she had no ability to resist the inertia of my 220 pounds. I shoved her into her room, and she indignantly slammed the door. No more than nine seconds later, the front door flew open; in rushed Charles and Astrid.

"We decided we didn't like going to church after all," Astrid said, glancing wildly in all directions. Charles hurried into the kitchen and seemed to make a thorough search of it. He came out and almost imperceptibly shook his head at his wife. As the three of us stood there shifting our gazes from face to face like gunslingers in a spaghetti western, Leni emerged from her room fully dressed. We sat down to a mostly silent pancake brunch, after which I left.

When I got home, I imagined the scene: Leni drops her bathrobe, takes a flying leap and latches on to me like a baby spider monkey, naked, her arms and legs wrapped around me, and at that moment Mom and Dad burst in. Catastrophe was averted by nine seconds.

I wrote Charles and Astrid a long, carefully worded letter in which I told them I believed Leni was in dire need of psychiatric help. To underscore the point, I related all the times she'd rubbed her chest or bottom on me, the night she'd tried to crawl into bed with me, and how she'd begun accusing me of hitting her. It was only a matter of time before she made worse accusations. I told them that I was sure this letter would end our friendship, but it had to be written anyway. They never responded. I wrote two more letters and received no answer to them either.

In 2009 I joined Facebook, specifically to try and see what had become of Leni, the youngest of my ghosts. When I did find her, it made me wish I hadn't. She was twenty-two at the time, one of those people who share absolutely everything about themselves. Under "Interests," she listed "Men" and "Watching cute guys." She was also deeply interested in wine and belonged to a quasi-Buddhist therapy group. A little research showed that a man in his late forties ran it; all the members were women in their early twenties. On the group's Facebook page, they each gushed about how they couldn't wait for the next one-on-one session with him.

Leni's Facebook account had a link to a photo-sharing service, where she'd posted thousands of self-portraits, close ups of her looking seductive in as many different ways as possible. She was alone in almost every image; there were less than fifty pictures of anyone else. Although physically attractive, she still wore her hair in the exact style she'd had when she was twelve, and she looked years older than her chronological age. In some of the shots, she stood in front of a mirror, pushing out her chest. One photo showed her pointing to a blob of thick, pearly white fluid on her chest and gazing at the camera with an arch, satisfied expression. She looked completely out of her mind. Everything I'd predicted for her had come true.

Only recently did I realize what actually happened: Charles and Astrid deliberately left me alone with their innocent, predatory daughter. I don't think they sat down and devised a plan, but they knew full well what Leni was likely to do if they were out of the picture for an hour and a half or so.

It probably went like the following.

"Honey, we haven't gone to church in a really long time. Why don't we go on Sunday? We don't need to take Leni; I mean, she's never been to church in her life. This is something you and I should do. Since Tom's coming over anyway, he can watch Leni."

And then ten minutes into the service, Astrid turned to Charles and said, "I just got the weirdest feeling that we need to go home *right now!*"

My friends had to get rid of me, either by telling me to never come back or by getting me arrested. I was proof that they were horrible parents. There was no way they could ignore how much more abnormally their daughter behaved whenever I was around. They handled everything wrong, right from the beginning – from her birth, in fact – but rather than confront their failures and try to help Leni, they had to neutralize me so that I couldn't harm their precious self-image.

I gave Charles and Astrid an out by writing my letters. They no longer had to use their daughter as literal jail bait. Instead, they just fired me because I was obviously crazy, saying all those awful, untrue things. The only casualty is Leni. Nobody seems to care about her except for me. Judging by her Internet postings she's been swept out to sea, with no hope of ever making her way back to shore.

I'm sorry, Leni. There was nothing I could do.

A Second Brush with a Psycho; Her Brush with Catastrophe

In 2007 I'd begun commenting incessantly on a political blog. From the spring of 2009, a woman I'll call Ariel joined the discussions. She was twenty-four and a prankster, posting under different names to yank peoples' chains. I could always figure out it was her, and when I did, I'd write, "You hold your water, young lady!" It was a notorious line from the movie *Sybil,* my way of telling Ariel I'd identified another of her playful multiple personalities. When I'd unmask her, she'd congratulate me: "Well done, sir!"

I was attracted to her ironic sense of humor and sadness. Like me, she couldn't sleep; we were always the last people on the blog every night. Sometimes we'd talk until three or four in the morning. She often left earlier for what she called her "nocturnal prowling." I'd close our conversations with a link to a music video, or I'd pass along some poetry. Being so young, she didn't know any of my favorite musicians and poets. In June of 2009, I posted this as my sign-off:

> *I hear you now, I hear you, shy perpetual companion,*
> *Whose deep whispers*
> *Never wholly fail upon my twilight; but for months now*
> *Too dimly quivered*
> *About the crowded corridors of action and the clamouring*
> *Swarmed ingresses where like squinting cobblers and worse creatures*
> *On a weary ship that moors in the dock, with grimy hatches,*
> *Cross-purpose jangles.*[4]

I intended to go to bed, but Ariel instantly responded with, "Do you have any idea what you're *doing* to me? Who *are* you?!" Yes, it was flattering. I had no plans to ever contact or meet her, so it was just a fun, interesting, completely out-of-the-ordinary line of communication with an intelligent woman who appreciated me.

"Don't think I'm anybody special," I wrote. "I just like good art." I included a YouTube link to Jeff Buckley's song "Grace" and told Ariel I'd talk to her tomorrow.

The next night, she posted a coded message that instructed me how to go back into the archives of the blog so we could have "private" conversations in long-dead threads that nobody read anymore. It took a while to figure it out. Once in the archives, we didn't reveal our identities but spoke candidly about our backgrounds, using pseudonyms different from our usual ones. I wasn't at all surprised to find out what we had in common. She said the experience had nearly killed her, and that sometimes she thought she could barely make it through the next minute. I assured her I knew exactly how she felt. While we shared our feelings, we concealed everything about ourselves except what we'd already discerned in each other. This led me to candidly describe all my failed relationships. It didn't have to happen to her, I said, because she was still young enough to learn from my mistakes. Ariel asked gentle, respectful questions about the women who'd meant the most to me; I told her about Carmen and Noreen, using only their first names and mentioning that both were now married. Ariel was very sympathetic.

"That must tear your heart out," she wrote.

"Not with Noreen, but with Carmen, it's as though we broke up yesterday instead of sixteen years ago. I've now been apart from her more than three times longer than I was with her, but nothing's really changed. There doesn't seem to be anything I can do about it, so I just live with it."

"You're making me very sad. You've had a lifetime of pain and loneliness. I'm afraid that's what I'm in for, too."

"Don't be sad," I responded. "This is my story, not yours. And I'm not moping around all day feeling sorry for myself. I've accepted my situation. If you don't do what I did, it doesn't have to happen to you."

On June 18, I told her that earlier in the evening Tim and I heard a tiny mewing on his front porch. We went out with flashlights and saw a black kitten in the bushes, out of reach. Though we coaxed for half an hour, it wouldn't come to us. In my neighborhood, people don't spay or neuter their cats. When a new litter is born, they take it out and abandon each kitten one by one in different places. This cat was little more than a baby. It sounded terrified.

Eventually, Tim put some sliced turkey on the porch. We went back inside and watched through the windows as the kitten came out and gobbled the entire plateful, an amount almost as large as it was. Then it fled.

Ariel asked, "Did it ever come back? Did you manage to save it?"

I told her I hadn't.

"I'm that black kitten," she said.

That made me so emotional and fearful for her safety that I did something very stupid: I told her my name. I posted it for a moment, along with a link to a photo of me I temporarily put up on Flickr, explaining that this was my way of proving that I was genuinely on her side and wanted to help her overcome her past. No matter what happened, she'd never be that kitten. She thanked me for trusting her enough to tell her who I really was and said she was overwhelmed. I then deleted the post and the photo without asking her to reciprocate with her own real identity.

Within a few days, Ariel began saying things like, "I'm going to be naughty tonight," or "I've put on my sexiest Goth costume, and I'm going somewhere you wouldn't approve." I'd mentioned to the blog commenters under my regular pseudonym that although I prefer women with no makeup, if they're going to paint their faces, the Goth look is what I like. I'm complicated.

Ariel kept trying to steer our private conversations toward discussing the debauched secret life she lived, even though I told her that trying to make me a part of that would defeat the alleged purpose of our speaking in the first place. It wasn't hard to figure out where she went on her "naughty" nights, since she was a fan of the photographer E. J. Bellocq. I said I neither approved nor disapproved of what she did, because I didn't know her. It was none of my business. She'd get angry, tell me how much I hurt her with my indifference, apologize, and berate herself for not understanding boundaries and not respecting my wishes or sensibilities. Then she'd do it all over again.

In early July, after the third time it happened, I wrote, "Don't you think we've both had enough? Seriously? I don't want to hurt anyone, and even if *you* do, there's no reason to. I just wanted to help you if I could. That's all. Should I be punished or made fun of or taunted for that? Aren't there more appropriate targets? Like, for instance, mean-spirited people? I'm just trying to improve myself here. Is that a good reason to try and mess with my head?"

"You have no idea what has been going on in my mind today," she responded. "You've made up your own story as to my actions. You have no clue what my day has been."

"That's true, but why can't you take it out on the 100 fake friends you said you have instead of the person who not only just wanted to help you but also took a giant leap of faith for you? You make everything I said to you seem trivial. Maybe it *was* trivial to you, but it wasn't to me."

"I have been an entirely private person for 24 years and you think suddenly I am going to know how to act? You are not in charge of me being fucked up or not. I was fucked up long before you and I'll be fucked up forever. You are not my babysitter!"

"I don't know what that means," I wrote.

"It is not up to you to see to my well being. And trivial? Screw you if I am not acting appropriately about my life! And how dare you throw my friends into this? I don't use your words against you! I am not a perfect person. I am not a good girl. I have never been. I will never act the way I am supposed to act because I have no idea what that is supposed to be."

"Well, then let's release each other. After I accepted that I could never be a husband or father, I never inflicted myself on anybody again. If you believe that you are incapable of knowing how to act with someone who cares about you, then the only thing to do is to not inflict yourself on that person."

After almost ten minutes, she wrote, "Okay."

When there was no follow-up, I added, "In the end, our problems are our own. Nobody is under any obligation to be with us or stay with us if they can't deal with our deficits. As you said, you might be in for a lifetime of loneliness, but I knew this about myself years ago. I'm sorry I can't help you. All I can tell you is that loneliness is survivable. You're a smart, creative, artistic person. There are compensations. I no longer pine for the things I'll never have. But I'm almost 47. Make yourself as hard as steel. Become as self-sufficient as possible. Then, if by chance you ever meet someone you can engage with, it'll be a bonus. There are worse things than loneliness. And you have friends. Don't take them for granted. You're luckier than most."

Another long pause, and then, "Do you know how?"

"Do I know how to do what?"

"Nothing. Okay. I can't write. The words aren't coming out. I'll do what you said. Bye."

She didn't post anything else. After an hour I left her with a quote from *Charlotte's Web*.

> I wove my webs for you because I liked you. After all, what's a life, anyway? We're born, we live a little while, we die. A spider's life can't help being something of a mess, with all this trapping and eating flies. By helping you, perhaps I was trying to lift up my life a trifle. Heaven knows anyone's life can stand a little of that.[5]

In September of 2009, as I furiously commented away on the blog in the middle of the day, the response to my newest post was this.

[My pseudonym] is really Thomas Edward Wictor. He lives at [address withheld]. His phone number is [withheld]. His e-mail address is [withheld]. He's a failed writer because [withheld]. He used to work at a magazine called *Bass Player* until they fired him. He's a whiny little bitch who has nightmares every time he goes to sleep and he pines like a dog for his ex-girlfriend Carmen, who dumped him for a wealthy [withheld]. He has to take anti-anxiety medication and he's fat because he stuffs his face thinking about all his failures. The only thing on his mind 24 hours a day is [withheld].

[Link to an old photo of me on an authors' Web site.]

Keep in mind that this was in the middle of a discussion on a hugely popular blog read by tens of thousands, and at that time I was the house cutup, the wit who kept everyone entertained. The commenters there kept telling me I should write a book. These were people I'd "known" for years. What to do? It was one of the worst moments of my life, the total exposure of everything, being stripped nude in public and then raped. But cornered rats fight to the death. That's the danger of giving someone no out. I therefore responded.

"Well, did a little detective work, did we, Ariel? Now you know everything about me. And now I know what you are, just not your real name. Let's see how big your balls are. I'm sitting here by my phone right now. Call me. Pick up the phone and let's have a chat. I'm betting you're too afraid. Really easy to sit there in anonymity and be all vicious and destructive when there are no consequences to you, isn't it, Ariel? Give me a call, dear. Let's hash this out voice to voice."

No answer. I wrote another post.

"Come on, Ariel. I know that's you. What, are you angry that I didn't want your sickness in my life anymore? Call me. You've got my number. I've got nothing more to lose now, do I? So pick up the phone, sweetie. I promise I won't be mean to you, which is what you're afraid of. Note the operative word, A-F-R-A-I-D. This is the most chicken-shit, petty, ugly thing you could've done, yet you actually thought you were worthy of my attention, much less my respect? Give me a call, lover. I'm sitting here right by the phone. Prove what a badass you are. Put on your Goth action-outfit and let's get it on!"

Finally, a reply: "Beg me."

"*Beg* you? For *what?* More pollution in my life? More sickness and evil and negativity? I'm not *begging* you, you pitiful wreckage of a human being. I'm *challenging* you. I'm publicly calling your bluff to prove to everyone here that I'm a better person than you are. Now that you've exposed me, let's see if you have the courage to meet me on equal terms. Give me a call. Let's see if you have the guts. I say you don't."

And then the moderator deleted all our comments. But Ariel wrote the same thing several more times and began assaulting me under dozens of pseudonyms. She called me a "fat, ugly, pimple-faced fuck," a "piece of shit," "a cowardly worm so jealous of others that you can't sleep at night," and someone who longed to "engage with an orangutan in the deepest jungles of Botswana."

Regarding the last bon mot, I didn't bother pointing out that orangutans are native to Asia, not Africa. "Ariel, aren't you bored with this yet?" I asked.

Someone named Anon wrote, "There is a very good chance that the person you think is doing this is innocent. It would be a shame to blame someone for something that person has never done. Don't say anything else that might cause an innocent person much more pain. She has never been your nemesis. Mischief making, yes. But nothing written in malice."

"I've always been the target of mischief makers," I responded. "It continues to this day. The only thing I ever wanted in this life was to not be assaulted. A very simple desire. Not hard to grant at all. Takes a little empathy, nothing more."

Pause. "Where's Thomas Wictor, the piece of dog shit? I think he's possessed."

"Ah. Pearls before swine, I see. Well, no demons here. Sorry to disappoint you."

A different personality commented, "You can have one of mine, Tom. I have ten."

"No, you're too rinky-dink to be possessed."

A third personality chimed in. "Take note, Tom. You've made a serious error here. You've made an oath enemy of a freeman. Everyone beware of Thomas Wictor. He's a crafty one. He stole my e-mail tonight. Tom, I'll be in contact with the Cyber Unit of my police department in the morning as my brother-in-law is an agent there. You'd better not disseminate or harm my daughters as their addresses are now in your possession. You'll be easy to track and persecute. Don't give out my girls' addresses."

"I'll wait for the cops to call."

"If you're lucky," the freeman said. "Cyber stalkers like you should be taken care of in other ways."

"This is what the inside of your head is like, isn't it, Ariel?" I posted a link to a YouTube video of the bar-dance scene in the French film *Calvaire*.

All she could manage was, "Ha-ha. That's hilarious."

"Your newfound hate has blunted your wit. Here's how I picture you." I linked to one of the funniest videos on YouTube, titled "[Angry German Kid] Heaven Hell and Keyboard remix," a brilliant piece of art that synchs the Teutonic bedlamite's berserk antics to Jacques Offenbach's "Galop Infernal," from his opera *Orphée aux Enfers* (*Orpheus in the Underworld*).

"Where's your nigger Jew girlfriend?" Ariel replied.

"See what I mean? Thanks for proving my point. Your psychotic rage makes you dull. Now you're about as witty as a hippopotamus rectum."

I changed my pseudonym several times, but soon I stopped commenting altogether because now it was our *Sybil* game in reverse: She kept figuring out who I was and bombarding me with insults or writing, "Hey Thomas Wictor. Nice to see you again! How's Tim doing? You still living in [withheld]? Still a failure because [withheld]? Keep in touch!" Though I hadn't given her any of my family members' names, she posted all their contact information, too. Every day she repeated what I'd told her about myself in our one-on-one conversations, when she and I were anonymous and I thought she was a tortured soul who needed to know she wasn't alone in how she'd been impacted by what she'd gone through. In 1996 Noreen had also taken my disclosure and used it as a weapon; this time it was broadcast worldwide.

The blog Webmaster tried to identify Ariel, but she had over forty IP addresses. She used anonymizing software that allowed her to purchase IP addresses in blocks. They originated in Europe and were bounced off at least four locations. The blog owner didn't want to introduce registration for commenters because it reduced traffic. Basically, Ariel couldn't be stopped. It didn't much matter to me that she trashed my name on the Internet. I'd long since thought I'd never publish anything again. My name was already mud, and besides, I wasn't the same person I was in 1996. I was angry but felt no pain or sense of betrayal because this *thing* had never been my friend; our relationship had been a crappy illusion. The situation was entirely my fault. I was ashamed only of my idiocy, not what she aired.

After I stopped commenting, she began posting under my real name, complaining of being fat, lonely, sad, and tortured by failure. She'd also compose first-person orations on my longing to relive what I'd experienced because I'd actually enjoyed it. This went on for six months. It brought back all the memories of Hazim shadowing Carmen and me across Tokyo. The Webmaster felt I had the right to know and therefore sent me each of her comments. Since I didn't react to Ariel and her posts were quickly deleted, in March of 2010 she upped the ante by writing detailed false confessions of illegal acts. Now it had to end, for the sake of people – including my family – who'd be linked to the worst sort of criminal. I went back in the blog archives to see if she'd left any clues. It was days before I found the key to her identity. One night during our private conversations, she'd said, "I have to tell you something."

I responded, "You were institutionalized."

She was shocked and asked me how I knew. I told her I didn't care. The only thing that mattered was that she felt better now. She thanked me for my understanding; I left her a link to Suzanne Vega's "In Liverpool" and said goodnight. After I signed off, Ariel posted this, which I didn't see until March of 2010.

> You never know how something posted here may change someone's opinion, ideology or life. My life was changed here tonight by something someone posted, and the feeling was so startling and true, that I want it permanently. I want to openly discard all the names that I have been posting under, and discover my own voice. In no particular order: *[List of fifty different pseudonyms.]*
> There are many others, but I cannot think of them right now. These are just the most recent. Thank you to the person who seemed to know me better than I know myself.
> Ariel

She'd clearly forgotten she'd written this, since she hadn't deleted it. I sent all the names – which I figured Ariel may have used before she bought her anonymizing software – to the Webmaster, and I received a message that made me slam my fists on my desk and roar in triumph.

"Got her! [Name, e-mail address, and hometown withheld]. You were right, Tom. She started using the anonymizer only after she went apeshit on you."

The Webmaster also told me she was a male commenter who'd attacked me viciously on the evening threads for months after Ariel showed up. So even as she claimed I'd freed her and was just such a spectaculicious, all-around groovy guy, she harassed me the entire time.

After a few weeks of *collating,* I guess you could say, I fired off an e-mail. Within minutes, the blog owner received the following message.

> Dear Mr. [withheld], I am writing to you regarding the situation between Thomas Wictor and myself. There has been a misunderstanding that I hope to have resolved. I realize that it is not your responsibility, but because I am being accused of doing things that I did not do, I am hoping that you will be willing to listen and look into the situation.
> I did have conversations with Thomas Wictor about many things including a shared history of [withheld]. It was good to talk to someone that I felt understood how I felt. It was a mistake to do this, I have unfortunately discovered, but that is what happened. I made it clear during these conversations that I had no desire to ever have more contact than to talk online. Thomas Wictor at one time posted his full name. I did not ask him to do this and never did anything with this information. After Thomas Wictor and I stopped writing to each other I did not attempt to contact him in any way. I realized that your site was not an appropriate forum for personal therapy.
> I continued to read your site, as I have over the past year. I did read the comments that referred to the fact that someone had posted Thomas Wictor's personal information, but the original comment by the guilty party had already been removed so I did not see what was written.
> I am not the poster of that information and have no idea how anyone got his personal information. I have never told anyone of my conversations with Thomas Wictor or shared his name with another person. It was my belief at the time, that the Webmaster would be able to find the identity of the poster and I would be shown to have not been involved. Apparently that is not the case as today I see that Thomas Wictor has been given my personal information by you or the Webmaster. I can accept that I made a mistake by talking personally about my past on the

internet, something I will never do again, but certainly, if I can be outed, there must be some way to find out who actually posted Thomas Wictor's information, so that I can be cleared of this offense.

As you can see from all of my past posts, besides using many names, I have never attacked Thomas Wictor or any of your guests. I am writing to you here, instead of trying to clear myself in your comments section because, as I said earlier, I have no desire to continue this event further.

It is my hope that you, or the Webmaster will be able to find out who it was that actually posted Thomas Wictor's information, as well as see that I have not been any one of the people writing harassing comments to him at any time and let him know what you have found out. I take responsibility for being stupid enough to think that Thomas Wictor was someone that was a friend, and that I could talk to, but I have never done any crime that deserves to be harassed by him or others. Thomas Wictor was also a willing partner in our communications.

Sincerely,

[withheld]

Entirely coincidentally, after she sent this mealy mouthed deflection of responsibility, the stalking stopped. Ariel apparently feared – though I can't imagine why – that I'd expose her. She'd told me *her* secrets when she was anonymous, and some of them are doozies. I uncovered others on my own. Her fate is in my hands. As the late psychiatrist Dr. David Viscott said, "The manner in which people screw you always lets you know the best way to screw them back."

Ariel is aware that after I learned who she is, I obtained an interesting video of her and found out where she lived, where she worked, and whose child she is. What she didn't know until now is that when I shared this information with Tim, he offered to pay her a visit. He goes on photography day trips all the time; I was absolutely terrified that he'd tell me he was off to shoot pictures of mountains somewhere but would actually get on a plane so he could meet Ariel in person. Not only is Tim inhumanly strong, his solution is always to directly address the problem. He doesn't believe in letting things build up. His philosophy is to instantly take action in order to get it out of the way. As he describes it, he simply hastens the inevitable conclusion to save time. He cuts to the chase. His opinion is that when someone goes out of their way to make your life miserable, they choose their own fate. It took a lot of persuading before he agreed to stand down. There was no need for him to lift a finger, since I have a full dossier on Ariel.

Two of Tim's favorite movies are *Taken*, starring Liam Neeson, and the spectacularly satisfying *Falling Down*, Michael Douglas's best performance. When Tim watched them with me, he laughed all the way through. And though he's not religious, he absolutely loves the Bible verses II Samuel 22: 38-43. They're his credo, you could say.

> *I have pursued my enemies, and destroyed them: and turned not again until I had consumed them.*
>
> *And I have consumed them, and wounded them, that they could not arise; yea, they are fallen under my feet.*
>
> *For you have girded me with strength to battle: them that rose up against me have you subdued under me.*
>
> *You have also given me the necks of my enemies, that I might destroy them that hate me.*
>
> *They looked, but there was none to save; even unto the Lord, but he answered them not.*
>
> *Then did I beat them as small as the dust of the earth, I did stamp them as the mire of the street, and did spread them abroad.*

I hope Ariel realizes what a lucky young lady she is.

Reconnecting with the Cardinal Ghost

After I joined Facebook, I searched out a lot of people, just to satisfy my curiosity about what had become of them. I didn't send any of them messages. Inevitably, I looked for Carmen and discovered her under her maiden name. We hadn't had any contact since 2002, when I told her it was too painful for me to talk to her. That was a lifetime ago. My career in music journalism had failed; my interview book had failed; my two novels had failed; my contribution to military history had been summarily rejected; and now a deranged young woman publicly flayed me to the bone every day. Being apart from Carmen was just another failure. It no longer burned like acid. I therefore sent her a message saying hello and telling her I hoped all was well. I didn't expect a response, but I got one immediately.

> Dear Tom:
> How good to hear from you. I finally gave up looking for you on the computer, and came close to sending you a note to your old address. It's funny timing that I should hear from you at this moment. I am thoroughly exhausted (reminiscent of the jet lag from my years in Asia). We just got home a few hours ago after traveling since 5 pm yesterday from Oregon. My kids and I spent the week visiting friends in Bend (we took the overnight train) and we're leaving for FL tomorrow morning (my in-laws have a place in Boca).
> One reason I wanted to contact you was to let you know that we euthanized [the cat we had in Japan] this past September. Her health suddenly failed and she needed help letting go. She was with me 21-1/2 years!
> I enjoyed hearing from you. I have to go now to unpack from the snow and repack for balmy weather.
> Please write again.
> Carmen

I did write again. Instead of being saddened by our cat's death, I was happy that she'd lived so long. She was a wonderfully eccentric being who named us. I was "Eh-eh," and Carmen was "Eh-eh-eh." There was absolutely no doubt because the cat always said "Eh-eh" when she greeted me and always said "Eh-eh-eh" when she greeted Carmen. I sent Carmen a poem I wrote on the spot. I've never been good at poetry, but I'm sure our cat wouldn't mind.

A Cat Named [withheld]

I once knew a cat named [withheld],
Who named me for her convenience.
She called me "Eh-eh," her reluctant warning.
It meant "Not a chance," the answer
To all my questions, though I think
It pained her to keep reminding me.
We watched the birds and played.
I had a rubber spider strung to a pole.
She hunted it in mad aerial loops
Five feet off the floor.
When she'd had enough, she'd tell me:
"Eh-eh. (Not a chance.)"
She came when she wanted.
She played when she felt like it.
She refused me quite often.
But just as often she landed on my lap

With a soft thump.
Sitting, purring, washing,
Pausing to make sure I understood.
"Eh-eh. (Not a chance.)"
Goodbye, [withheld].
Thank you for those chances.
They live on in me, as do you.

Carmen responded.

Eh-eh.
Thank you for creating this painfully beautiful poem.
You have stirred my memory - I would not have otherwise recalled these particular images. Most of all, I miss her scent.
Bless you, bless her.
Eh-eh-eh.

My response to her.

You're welcome, and bless you right back.
Happy New Year to you and yours. Get home safely, and have a terrific 2010.
Cheers,
Tom

The Poet Who Saved My Life

In January of 2009, I discovered the poetry of Stephen Crane. I'd known him only as the author of *The Red Badge of Courage*. His poetry was the best I'd ever read. I bought a complete collection of his poems and read it almost every day for weeks. Afflicted with tuberculosis, he died at twenty-eight. He did as much as he could in his short life, including being a prodigious lover. Virtually everything he wrote spoke to me. His thoughts seemed in perfect sync with mine, but he lacked the rage and bitterness I felt at the way my life had turned out. In fact, he warned against those corrosive emotions constantly. On bad days, I'd pick up my book and read Crane until I felt better.

All of his poems are untitled. This is the one that compelled me to write to Carmen in January of 2010.

I wonder if sometimes in the dusk,
When the brave lights that gild thy evenings
Have not yet been touched with flame,
I wonder if sometimes in the dusk
Thou rememberest a time,
A time when thou loved me
And our love was to thee thy all?
Is the memory rubbish now?
An old gown
Worn in an age of other fashions?
Woe is me, oh, lost one,
For that love is now to me
A supernatural dream,
White, white, white with many suns.

A Brief Exchange

Hey Carmen:

Let's talk art! My current favorite singer is Róisín (pronounced "RaSHEEN") Murphy. Ever heard of her? She's Irish and the model for Lady Gaga – except Murphy is brilliant while Gaga is meh. Here's my favorite Róisín Murphy song: "Ramalama Bang Bang." *[Link to YouTube video.]*

Her former band Moloko is also brilliant. Just plug "Róisín Murphy" or "Moloko" into YouTube and have a blast. "Primitive" and "Overpowered" are also great songs. See if you can find her acoustic version of "Overpowered," sung on the street in London with no mics. Amazing.

Movies? The best new one I've seen recently is *Crank,* with Jason Statham, the sexiest man alive. Mostly I'm into really old films. The new stuff is so boring it's unwatchable. I'm working my way through the entire Greta Garbo catalog. I'm also into Korean films. *Old Boy* and *I'm a Cyborg but That's OK* are two of the best films ever made. If you still have the same bizarre tastes you had when I knew you, I think you'll love them, especially *Cyborg.*

My favorite book is a collection of Stephen Crane's poems. He's best known for his novel *The Red Badge of Courage,* but he's one of the greatest poets who ever lived. His poems are all numbered instead of titled. Here's my favorite, which I'm going to use as the epigraph in my next novel, about a man who dies, goes to hell, is pulled out by his guardian angel and given a second chance, but starts to screw it up by once again becoming a slave to anger, hatred, and bitterness. It's going to be a very funny, inspiring story. Seriously!

A Stephen Crane poem that I've taken to heart:

> *There was a man with a tongue of wood*
> *Who essayed to sing,*
> *And in truth it was lamentable.*
> *But there was one who heard*
> *The clip-clapper of this tongue of wood*
> *And knew what the man*
> *Wished to sing,*
> *And with that the singer was content.*

That's all we really want, isn't it? To be understood. Crane speaks to me like no other poet. He was only 28 when he died of tuberculosis. In 2007 I was diagnosed with a possible brain tumor or multiple sclerosis, as evidenced by swollen optic nerves. Luckily it turned out to be pseudotumor cerebri, a treatable condition, but it left me with diminished eyesight. I try to be grateful for every day above ground, and I try to be a better person. I was on that trajectory for a long time before 2007, but that was a real banner year for self-examination.

Best album in my collection? *Songs in Red and Gray,* by Suzanne Vega. Best song on the album? "Widow's Walk." *[Link to YouTube video.]* I'm really into beauty right now.

Best,
Tom

Hi, Tom

I'm sorry to learn about your intracranial scare and resultant (and progressive?) vision loss. The closer we get to nonexistence the more provocative and exquisite existence becomes..... neh?

C.

Can you dance like this in high heels? *[Link to YouTube video of Róisín Murphy dancing.]*
 Tom

Tom:
O.k. I LOVE her.
She's my new girl.
Lady GAG has nothing on Missy Murphy.
C.

Ha! I knew you'd love her. She also does a music/dance style called "Northern Soul" that I find amazingly moving for some reason. I think the idea behind this video is that she's all alone, fantasizing that she's leading this fabulous life, which is a theme I've always found compelling. *[Link to YouTube video of "Familiar Feeling."]*

There are two more that I watched a while ago but very stupidly forgot to bookmark. I'm not sure if they're Moloko or Róisín alone, but I'll see if I can find them... Aha! Found them. They're both Moloko. The first is a great song but an even better video. "Forever More." Look how she dances! She may just be the coolest human being on the planet. *[Link to YouTube video.]*

The second one, "Take my Hand," never had a video made for it, but it's one of the best songs ever written. It has that weird inevitability that great art always has, as though it existed somewhere in the ether and the band tapped into it, bringing it down intact here to us grubby humans. *[Link to YouTube video.]*
 Enjoy!
 Tom

Tom:
Thank you for these awesome links. "Forever More" is my favorite (especially that move at 45 secs).
She has an anti-diva vibe oozing with unapologetic strength and talent.
Are you still bass playing?
C.

I haven't played in years, but I'm going to pick it up again someday. I play in my head a lot. I had an 8-string made for me by Fat Dog at Subway Guitars in Berkeley. It's pretty amazing. Slaps great, and you can make it drone like a sitar. Still have the Sting Ray you bought for me in Japan. Best bass I ever had. I spend most of my time writing now, but I expect to play again someday.
 Tom

• • •

I then found something I thought would blow her mind. It was a live version of Art of Noise's "Close to the Edit," our favorite song in Tokyo and San Francisco. We'd tried for ages to play the bass line ourselves but thought it wasn't feasible, since the original had been done with a sequencer. I thought she'd go wild that someone had actually accomplished the thing we'd tried so hard to do ourselves. I sent the following message.

That's Trevor Horn on the bass. Remember we didn't think it was humanly possible to do a live version of this bass line, but here it is! *[Link to "Close to the Edit" by Art of Noise, played live at the Prince's Trust of 2004.]*

Her answer.

> Hey, there.
> Most things from my past usually ring a loud bell in my head when they
> cross my path after so many years, but the Art of Noise and that particular tune
> ("Close to the Edit") rang such a dim bell it was maddening!!! Such a painful
> blurry feeling.
> Thanks for sending it.
> C.

At first it made me as sad and horrified as I'd been the day we broke up. How could she
not remember our song? Then I got the impression that using the phrase "painful blurry
feeling" was her way of telling me to back off, that I'd crossed a line. It didn't make me
angry, though. The last thing I wanted to do was muck up her life by reminding her of a
long-gone, ultimately valueless span that had no bearing on the person she was today. So I
finally yielded to reality, the way I should've in 1994. I stopped writing her. What I'd had
with her would remain my supernatural dream.

  Still, my decision didn't solve anything from my perspective. It was merely giving up.
I walked in Stephen Crane's shoes.

> *Places among the stars,*
> *Soft gardens near the sun,*
> *Keep your distant beauty;*
> *Shed no beams upon my weak heart.*
> *Since she is here*
> *In a place of blackness,*
> *Not your golden days*
> *Nor your silver nights*
> *Can call me to you.*
> *Since she is here*
> *In a place of blackness,*
> *Here I stay and wait.*

Despite the pain it caused, touching base with Carmen gave me the strength to endure
Ariel's relentless evil. For the first time since 1994, I went into my filing cabinet, pulled
out all my correspondence with Carmen, and read through it. I found a card that showed
an underwater photo of two manatees swimming side by side, the smaller one nibbling
the larger one's flipper while the nibblee appeared to smile. From the distant past, Carmen
spoke to me through elegant, rounded handwriting in blue ballpoint and purple, green, and
red felt-tip ink.

> Dear Tommy,
> I don't see what you're getting so upset about... It's only another birthday!
> Happy 29th Birthday.
> Love you (still),
> Carmen
> 6 Aug 1991

To my surprise I laughed. Though Carmen had assailed me as viciously as Ariel did, it
wasn't to hurt me. I now realize it was to drive me away. Most people can't explore or even
share the depths with you. They didn't sign up for that. Sixteen years of living, rumination,
brutal honesty, and racking up tremendous losses finally allowed me to understand how
this natural law had nothing to do with me. Carmen's inability to accommodate my

circumstances and the way she lashed out in panic were no more volitional or cruel than someone being unable to travel by yacht because she always gets seasick. Once I was no longer in her life, Carmen apologized and admitted that what she'd said wasn't true. She'd also never used Noreen and Ariel's line of attack. Even in her anguish, hatred of what I'd wrought, and desperation to break free, she spared me because she's a kind person. I don't count what she said in our final fight; those were generic putdowns angry women often use against their men, especially when the relationship has augered in.

The manatee card was tangible evidence of a sublime era in which I had all I needed. Ariel could mock me on the world stage as much as she wanted, but she couldn't take that away. One thing's certain: Nobody has ever given her such a card, and nobody ever will.

I still have mine.

The Cardinal Ghost in Video and Film

Carmen is portrayed perfectly by Róisín Murphy in Moloko's music video – not the live performance – of "Fun for Me"; by Julia Louis-Dreyfus in the outtakes of *Seinfeld;* and by Jennifer Connelly in the 2003 movie *Hulk*. The film even takes place in San Francisco. Carmen and I had been to most of the places shown.

All three small, dark-haired women capture Carmen's studly mannerisms and body language, but each represents a different aspect of her triune personality. Murphy as a prancing nurse embodies the sexy, campy artist-performer. Louis-Dreyfus is the horse-laughing comic with a penchant for crying and rushing without warning into your arms. Connelly – who in this role bears a spooky facial resemblance to Carmen and has the identical vocal timbre – exhibits the sadness and detachment that were always right under the surface.

Though I regularly watch "Fun for Me" and the *Seinfeld* bloopers, I've seen *Hulk* just twice because some of the scenes are so excruciating I kept having to stop the movie and take a break. That's my life on the screen. Eric Bana destroys everything with his uncontrollable rage, costing him all he loves, and he can't conquer his past. Connelly is his only desire. She tries her best, but he simply poses too much of a threat. Knowing full well her actions are wrong and agonizing over them, she rationalizes her betrayal of him. His only option is to give her what she wants: his departure.

After the second time I watched *Hulk,* Tim asked, "Why do you do this to yourself?"

My answer is, "You had to have been there." Otto Dix would've understood, I'm pretty sure. We do things until we no longer need to do them, can't bear to do them anymore, or realize that doing them is pointless.

It's just a movie, I know, which is the reason I was able to watch it only twice. It was fiction. The actors are content, safe, and well paid. Nobody was really driven away and had to live with that for twenty years.

Flashback: Why I love Butch Women

I went to a club with a publicist to see the band whose bassist she wanted me to interview. Everyone said the publicist was a lesbian, but I knew she wasn't. She was jaw-droppingly beautiful, a twin of the actress Andrea Parker, and she always wore suits. People assumed she was a lesbian because she was as hard as an Abrams tank and could be just as terrifying. This night I got to see her in action. She wore jeans instead of her usual suit; I'm sure she was or had been a dancer.

As we walked past the bar, we approached a group of six men who stood in our way. They all held mugs of beer. The publicist was in front of me; when we got to within a few feet of the men, they stared at her and nudged each other. She didn't slow down, her heels clocking on the floor like a metronome: *tok-tak-tok-tak-tok-tak-tok-tak.* It was just like the scene in *Point Blank,* where Lee Marvin is on his way to his wife's apartment to murder her boyfriend.

Since it was clear the publicist was going to walk right through or over the men, five of them stepped back, but one – a flushed guy in his late twenties – refused to move.

"Hey, hey, hey! Where you goin', baby?" he roared.

She turned sideways and slipped by him. I've read that when men do that they point their chest toward the person they're avoiding, but women point their chest away. The publicist pointed her chest toward the yelling guy. When she'd passed him, he pivoted, cupped one hand around his mouth, and yelled, "Nice *ass,* bitch!"

The publicist stopped cold and I almost crashed into her. She spun around and headed straight back toward the drunk, zeroing in on him like a guided missile. In the time it took her to reach him, she tucked her little handbag into the waistband of her jeans, putting it into the small of her back out of the way. Now both her hands were free. She pushed her bracelets up her forearms and stopped right in front of the hapless, red-faced lout, who grinned uneasily.

"Uh, hi," he said.

"What did you say to me?" she asked.

The drunk visibly shrank, his smile somehow going rigid and quivery at the same time. Tall and blonde, he wore a white button-up shirt that spilled out of his low-slung khaki Dockers. He seemed horribly defenseless; when he looked to his friends, they examined the floor, the ceiling, and their beer mugs. This was his own little shindig, which he could enjoy all for himself. Turning back to the publicist, the guy shrugged and raised one hand, an appeal for calm. "I didn't say anything. Really."

The publicist snorted, looked him up and down, and stepped around him to examine his rear. He sagged even more, gripping his beer mug with both hands, like a toddler with a sippy cup. The publicist put her hands on her hips.

"Nice beer gut," she said pleasantly. "Nice double chin. Nice soft, flabby, *droopy* ass."

He appeared to digest her words and then silently raised his mug and toasted his annihilation with abject gallantry. His friends coughed and cleared their throats. The publicist gave him three more seconds, turned, and walked away.

I could easily have eloped with her on the spot, but she already had a great man in her life.

A Final Excursion into Military History

In July of 2010, the editor of my flamethrower books asked me if I wanted to write a book about German assault troops of World War I. I didn't, but when a publishing house queries a writer, it's always a good idea to accept. I decided to make it the definitive volume on the topic, as my farewell to the field. It would be different from the hundreds of other volumes in that it would include entire orders for shock-troop missions, translated into English. There would be no interpretations or opinions inserted by me, the writer. I'd just put everything out there and let the reader decide.

My heart was not at all in the project, but I was still too afraid to try and sell the novel about the suicide of my best friend. I decided that being the author of a trilogy about World War I flame and assault troops would be a good thing. I've always liked threes: trilogies, triptychs, trinities, Cerberus, and so on. Plus, I'm the third child in my family.

One of the most unforgettable TV shows ever aired was *Trilogy of Terror,* a three-part horror movie from 1975. The first two segments are okay, but "Amelia," starring Karen Black, will stay with you forever. Richard Matheson wrote it, based on his short story "Prey." If you have the opportunity, just buy it. Take my word for it. You won't be sorry.

Flashback: Opening the Doors of Perception

I interviewed a great bassist by phone. The publicist arranged for me to call at 10:00 A.M., which I did. I got a busy signal – for two hours. Eventually, I connected and spoke to the bassist for about forty-five minutes. Here's the transcript of two minutes.

What drew you to the bass?
[Laughs]. Ahhhhh. Like, oh wow, man. Uhhhh. You know, I just think of, like, some bass lines that stuck in my head that just, I mean, that, I mean, it just... You know, that big-bottom thing, you know, uh, just, like... Genetically, I'm drawn to it. You know, I mean, I've *got* a big bottom! [Laughs.]

B'doom-chik.
[Laughs loudly.] Ahhhhh, yeah, you know, I just think without even knowing what, which, which instrument was the bass, I was just so drawn to stuff like, like, like, you know... I'm totally into the Jackson Five, you know, so it was like, *dum, dih-dih-dum, duh-duh-duh dum, doo-doo-doo, doo-doodle dee doo, doo doo, dum dum dum.* [Laughs.] You know?

So you found yourself singing bass lines instead of other parts?
Yeah! Yeah! I really did! You know? And of course there's the *Barney Miller* thing, you know? [Laughs.] You know, and, um, you know, I, I, I just think that, um, there were so many bass lines that... uhhhhhh... really... were in my head that I didn't know, uh, were bass lines [shouting] *until I got a bass!* [Screams with laughter.] I realized, you know, you know, those, those notes that are like, uh, subliminal? [Laughing loudly.] Those! Are! The! Ones! [Laughs, gasps for breath.]

Those are the ones.
[Laughing.] Yeah! I was a latecomer to the bass thang, you know. My basic thing was, you know, I had a lot time on my hands, you know. I was growin' pot, and so... [Laughs for five seconds, then speaks while laughing.] I had to! Stay home! A lot! And watch! The pot farm! [Laughs, takes deep breath.] And I wanted to learn how to play an instrument, you know, or do somethin', you know, because, you know, it doesn't really... I mean, you can't go, like, you know, like, uh, pick up and travel and, and, and come home, you know, when the plants are all done. [Screams with laughter, coughs, speaks while laughing.] So I had to! Stay home! A lot! That was, uh, really... kinda... how I got started, you know?

How did you get into songwriting?
Started takin' some classes about, like, uh, you know, just, just, you know, racism and sexism and all that shit, you know, just trying to figure out, "Well, fuck, you know, what, what, what part does music play in shaping our, uh, you know, societal values and stuff?" Having been really a singer all my life, you know, in some form of another, you know, I had never thought about that. I never thought about, uh, how, uh, like, you know, like, uh, songs like, uh, "Brown Sugar," uh, "Take a Walk on the Wild Side," you know, like, uh – And I like *both* those songs! [Laughs.] They're great! [Screams with laughter.] You know, but, how that gets into our... uh... psyche. It just, uh, you know, uh... "Shake, Rattle and Roll." Or just, uh, you know, "Indian Reservation." Shit like that, you know. Songs that, uh, you know, that, uh, like, we all sing... For me, I sing them *mindlessly!* [Screams with laughter.] I don't... I... [Gasps, coughs for ten seconds.]

I transcribed the entire forty-five minutes instead of only the parts I knew I'd use for the article, which was my usual practice since transcribing takes a lot of time and energy. Then I sent the transcript to the publicist, who called and said, "Please, *please* tell me you're not going to publish this."

I promised I wouldn't.

So don't tell anybody you read this, okay? I appreciate it.

The Cat Who Saved My Life

On August 22, 2010, a skinny, black, feral cat showed up in Tim's back yard. He didn't run away when I spoke to him, but he obviously didn't want me to approach him. After I talked to him for about ten minutes, he sauntered off. The next day he was back, and this time he came right up and sat in my lap. I called to Tim through the screen door, "Come out and see. We have a visitor." This cat looked eerily like Tim's beloved cat Syd. His death from heart disease in 1998 was protracted and traumatic for Tim, who said he never wanted another cat.

After a couple of days of feeding this cat, we let him into Tim's house. He casually wandered in as if he knew the place, settled on the sofa, and took a long nap. We had to keep him, and we had to name him Syd the Second. As soon as we got his weight back up, he became a monstrosity. He bit and clawed us without warning; he was afraid of toys, hoses, power tools, appliances, all other people, and throw rugs. I couldn't figure out why he'd take so long to go in and out of the cat door we installed, and then I realized he thought the furry throw rug was an animal. He was scared of it. When I took it away, he was fine.

Since he was terrified of bottle rockets, we think people shot them at him when he was a kitten. His problems were endless. He had violent, thrashing, hissing nightmares, and he hated boxes. After a little research we learned that a favorite game among some people here is to put a cat in a cardboard box and play soccer with it.

It took eight months to socialize him. During this period he had lapses in which he'd bite or scratch us and then run out of the house and crouch under what we called the Sulking Tree in Tim's garden, depressed because he'd let us down again. Sometimes he'd sulk in the rain. We never hit him or even yelled at him, but Tim was tempted to take him to the pound several times. Tim's patience paid off when Syd finally became nice and trustworthy. He even had an odd sense of humor, charging us sideways in that crabbing, Halloween-cat stance, as though lampooning his former ferocity. When I rolled a little rubber ball toward him, he'd cock and whirl his head all around watching it; he seemed to be pretending that he had no idea what it was. In the evening he'd leap through his cat door and gallop into the kitchen with a triumphant meow, as if making an entrance. He was a jovial little crank when he wanted to be.

Syd spent most of his time outside. We knew the risks, but we felt it would be cruel to lock him inside all day. Besides, he was street smart. We'd figured out that he was the tiny black kitten we'd given sliced turkey in January. He'd remembered the one place where someone was nice to him, and when he was on his last legs, starving and desperate, he'd returned looking for help. Having spent his whole life outdoors, he avoided cars and yards with dogs. I established a ritual with him; before I went to bed, I'd go outside and call, "Where's the kitty? Where's the puss-puss?" and he'd come running with his distinct, breathy meow. He'd sit in my lap for fifteen minutes or so, ramming his head into me and purring loudly. In the morning, we'd greet each other again the same way, and then he'd patrol the three properties he owned: my parents', mine, and Tim's.

On August 21, 2011, we noticed that Syd was very short of breath. We took him to the vet in his cat carrier. He was afraid, giving us that pitiful, moaning alarm call that cats use. We talked to him and he put his paw through the wire carrier door to touch Tim's hand, which calmed him. Tim and I explained to him why he was going to the doctor, and we sent mental pictures to him to try and help him understand. The vet told us we needed to leave him overnight. When he called us the next morning, he asked us to come to his office. We knew it would be bad news.

Syd's lungs were full of tumors. There was no hope. I left the room when he was put to sleep because I began getting very upset and I didn't want to scare him. But Tim held him and whispered in his ear as he died that he could come back anytime. Tim said Syd wasn't afraid; it was all very peaceful. He left us August 22, 2011. We'd had him exactly one year, to the day. The vet sent us a sympathy card, which was very nice of him.

In that short year Syd taught me a lot. We didn't save him; we gave him the means and opportunity for him to save himself. He did so through sheer force of will and the desire to improve. What he wanted more than anything was to be a good cat. In the end, his phenomenal character came through, and he overcame his demons.

He died in the afternoon, and that night I went out and called, "Where's the kitty? Where's the puss-puss?" In response I heard a breathy meow, clear as a bell. It made me laugh because I fully expected it. Later, as I lay on the sofa, I felt a weight on my chest and fur against my arm, and then it dissipated. I think he's okay, wherever he is. He had a year of safety, good food, and care, which he never would've experienced if we hadn't adopted him, and he was happy and calm by the time he left us. Even though I miss him, the pleasure he gave me from knowing him outweighs the pain. After he died, I think he fought as hard as he could – the way he fought all his enemies, real and imagined – to let us know that he was all right. Tim also saw him sitting in the garden for just a second, sweet and jaunty, his tail switching. He wasn't quite finished, though.

Tim and I meet at his house for conversation when he's in the mood. He sits in an armchair on one side of his living room, and I sit in one on the other. About a month after Syd died, we spoke about how that was the day it hit both of us hard that he really was gone. It was tough to express those feelings to each other. As we talked, I noticed a tan, pea-sized ball on the floor right in front of my feet. It was glaringly obvious against the deep maroon of the Persian carpet. When I picked it up, I saw that it was a cat kibble, made by Science Diet. That was the first food we bought for Syd, and he loved it. After the bag of Science Diet was consumed, we switched to Purina, the dry food shaped like starfish. Tim hadn't had kibble in the house for over nine months; the rug had been vacuumed many times since the last time we served Syd his Science Diet; I'd had dozens of conversations with Tim during the kibbleless period, sitting in that armchair; and the chair is over twenty feet from where Syd ate in the kitchen. I hadn't seen that kibble when I sat down, even though it stood out like a little beacon. I gave it to Tim. He keeps it carefully packed in a tin breath-mint box.

Syd wanted to change. He wanted to be good. Once he realized he didn't have to battle for every scrap of food or safe place to sleep, he changed on his own. He was happy when he died, but only because *he'd* made the choice to become a good cat. He's still a good cat, apparently, with a need to console and reassure.

So thank you, Syd. Like Tim said, you can come back any time you want. We'll be expecting you.

Shark-toothed Man and the Hollywood Jamboree

In the parking lot of a Hollywood drug store, I came across a 400-pound black woman about seven feet tall in the midst of a slow-motion square dance with a tiny, hideously ugly, monkey-like man who chanted, "You stupid! You big stupid! You damn stupid!" They circled each other, round and round and round. Thinking it might be some kind of domestic thing that'd reached critical mass, I waited to see if I should duck under my car to dodge the bullets. A young white woman appeared and joined the giantess, who produced a cell phone and made a call. Monkeyman slowly walked away, the giantess following.

At that moment, a deputy sheriff pulled up in his cruiser, and the white woman ran to his window and began excitedly explaining something with a lot of pointing and waving. The cop drove over to the walking pair and rolled alongside them, not getting out and not talking to them. Monkeyman inched toward a van and climbed in. The white woman joined him; the giantess got into another car; and everyone drove away in different directions. As I stood pondering what I'd just seen, a bearded man approached and said, "Hey, don't worry about all that. Stone'll take care of it. I know Stone. He's a good guy. My name's Jesse, by the way."

He held out his hand, so I shook it. It was colossal and so rough it felt barnacled. "So you married or a single guy?" he asked.

Of course. "Single," I answered.

"What, you don't like kids?"

I didn't say anything.

"How about sex?" he wondered. "You like sex? Me, I like sex a lot." He laughed, opening his mouth as wide as it would go, like an attacking Great White shark. In fact, all of his teeth appeared to have been filed to points. "*Eeeeeeeyow,* do I like *sex!*" he snarled, winking one coal-black eye in a blithering spasm.

"Okay," I said. "Gotta go now."

"So, where do you live?" he asked, taking a step toward me. "You live around here?"

"I live around," I said. "Goodbye."

"Hey, maybe I'll see you later?" he yelled after me.

"It wouldn't surprise me at all," I said. In the drugstore, I took my purchase to the only checkout stand open. An old man in front of me flipped through a newspaper looking for a coupon. There were two cashiers at the register.

"Is this *my* pen, or is it *your* pen?" one screamed.

"It must be *your* pen 'cause I got *my* pen," the other one howled.

"No, here's *my* pen, so whose pen is *this* pen?" the first one roared.

"That ain't *my* pen, and it ain't *your* pen, so that's got to be *someone else's* pen," the other one bellowed. The old man mumbled on and on, shuffling his newspaper, while a stinking guy in a filthy T-shirt stood in line so close behind me his breath tickled the hairs on the back of my neck. Finally, the old man found his coupon and clawed through his pants forever before he acquired his money clip. When the cashiers discovered that the register didn't have any paper for the receipt, one went over to a closet for another roll, which took her ten minutes to install.

Once she'd rung up the old man, only then did he explain that he also wanted to leave a roll of film for processing, which he tweezed out of his chest-high pants. The cashier dropped it in an envelope and the old man said, "Do you want me to put my name on the envelope? Should I do that?"

"No, put *my* name on it!" the cashier screeched, and she and her partner exploded into thunderclaps of laughter. The old man crouched over the counter on his elbows, settling down for the night, crossing his ankles, getting comfortable as he tried to figure out how to write his name on the envelope. A third cashier walked up to me, snapped her fingers right in my face, and said, "I can help the next person in line." I followed her to her register.

Outside, there was no sign of my would-be lover, the bearded sharkman; I headed for my car. Two big, black pickup trucks pulled in next to it and two men got out simultaneously. One was old, the other young, both wearing jeans, blue work shirts, red baseball caps, and heavy black mustaches. They walked toward each other, their hands out, and they had identical limps. The left leg of each was as stiff as a baseball bat. They shook hands and went into the drugstore, limping along asynchronously like a complicated, geared machine.

In September of 2011, exactly fifteen years later, I stopped at a gas station about ten blocks from my house. My career in music journalism was long over and I was ready to scrap my niggling career in military history. As I filled my tank, the shark-toothed man suddenly popped out from behind one of the pumps and said, "Hi! That's a nice beard! How long did it take you to grow it?" He hadn't changed in the slightest. He may even have been wearing the same clothes.

I started laughing and said, "I've had it since I was born. I'm a werewolf."

He laughed, too, and walked toward me. I got in my car and drove away, still laughing. He'd spent the past fifteen years methodically working his way through thirty miles of communities to find me. Any second now he'll knock on my front door.

Flashback: I Didn't Like That Bassist Anyway

The record label called one day and asked if I wanted to see the band's concert. I didn't really want to, because I hate being swept through sluices in a crowd. I avoided going to concerts whenever possible, a somewhat self-defeating attitude for a music journalist. Also, the bassist and I hadn't gotten along. At one point I'd asked him one of those challenging, theoretical what-would-you-answer-to-people-who-say questions, and he apparently thought I was telling him what *I* thought, because he said, "Fuck. *You!*" and glared at me for several seconds before answering. He then brought up that statement about ten more times during the interview. He had horribly rotted teeth; maybe he was irritable from the pain.

Eventually, I decided I'd better go to the concert because there was no telling when the ride at *Bass Player* would be over. The people at the label told me I was on The List, but since I'd been turned away many times at concerts where flacks had *said* they'd put me on The List but hadn't actually bothered to do it, and since I'd once been given tickets for seats about six miles from the stage in reward for conducting what the label said was the best interview of the bassist's career, I didn't expect anything at all from the pot-smoking, green-haired former dominatrix handling the band.

The night of the show, I drove the half hour to Pomona, arrived at the hall, checked with the List Guy, and was dumbfounded to be handed a yellow vinyl hospital bracelet. "That'll get you into the party afterward," the man said. I went inside and saw that there was a really cruddy band as the opener. I now had a dilemma: I possessed an advance copy of the *Bass Player* issue with the article on the bassist, but since I'd expected to be given either just a crappy general admission ticket or the bum's rush, I hadn't brought it with me. The only solution was to go home and get it. I asked the doorman to stamp my hand, and he pointed to my yellow hospital bracelet.

"You don't need your hand stamped. You can come and go all you want with that." With this incredible passport in my possession, I therefore got back in my car, drove all the way home, and plucked the magazine from my elderly mommy's fingers, telling her "I'll get you another, Ma."

Reading that last sentence might make people think I lived with my parents while I was a music journalist. How absurd! What nonsense! I lived next door to them.

Now, I'd have a function at the party: Purveyor of the Advance Copy. Maybe I could even get the evil-tempered, rotten-toothed bassist to crack a frosty smile, once he saw how well the piece turned out. I drove back to Pomona and tried to walk past a different doorman, holding up my braceleted arm. He grabbed me and yanked me to a halt.

"Hey, where the fuck do you think *you're* going?"

I pointed to my bracelet and said, "The other guy told me I didn't have to get my hand stamped because I have this all-access bracelet."

"There's no fuckin' all-access bracelet, asshole. If you had all access, you'd be wearing a pass around your neck. Now get the fuck outta here!"

"Look, I interviewed – "

"I don't give a shit! Get *outta* here before I kick your *ass!*"

He had a shaved head, his black T-shirt barely containing his massive torso. His upper arms were bigger than my thighs. I went over to the ticket window, but it was closed, with a "SOLD OUT" sign propped up against the glass. There were no other entrances to the hall I could find, so I drove home and gave my mother back her copy of the magazine. I told her what had happened.

"I didn't like that bassist anyway," she said. "He looks really mean in the photo."

The Third Really Weird Disease

I've always had tinnitus and sinus trouble, but in the fall of 2011 the ringing turned into what sounded like a vacuum cleaner running in my left ear. The ear felt plugged all the time, and sometimes I'd lose most of the hearing in it. I did a lot research and figured I had allergies. All the symptoms could be explained by allergies and chronic sinusitis. Then one night I got so dizzy I had to immediately take to my bed, bathed in sweat. It was the worst dizziness I'd ever experienced.

What it felt like was sitting in a swivel chair that spun at about 500 revolutions per minute while also being rotated end over end on two or three different axes, as my head hung over the back of the chair, a full sack of cement lay on my chest, and a pair of giant hands pushed down on my shoulders. It lasted for hours. Over the next month, I had several of these attacks, some of them culminating in me projectile vomiting. Before I went to see my ear, nose, and throat specialist, I did more research, and I discovered a terrifying affliction called Meniere's disease, which is incurable. Nobody knows what causes it, and many people don't respond to treatments. In worst-case scenarios the victim is utterly disabled and must undergo an operation in which the vestibular nerve is severed.

I went to the doctor on October 7, described my symptoms, and said, "As long as it isn't Meniere's disease, I'll be okay. That's the only thing that really scares me."

He looked me right in the eye and said, "I'm sorry. It's Meniere's disease." He didn't have to run the usual gamut of tests because it turns out he's the West Coast's premier expert on the ailment.

This was the big one. I'd always come through my previous health scares, but now I'd gotten the diagnosis of an incurable, incapacitating illness that could last the rest of my life. If you want to see the best cinematic portrayal of someone receiving terrible medical news, watch *Joe Versus the Volcano*. The scene in which Tom Hanks is told by Robert Stack that he has a "brain cloud" is one of the most heartfelt, deeply moving representations of what it's like to be informed that your life has just drastically changed for the worse.

I was started on a program of potassium-sparing diuretics, diazepam for the attacks of "rotational vertigo," and an insanely low-salt, low-fat diet. I can't consume more than 2000mg of sodium per day. To give you an idea of what that means, one McDonald's cheeseburger – the little, flat kind – has about 850 mg of sodium. I can't have any MSG, any artificial sweeteners, any alcohol, any caffeine, any chocolate, any aspirin, and any foods with the single-compound version of the amino acid cysteine, which means apples, onions, garlic, and oatmeal are off limits. And MSG is put in food under millions of euphemisms, thanks to lobbying of the FDA by food processors. If it's called "natural flavors," "natural flavoring," "malt flavoring," "vegetable protein," "yeast extract," "autolyzed yeast," "hydrolyzed vegetable protein," "calcium caesinate," "whey protein," or "textured protein," it's MSG.

Basically, I can't eat any fast food, restaurant food, or any food with a label. Plus, I have to do twenty minutes of cardio a day because increased circulation helps reduce the symptoms. Even so, I'm guaranteed to lose at least some hearing, and since Meniere's is an autoimmune disorder, stress can cause attacks. I'm essentially housebound until further notice. I also get daily headaches that build to full-on migraines a couple of times a week. The good news is that the disease usually goes into spontaneous remission, and I can take short trips to go shopping or run errands. But my days of cross-country driving are over. Book tours are out of the question. Dinner with friends is impossible.

Worst of all for a writer, the disease causes a condition called "brain fog," which does sound eerily similar to Joe Banks's brain cloud, except this is real. I have trouble concentrating and speaking sometimes, and it takes me about three times longer to write anything now because I have to go back and correct elementary grammatical and spelling mostakes.

Mistskes.

Mistakes.

Those first two attempts are 100 percent genuine.

Why am I so happy, then?

Endnotes

[1] "De-Lazari, Alexander Nikolaevich. *Khimicheskoe Oruzhie na Frontakh Mirovoĭ Voĭ 1914-1918 gg,*" http://supotnitskiy.ru/book/book5.htm (accessed May 12, 2012).

[2] "The Theory of Harmonic Rhythm," by Stephen Jay, http://stephenjay.com/articles/hr.html (accessed May 2, 2012).

[3] www.leslieditto.com

[4] Edmund Blunden, "On Reading that the Rebuilding of Ypres Approached Completion," in *Undertones of War* (New York: Harcourt, Brace, and World, Inc., 1928), p. 246.

[5] E.B. White, *Charlotte's Web* (New York: Harper Collins, 1952), p. 154.

Interlude with Scott Thunes
Happiness

When I was a kid, I lived in a really bucolic area. I was in a valley; there were tons of suburban-type houses, but nature was exactly five minutes away. I lived between what I used to call the "dry side" and the "wet side." The wet side was where I had tons of redwood trees and beautiful green growth of every description. There were no brown grasses – that was on the north side. So there are two different experiences you could have: it rained a lot, so there was a lot of indoor stuff, but there was also a lot of walking around in the fucking rain. We'd get stoned. We would take acid and we would walk amid the hills. Actually, first we would walk up into the hills and *then* we would take acid. We would get very high, and we would commune with nature.

The first three or four times I did it, had a couple of bad trips, fake suicide and what have you, but I had my friends, and we'd take care of each other. Saw a lot of people having a lot of really bad experiences, but most of the time it was purely recreational and fun. We knew from our parents that you were supposed to open doors of perception, but we didn't really care about that at the time. It was purely recreational. After a while, of course, it became un-recreational. It wasn't any good. You started having nothing but bad trips, and you stopped. Took a couple of years. But the point is that we would go out into nature every day. Every single day we would walk up into the wet side, and go into hills and cruise around behind people's houses and adventurize that way. It wasn't discovering new lands as much as going into people's beautiful back yards, and their houses and stuff, and seeing what was going on.

Coming out here, out in the middle of nowhere, we would just sit and surround ourselves with this tree stuff: trees and rocks and water. We were completely and utterly surrounded by it, all the time. I always hated the American suburban ethic. I was raised in Los Angeles, and when I came up here and supposedly became a hippie, my whole idea was the world is going to fall apart. It's going to be nuclearized and dead in a couple of years. I don't have to think about anything. I'm not going to think of any future growth because I'm going to be dead in five years. None of this shit really matters. Being a musician was definitely part of that. It was instantaneous gratification.

I never thought about the future. I knew that there wasn't going to be any. So everything was purely instant gratification on every level. Nature was the best way to do that. You know, I wasn't really getting laid as much as I liked. I had a girlfriend, and then I didn't have a girlfriend. All that was really tense, and really weird, but nature was always there. It was always a given; you always knew it was going to be there. When I moved to Los Angeles and lived there forever, I knew this was all still here. I came up and visited, and every time I visited, it was all still here. Everything's exactly the same. Twenty years later, it's exactly the same.

If I wanted to, I would come out here more often, but when I'm working and at home, I don't think about it. There's absolutely no reason for me to leave my house. There's not a piano out here. No matter what happens, I've got a computer; I've got my beautiful wife; and I've got an acoustic piano with tons and tons of music that I still can't play yet. And I enjoy sitting around and playing the piano so much, even fitfully, going in and playing a couple of notes and then leaving. I've always got that option. But out here, I don't have any option. Still, I have to bring people out here to show them what's going on. The only time I come out is when I'm showing people who don't live here what it's like.

Georgia and I probably wouldn't come out here at all if we weren't showing people. She goes out and walks around in nature as exercise, and there're so many beautiful places to do it. You might as well drive to Phoenix Lake, walk around it, or run, depending on how excited you are, but I can't even get my shit together to ride my bike to work, which I was really excited to do because it's only a fifteen-minute bike ride. But I'd much rather stay in bed that extra ten minutes with Georgia. I'm late to work every day, at least by two minutes, just because I'd much rather stare at her and smell her and just hang out with her. There isn't anything better than that.

Everything that has happened in the world has shown me that the only thing that you can do is get pleasure where you can find it. Most people, they have tons and tons of time to bore themselves with the microscopic intricacies of getting out into nature by driving a thousand miles to get somewhere that they aren't at, you know? There is so much stuff that is right here that I can't even begin to slightly access. I don't have time. Between the pleasures that I know I can have within exactly ten feet of my face, there's no reason to come out here. I love people experiencing this pleasure, especially when they come from Los Angeles, because the only people who come to visit me are my friends in L.A., so it's perfect because they get off on it in the most extreme way and that reflects on me incredibly well, in three or four different ways.

I'm smart enough to live here. I got out. They're still there. So no matter how cool they are, and no matter how cool their lifestyles are down there, they're still fools. And I can reflect on that in an interesting way, because I stayed down there, totally willingly, for six and a half years, as an adult, knowing that this was here. When everything kind of fell apart in L.A., I finally decided to go and actually move up here. I was going to come up here anyway, but things wouldn't have been as good. I probably would still be living in Berkeley with an ex-girlfriend. Those tons of tension would be in full force, you know, so everything turned out incredibly well, but it didn't happen because I moved up here. It's totally separate. All the other cool lifestyle stuff happened separately from my moving up here. Very weird.

So: How do my wife and I try to interact with other people, knowing that they think we're too cocooned, or something like that? Wow! It's difficult, at times because I want everybody to be as happy as I am, and I'm not threatened –

That's not what you asked, I know. You asked if other people are threatened by us. But I'm trying to access it from my own experience.

The whole idea is that whatever those people are doing that are coming into my universe and seeing how happy I am, I must force myself to not play it down because it is the most important thing that's ever happened to me. It's one of the rarest things in the world that

I've ever heard of: a happy marriage, let alone two people who never argue. Two people who don't have that constant underlying tension. If there *is* tension, if it is there, please show me what it is. I have absolutely no problem in finding out what the hell is going on. I know I'm sublimating tensions from a million years ago, and I know it reflects interestingly on our relationship, that a bunch of my subtexts are being played out every day.

If I want to talk about my psychosexual weirdnesses I can, but I don't know exactly what all of them are, and I don't know how I'm keeping her down, or what have you, but from the external point, it is very difficult for me to make sure that I am being exactly as happy as I am. I want to be with her all the time. I am consciously aware of the fact that most people don't have what we have, and I have to play to them. I want [withheld] to be happy when he comes up here, but not only has the past three times he's come up here been fraught with tension because he's breaking up with his girlfriend, but I'm angry at him for not letting it go.

He can be happy up here, not based on any relationship weirdness. Everybody else is kind of the same way because I don't know anybody who has what we have, and everybody comes into it thinking, "They must be hiding something," and it's very difficult because there's no way I can show them. My friends all know that if I have a problem, I'll discuss it with them. Every single relationship I've had, I've said, "She's driving me absolutely fucking bananas. Every single thing she says makes me want to kill her." Every single woman I've been with has forced me to have "trouble talk" with my friends.

This relationship? Nobody ever gets anything. I have nobody that I need to dump on. I don't go outwards searching for people to bring into my universe so that I can dump my negativity on them. And realizing how much time I spent doing that in the past gives me the willies, realizing how ugly it must've been to everybody else. That's normal, but now that I'm in this marriage, I have to think in terms of what am I going to get from people when I hang out with them? Which is why I don't hang out with anybody, because nobody's as interesting as Georgia. Everybody drives me crazy. After a couple of minutes of listening to them talk the kind of talk that most people normally have, it drives me up a wall.

Before, I was very interested. I like gossip; I like seeing that other relationships are going through interesting changes. I want to know what they are. I'm very concerned when somebody isn't happy, because I'd like to talk to them, to see if there's any way I could say to them, "You don't have to be stupidly in love, in pain. You don't have to. There's no point in it whatsoever." Eventually, something happens, where somebody proves themselves to be the kind of a human that you can't deal with anymore. At some point in time, every single one of my friends has done that, but I still enjoy them because they're smarter than everybody else.

But when they start playing "normal," I pull back. I can't play normal. I'm not going to waste my time. And I have a big problem with people who are very nice and very dull. You're supposed to enjoy humans, and people are supposed to be nice. You finally find people who are nice, and they're dull. They don't have anything to discuss. I have some friends from Los Angeles who come up and visit. They're very nice, and the guy is old-school "trouble relationships," and he's very intense. He's very smart, with a very high artistic level, and all of us are used to having very deep artistic and psychological and physiological and psycho-whatever conversations. We always get really in depth. But he's also kind of frivolous and can be kind of goofy.

But the past four or five times they've come up to visit, I immediately recognized that the only types of conversations we have are the two lowest types – stories and jokes. That's what's weird about being with Georgia. You have to – After you get off work and she gets home from school, you gotta tell what happened during the day. When I was with my previous wife, I didn't want to hear her stories. I didn't want to hear her talk for forty-five minutes straight about what happened to her at the fucking office. I couldn't stand it. I couldn't deal with it. Being with Georgia, I'm interested in what happens at school. When we go out and have recreational communication – stories, jokes, what have you – that's one thing, but we very rarely drop the ball with each other. We have trained each other to know. I'm not going to bore her, and she doesn't want to bore me.

So many other people don't care about adjusting to wherever they're going. It's like, "This is our life. We present it everywhere we go." Georgia and I sit around, and as soon as somebody tells a story, we look at each other and we go, "Hmmmmm." And at what point do you say, "Uh, you're boring the fuck out of me." I have a relationship here that is based on a higher level of communication. She wants to experience and communicate and trust and train and inform and delight, and nobody else wants to delight. They want to amaze and astound, and perform. We don't have time for it.

• • •

When Tom came over to my house – bless his massive little heart – he was a little cucumber of a muffin. All tender and sensitive. He cared so much! It hurt to watch. I tried to break him. Nope. No such luck. He sucked me dry and watched me turn from a vitriol-filled cupcake into the man I am today. Without him – and the physical love of a good woman – I would be banging on doors of all the clubs in the Tenderloin, looking for my lost karma.

As it stands, I have not only gone back to the source for many of my Zappa memories (Tom wrote about me telling him I'd not listened to these albums for ten years, something about horn players being all over them or not having had enough sex on the road) but since then, I've been the happy recipient of an 11-day stint with Zappa Plays Zappa, playing several of my favorite songs in the universe, in, like, ever (as the kiddies say). Also, another book-writing friend of mine – Andrew Greenaway – wrote an oral history of the ill-fated 1988 band, using interviews with all of the concerned members (except, notably, the drummer, who shall remain nameless [and I prefer that he does. Thanks. Vulcanism!]) which caused me to attempt to recall many other elements of my time with Frank all those many years ago.

Over the past couple of years, the Zappa-stuff has come back, big-time. I sat in with ZpZ *[Zappa Plays Zappa; see next chapter]* a couple of times and Gail – bless her heart – invited me to come to London for the Roundhouse Zappa 70th Birthday celebration. I was feted with a sit-down "seminar" with Jeff Simmons (early bassist and guitarist with Frank), several songs of sitting in with the band, watching a full length orchestral performance of some of his music, and got to stand next to my wife next to the stage watching my wife's and my favorite British comedy group – The Mighty Bush – open up for ZpZ (and me, technically). Beers were purchased, I met many fans, heard many stories, and ate wonderful food, then got paid and had my plane ticket bought for me.

Then, I got to see my good friend, internet sensation (and ex-Special New Friend, 1988) Dr. Dot mention the size of my penis in print, met Ian Underwood, and leave my family for the longest time ever in one chunk (almost three weeks) since starting my family 12 years ago, because of MUSIC.

So, after all the horrible things that happened to me I refuse to apologize for being me, being sensitive and hating all the stupid shit that happened to me even though I still have my health, my limbs, a family and some friends, and a house. I have suffered very little as compared to many in the rest of the world, but I'm not a "Children are starving in Korea" (thanks, Alice!) type of guy. I'm a privileged white guy living in Marin County. I know how much it sucks to hear the whingings of some hack. But my experience is extremely similar to Tom's in that we got screwed by the people we loved and purported to love us. We got screwed by people who couldn't care less for any other humans than themselves and LOVE to screw us. We're also – really, actually – happy people.

Even I was happy having had stuff happen to me that caused me to stop playing. I was really actually enjoying myself a lot at the very time Tom interviewed me. He'll remember the endings 1: "And everything else is secondary to happiness, and I don't want to come off like some Zen, hibernating monk. It's not that I stepped down off the mountain to live in the forest" 2: "[Everybody] just wants to be in a rock band. They want their musical ideas to be valid. I'd rather have my life be valid than my musical ideas. I think that's about it." And my favorite: 3: "...why would anybody want to interview a happy person?"

So, having slightly debunked that small element – easily misinterpreted, sure – I'd like to go on record by saying that it's about gat-dang (let's see if THAT passes the swear-filter) time that Tom has gotten his due, and we should all be forcing him to finish up whatever "novel" he's putting together so we can finally read the roman a clef of Scott's life told in flashback from the insane asylum.

Two things: I'm playing around California (also sporadic ventures across the US) with 20 year veterans of rock, the Mother Hips. I really love what we're doing and look forward to many more gigs with them. Please come see us play. We're awesome rock and roll. I use a 1965 Precision bass I got from an ex-girlfriend. Also, I was recently given (traded a '72 Gold Top Les Paul Signature Bass for it, actually) a 1990-era A/E Precision, fretted. I use that a lot. It's truly an amazing instrument.[1]

Endnotes
   [1] "Interviewing Bassist Stories," (accessed May 18, 2012).

Anthology Seven
The Great Un-haunting
2012

There was a man who lived a life of fire.
Even upon the fabric of time,
Where purple becomes orange
And orange purple,
This life glowed,
A dire red stain, indelible;
Yet when he was dead,
He saw that he had not lived.

Single, Housebound, and Happy

The strangest thing happened after my diagnosis of Meniere's disease: My chronic anger fell away almost overnight, leaving only occasional, acute, short-lived attacks of temper. Everything I still had – what health, faculties, and ability to write that remained – became much more precious, and it dawned on me how lucky I'd been to have experienced so much that was beautiful and inspiring. I was flooded with fantastic memories, such as the time I sat for hours on a wall of the Hohensalzburg Castle in Austria, gazing down at the couples sitting at the outdoor cafés and marveling at how the big fountains, cobblestones, and street lamps were a weird grayish-green color, tinged with gold in the light of the setting sun. Or when I met a shockingly handsome Frenchman named Geoffroi on a ferry from Korea to Japan, and we talked for seventeen hours straight about everything you can imagine: medieval European cuisine, super reactors, music, economic theory, art, marine life, UFOs, fruit cultivation, linguistic morphology, world-changing inventions – it may be the best conversation I've ever had.

Or the day I diffused a brewing fight in a liquor store between a tattooed Mexican gangbanger and an Arab cashier who spoke broken English. The gangster was barely intelligible even to me; after trying four times to get his pack of Marlboros, getting more and more steamed, he turned to me and shouted, "*Dude's straight retawded!*"

I said, "Hey, hey, hey! Take it easy! Your veins are sticking out and your head's gonna blow up, *pshww!*" I made a big, splattering explosion in the air with my fingers. "We'll have to clean it off the floor with a *mop!*"

For a couple of seconds the gangster gave me the stinkeye. Then he laughed once – "*Hop!*" – and said, "Yeah, okay, you're right. I don't want nobody cleanin' my head up off the floor with no mop." He shook my hand and apologized to the clerk.

Looking through the past few years of my daily scribblings, I found the funniest, most life-affirming performance art I've ever seen, which appeared in the middle of a vicious, pro-forma flame war on a long-defunct political blog. I'd copied and pasted it, and now I couldn't stop laughing at its brilliance. Whoever "Chris" is, I hope he or she appreciates what a timeless classic this is on so many levels.

Willy: i love to argue with you people and expose your simple minds its so much fun for me. it obviously has nothing to do with this thread but nevertheless it's great fun to expose your hypocracy.

Chris: Willy, you and I are going to have to get together. These people drive me crazy. I was just arguing with one at a Subway sandwich shop tonight and he told me to go to hell. Then I made the point about racism against blacks, because he said blacks were okay but he wasn't for gay rights, and I said "Okay, well, what if a naked heterosexual black guy was running down the street with a vibrator in his buttocks?"

He didn't know what to say and again my point is that these people are hypocrites.

Willy: chris it sounds like we would agree on many things. if a politician is in a party that speaks hate and unequality why would i beleive in them or their message. they think that they are better than a gay or a black, or mexican, or asian, or my fellow ancestors who are american indian. chris thank god for people like you who can see we are all human beings who deserve rights and deserve liberty and happiness.

Chris: I've read some of this thread so far. It's hard for me to read that many words together but I'm trying. When I haven't intaken enough vitamin E I get real bad stigmata. I saw the part about your ancestors being Indian. That's cool because I'm 1/8 Indian. Which tribe are you?

Willy: My ancestors where cherokee and the lightfoot tribe. what's yours?

Chris: Mine are Chickatoo.

Willy: oh thats cool. i live in illinois where are you from?

Chris: I lived in Oklahoma for a while then moved to Kentucky then back to Oklahoma then I took a job that had me traveling delivering Styrofoam peanuts across the country but we ended up delivering to some really rough parts of town so Anthony fired me for complaining about it. I am looking into getting a job as a guillemot egg collector but it's hard to get into and I don't know if I have the hands for it.

I have to admit that I don't have a job right now but I will soon so it's not like I'm homeless. Right now I'm living at an RV park till next week outside of Kansas but we are heading to Detroit in five days. I heard the job market is a lot better up there.

You like Illinois?

Willy: not realy people seem very close minded here lol. theres a lot of small mentality here and not much job opportunity. i plan to move somewhere where people are more accepting, more polite, just more positive. i would love to be in that kind of atmosphere.

well i gotta eat soon chris but ill be back in a bit if you wanna chat more. i wish you luck finding a job and everything. hope you can find a good opportunity with some future growth.

Chris: Good luck to you. I hope you find a spot. It's pretty cold to be in the cold area but there is now a fire burning brighter than any man-made fire on this continent.

I have to get off the computer now. My dad didn't charge the battery so we gotta hook it back up and wait till morning. I'll talk to you soon if I can get through all of the elephant waste on here.

I wish they could feel what you and I feel coming from this super-intellectual geniusly diplomatic political figurine.

Thank you, Chris. You helped me stop foolishly squandering my limited resources.

Since I'd now have to spend so much of my time in my house, I began building up my DVD library. I also began scouring YouTube for music, in the process discovering the work of David Amram and Australian composer Tony Hayes, who uses a Fender Bass VI. Amram's full-length version of "Theme from the Manchurian Candidate" is one of the most sublime compositions I've ever heard, and Hayes's "Diana Dors. Solo Fender VI Bass" and "The Drummer - from a Fender VI" are dumbfounding in their perfection. The music of these two artists expressed my mood perfectly; it was the soundtrack to my life.

The song that instantly became part of my being is Morcheeba's "Everybody Loves a Loser," a lush, Motownish throwback that simultaneously kisses off a hopeless failure and cocoons him in protective, affectionate sympathy. It's an astonishing tune, from its brass-heavy instrumentation to its adroit lyrics and the poignant melody of the chorus. The key, however, is the vocals of Skye Edwards, which give the loser the courage to forge ahead even though – and this is the ingenuity of the piece – he'll always be a failure. It's not even that Skye forgives him for being a loser; she's simply explaining his fate to him, with the objectivity of a goddess, reassuring him that he won't be alone and doesn't have to be sad. Soon enough it'll all be over. "Everybody Loves a Loser" is unique in the history of pop music, as far as I know, in that it's a death sentence conferred with genuine fondness. Skye Edwards deeming you a loser is not only bearable: It's a benediction.

When I finished my last military-history book, I turned it in to the publisher and tried to figure out what to do next. This time, I wasn't afraid of my future because so much of it had been laid out for me. It'd be a radically limited future, but I wasn't angry. I hadn't received the news Orson Welles does in his stunning masterpiece *Touch of Evil,* when Marlene Dietrich tells him he has no future because it's all used up.

I was happy that I was still alive, still healthy except for my incurable autoimmune disorder, and could finally see how wrong I'd been about so many things. There was a lot to clean up. I began with someone I'd hated for almost seven years.

A Test of Character from God?

In late 2011, I'd bought a postcard on eBay. Nobody else bid on it, which was odd because it's a rare and valuable image that shows technical details of the assault order worn by German flamethrower troops in World War I. Such an image has never been published in any book. I got it for $11.00.

When my postcards arrive, the first thing I do is scan them at 1200 dpi so I can slowly examine them for the tiniest detail. I noticed that the two vehicles in the photo had placards on the sides that identified these assault troops as a platoon of the same flamethrower company to which the father of Lew – my old scourge and erstwhile coauthor – belonged. How ironic, I thought. Lew the Hitler-voiced chicken would give his right arm for this photo. I slowly traversed the scan of the card because I try to memorize each face. This helps me buy future postcards. I've acquired hundreds of valuable postcards cheaply because I recognize faces. Sometimes the insignia is hidden, throwing off other collectors, so I get them for a song. My memory for faces is my secret weapon. There were 3000 men in the German flamethrower regiment, which actually isn't a lot of faces to memorize.

In this postcard, the fifth face I saw was that of Lew's father. There was no question. To make absolutely sure, I compared it to the photo Lew sent me while we still ostensibly wrote a book together. It was the same man. Because of the insignia, I knew that the photo was taken after July 28, 1916. The photo showed wet and cold weather, and men in heavy coats. This particular flamethrower company fought only in the late spring, very early summer, and winter of 1916. I knew the exact day Lew's father was severely wounded in the Battle of Verdun: It was very late in the year. After that he was never fit for flamethrower duty again.

The photo shows Lew's father riding in the lead vehicle with the flamethrower operators, while the second vehicle carries the grenadiers who protected the flamethrower squads. Lew's father was wounded on the first day of the platoon's winter deployment. Therefore this has to be the date of the image. It's not a training photo; the men are armed with live weapons, and there are plenty of grim and frightened faces. It's undoubtedly a pre-mission photo, taken right before the platoon went to fight on the Dead Man and Lew's father met his fate.

I felt morally obliged to tell Lew I'd found a photo of his father taken the day he was wounded. It gnawed at me to keep something so meaningful from a person. I asked several friends what they'd do in my situation, and they all had the same advice: Don't say a word. Look at the damage he wrought to you before. You'd be crazy to get enmeshed with him again, and you don't owe him a damn thing. Tim was especially vehement, telling me that he'd be *extremely* disappointed in me if I invited Lew back into my life in any way because it'd prove that I was incapable of learning. I completely understood, but this was Lew's father. What if letting him know I'd found this photo brought him a measure of peace?

Lew was my worst ghost, in the sense that he was the only one who made me seethe and clench my jaw. This began haunting me without letup. Finally, I posted the photo on a World War I forum with a title that would grab Lew's attention. I asked him if this was his father. He confirmed with much stupefaction that it was. I offered to send him a CD with high-res color scans of the image – it's a pleasing sepia tone – for him to use as he wished. He politely accepted and thanked me. I sent the CD; he acknowledged receipt; and we've had no further contact.

Farewell to the Bass

In late February of 2012, I finally admitted that I'd never play the bass again. I'd known it for ten years but simply refused to face the fact that I'd lost something else I loved so much. Osteoarthritis made it impossible to play anymore. It simply hurt too much. Over the previous ten years, every time I played more than a few minutes, the bases of my thumbs hurt so badly that I had to take painkillers. I think it stems from the double thumb dislocation I suffered when I worked on the shore-support base in Norway. Though I could still type, I couldn't play the bass. Yard work is hard, too, as is vacuuming and writing longhand.

I'd held on to my Sting Ray because Carmen had bought it for me. Like Robert De Niro and his watch in *Midnight Run*, I just couldn't give it up. Now I felt it was time. In 2001 I'd made a video of myself playing Gentle Giant's "Mobile," one of my favorite songs. It's got a diabolically difficult bass line – not as hard as the live version of "Free Hand," but close. After twenty takes I got it 98 percent right. I decided to post it on YouTube under the title "Gentle Giant 'Mobile' bass cover," the only video I plan on ever uploading. Then I contacted everyone I'd known in the music industry who'd left me with positive memories and invited them to watch the video as a celebration of my departed skill. It was the high point of my bass-playing ability, and I wanted to have a wake for it. Everybody I contacted responded with kindness and admiration. It was a thoroughly rewarding experience without a hint of sadness.

One of the most moving e-mails was from Mike Keneally.

> At your request, I am refusing to be sad; instead I praise your mofo self for KILLING on that wonderful tune :) and I am grateful to have had any small thing to do with facilitating the Thunes interview, a classic of all time (a true piece of art – for which you suffered commensurately I know – the result is beyond magnificent). I sincerely hope you're doing well!

I'm doing great, Mike. Having you dub me a killing bassist and an artist is a tribute beyond my wildest dreams. Thank you.

Special Mention: Mr. Cranky-pants

I interviewed Bryan Beller several times in my career. He's a remarkably thoughtful person without being mawkish about it at all. He regularly sent me holiday greeting cards, even after I dropped off the face of the music earth. I kept them all.

It was clear my goose was pretty much cooked at *Bass Player* when they stopped giving me tickets for the annual winter NAMM show in Anaheim. This happened after the guy who killed all my articles replaced Karl Coryat. The first year I didn't appear at NAMM, I got a call from Bryan, asking me why he hadn't seen me. I told him *Bass Player* hadn't given me a ticket.

For the next few years, until I asked him to stop, Bryan sent me NAMM tickets without comment. They'd just appear. I finally asked him to stop because I knew *Bass Player* would never let me interview him again, and I didn't want to become an embarrassment for him. Bryan would never be embarrassed by me personally, but as he rose ever higher in the music world I didn't want his peers to ask him why he continued to associate with that useless has-been.

When I contacted Bryan and told him I could no longer play the bass and wanted him to watch my "Mobile" video, he complimented me on my playing and wrote, "I'll be your hands for you."

Thank you, Bryan. And take care of my hands!

Message to the Cardinal Ghost

On March 9, 2012, I contacted Carmen for the first time since 2010 to tell her that I couldn't play the bass anymore. It was my way of letting her know I'd finally come to terms with everything. I figured this would be my last communication with her.

> Hi, Carmen:
> Hope all is well with you and your'n.
> You bought me this bass. It was hard to part with it because it had such a great sound and there were such great memories attached to it. I'm cleaning up loose ends and simplifying, though, and I haven't been able to play for years now. So I sold it.
> But to commemorate the bass, and you, and the way I used to be able to play, I posted my first and last YouTube video. It still bugs me that I wasn't able to get this bass line 100 percent, but maybe in the next life.
> Thought you might want to see it. Prog isn't for everyone – I know, I know. But Ray Shulman is my hero. Funnily enough, he doesn't play bass anymore either.

[Link to "Mobile" video on YouTube.]
Take care,
Tom

Her reply.

> Hi, Tom.
> I was just thinking about you last week! I was listening to a This American Life podcast and the monologist's observations/humor reminded me so much of you.
> Thank you for sharing your Youtube performance with me. How very sad that you no longer have your prize bass, and even sadder that you no longer play.
> Your performance on Mobile is masterly. It's obviously a challenging bass line and you play it well and with ease!
> Good to hear from you.
> Carmen

When I wrote that message, I fully intended to sell the Carmen bass. It seemed the only way to release and be released. I told Carmen I'd already sold it because I didn't want her to feel any conflict or discomfort over the idea of the impending departure of this instrument that had meant so much to both of us. The most humane, considerate thing to do, I thought, was to present her with a fait accompli. That way, too, she wouldn't misunderstand and think I wanted her to talk me out of it.

Reconnecting with the Collateral Ghost

I also sent a message to Scott Thunes, thanking him for the two great interviews he'd given me and inviting him to watch me play "Mobile." We'd e-mailed each other only once or twice since 2003. I stopped following music in 2003, so I didn't know that Scott had written "Kids These Days," a Soapbox commentary for *Bass Player*. It appeared in the April 2009 issue, which included a feature article titled "Frank Zappa's 'Alien Orifice,': Scott Thunes's Complete Bass Line." The author and transcriber was none other than Bryan Beller; his piece brought me full circle in about eight different ways. "Our Wildest Transcription!" proclaimed the magazine cover. Scott's own essay was illustrated with a photo of him as a bearded, bespectacled professor posing in front of a whiteboard covered with a partial transcription of the Beatles' "Day Tripper," his pointer aimed at the word "Bass." In the article – about the joys of teaching music to children – Scott referred to himself as the "luckiest ex-bass player on Earth." He'd made his peace with my former home in music journalism, which ameliorated so much for me. The article ended with an acknowledgement that he wanted a gig. Though this admission was presented tongue-in-cheek, I knew he was utterly serious.

That gig came in March of 2011, when Scott began playing with the Mother Hips, a San Francisco-based outfit formed around the core of guitarist-singers Tim Bluhm and Greg Loiacono. They describe themselves as "original California soul." After I read about the Mother Hips, I watched a few videos on YouTube of Scott performing with them. They were very good, if not precisely to my taste. It seemed that Scott's unique talent for accompaniment, improvisation, unconventional note choices, and expression of emotion could've been better utilized. Still, I could easily see the appeal of the band.

A big surprise was learning that in December of 2011, Scott had landed another gig, hooking up with Dweezil Zappa and performing live with him in a show called *Zappa Plays Zappa,* a showcase of Frank's work. Things I never thought possible for Scott had come to pass. While it was great that he'd decided to play again, it made me realize how truly unfair and destructive my obsession with getting him back into music had been. It was only marginally destructive to Scott, since I badgered him just a handful of times; even so, I was ashamed to admit to myself that I'd tried to force my desires on him instead of letting him do things his own way, in his own time. The nadir of our relationship – when I fled his house at 11:00 P.M. in 1997 to drive all the way back to Los Angeles – was the result of my pressuring, but we both surmounted that genuinely ghastly experience. Mainly, the damage I inflicted was to myself, which is as it should be. All that brooding and being haunted no doubt contributed to my immune system blowing up. I don't regret my concern for Scott, but I regret the way I'd handled it. My approach wasn't good for either of us.

In response to my outreach, Scott sent me a very nice e-mail that I choose to keep private. Suffice to say, he blamed me for nothing and had only good memories of me. He said nothing about my "Mobile," video, however. After a couple of weeks I asked him if he ever planned on watching it.

"Yes, my dear friend," he wrote back. "I will be very happy to do so. But I gotta build the pressure up to manageable proportions. You're still too pliable. Gotta catch you at the breaking point."

I then watched a YouTube video titled "The Mother Hips/Stoned Up The Road → Magazine," that featured Thunes playing with the Mother Hips at The Hole In the Wall, Austin, Texas, on March 2, 2012. The two songs themselves are superb, but to my almost delirious amazement Scott's playing was as brilliant as anything he'd done in his so-called heyday with Zappa. He'd lost absolutely none of his skills and may even have improved. Although a fifteen-minute video, I watched it three times in a row. He'd used his fingers with Mother Hips in other clips, but in this one he showcased his absolute command of the pick, flying all over the neck of the bass and improvising endless aural masterpieces that existed for only a second and then vanished. The astonishing thing to me was that his long hiatus had done nothing except magnify his talent.

Watching that video made me as happy as I was when I first heard the live version of Gentle Giant's "Free Hand."

Unburdening

On March 23, 2012, I opened an account at the discussion forum Talkbass.com under the name Arthritic_Tom and began a thread called "Interviewing Bassists Stories," in the sub-subforum "Bass Humor & Gig Stories." My plan was to write a dozen or so descriptions of what it was like to interview bassists, what went wrong and what went right, receive some "Cool story, bro," comments in return, and then I could put that entire chapter of my life behind me. I wanted to get a few things off my chest, without mentioning any names. It was a way to clean up, the way I had with Lew. I was shocked when the readers at Talkbass.com loved the stories and kept demanding more. This account was in my first post.

> And I interviewed a band with a hot female bassist who I discovered in the course of the interview hadn't actually played the bass on the debut album. I stopped the interview to call my boss to ask what to do, and band's female agent came shrieking down the hall toward me like a murderous lunatic. I aborted the interview, and the record company and publicists made the magazine miserable for weeks. Initially my bosses stood by me, but the pressure got so great that I'm pretty sure it contributed to the end of my career.

The readers were especially interested in that story, particularly after I wrote that the bassist was famous for writhing, bumping, and grinding in a really contrived way onstage, as though her own playing is so good it makes her lose control of her body. "There are videos of her all over YouTube, doing all her patented kinky, porny moves as she lumbers through another dull song," I wrote. I didn't like her at all when I met her. She had a totally affected languidness and spoke in the lazy, self-satisfied monotone of someone who'd just spent five hours with the best gigolo money can buy. Her problem was she'd swallowed her own press about how smokin' she was, and she expected me to kneel in praise of her exalted hotness. She was easily the most boring person I ever interviewed. For most of the short time I spent with her, she spoke about the fact that she has two X chromosomes, repeating three times, "Words are hard."

Since so many people wanted to know more about that interview, I now present the transcript of the actual moment when she revealed what was apparently supposed to be a secret.

I think there is a difference between masculine and feminine, and I'm really trying to support the feminine way of music. I don't like to compete with the masculine way. They're just two different ways.

Well, would you – Words are hard, *I know, but would you be able to put into words what the difference is?*
Well... [Long pause, clears throat.] It's just, it's just the same way a man articulates and a female articulates. [Ten-second pause.] You automatically know if you're talking to a man or a woman. I think if you let go, you can hear the woman inside music, and you can hear the man inside music. I'm definitely trying to not sound like a man.

I'd sort of like to get into that a little, because when I listened to the CD, I noticed that there's a definite tone-thing going on, and I'm wondering if that's deliberate on your part, in the sense of trying to have a more feminine approach.
If we go back, I am actually not, not playing on all, all the songs.

Oh. Okay.
So what you hear live and what you hear on the CD are two different things, definitely, uh, as far as, uh, my interpretation of the sound, but, uh...

So how many songs on the CD are you playing on?
Well, on the CD, I'm playing [a different instrument].

Okay. Okay.
[Withheld] plays the bass on the CD.

Huh. Hmm. Okay. Umm, let's see... Um, I'm kind of thrown for a loop here. I didn't know you didn't play on the record. Nobody told me that. That sort of puts a big monkey wrench in this. I'm going to have to – I – My questions are all kind of irrelevant now.
No shit?

Listen, uh, let me talk to my editor, okay?

I stopped the interview to call my boss for advice on how to proceed. What should I do? Should I say that due to extreme sexiness, the woman couldn't actually play on the album, so a more unlovely male had to step in? The publicist and label bombarded *Bass Player* with complaints because my refusal to lie interfered with the launching of a new "supergroup." I was taken off the story and another writer was assigned. He deftly sidestepped the whole issue by saying something like, "She became bassist for [the band], and then they released their first album." Factually correct.

And it worked. To this day people still think Ms. Sexy Writher played the bass on the CD. But she didn't.

Flashback: Another Reason I Hate Mountain Bikes

I interviewed a very successful musician and arranged to photograph him at his manager's office. The band was so busy it had only an hour to spare. I wanted to go along with the photographer because I love photo shoots. Precision appeals to me, and I'm fascinated by how lighting and lenses create completely different images. The day I set up the shoot, the manager told me six times to not be late. I arrived at the photographer's house thirty minutes before we were to be at the office, which was only a few blocks down the street. In his back yard, the photographer worked on a mountain bike.

"Come on, let's go," I said.

"In a minute," he answered. He picked up nuts and gears, examining them like an archeologist poring over bits of an amphora.

"*We have to go!*" I yelled.

"Just a second."

There was nothing I could do. I knew he'd decided to sabotage me because that's what friends do in Los Angeles. I gave in to my fate. He tinkered away until the exact time we were supposed to be there, and then he slowly gathered up his equipment. We showed up half an hour late. The manager was hysterical. "What did I tell you?" he bellowed. "What did I tell you? Did I tell you how important it was to get here on time? *Did I?*" He was like a Hollywood mobster, about to blow out our brains.

I went to the bathroom to wash my hot face as my photographer set up, and I heard a deranged howling from inside one of the stalls: "No, we can't now because the photo shoot is gonna be late! I'm sorry! It's not my fault, so stop talking to me like that!" The lead singer of the band came stomping out of the stall with his cell phone and shoved past me without a word. When I came out, the manger said, "You got ten minutes. That's it. Go!" So we did a ten-minute photo shoot.

As my photographer drove me back to his house, he muttered, "They weren't very happy, were they?" I wanted to take his tripod and smash it into his face and then make him eat his mountain bike. That day I lost ten pounds from sweating, easily.

When the article was published months later, the musician was so happy with it that he invited me to his band's show. I was conflicted because I was interested only in his solo material. Also, the manager seemed like nobody to mess with. I asked the musician if it was a good idea to invite me, and he assured me that all was forgiven. They'd even loved the photo that appeared in the magazine. The manger would laugh about it with me, he promised.

With no way to gracefully decline, I accepted. He FedExed me two all-access passes the next day. These were *real* all-access passes, laminated in plastic with a photo of the band leader, his name, the date of the show, and the words "ALL ACCESS" stamped in red across them. Each pass had a hole with a little metal grommet at the top, with a woven green cotton cord laced through it so you could hang the pass around your neck. It was the real thing, a totally professional job.

Since I didn't know anybody who liked the band, I asked the photographer who'd almost torpedoed the shoot. He agreed, claiming he wanted to get back in the manager's good graces. Los Angeles is a very small town in some ways. Every torpedo you fire at an artist, publicity firm, or manager has a way of circling back and hitting you. We arrived at the show and breezed past layer after layer of security. Those passes really worked. We had decent seats and after watching a bit of the show, the photographer said he wanted to go backstage to find the manager and apologize. So we went down to the stage and were let in through a gate by a security guard. The first person we saw was the band manger. His eyes almost popped out of his head.

"*You!*" he shouted. He turned to a guy with a walkie-talkie and said, "Get these fuckin' assholes *outta* here! *Now!*" A wall of very large men trundled grimly toward us, but we stayed a few steps ahead of them and went back out the gate under our own steam. Since there was no point in staying to listen to music we didn't like, we left.

"Guy's got a long memory," was the photographer's only comment in the car on the way back to his house.

The Collateral Ghost Un-ghosts Himself

On March 27, 2012, Scott Thunes began commenting on the Talkbass.com thread "Interviewing Bassists Stories." It was the first time he and I had interacted publicly since 2001, when we did a reading for *In Cold Sweat*. The following are excerpts of our exchange. I've edited them somewhat to improve the flow, and I took out my silly all-capital screeching because it looks really stupid in a book.

> **yep_scotthunes:** Priceless. Classic Tom. The best parts of *In Cold Sweat: Interviews with Really Scary Musicians* were the introductions. To the book and to each section. I re-read them over and over, having 'lived' my section and not caring too much about the other guys (sorry!). They were the only 'written' parts of the book that were "TOM", as it were, and I loved them. Tom got in touch with me a month or so ago, and because I'm actually forced to leave the house, now, every couple of days - and I really didn't know what to say to the house-bound buffoon - I didn't write him back immediately. I'm glad I waited, 'cause this happened and he told me about it today and I'm so fucking happy about it. Tom's stories are things that I wish happened to me so I could write a book about my life. I feel my life and stories are completely boring - because I actually lived ROCK I know for certain how terribly life-sucking the soundtrack to that lifestyle is. Hell, I wrote some of it!
>
> He tried to get me to agree to let him 'ghostwrite' the book with me, doing interviews and transcribing them, much like the *BP* interview went. But I wanted to go my own route, and now I'm the lesser man for it (I've yet to start that book). Tom, you were right, and if we'd followed our hearts, we'd be wiser and richer for it. As it is, we must suffer with our decision and try to make the best of it. Please don't hate me for assisting in the ruination of your career. You bettah off! That said, I'd like to thank him for hepping me to this thread. I agree with everything all of you have said. He IS the man, and he deserves the cookies (I'll tell you the story someday, Tom. It came from Marty S).
>
> Georgia says hi! Oh, and HI everybody! Thanks for hosting this little party... OOOH! I knew I was forgetting something. The reason I just registered was so that I could remind Tom to tell the story of the guy at the Guitar Center who stood next to him while he bought picks (right after the article came out). Not to toot my own horn or nothing, but I WAS the guy that almost got you killed for nothing, so, you owe me... or something....
>
> Tell it! Tell it! (like with the dialogue and everything like a screenplay like you do so well!)
>
> **Arthritic_Tom:** What's this "*we* should've followed *our* hearts" crap? *You're* the one who refused! I *told* you to write the effing book with me, didn't I? I *told* you we'd mop the earth together, but *noooo!*

"Who are you to tell me how to live my life! Harrumph! Waaaaah! Nobody tells me what to do! So there! How do you like them apples, eh? Besides, what've you done for *me* lately, huh? Change my diapers, dammit!"

I didn't ask about Georgia because I don't read about my heroes. I was afraid to ask. Thank God she's still with you. Tell her I love her deeply for everything she did for me. Your kids won't remember me, but tell them hi. There's a phrase you may have heard: "God did a little dance around him." Miraculous talent, unbelievable intellect, the undying love of a perfect woman, and beautiful children. No fair. Why do some guys get all the breaks? Who do I have to kill to get a life like yours? You're going to have to e-mail me the details of the pick story. I told you I've blocked most of that period out. It's on the tip of my tongue, but still too hazy to flesh out. Bastard.

yep_scotthunes: Oh, don't worry. I was kidding. I'm perfectly happy to have it done 'my way or not at all'. For instance, I fucking HATED *The Real Frank Zappa Book.* And no, not just because it didn't mention me at all. But because it was so plastic, even though it was 'in his voice'. His voice was perfectly described in *Them or Us,* the stupid gigantic waste of paper, copied directly from his home's dot-matrix printer. It was ungainly, and horribly overwrought, but it was what he wanted it to say and it said it in an uncopyable fashion. But that book. It was so dry and lumpy and sad, really. I have a deep fear of coming off that way. So, no. I'm happy the way it turned out. And I'm happy we get to start over again. Now, could you tell the pick story, please?

dhsierra1: this is too cool, thanks for joining in, Scott, not to overdramatize things but this is an important piece of music history coming together before our eyes. Seriously.

Arthritic_Tom: Don't encourage him! He's like a, like a...

He's like some kind of ancient machine that you'd heard about, that had been assumed lost forever, and there were all these legends about what it could do if only it could be found and reactivated, so you called around and spoke to some experts who gave you hints and little details here and there, and then you had to gird your loins and plunge headlong into the jungle, hopefully not dying because you were no explorer, you were just an enthusiast, and then by God you found the thing almost fully buried in the dirt, and you dug it out, brushed it off gently, started it up... and then it started chasing you!

And you were screaming, "Wait, wait, wait! I'm the one that unearthed you! I'm your friend!" And it was gaining on you, with these whirling blades you didn't see before, and you crapped your pants in terror because you realized that this machine saw everyone as an enemy, just like in the ancient days when it was first built and it was fighting nonstop for survival, so it's still in survival mode, and it bears down on you and you close your eyes and scream –

And then it picks you up and kisses you with its metal lips and goes, "Ha-ha! Just kidding! Of course you're my friend. I knew it the whole time! Just messin' with ya!" So you're lying there with your pants full of crap, your heart ruptured from the terror, and right after you die, *that's* when the machine starts to do what it was built to do.

So don't encourage him. Not unless you have an I.Q. of about 370, lightning reflexes, and the ability to think ahead by decades.

yep_scottthunes: Dude. It's all good (as the kiddies say). I apologize for getting you all riled up, but I never meant for it to be taken seriously. My story is my own. It was always mine to fuck up. Your generous and gracious offer was the best thing that had ever happened to me (besides Georgia) up to that point in my post-Zappa musical life and I thank you for it. But it was not something I would ever have enjoyed, seeing as how my wife was always up my ass for not writing enough (still is) and my story needs to be told by the asshole that lived it. Your assistance would have made a book that could not have been created by me. My musical life story is dull, lifeless, and means absolutely nothing to anybody. But a story I wrote? It would be as great and as interesting as a story YOU wrote, about anything, really.

As long as I don't write that story, it remains the great story, greatly told. As it is, I'm spending that extra time that could have been applied to sitting down and writing to drinking beer, loving the wife (heh heh), inputting Hindemith into Logic, playing video games, and helping put the house into some semblance of order (along with my various teaching duties and the rock and roll that has permeated my life as of late [Go, Mother Hips!]). The second I start to write that book will be the first day of the rest of my life.

Arthritic_Tom: Aha. My memory has been refreshed. A certain someone has reminded me of an encounter that I had utterly erased from my aching brain. I was buying picks at the Guitar Center, and as I was signing my name on the check this massive goon standing next to me was apparently in the habit of peering at everyone who signed checks, because he did one of those Warner Brothers cartoon *yubbity-yubbity* double takes and stared into my face, the gears slowly clicking in his prehistoric skull, his lips moving as he pronounced my name to himself, and then suddenly he says to me, "Hey! You called me a moron! I oughta kick your *ass!*"

Since I hadn't actually said anything to him, I didn't know what the eff he was talking about. "Me? When?"

"You wrote that all bass players are morons!"

Oh. My. God. He was talking about the pull quote from the Scott Thunes interview, "Requiem for a Heavyweight?" in *Bass Player.*

"No, I did not call you a moron. The person I interviewed, Scott Thunes, said that bass players are by definition morons."

"Yeah, well, *you wrote it!*"

So I have to *die?* Is that it? As I recall I finagled my way out of a physical confrontation, but talk about the backfiring of an attempt to disprove a statement made about a particular group. "You think we're all morons? Well, I'll be even more moronic than you can *imagine,* then. Whattaya think about *that?*" For the record, I understood Scott's quote to be in the context of what was required of bassists by the restrictions imposed by the various forms of music being played and the people writing that music, most of them not being bassists. Scott could have phrased it, "To be a bassist, you're expected to be a moron."

It's so ironic because all these years later I find myself seething at the way people willfully misunderstood and refused to educate themselves. For God's sake, all you had to do was listen to *Make a Jazz Noise Here* to understand that this is a person who is capable of conveying more emotion with that limited instrument than entire ensembles. He obviously didn't think that you're a moron for wanting to play the bass, because look at his body of work! It's unparalleled, and it's all on the bass! How hard is that to understand? I said that to literally hundreds of bassists, and none of them would listen to the CD! None of them! I begged them. I pleaded with them. What the hell is wrong with you? Listen to the music! Why won't you do that? Christ, the roles are totally reversed. I'm now the raging, frustrated, housebound desk pounder, railing at the idiocy I see, and Scott is happy, out there playing beautiful music again. It's just too funny.

yep_scottthunes: Wait. Bass players...you knew...were offended I called them morons - but not really - and wouldn't listen to Frank Zappa's music, the last live music he produced on this Earth... because I played on it? After pleading with them? You're actually saying this... Man, after all the things I've said, done, and even regret, I've probably only said to myself a couple of times "I don't think I went far enough". That is definitely one of those times. That quote is easily one of the most UNDERSTANDABLE things anybody has ever said about the bass, and you're telling me that people use that as an excuse to not listen to music? What. Are. Their. Phone Numbers.

Arthritic_Tom: No! No! Stop it! No! You are *not* to go off on another years-long festival of rage because a bunch of completely unimportant strangers are so tribal and immature and insecure that they're impenetrable. Nobody allows in new information. Don't you get that yet? I didn't understand that when we first spoke, but now I accept it. Why can't *you* accept it? Yes, I begged your critics to listen to *Make a Jazz Noise Here,* and yes, they wouldn't because you were the guy playing the bass. So what?

Since I last saw you, I've become the world's leading expert on World War I flamethrowers. I've done research that has astonished the three people on the face of the earth who appreciate what I've accomplished and the history I've saved from being lost forever, but the entire rest of the field of military historians don't care, and they hate me for providing facts that disprove their preconceived notions. So what? I don't care about them now either. They're buffoons, if that's their attitude.

So no more of this "How dare these ignoramuses be ignoramuses!" They say what they say because that's their job, just like a cow's job is to say, "Moo!" Anyone who dismisses your playing without ever having heard it is not worthy of comment, much less anger. So enough.

yep_scottthunes: Man, you don't mind if I alternate puking from tension into a little bucket and crying hot tears for all the lost years, do you? No, I didn't think you would. (this is a joke. I am not doing any of the above. This has been a preemptive irony-free-zone prophylactic statement) Before I get to the meat of my post, here, I'd like to thank you for the kind words, the statements of appreciation for me and my daughter, and everything you've said that isn't derogatory. Even derogatory's good, nowerdays (no press is bad press, yes? yes!).[1]

As I participated in this back-and-forth with Thunes, I screamed with laughter. I felt years of poison drain from me. The thread also brought back memories of incidents I'd completely blocked out.

Rage Flashback

On June 24, 1997, I interviewed Black Sabbath bassist Geezer Butler about his terrific solo album *Black Science*, a radical departure from his previous work. The album was released a week after I conducted the interview. This article was one of several in the can when Karl Coryat was replaced as editor of *Bass Player*. Since the article didn't appear for over a year, I assumed Karl's successor had killed it, as he did with so many of my pieces. By the middle of 1998, I knew that no amount of arguing would change his mind; I therefore said nothing. What happened to the article was actually much worse than it being killed.

It was published in the March 1999 issue of *Bass Player,* with a new introduction that takes note of Black Sabbath's 1999 reunion and tour. However, the rest of the piece was unchanged. It was all about Butler's solo album, concentrating on the personnel of that effort, guitarist Pedro Howse and vocalist Clark Brown. It describes a two-year-old solo album, not the reunion tour. The editor killed the article when it could've helped Butler sell his solo CD, and then he reanimated it into a zombie and used it two years later, when the original lineup of Black Sabbath had reunited. In other words, he pulled off the incredible feat of making the piece utterly worthless for every single person involved, including all the artists, the label execs, the Sabbath tour promoters, the staff of *Bass Player,* himself, the advertisers, the writer of the article, the fans, and the general public. Come to think of it, he made that article worthless to the population of the entire planet, which has to be a first in journalism.

He made me look like a lazy, imbecilic asshole treating a legend with total disdain. Geezer Butler deserved better.

A Warning from the Prince of Hades

As the thread at Talkbass.com grew and grew, I became involved in another deeply gratifying and illuminating experience, this one in the field of military history. I'd sent a scan of a photo to the German Firefighting Museum in Fulda, asking if anyone there could identify the man in question as the commander of the German flamethrower regiment of World War I, Major Bernhard Reddemann, known by his troops as the Prince of Hades. Dr. Rolf Schamberger, director of the museum, answered me. First, he expressed his happiness at establishing contact with me because he said my work in the field was so important that he considered me a colleague. He then confirmed that the photo was indeed Reddemann.

We had a long series of exchanges, in which we compared notes on Reddemann, Germany's most famous firefighter before the war. In 1915 Reddemann invented shock-troop tactics, a break from the military tradition of skirmish lines. Reddemann's men advanced in small groups instead, using the natural terrain as cover and keeping within shouting distance of each other. They bypassed strong points and took the assault as quickly and deeply into the enemy position as possible, leaving the hardest targets to be mopped up by succeeding waves. Reddemann also originated the modern special-operations methods of relying on surprise and building full-sized mockups of objectives so that the attack could be rehearsed for days or weeks ahead of time.

By the end of the war, the Germans had trained their entire army in shock-troop tactics. The U.S. military expanded the tactic into a strategy in the Pacific in World War II, calling it "island hopping," and General Tommy Franks used it during the lightning-fast race to Baghdad in 2003, during Operation Iraqi Freedom.

Reading Reddemann's postwar memoir, I'd gotten the impression that he was an angry, bitter man. During and after World War I, the flamethrower was excoriated as an example of "Hun frightfulness," a terror weapon. However, even a cursory study of the use of flamethrowers showed that they saved lives far more often than taking them. When assaulting a fortification, the attacking force might use grenades, machine guns, explosives, mortars, and light artillery fired point blank, creating large numbers of casualties on both sides. A flamethrower squad, on the other hand, could usually induce an entire garrison to surrender merely by squirting one jet of flame into the air where the defenders could see it. Reddemann sneeringly referred to his detractors as "weak sisters" and "old maids" who had no clue what they were talking about. He correctly argued that flamethrowers are more psychological weapons than anything else.

Although Reddemann clearly originated shock-troop tactics, the credit was given to both a younger, more glamorous German army captain and a French army captain. Reddemann, the middle-aged major of the reserves and cobbler's son – who had hobnobbed with the Crown Prince during the war – was himself bypassed, but by history. One humiliation Reddemann endured really hit home: In 1928 he sent a courteous letter to the American Chief of the Chemical Warfare Service, Brigadier General Amos A. Fries, taking issue with the ludicrously inaccurate statements Fries made about flamethrowers in his 1921 book *Chemical Warfare*. Reddemann's letter was several pages long and included factual refutations and testimonials by German generals. Fries never bothered to respond, instructing the Berlin attaché to thank the major for his interest – misspelling Reddemann's name in the process – and making the preposterous, dismissive claim that the Germans never attacked American troops with flamethrowers.[2]

Dr. Schamberger of the German Firefighting Museum told me that after the war, Reddemann's influence in the world of firefighting collapsed. He failed in his attempt to develop modern firefighting equipment and became a persona non grata in the community of firefighters, likely because of his role in developing flame weapons. Once Germany's most admired firefighter and a war hero who consorted with royalty, he became a pariah overnight and then a chronic failure. In all the photos I've seen of him taken after the war, he looks ready to explode with rage, his mouth clamped tightly in an ugly line and his eyes glaring.

I learned that Reddemann joined the Nazi Party in 1932. After his death in 1938, his widow never mentioned him once to her family, even though she lived until 1975. Today, nobody even knows where Reddemann is buried. He's become an unperson. Among American and British military "experts," he's known almost universally as *Hermann* Reddemann, who was in reality a Berlin physicist. An assistant to Dr. Lise Meitner, Hermann was killed fighting for the German army in World War II. I'd corrected several historians, but they refused to accept that they'd used the wrong given name for years.

My interest in Reddemann had admittedly become an obsession. After corresponding with Dr. Schamberger, I realized that Reddemann was another ghost. As with Thunes, my sense of injustice compelled me to right wrongs; in this case, I wrote three books that laid out the case for recognizing Reddemann's significant contributions to military science. When my books were ignored and my ideas denigrated, I'd become as angry and bitter as the Prince of Hades himself.

The photo of Reddemann I'd sent to the German Firefighting Museum was taken in 1916 and shows a pleasant, middle-aged officer clowning with a corporal. He bears almost no resemblance to the snarling older man of later years. The warning by this ghost was the first that sunk in. In fact, when I realized my motivation in writing about him, all the anger I felt at the anti-reception of my books simply evaporated. It was a wonderful, absolutely liberating moment.

Demanding Satisfaction

On March 28, 2012, three weeks after I'd asked Scott Thunes to watch my "Mobile" video on YouTube, I began posting about it on Talkbass.com. What follows are edited excerpts.

> **Arthritic_Tom:** As always, Scott Thunes is being obstinate and perverse. I asked him to watch my farewell-to-the-bass video, and he won't! He gave me more of his patented incomprehensible twaddle, something about having to force me to the breaking point first, and I'm just not going to have it.
>
> He's been complaining about my praise of his playing for 15 solid years, and now that I've given him the chance to critique me back, he refuses! Well, too bad. For once in our relationship, *I* want what *I* want. I want him to spend four

minutes watching me performing at my peak as a bassist, and I want him to post his reaction – good, bad, or indifferent – here, on this thread. I don't want a private message or private e-mail. I wrote about him publicly, and he damn well is going to write about me publicly, too.

What I want is feedback on my bass playing from the person who may know best in the world what bass playing means. This video is very important to me, and Scott Thunes is going to tell me what he thinks about it! Most of all, I want to know how it makes him feel. I want to know if my performance moved him in the slightest. The way you can help me is that all of you – posters and lurkers alike – can inundate his message box with the question, "Will you watch Tom's farewell-to-the-bass video?"

Guilt-trip him! Ask him how he can be so callous to *me,* a pitiful remnant of what I once was? How can he do this to an arthritic, dizzy, housebound projectile vomiter who can't even play his beloved bass anymore? Scott has been known to feel regret about his actions on occasion, so maybe, just maybe – probably not – but maybe we can force him to bend to our will just this once.

CGramazio: It's like a bass version of *Field of Dreams.* All Scott has to say is, "Hey rookie, you were good."

Arthritic_Tom: See? See? How hard is that for him to get? You've hit the nail exactly on the head. Perfect. Can't I get a little validation before I vomit myself into a soundless void? My mother always said, "I'm proud of you." But Mom doesn't play the bass. What I want to know is, Do I merit praise from a guy who has mastered the instrument like nobody else I know? This is the chance of a lifetime.

NWB: Tom, please bear with me here. I mean no harm. Why is it that Mr. Thunes's opinion on your video is so important to you? What do you expect him to write? I'd like for you to think about that. Mr. Thunes has free will and may choose to do or not do whatever he wishes regardless of expectations placed on him.

Arthritic_Tom: You're talking to someone who knows that better than any person on the face of the earth, with the exception of his family. I know he has free will. I don't care. He's going to comment on my video publicly because I *demand* it from him. I *have to know* what he thinks about it. I don't *expect* him to write a thing. I *want* him to write something about it here, and I want it soon. I'm tired of waiting for him to figure out the most esoteric, pretzel-logicky, abstruse rationalization for why he doesn't do things.

All of that was fine and dandy 15 years ago, but the roles are reversed now. I knew he was happy on a personal level 15 years ago. I met his wife Georgia. Like Scott, you'll never, ever meet anyone quite like her. If you were in a car accident and they had to amputate your entire body, leaving you only with your head, Georgia could still make you happy. I get that. But no matter what he said to me, I *knew* he couldn't possibly be *artistically* happy unless he was playing.

I'm now having to rethink my view that *Make a Jazz Noise Here* is his best work. ["Magazine" with the Mother Hips] is unlike anything I've seen. And you can only make that kind of music when it's fulfilling. So, he's now achieved actual, heaven-on-earth happiness because he's fulfilled on all levels. Don't get me wrong; I believe him when he says if he'd never played again, he still would've been happy. But how the hell can someone have a total hiatus from his instrument and then come back without having lost even an iota of his talent? The only answer is that it was there inside him the whole time, waiting to come out again.

So, he's gotten there, finally, the way I always hoped he would. He's going to be okay now, and I can stop worrying about him. Now, he has to tell me what he thinks about my video. I've had to give up the bass, and I've given up writing about music, and I've already lost some of my hearing and may end up losing a lot more of it. So I want him to tell me, like CGramazio said, was I good? He can even tell me I was bad! It doesn't matter. The circle must be closed, and then I can finally let it all go.

I want the opportunity, for once in my life, to be told by a master of anything, what he thinks. In fact, I *demand* that opportunity. This is the equivalent of having the chance for Christopher Hitchens tell me what he thinks about my writing. But he doesn't *have* to do it. I have no control over him, and I won't think any less of him if he declines. He likely *will* decline because I'm putting a lot of pressure on him. He doesn't like to be pressured. But I don't care. This is the chance of a lifetime, and I want it.

NWB: Tom, the reason that I wrote that is because I admire your writing and your thoughts. My intent is to be as helpful as I possibly can through my words. You never did answer as to why Mr. Thune's validation is so important to you. I only ask this because my life experience has taught me that viewing myself through the judgments of others is not a good road to take. It's a road that leads to inevitable disappointment or worse.

Arthritic_Tom: Actually, I answered your question in detail. And you're misapplying the term "validation." I'm not asking to be "validated" by Thunes; I'm demanding that he tell me his opinion. As I explained, if he refuses, fine; if he says it sucks, fine. His recent return to music has proven to me once and for all that he is a master at his art. I've never had the opportunity to have a master in anything give me his opinion on something I did. The nature of my relationship with Scott is that I can demand this as rudely and inconsiderately as I have, and he can as rudely and inconsiderately refuse to cooperate. And we'll both be fine with it.

What I have here is an opportunity to see beyond the usual borders of experience. It's like standing outside a door that shows you what lies beyond this life. You *have* to open it, even if it means you find out there's nothing behind it. I was damn sure before, but now I'm 100 percent convinced (sorry, Scott) that Scott Thunes is one of the greatest bass players ever, and I want to know what he thinks about my own playing. I'm not asking him to "validate" anything. Believe me when I tell you, whatever he does or says is going to be fine with me. I can't explain my relationship with him. But it works.

So don't worry about me. I understand that you're trying to be helpful, but this is going to have a happy ending one way or another. Thunes of all people knows that his opinion of my playing isn't going to change anything. I can't play anymore, and I don't view him as a bassist; I view him as a man who plays the bass. I wouldn't ask anyone else. I'm only asking *him* because I know he understands, and despite all my *Tiger Beat* fawning, he's going to do what he wants to do, as he always has. He and I both know that. So whatever happens is the right thing. There is no possible disappointment, anger, or resentment headed my way. Seriously.

CGramazio: And herein lies the problem with the request for validation (and don't get me wrong, I fully feel it and get it). My nod to *Field of Dreams* works on a metaphorical sense, but it can't really work in truth. My thought is that Scott would honestly think, "How can I tell you if you're any good." "Does it even matter." And we know it matters to you because he's your Shoeless Joe. But the subjective nature of the art leaves it impossible to define good or bad when you step out of the so-called "technically adept" realm. His only assessment can be, is this your true self on the instrument?

Arthritic_Tom: I predict that Scott's response – if it ever comes – will be very similar to yours. And that's excellent. All I want is an opinion publicly expressed, not only because he is my Shoeless Joe, but also because I've written about his playing publicly, and now I demand that he do the same about mine. He's blogged about my interview and book many times. What I'm looking for is *not validation*. I'm looking for a coda.

And he's the only one who can provide it, whatever that coda turns out to be. When he provides the coda, I can happily put my last demons and ghosts to sleep. Even if he refuses to comment, that's a coda, too, and it will be perfectly in keeping with all that's gone before. A public refusal to comment because it's not appropriate since art is subjective, or since I'm putting too much stock in his opinion, or because he fell asleep 30 seconds into it is fine.

But at this time and place, after this weird, bizarre, hilarious, unexpected thread that has gone completely out of control, I decided that I would make an unreasonable demand, just to see what would happen. Just two months ago, I wouldn't have done it. I'm not the same person I was two months ago. It's weird but gratifying. All will be well, no matter what happens. Trust me. No coda is itself a perfectly appropriate coda. But the demand had to be made. And it had to be a demand, not a request.

CGramazio: It'll be the most eagerly awaited coda in some time. He's just letting the tension build.

Lady Kayri: I would like to add that I can understand your desire to have Scott comment on your work. After over three years of lessons, the one that stands out in my mind was the time after I'd managed to keep decent time, and not hit too many wrong notes, on a piece while my instructor accompanied me on guitar. He told me after the lesson was over "You done good today." Really made my day. (Mind, my instructor is very sparing with praise anyway...) Did I have to have that comment for my continued well being? Would I have stopped studying in a snit if he hadn't said something? Nope. But in a very real way it completed something for me, told me that the time I'd spent working and practicing was not in vain, and that he recognized how much I had progressed since I started studying with him.

Arthritic_Tom: Makes perfect sense. "It completed something for me." Completion. I hate, hate, *hate* the term "closure," because people always misuse it. You hear some reporter asking the mother of a murdered child if something brought her "closure," and you want to scream. But there *is* real closure. Losing a career and the ability to play an instrument can't be compared to losing a child. There can be closure to the first two, not to the second. There can be codas to the first two.

jeffbrown: I saw that a famous bassist commented on your YouTube video. He's right. Well done.

Arthritic_Tom: It's the coda I was talking about. Very nice to have gotten it. I've figured out why it was important to hear it from him: It made it all real. It confirmed that there once was a time when I soared. It sounds counterintuitive, but I can better deal with losses when I know that what I lost was real. I *had* to know. I had to know if I were suffering over the loss of something that was real or never existed.

The confirmation that I've suffered a real loss and not something imaginary has made me finally at peace with it. The wonderful memories of that which I've lost are therefore real, too. My fear was, What if I'm mourning a self-delusion? Wouldn't that make me the biggest jackass ever? So, it's actually a relief to know for sure, from a master, that I suffered a real loss. It makes me more grounded. It enhances my clarity, and clarity is all. As you said, when we finally enter the mode of complete acceptance, we can move on.[3]

A Windup and a Pitch

By this time readers had inundated both the thread at Talkbass.com and my mailbox with requests that I write a book about my experiences. I told these nice, enthusiastic people over and over that I didn't want to set myself up for failure yet again, that I'd simply begun that thread to vent, exorcise, and entertain before moving on to the next project. Eventually, however, they wore me down, and I alerted my editor, Bob Biondi, to the thread. Bob is a huge Zappa fan; I asked him if he thought there was potential for a book.

In the meantime, I continued posting stories, convinced that this would be the last time I spoke publicly about them.

The Hardest Interview of My Career

In January of 2000, I was assigned an interview with bassist David Vincent – a.k.a. Evil D – of Genitorturers, a band popular with followers of fetishism, bondage, and sadomasochism. Genitorturers audience members participate in the live show, during which people engage in sex acts and are pierced, cut, whipped, and crucified. I planned to refuse the interview, but then I listened to the music and found that most of it is very good. *Sin City,* for example, is a terrific CD. This made me even less enthusiastic about doing the interview. Since these were fine musicians, they did what they did because they liked it. With a kind of jittery numbness, I accepted the assignment.

Articles about Genitorturers never addressed the issue of why a band would make extreme pain a part of their show. I wasn't going to ask, either, because this area of sexuality scares and saddens me. In Tokyo I met a beautiful South African woman of Indian extraction. She was smart, funny, friendly, and so attractive that my chest hurt when I was near her. I don't know where I got the audacity, but I asked her out for a drink, and she accepted. The evening went like a dream until the subject of previous relationships came up.

"My last boyfriend was just wonderful," she said in her clipped British accent. "He absolutely adored me. He told me I'd ruined him for anybody else."

"Why is that?" I asked.

"Because I used to dress up in a leather bustier, crotchless panties, and stiletto heels and whip him as he jumped in and out of a tub of cold water. Oh, Tom! You should see your face!" And she produced a tinkling, delighted laugh. She should've seen her own face. I'll never forget it as long as I live.

David Vincent spoke to me for an hour. The excerpts below represent the most grueling moments I experienced in my career as a music journalist. Although Evil D was civilized and considerate, I trembled the entire time.

We have a pretty reputable stage show that goes along with the band. Have you ever seen us before?

No, I haven't.
Oh, boy! Well, you're in for a treat! You've gotta come see us on this tour.

Well, um, the thing is... I guess, I guess... Now that you've brought this up... Okay, just on a personal level – I've heard a lot about the show, and from what I've heard, it's something that I don't think I want to see.
Oh, no!

You know, in terms of sewing eyes shut and sewing mouths shut and crucifixions and all that, it's something that would, I think, give me nightmares, actually.
[Laughs.] Well, look: It's all in good fun, number one. Number two, it's not so much a circus sideshow, as it were. There's actually a story line. It's almost more of a Vaudeville kind of thing.

Okay, I mean, this is strictly a journalistic question. It's not meant to be, you know, combative or anything, but it would seem to me, just from reading a straight description of all that, that if you have to get to the point – to make social commentary or to create art – where you're actually doing that, it would seem that, that you've sort of admitted that people can't, people can't sort of use their imaginations anymore. You know what I mean? If you're actually doing it, then how much of a commentary is it, really, because it seems like you're sort of hitting people over the head with a two-by-four.
That's a good question. That's a fair question. And I would say this: I don't think there is ever a reason to do something unless you're going to *really* do it. Okay? That's one part of it. Number two is, I'm an old Alice Cooper fan; I've always been into show, and into grandiose, and into larger-than-life, and into just completely being entertained. Now mind you, I'm a musician. And the musicians in the band are separate from the show, apart from our singer.

But didn't Alice Cooper mime things rather than actually perform them?
Alice Cooper did mime some things. Back in the older days, he performed a little more than he mimed. And then he got it down to a point where yes, there was more miming going on. But this is something that our singer takes very seriously.

Right. I know there's a whole sort of, I guess you would call it a milieu, that the singer belongs to. [Pause.] Uh, the show is, uh, very interactive, isn't it?
It is interactive with the audience. People come to the show early and interview with some of our stage performers to actually see whether or not they can take part in things. There are people that are involved in a certain lifestyle, and this is kind of a lifestyle game for them. This is something that our singer has been into ever since I met her. So it's part entertainment, it's part interactivity, and it's part making people feel a part of things. If it's up to me, to gain five fans would I remove certain things from the show that make other people happy? Absolutely not. You know, Alice Cooper's at the point where, you know, he doesn't hit women anymore. [Pause.] That came across weird. [Laughs.]

No, I understand.
In other words, he doesn't have violence or blood on stage anymore because he doesn't want his kids to see that. He doesn't want his kids to grow up and say, "Hey, Daddy, you're teaching us this, but then you're up there doing that." But

with us, when they come see us, yeah, we've had people get sick and leave. So? That becomes even more entertaining. It just amps everything up.

Okay. I see.
Is that fair enough?

Yes, I understand.
What I do with this band is I'm a musician, and I'm a composer, and I'm a songwriter. Okay? That is my focus. That has always been my focus. I don't participate in the stage show myself per se. Some of the wild parties afterwards? I'd be lying if I said I didn't participate in those. But when I'm on stage, and when I'm in the studio recording, and when we're rehearsing, I'm all about music. I'm serious, I'm passionate, and that is my main focus.

To be a perfectly fair and objective person, I should go and see your live show. To be the best journalist I can, I should go off and see it. But I have a weak sort of tolerance for the infliction of pain. I can't deal with it. I'd be one of those people everyone would be laughing at, fighting my way out of the crowd, you know. So it's kind of a conundrum because I would like to see you play.
Well, maybe we can figure something out. Maybe you can stop by for a sound check, and we'll run through several songs for you. Hey, dude, I can completely respect all the things you've said about that, and I wouldn't want to force the issue.

Well, I've interviewed people with some pretty outrageous public personas, and the ones I really respected were the ones that if I said, "This is shocking to me," they said, "Of course it is! It's meant to be shocking. I perfectly understand why you feel that way." Then I knew that they had their heads on straight. When they said, "Well, what's shocking about it?" then I knew that it was an area that I didn't want to get into with them because if somebody says, "I can't understand why you're shocked by this particular infliction of this or that," then that's not somebody I could really deal with. But when somebody says, "Of course I understand you're shocked," it's different. So you know, I would definitely love to see a sound check, if that's possible.
That's cool. They're usually later in the day.

Excellent. That'll be really cool.
So, hey, man, it was great talking to you.

Yeah, it was great. You did a very impressive job, if I may say so myself.
Well, cool. It's kind of a double-edged sword. Bands that sell twenty times the number of records that we do can't draw as much as we do. I understand that the show is a good part of our drawing power, and I also understand that the show is the main reason why in some areas people will, will just refuse to work with us. It's not because we're bad people. I mean, I'm regular, nice guy. [Laughs.] But at the same time, we have fanatic fans that are just crazy about us.[4]

After confronting what was for me extremely unpleasant subject matter and having the good fortune to encounter an artist who explained why what he did was art and cheerfully offered to accommodate my sensibilities, the opposite-editor at *Bass Player* excised all the material I excerpted above. He also changed the title to make it look as though I were making fun of Vincent, who'd given me an hour of his life and a thoughtful, intelligent interview. I was handed an assignment I didn't want, and as my reward for completing it successfully the editor removed all the material that had been so tough for me to get and once again made me look like a vicious backstabber.

Saying Goodbye to Military History

In early April, I resigned from military history after another interminable argument on a discussion forum. It was a long time coming. In May of 2010, British enthusiasts had discovered the remains of a Livens "Large Gallery" *Flammenwerfer* used in the Battle of the Somme on July 1, 1916. It was a ridiculous weapon, fifty feet long and assembled in underground mining galleries. When fired, the nozzle was rammed up through the earth with a hydraulic jack, emerging from the ground like a submarine periscope. It then automatically traversed from side to side, spraying its 300-foot tongue of flame. A French historian e-mailed me and asked if anyone connected to the excavation of the weapon, the subsequent building of a working replica, and the documentary made about the whole enterprise had contacted me.

I just laughed. Why would they? They had all their pedigreed experts to advise them, and as a result they got virtually everything wrong. The newspaper articles about the device provided inaccurate information about the range, duration, capacity, effectiveness, and even the purpose. But by that point I didn't care anymore.

The conclusion that Dave, the Best Therapist in the World, had reached about me in 1999, which resulted in our mutual decision to end our sessions, was that my patterns were too ingrained. My best hope in life was to become more adept at recognizing that once again I'd gotten myself into my usual situation, which would then allow me to extricate myself sooner. It was a discouraging diagnosis. However, while it took me ten years to leave music journalism, it took only five to leave military history and stop posting on political blogs, a 100 percent improvement.

Here are excerpts from my resignation letter to my fellow military historians, posted on a blog.

> Excellent job of completely missing my point. I've never said, "I've said it, so it must be true." I've said we've gone over this many times in this very thread, and I'm tired of explaining my theory, which I've said over and over is just a theory. However, I've laid out concrete circumstantial evidence for the theory, and not gotten any rebuttals except, "I just don't believe it." Not very impressive, I must say. That tells me that there's an idée fixe at work here, and when we're dealing with that, there's nothing I can say to change anybody's mind, so there's no point in going on about it. "I don't believe it because I don't believe it" is just as inflexible and illogical as "I've said it, so it must be true."
>
> Don't whine to me about hostility. I've had a boatload of it directed my way for no reason at all, along with derision and bizarre pretzel logic. I'm just giving back what I've been getting. I never said I don't like people questioning my work. But show me a thoughtful, detailed, non-snarky post where someone respectfully presents an opposing viewpoint along with their own factual evidence to back it up. I'll wait.
>
> I've presented tons of circumstantial evidence, and those who think my ideas are all wet have done no such thing. That's why I've finally lost patience. Who needs this? Seriously. If you can't understand my impatience, too bad. Did anybody offer anything in the nature of a serious discussion about my photo? Of course not. It was just the usual mocking one-liners. I thought people would be genuinely interested. My mistake. So if you've got a problem about how this has devolved, take it up with the people who turned it into some weird, completely uncalled-for pissing contest, the way all military-history forums are. I originally

got into the field of military history to share information. I've discovered that my approach is not welcome because people aren't interested in new ideas, so that's why I'm not going to waste any more time on it. This was just the last straw, that's all.

I linked some of the responses here to [Talkbass.com], and people were utterly shocked at what they called the most amazing head-in-the-sand attitude they'd ever seen. It's endemic in military forums. That's fine. You don't see it because the culture has taken you over, apparently. But I can still think for myself. I've enjoyed some of my time in this field, but in the end it wasn't any more rewarding than music journalism, so it's time for me to stop messing with it.

My three books are out there for anyone who wants to read my retarded theories and the many, many, many pieces of evidence I use to back them up. If anyone ever has a substantial argument against them, with their own counter-evidence, I'm willing to listen. But I'm done with laughing emoticons and one-liners. Who needs it? It's a gigantic waste of time on my part because there's no engagement. I don't mind engaging with people, but this adolescent, endless snark has taken all the pleasure out of it for me, so I'm moving on. Big deal.

Home Run

On April 9, Bob Biondi sent me an e-mail after beginning to read the "Interviewing Bassist Stories" thread at Talkbass.com. It said in part, "Love this!!! I'm half way through and want to do the book! Pull a proposal together at your leisure. Fantastic read!"

The offer was confirmed on April 11, even before I submitted the proposal and signed the contract. What began as the closing of a door finished with the opening of a much larger one, more of a castle drawbridge. It may be the most bizarre, hilarious, inspirational moment of my life. I still can't quite believe it. To justify my editor and publisher's confidence in me, I present four of the more memorable stories from my failed career as a music journalist.

Among my Betters

My interview with a bassist of a British pop band was to take place in the lobby of the most exclusive hotel in West Hollywood. I'd never been there, and it took me a while to find it because it's very discreet: No name and no number on the outside of the building, with the driveway hidden behind a giant metal sculpture of a door. After several trips up and down Sunset Boulevard, I finally maneuvered myself into the right place behind the door-sculpture. I surrendered my car to an enthusiastic valet in late middle age, who yelled, "Thank you, sir," as he vaulted past me into the driver's seat. He disappeared around the corner on screeching tires; before I could protest I was waved out of the path of an oncoming Toyota Land Cruiser. Behind the wheel was a wan, pants-suited blonde woman with a cell phone jammed to her head. She stopped, got out, gathered up two briefcases, and turned her car over to the valet all without interrupting her conversation.

I went into the lobby of the hotel, where I was to wait for the tour manager, a guy named Chris whom I was told looked just like Mr. Clean. The massive, sparsely decorated lobby reminded me of something out of Woody Allen's *Sleeper*. It was all in white, with glossy linoleum floor tiles cut to look like wooden planks and a few angular love seats here and there. There were white linen curtains that hung halfway to the floor in a couple of places, hiding nothing behind them. They were just there to break up the warehouse emptiness. A few rectangular white-painted cement columns served the same function. The ceiling was studded with recessed baby spotlights, and what I thought was an office turned out to be the elevator shaft. It was enclosed in enormous green-tinted glass sheets behind which hung more of the white linen curtains. The double doors of one elevator opened, disgorging far too many passengers for such a small enclosure, like a circus clown car. It was very disconcerting.

As well as love seats, the lobby also held wooden rocking chairs, some padded benches, and a luxurious cloth-covered armchair. Every effort had been taken to make the lobby a fashionable place to wait, drink, talk, deal, and be seen. Since the few chairs dotting the Arctic wasteland of the floor were so far apart, however, I felt weirdly exposed when I sat down, as if I were stranded on an ice floe. Quiet, synthetic world-music wafted from hidden speakers, and the dozens of wandering hotel staffers – men and women alike – all wore identical oversized linen suits in beige.

At the information desk, which was just a plain kitchen table, a hoarse woman with a tough, simian face gave advice to two guests, obviously models or actresses. "You're doing it the right way. Okay?" she rasped. "Just keep going the way you are. Okay?" She was rude and seemed disgusted, but her listeners, both wearing tiny skintight T-shirts and those awful bell-bottomed stretch pants that give even the slimmest women enormously wide breeder-hips, nodded gratefully and said, "Oh, ya, ya, okay, ya!" The guests were all either aging Players, aging power-hags, buff young studs, or emaciated young women with colossal breasts. Suits were very in, as were cell phones carried in the hand. No one kept their cell phone in their purse or inner suit pocket. Did that mean they answered them immediately? No. They just let them ring. The lobby buzzed, chirped, tinkled, beeped, trilled, and sang continually. Outside by the pool, youthful Eurogigolos sunned themselves while talking on cell phones. They all had dark glasses, sideburns, and greasy hair. Though shirtless, they wore dress pants and dress shoes, a style copped from Bacco Bucci magazine ads.

As I waited, I asked the guy sitting on the other side of the love seat if he was Chris, because he had a shaved head and an earring. He said – and this is a quote – "No, sorry. I'm waiting for some lawyers I'm going to trick into signing a band I represent." He showed me a press kit, detailing his lie that another label clamored for his threesome of soulful and yummy Panamanians who sounded like Boyz II Men. There was even a fake CD cover. Everything in the press kit was phony, he explained. His gusts of excited laughter smelled horrible, as if he'd been eating road kill. From what I gathered, he'd meet a lawyer representing the band and lawyers from the dupe-label, and they'd all thrash it out in the hotel restaurant. When an inoffensive-looking man in Dockers showed up and shook hands with my pal, I was tempted to say, "Do you know what he's got planned for you?" But I didn't.

The two went and sat across the room, where two others joined them. One, a fat, middle-aged guy in a baggy linen suit, spoke so loudly he drowned out the Muzak. He began yelling, "I wouldn't have shot 'em; I would've humiliated 'em. I've got friends in the military and they can get me a fuckin' bazooka." He stood up, clenched his fists as if aiming a weapon, and screamed "*Boom! Ba-boom! Boom!*" His gravelly voice bounced off the sheets of glass and polished linoleum, echoing and magnifying in the tomblike lobby until it sounded like four or five howling boors held court instead of just one. I looked around; not a single person in the lobby – and there were about twenty-five – batted an eyelash.

The fat man wasn't finished. "I woulda took an AK-47 and had those fuckers beggin' me to *piss* on them," he bawled, standing again and grabbing his crotch. His three companions laughed hysterically, wiping their streaming eyes. The fat man went on and on, telling more stories and jokes about turds, anuses, genitalia, and guns. One joke, full of Yiddish and Irish accents and fake Latin incantations, was about a man who dresses up like Jesus in order to butt-fuck a nun; when he's done, he rips off the costume and says, "Guess what, Sister, I'm the guy on the bus!" The nun then rips off her habit and yells, "Well, guess what, asshole, I'm the bus driver!"

The four of them made more noise than I would've thought possible for so few people, roaring, pounding the arms of their chairs, and stamping their feet. A waitress approached to take their drink orders; the fat man asked what was available and then told the woman to bring him what she thought would best fit his personality. It was a form of flirtation in which he asked questions and then cut off her answers with his shouting, rapid-fire shtick. His buddies shuddered in gape-mouthed admiration. The waitress just smiled. She had a huge plume of tangled honey-colored hair and a thick layer of pancake makeup partially concealing the intricate tattoo on her right shoulder. Cheerful and remote, the waitresses all wore sleeveless one-piece tubes of semitransparent material, miniskirted white outfits that clearly showed their nipples and microscopic panties.

The amenities over, the fat man suddenly began speaking with quiet dignity, his riotous crudity gone in a flash. Leaning forward with his elbows on his knees, he looked deeply into the eyes of the other three. He was a lawyer, he explained, who'd done everything: promotion, managing, playing keyboards on albums, and representing some of the biggest artists in music. His recitation of his accomplishments sounded like a eulogy, his expression humble and reverent. He had a thick pad of coal-black hair attached above his left ear and laid flat on the top of his head like a hinged lid, and his wrinkled brown face with its large nose and high cheekbones gave him the look of a friendly old Sioux Indian chief.

I couldn't follow their conversation, which slewed all over the place. From talking about the Indian chief's résumé, the group went on to discuss a hip-hop star I'll call Planet Aptitude. One of the men was Planet Aptitude's lawyer, agent, and friend or brother-in-law; I couldn't catch the last relationship. The Indian chief announced he was doing an album for charity and wondered if Planet Aptitude would be interested. "Is he a nice guy?" he asked, two seconds after one of the others had said, "Planet Aptitude's a nice guy." Planet Aptitude's lawyer-agent repeated that yes, Planet Aptitude was very nice. "Would he do something like that?" the Indian chief asked. He stood and removed his jacket, folding it carefully across the back of the chair so that the designer label inside showed. Planet Aptitude's representative asked what the charity would be. "Child abuse," said the Indian chief. He described the accompanying video, which he said would show that mothering skills were not innate, but were acquired, "just like going to McDonald's." It was a horrific document, this video, and one that had moved the chief tremendously. "We've got to do something about this... this *plague!*" he cried.

The three other nodded gravely. Without warning, everyone began dropping names in a deafening clatter. Mary J. Blige; Tony, Toni, Tone; Toni Braxton. They all knew them or represented them or worked with them. I became distracted when two young guys with neat short hair, short pants, T-shirts, and sandals pulled up two rocking chairs and sat down about six feet in front of me. They produced gigantic cigars, clipped off the ends and lit up. Once they got the things cooking, with all the requisite sniffing, licking, twirling, and sucking, they began tapping the ashes on the floor. I looked around and saw that most of the smokers in the lobby were doing the same. There was a long table to my left with tall bar stools around it. The older-looking crowd on the stools all seemed to know each other, and they all flicked their cigar and cigarette ashes everywhere, despite the many ashtrays. One old fellow tossed the butt of his Havana on the floor and ground it out with his heel, leaving a huge black smear. I now knew the reason for the linoleum, which is much cheaper to replace than exotic hardwood is to refinish.

I went to the bathroom, which had an *M* on the door formed by a beam of light shining through a stencil hidden somewhere in the ceiling. It was an unusual touch, but I was too tired to try and figure out exactly where it came from because I'd been waiting over an hour at that point. Though the bathroom was beautiful, with black marble surfaces and gleaming chrome-plated fixings, it was filthy. The floor and walls around the urinals gleamed with carelessly splashed droplets; the toilets held their terrible contents unflushed; there were puddles of water all over the sinks; and wadded-up paper towels were piled everywhere except in the trash receptacles. As I took it all in, someone unlocked one of the stalls and came out, not bothering to flush. He blew his nose noisily on a paper towel, which he threw into the sink, and nodded curtly as he walked past me out the door, neglecting to wash his hands.

I'd heard that the best hotels and restaurants don't have to change their rolls of toilet paper very often because they're not used up all that quickly. That's not surprising. The rich and successful Players I've observed at parties tend to smell as though they can't be bothered to bathe. It's not hard to go the remaining distance and imagine that they don't wipe or that they just unzip and let loose as soon as they walk into the bathroom, spraying everything in sight.

Back at my seat, I watched a woman on one of the couches juggle her cell phone and a fat cigar. She wore a pants suit and tiny John Lennon sunglasses, her cawing voice occasionally going cottony from the hits she took on her stogie. I wondered what would happen if I went over to her and said, "I'm sorry. I just had to tell you that you look like a perfect jackass." Actually, I realized that *I* was the one who looked like a jackass, outfitted as I was by Ross and K-Mart. Most of the younger women in this realm resembled Italian porn stars, with racy platform shoes, plucked eyebrows, deep tans, and smooth bellies pierced by jewelry. Young men tended to have Ku Klux Klan sideburns and the giddy, chattering, oily vibe of Quentin Tarantino, with that absolute inability to listen. The older women looked dangerous, and the older men seemed to be on another planet.

There was a choking stench like fermenting garbage by the telephones, though it had no visible source. I saw two children while I waited. One was a serious little boy of seven or eight holding the hand of a wild-eyed, unshaven man who looked exactly like Mehmet Ali Agca, the mad Turk who shot Pope John Paul II. He had to be a writer. The other child was a blonde fourteen-year-old girl in a thong bikini. She came in from the pool and stood dripping in the lobby, her hands on her cocked hips. A tubby middle-aged man in a golf cap walked up behind her and stood silently, staring down at her butt as he played a vigorous game of pocket pool. After a few seconds, the girl turned around and jumped slightly as she saw him. "Thare ya arrrr," she drawled in thick L.A.-speak. "I thought ya'd alraady gone up? I was ginna hold tha alavaterrrr fer ya?" Her companion gulped and followed her dumbly into the elevator, never taking his sweaty eyes off her little tail.

After an hour and a half, Chris the tour manager showed up, informing me that the bassist would be an extra hour late. He offered me a beer, and I almost took it but decided that the lobby of this hotel wouldn't be the best place for an event as momentous as my falling off the wagon. When that happens, I'm going to be in my own VIP suite, surrounded by good-looking prostitutes, with a gorgeous private bathroom for me to befoul, my lips wrapped around a massive, stinking cigar, a cell phone in my hand, and an interviewer waiting patiently for me downstairs.

Like Zappa but Funnier

One day I got a call from someone representing a band I'll call Cloaca. She got my name from my friends Roger and Dolores. This rep invited me to a party where Cloaca would play, and I should go because the band was the object of a massive bidding war between major labels due to its amazing originality. Cloaca had already been promised interviews in *Vanity Fair, Harper's Bazaar, BAM,* and *Rolling Stone.* Like Zappa but funnier, the rep said at least a dozen times. She promised to send me a publicity package and a demo.

The weeks passed, and nothing came in the mail. Finally, the day of the party, I got an invitation that said, "Free food! Free Drinks! Gawk at People! Meet New Friends!" Written discreetly in the lower right-hand corner was "Live music by Cloaca." There was also a pen and ink logo, in which the letters comprising the band's name were worked into a sketch of a writhing woman, her mouth agape and her head thrown back. She was either in ecstasy or the corpse of a murder victim; it was impossible to tell. The cartoon woman's breasts were bare, complete with erect nipples. It looked like the work of a talented seventh grader, and there was no demo or bio accompanying it.

I was the first guest to arrive at the house in Hancock Park. The homeowner was a tiny bespectacled fellow with a dramatic Italianate name. Initially he gazed at me blankly. I was told he was a writer for *Star Trek: The Next Generation,* but when I said I wrote for *Bass Player,* he did a double-take and lunged for my hand, squeaking, "Awesome!" The house was gigantic and fashionably bare, only the TV room showing any signs of habitation in the form of books and knickknacks. The rest of the place, including a room that'd been painted the crimson of arterial blood, had only a table here, a shelf there, or an antique leather trunk over in the corner. A young blonde woman in a black sleeveless, backless, chestless blouse – basically, it was just a bra with shoulder pads – carefully arranged dozens of candles in drinking glasses all over the floor. I watched her nudge one candle along a stair, moving it micron by micron with her high-heeled platform shoe. She fussed over it for five minutes, standing back and frowning, again and again, until it was perfect.

Outside, the huge yard was lit by scores of smoky Tiki torches. Two wet bars and an ad-hoc stage were set up near the pool, with three or four tables holding metal trays of chicken and rice, massive bowls of salad, and platters of cake and halavah. There were tubs of iced beer, but no soft drinks in sight. The only non-booze I was able to score was an airline-sized glass of Diet Coke, poured for me by a shocked bartender.

I quickly made friends with Cloaca's soundmen, four young guys from Kentucky attending their first Hollywood party. They were in a band of their own and let me know within eight seconds that Geffen Records had been sniffing around. As soon as they found a bass player, they'd get signed. We talked about Cloaca, and I was again told how amazing and original they were, though Phil, the head soundman, disclosed a little secret: Choo-choo, the bassist, had been playing less than a year. "But she has a great feel for the instrument," he promised. "It's not really what you play, either. It's how you play it. I mean, you know that, I'm sure. The bottom line is, they're amazingly original. They're like Zappa but funnier."

This led to a debate about integrity versus selling out. I said that having failed miserably as a musician, if I could do it over again I'd be as commercial as possible. Once I'd made my money, I'd then switch over to doing the music I wanted to do. One of the soundmen, a kid in a hockey jersey and a Woody Allen tweed hat, paused between gulps of beer. Earlier we'd discussed his hometown, where once you got high with someone, you were buds for life. He'd asked me if I got high; I said no; and he'd slumped in disappointment. He now shook his head and slushed, "I dishagree wish you. I dishagree. Never shell out. Never compromizhe. I mean, did *Jesus* shell out?"

Cloaca was scheduled to go on at 9:00, but they didn't play until 11:15. While I waited, I spoke mostly to the Kentuckian soundmen, watching them hit on the nubiles that began flooding into the backyard at exactly 10:00. These women were slickly tanned and arrived in flocks, as if they'd been released from hidden pens. The yard eventually became crammed shoulder-to-shoulder with people, none of whom had been invited, none of whom had ever heard of the band, and none of whom knew the host. I determined this by shuttling from group to group, eavesdropping. Most of the guests said they were writers and directors. One enormously fat young guy walked up to two other men and said, "Hi, I'm Bob. I don't know anyone here."

"Hi Bob," came the answer. "I'm Terry. I don't know anyone here either." They shook hands and Terry introduced Bob to Mark, his pal. All three were flushed and sweating in the cool night air. They had a pickled, waterlogged look.

"So whattaya do?" Bob asked his two new friends.

"We write for the WB."

"Great," Bob grunted. "I write for Fox." He waited, but Terry and Mark just stared at him. "Aw, you know!" Bob shouted. "*Simpsons? Married? Melrose?*"

Terry and Mark nodded and murmured, "Oooooh."

Bob then told a long, enormously complex, enormously dull story that ended with the punch line "I wanted strawberry shortcake, not frog's legs!" It had to do with a writing assignment he'd once gotten, but it was so full of boastful pleading and incontinent name-dropping I tuned it out word by word. No one listened to him, and from the way his head twitched and his eyes rolled he appeared to want desperately to stop talking.

Before Cloaca went on, I was introduced to the drummer, who bent my ear for twenty minutes on what a great band they were. "I've been playing for seventeen years," she informed me twice, "and I wouldn't play in a band unless they were good."

I was introduced to Choo-choo the bassist, who like the rest of the band may have been in her thirties, but she looked to be about seventy years old, with at least three face-lifts in her history. Her lips were stretched into a perfectly straight line, and her nasal-labial folds – the lines that normally bracket the mouth – had been pulled upward until they were horizontal, right under her cheekbones. When she turned to the side, there was such disconcerting weirdness going on in her profile she looked like a reconstructed burn victim. I was told she'd paid for the entire night, arranging it all herself. No agent or manager had had anything to do with it. Plus, she'd also just built a recording studio in her home. She was also the one who'd gotten all the coverage at *BAM, Rolling Stone, Vanity Fair, Harper's Bazaar,* etc.

The drummer told me how the band had been discovered: Choo-choo, an animal lover, was in her BMW on Laurel Canyon Boulevard at 3:00 A.M. She found a wounded dog in the road and parked perpendicularly to block both lanes of traffic while she aided it, kneeling on the asphalt in her black leather pants. The dog had a tag with a phone number, which she called. It belonged to a famous producer, who said – once his pet was safe in his arms – "How can I ever repay you? Dinner, maybe?" So they went to a restaurant, and in the course of the evening, the producer said, "I produce for rock bands," and Choo-choo said, "Why, *I'm* in a rock band!" And the producer said, "Well then, I've got to help you!" And now Cloaca was about to take off.

Delivered in a cloud of halitosis, the account concluded with, "We're just like Zappa but funnier." The drummer described Cloaca as being more performance artists than musicians, except her. Even though they weren't really musicians, they sang funny songs about penises, like Zappa, but not the way other people might sing about penises. They sang about penises in a different, funnier way. They were amazing and original, and just because Choo-choo had only been playing bass less than a year, I shouldn't be put off. The lead singer had just finished starring in a Broadway play, too, and was back because she loved the band, believed in it, and was committed to it.

When Cloaca finally took the stage at 11:00, they simply stood there, not tuning their instruments, not checking anything, instead milling, drinking, smoking, laughing, and talking. The yard was so crowded I had to stand on a rock wall to keep from being touched. People crashed through the garden and climbed like commandos over the wall, trampling the flowers and brushing against me as they tried not to spill their drinks. Below me, a guy puffed on a giant cigar, his stench wafting directly up my nose no matter where I turned my head. In the darkened yard, the only sounds were an occasional "Ow! Yow! Ow-ow-ow-ow-ow!" There was no music, the guests packed in so tightly the heat nauseated me.

At 11:15, a thin, dismal wail drifted out from the stage, supported by an unsteady *boom-chicka-boom-chicka-boom* from the veteran drummer. The Broadway-trained actress-lead singer strutted, squatted, and whipped her dreadlocks, grimacing, snarling, and flailing away on her guitar, a dynamo of coiled energy and sexual tension. She did everything required of a great front person except sing on key. The negligee-clad percussionist and didgeridoo player swayed dreamily atop a table. I thought her function was purely decorative, but she actually played her instrument once. All I made out was an asthmatic *poot* that didn't in any way resemble the goose-pimple-raising drone created by an Aboriginal master.

The two "gorgeous back-up singers" turned out to be a sullen, girthy redhead and a gnarled biker mama. They chanted "Ya-ya-ya-ya-ya-ya-ya" behind every song and later stripped down to their underwear, the drummer trying to accompany them with a bump 'n grind. At least twice, the band stopped in the middle of a tune and started over because everyone played or sang at different tempos. The lead singer kept chuckling, "Thanks for your patience."

Best of all was Choo-choo the bassist. Fretting the neck with only the index finger of her left hand, hooking the thumb of her right hand over the top edge of the instrument, and plucking the notes with her right index finger as all the strings rang out undamped in a roaring cacophony, she looked as though she hadn't been playing a week, much less a year. Her long, splayed arms and hunched, purse-lipped concentration made her look exactly like a trained circus ape; her performance was as unnatural and heart breaking as that of an orangutan forced to ride a tricycle.

"What the fuck *is* this?" somebody below me yelled.

It was obviously a first wives' club. Choo-choo got a nice, fat, California community-property settlement when her hubby dumped her for a newer model, and then she decided to go out and buy all the things most musicians have to work like dogs to get. The most pitiful detail of all was that the band had security, blimp-like bodyguards in case the crowd of aging Industry drunks – who probably knew every single celebrity in Los Angeles personally – got swept up in star fever and rushed the stage. I bailed after four songs.

The next day, I learned from Roger and Dolores that leading up to the party the Hancock Park house had been the site of countless three- and four-day events in which the best escorts money can buy were made available for label heavy-hitters. Contact took place in every one of those empty rooms, out on the grass, in the pool, and so on. Most of the women at the Cloaca party had arrived at the same time because that's when they'd been contracted to show up. Choo-choo paid for them, too. I heard that after I left, she apologized to the crowd, saying, "We suck tonight," and some guy yelled, "Me first!" People then began chanting, "Take it off! Take it off! Take it off!" Cloaca was never signed. I don't know if they ever even played again.

All I can think of today is this: What would've happened if I'd attended that party with Scott Thunes?

The Most Fascinating Career in Bass

Herb Gordy began as a brilliant jazz acoustic player and finished his career playing in Disneyland. Of course the anti-visionary editor at *Bass Player* wouldn't let me use the best material on Herb; we weren't in the business of entertaining people, since music isn't entertainment. Herb is a cousin of Berry Gordy who played with Earl Bostic and Red Prysock and arranged for Cab Calloway and Lavern Baker, all under the name Herbert Gordy. You can find his jazz recordings on YouTube.

In the mid forties, Herb – a rare left-handed standup bassist – put phosphorescent paint on the edges of the body and sides of the fretboard of his bass so that when the lights went down, the audience saw a green, glow-in-the-dark outline of the instrument. Later in the forties, Herb played with Tiny (Mac) Grimes and His Rocking Highlanders. Grimes was an electric guitarist who had his all-black band play in kilts and Tam o' Shanters. At different times the band included saxophonist Red Prysock and vocalist-pianist Screamin' Jay Hawkins. They sang open harmonies in the style of the Four Freshmen. One night at a club in New York, Herb was violently accosted by a drunken Scottish tourist, angry that Herb wore a kilt.

"What clan are ye?" the Scotsman yelled.

Herb had no idea that the tartan pattern – the "sett" – of a kilt signifies individual Scottish clans. Being a black American man born in the 1920s, he snapped, "I ain't no Klan!"

"What clan are ye, I said?" the Scotsman shouted, and then he was buried under a dog pile of bouncers who roughed him up and threw him out.

Tiny (Mac) Grimes and His Rocking Highlanders got their big break one night in Chicago. They were scheduled to play at the Edgewater Beach Hotel and would be followed by Sophie Tucker. The Highlanders would play several thirty-minute sets after an opening act. If all went well, the booking agent had other great jobs lined up. Grimes was so excited that he had a few drinks to calm his nerves. He didn't eat anything because he was too nervous.

The opening act consisted of a violinist, an accordionist, and a bassist walking around the diners, playing quietly. While they performed, the maître d' – a smooth, well-spoken gentleman – approached Grimes and said, "Mr. Grimes, would you please play nothing but soft music during this first set because this is our dinner hour?" Brush-type music, Herb called it. Always quick tempered, the stressed and now drunk Grimes blew his stack and said, "You don't tell me how to run my goddamn group!"

What Grimes didn't know was that in Chicago, the maître d' actually *did* run his goddamn group. He ran everything in the hotel, including the band. Instead of arguing, the maître d' got on the phone to the musicians' union headquarters. As he did so, the Highlanders took to the stage. Grimes plugged in his electric guitar, turned it all the way up, and played Benny Goodman's "Flying Home" as loudly as he could. The rep from the musicians' union came and watched. After the first set, he pulled the Highlanders' union cards, paid them for two weeks, fired them on the spot, and sent them packing.

Herb went to California in the mid 1950s. He arrived with Earl Bostic, who bought a home in Los Angeles and opened a restaurant. Bostic's six-piece band traveled the state nine months out of the year in two Chrysler station wagons. When the nine months were up, Bostic drove the band to Union Station, paid them, and told them to return in three months for the next tour. "Just like we were a baseball team," Herb said. For the ten years that he lived in California, until his death in 1965, Bostic – born in Tulsa, Oklahoma – was pathologically afraid of earthquakes.

When I interviewed Herb, he was bassist in the Royal Street Bachelors at Disneyland. He founded the trio and played with it for thirty years. Herb told me several stories about the Happiest Place on Earth. He and his two fellow musicians were the only employees allowed to have mustaches. They got their name from Walt Disney himself, who was horrified at the thought of naming them after the awful, debauched, sexy Bourbon Street in New Orleans. They were the *Royal* Street Bachelors instead.

Sarah Ferguson, the Duchess of York, scared everybody during her visit to the park because she had a gigantic armed security detail of agents from Scotland Yard, the Anaheim Police Department, and the FBI. The plan was for her to go right to Club 33, the private establishment beside the Blue Bayou restaurant and the Pirates of the Caribbean ride. However, as soon as the Duchess saw the ride, she announced that she wanted to go on it instead and then eat in the Blue Bayou, which set off a panic among her entourage because they hadn't cleared any of the area. They ended up hustling her inside and letting her ride one of the boats by herself, the craft in front and the one behind filled with security. She then ate alone in the restaurant, surrounded by her guards.

Herb's fondest memory of working in the Magic Kingdom was when a British symphony orchestra toured the park. One of the orchestra's ten bassists was a young woman at least six feet, three inches tall. She'd never seen a left-handed acoustic bassist before and asked Herb if she could play his instrument. He handed it over, along with his bow, and she proceeded to play a flawless, right-handed rendition of Rimsky-Korsakov's "Flight of the Bumblebee" even though the bass was strung left handed.

"Never seen anything like it," Herb said.

The Disneyland gig resulted in Herb's trio being hired to play at celebrities' private parties all over southern California for almost three decades. John Wayne and William Holden were two big fans. Rosalind Russell saw the Bachelors at the park, arranged for them to perform at her party the next month, and then died before the party was thrown.

As Herb pointed out, "We didn't get to play for her."

Repayment for the Best Interview Ever

After "Gene Simmons: Call Him Doctor Love" was published in *Bass Player,* I did something for the first and only time in my career as a music journalist: I asked a record company for tickets to a show, Kiss at the Great Western Forum in Inglewood. I figured I'd earned it. Two weeks went by, my self-esteem withering a little more with each passing day. The tickets finally arrived the afternoon of the concert, my name misspelled on the envelope. By that time, my date had long since bailed, so I went by myself. I thought ahead and parked in a semi-distant lot instead of at the Forum, where about 15,000 tailgate parties were in progress. I made my way through the swarms of scalpers, who'd changed their sales pitches from when I was a college-aged concertgoer.

"Ticket?

"No, thanks."

"Motherfucker."

At the entrance to the stadium, I had my sides, armpits, and buttocks fondled by a disgusted security guard. Inside, I became aware of several things. One is that concertgoers are cattle, herded and prodded through concrete portals and chutes to meet their destiny in chaos and foul, slippery floors. I also learned that for Kiss fans, time is meaningless. I saw hundreds of men my age or older, in black T-shirts stretched over enormous paunches that hung in front of them like sacks of cement. They hurried by with giant cups of beer and cardboard boxes filled with reeking cheeseburgers and fries, ready to power-gobble like growing children. Many of these guys had shoulder-length hair sprouting from the sides of their otherwise bald heads, and the majority were there with their buddies instead of wives.

A few doffed their shirts before the show even started. The Who's "Won't Get Fooled Again" played on the PA, and they danced to it at their seats as if it were the first time they'd heard it instead of the ten millionth. Conical, beer-bloated man-breasts flapped and bounced like the boobs of the best exotic dancers. I felt a rush of déja vu and realized the last time I'd seen these guys was in 1981 at a Clash concert in the Seattle Kingdome, where I'd had to save tiny Joe Cady from being trampled flat in the rush for the festival seating. All of us were nineteen or so back then, and here we were again, together once more in our mid-thirties. I felt a moment of swooning panic, sure I was back at my hellish college, still floundering around as I tried to figure out what to do with my life.

In the Kiss Army, the Women's Movement is as dead as Helen of Troy. I saw the most physically repulsive guys in the world walking hand-in-hand with taut, blonde, cheerful, siliconed cuties, leading them smugly into the fenced-off VIP areas in front of the stage. The women flounced along with pride, their heads high. There's something almost sweet about someone who does whatever it takes to get what she wants. Looking at the men they were with made me admit that those women really earned their seats and passes.

My own seat was in the stratosphere. The stage resembled a neat, toy-like science project, a collection of black matchboxes, test tubes, and saltshakers. I could barely make out vague, tiny movements as the roadies fiddled with the equipment. Up where I was, the women were crammed into miniskirts, jeans, and black leather pants tight enough to damage circulation. These ladies weren't the cheetah-like trophies of the VIPs. One woman in front of me wore white vinyl pants and a tiny halter-top. Her stomach slopped over her belt like an empty brown wineskin. When her male companion slapped her butt, which he did every few seconds, the way you slap the haunch of a good dog, her entire body jiggled. Her *back* jiggled. A ripple ran from her backside all the way up to the top of her head, rebounded, and swept down to her ass again. She drank five enormous cups of beer while I was there. When she turned around I saw she looked exactly like Leonid Brezhnev. She was about twenty-seven years old.

The opening act was a group of nice kids who called themselves Stabbing Westward. After listening to their contemptuous, obscenity-laden rants at the bored, restless crowd, I figured the name had to be a sexual reference. Their songs were all identical, an earsplitting throbbing interspersed with crashes, clangs, roars, and node-embellished yowls. Everything was played in the same muddy key. The band hopped unhappily around the stage, their legs together and their arms held straight down by their sides, and they whipped their heads up and down like crazed iguanas. Then they left, the lead singer snarling, "Enjoy the rest of the shooooow!"

During the intermission, most of the people in the crowd began smoking pot. They also started winding themselves up into a stuporous frenzy, like zombies trying to slam dance. The spirit was willing, but alas, the flesh was weak. I wondered what was going to happen when the concert ended, because everyone was drinking, getting high, or both. That guy over there, the one with the tattooed neck, the Megadeth T-shirt, the hair that had been cut with Playskool scissors, and the rotted, gap-toothed grin – the one swaying and coughing and roaring "*Paaarrrrty*" – was he the designated driver? He must've been, because he was much better off than his comatose pals. Thousands of weaving, careening vehicles would be unleashed on the streets and freeways as soon as the show ended. I felt doomed.

Suddenly, the lights went out, the audience lurched bellowing to its feet, and a voice warbled, "Lehdies an' gennelmen, yoo ast f' the best, yoo got it, th' hottes' ban' inna lan' – KEEISS!" The floodlights snapped on and a giant curtain with the band's Nazi-ish logo on it fell to the stage floor, accompanied by explosions as loud as municipal-strength fireworks. And there they were, the four of them, playing "Deuce." The guy next to me yelled "All right! Rock and roll!" He took out a pipe and had a few hits of pot or meth or crack. He was at least forty-five years old, with a swollen red face and a ghastly hair-weave. On his third hit, he gagged on his smoke and dropped the pipe, giggling "Whoopsie!" as his knees folded and he collapsed into a boneless pile on the cement floor. After a few seconds he pumped his fist feebly. I assumed he was still alive, though it could've been just a final reflexive spasm.

The audience began singing along with the band, which was unfathomably *loud*. To recreate Kiss's sound, at least to my plugged, oversensitive ears, take an empty fifty-five-gallon oil drum, drop a switched-on Black and Decker circular saw into it, add an old-fashioned upright vacuum cleaner also switched on, and toss in a live cat and a double handful of steel ball bearings. Put your head into the drum, have a couple of friends bang the sides with sledgehammers, and scream "*Waaaaaaaaaaaaa*" at the top of your lungs. My ears rang even with the plugs, a first for a stadium show.

I left after only four songs, woozy with secondhand pot smoke. The people around me were so relaxed they'd lost control of their bodily functions, puking like faucets or letting rip with sulfurous cheeseburger-farts of unimaginable pestilence. Body odor combined with the smells of spilled beer, vomit, intestinal gas, and weed to produce a miasma I could actually taste when I breathed through my mouth. I also knew if I stayed until the end, it would take three hours to get home, if I even made it at all with these thousands of impaired, middle-aged kids driving like bats out of hell, flooring it to be the first out of the parking lot. My mission to experience a Kiss concert was an abject failure.

Still, I'm forever grateful to Gene Simmons for the terrific performance art we created together.

One Last Duty to Carry Out in Music Journalism

On April 14, 2012, I sent a letter I should've written in 1997. Judging by the difficulty I had going through with it – especially after the recipient's gatekeeper told me I shouldn't send it because it came across as completely insane – I realize now that it would simply not have been possible at the time.

> Dear Ray:
> Interviewing you was the proudest moment in my career as a music journalist. The first Gentle Giant song I ever heard was the live version of "Free Hand" off *Playing the Fool,* which was played for me in 1981 by my college roommate, a punk rocker of all things. I had been playing the bass for a couple of years at that point, and listening to you shred that bass both exhilarated and depressed me. I knew now how high the bar was set. I was eventually able to duplicate most of the live version of "Free Hand," but there were always passages that eluded me. In the next life, hopefully.
> I've been offered a book contract for my memoirs, *Ghosts and Ballyhoo: Memoirs of a Failed L.A. Music Journalist,* which will be published by Schiffer. It'll chronicle my ten years in the deranged fleshpots of the Los Angeles music and entertainment world, my descent into all-consuming rage and ultimate physical collapse, and my pursuit of Frank Zappa bassist Scott Thunes, who had – like you – not played his bass in years. Unlike your story, I felt that his was tragic, and I brooded about it for fifteen years, trying to persuade him to allow me to ghostwrite his memoirs.
> The book will be about being haunted. Scott Thunes haunted me, and the way my new editor at *Bass Player* callously and laughingly killed my article about you haunted me right up until I got my book deal. I was never able to tell you that the article was killed, because it was a continual source of shame and rage at the sheer injustice of it. You had spoken to me in good faith, and my magazine had repaid you by tossing the article in the trash.
> In the book, I'm going to tell the story of finally interviewing my bass idol and having the article killed. Ironically, you – like so many other bassists I interviewed – had set a terrific example for me on how to overcome reversal of fortune with grace and dignity, but I wasn't able to perceive the warnings you and the others gave me. The lesson of my book is this: If it's not a good fit, you must make a change.
> The publishers want a photo insert, which I'm going to devote only to people who've had a positive influence on my life. If you agree, I would like to include you. It can be any photo you want, current or vintage, with a bass or without, a band photo or you alone, print or high-res scan. When the book is published, I'd like to send you a copy.
> I realize I wasn't responsible for what happened to your interview, but it was – until just a month ago – one of the most deeply shameful and haunting episodes of my life. I've now been able to put it behind me. I've finally banished it.
> If you prefer to not be involved in this project, I fully understand. I'd still like to send you a copy of the book, though.
> With much respect and gratitude,
> Tom Wictor

When Ray's representative contacted me, I wrote to her that the gatekeeper had said the letter made me appear unbalanced and possibly dangerous. I'd requested that he send it to Shulman anyway because everything I said in it was true and I couldn't sugarcoat the past. Ray is free to think I'm insane, as is everybody.

Her reply.

> I totally relate to a lot of these things you went through fighting hard to get assignments for your favorite artists, and perhaps feeling a bit of shame for articles that get killed along the way. I think that's a great note you sent.
> You've got great style.

An Aphorist Reaches Out

As I purged myself of so much that had tormented me for so long, I got an e-mail from Lola, my high-school friend from Norway, who'd suggested I take up the bass. We hadn't spoken in years. Her timing was amazing. The last time I saw her was in 2001, when I visited the Bay Area. We went to a club to watch a jazz band with an electric bassist we'd heard about. He'd developed a playing technique of putting his thumb and forefinger together, as though he were holding a pick, but it was just his fingers. Lola was all hyped up. Unusually, she wore a tight, red satin dress and heavy makeup. For as long as I'd known her, she'd been a tomboy.

The lights went down in the club, the music started, and *zowie!* This bassist was a genius. He was a blistering soloist but had Thunesian taste. I couldn't wait to pitch him to *Bass Player*. He had CDs available, so I figured my editor couldn't say no.

He did, of course.

After we left the club Lola bubbled over. "Wasn't that a great band? I loved the vocalist's technique. You know how you project like that? You squeeze your butt cheeks together. Listen."

And she let out a piercing, operatic, pitch-perfect high note that she held for about twenty seconds. When she stopped, a homeless man with a full shopping cart across the street yelled at us, "Jesus Christ, shut the fuck up! What's wrong with you people?"

Lola and I went to a doughnut shop and had chocolate-iced buttermilk bars that were about two minutes old. They were crunchy on the outside, soft and warm in the inside, the best doughnuts I've ever eaten. I told the Cambodian storeowner that he was a national treasure.

"For making doughnuts?" he said. "Man, are *you* easy to please. Your wife must love you."

In her e-mail, Lola wrote that she really needed to talk to me about my past. She said she'd understand if I didn't want to get into it. Her message ended with, "I know you are intelligent and well read enough to understand what I am referring to. You are the one who directed me to Alice Miller's books."

I sent her my unlisted phone number and told her to call me because she was my friend and I loved her. She phoned immediately and we caught up for about twenty minutes. As always, there was no awkwardness between us. I then asked her what it was about my past that she wanted to talk about.

The discussion was much harder for Lola than it was for me. I was very careful – not only for her sake, but for mine as well. I lost Carmen over just such a conversation. Therefore I only listened and asked questions. I no longer describe my past to anybody because doing so has always brought me grief. Only two people didn't change after I disclosed the details of what happened to me. One was my therapist, and the other is Scott Thunes.

Lola and I spoke for an hour and came to no conclusions, but I told her she can call me any time. She has more talent than anyone I've ever met. Since we've reestablished contact, she's now my most enduring friend. I was seventeen when we met, and she was fifteen. She can play any instrument, sing, draw, and she's a terrific athlete. The most striking aspect of her complex personality is her vastly superior intelligence; she's as curious and famished for information as Carmen was when I knew her. Over the past thirty-three years we've spoken often about relationships, fate, and free will. We have similar beliefs, but she reacted to her difficulties with sadness rather than all-consuming rage.

She's the originator of one of the most profound aphorisms I've ever heard, which she told me in 1992. I finally accepted it in March of 2012.

> Even if you're lucky enough to find your soul mate, it doesn't mean that both of you will be ready for each other at the time.

Truer words were never spoken, Lola. In August of 2012, I authored a follow-up aphorism that I'm sure you'd appreciate.

> The mandate that two people are supposed to be together can expire.

I Mean It: I'm *Not* a Music Journalist Anymore!

When I was a music journalist, I'd get unsolicited CDs in the mail several times a week from artists and labels pushing a new release. Some of them were beyond belief. I once took a punk CD and played random spots on every track for Tim: They were all identical. It was as though the entire CD were just one unbroken blast of spluttering, meth-head shouting; two-chord guitar played by an eleven-year-old; machine-gun bass; and that polka drumming that punk bands do, *oompa-oompa-oompa-oompa,* all at 500 beats per minute.

There was a quartet of toothless, middle-aged, death-metal truckers from the South, whose press release was riddled with f-bombs and racist epithets. They were ugly, bad, moronic, and agonizingly boring. Their songs had titles like "Gator Shit," "Pussy Grease," and "I'll Fuck Your Ass, Buddy."

Another quartet of chubby, old boys with rock-star dreams posed with three-quarters-naked sluts half their age for the CD insert, everybody smeared with food. The music was abysmal, a dozen tinker-toy caricatures each written in about two minutes, celebrating porn, drugs, homophobia, men who want to breast feed, masturbation, voyeurism, hatred of law and order, and finger fucking. In the credits the artists all thanked their families.

Some bands had a sledgehammering, anti-Christian message in every other track; political protest bands promised that their horribly banal music would end war forever; wall-of-guitar corporate rockers churned out anthemic snoozers that I completely forgot two seconds after they ended; and one band with an obscene name was composed entirely of homely girls with raccoon eyes, singing off key about how they wanted to be degraded receptacles for bodily fluids. Each CD was worse than the last. I wanted to write the publicists and labels and say, "Look, next time take all the money you want to spend on your latest purveyor of sewage and just send it to me. These people aren't going to make you a penny. What in God's name are you thinking?"

For some reason I was inundated with CDs from a particularly awful but successful band fronted by a chinless poseur who drove me crazy with his supermodel-skinny thighs; his necklaces; his awkward, hopscotch prancing on stage; and his smug style of singing, especially the hipster-megadork way he delivered the word "momma." I never understood why the band was so huge. Finally – thank God – they went "on hiatus" and I stopped having to throw away CDs that I never even bothered to unwrap.

I still get CDs to this day, even though I haven't written a thing about music since 2002.

Some **Will**

A great bassist and extremely attractive woman told me this.

"I never went out with musicians, at least not the typical L.A. guy. They always say, 'It's not gonna work if both of us are in music. If you really loved me, you'd give it up. We can't both be chasing a career because then we'd be pulling in two different directions.' Besides, you always end up supporting them. It starts when they say, 'Uh, I don't have any money today. Could you buy me a cheeseburger?' Then, it's 'I don't have any money for gas. Could you lend me twenty bucks to fill up my tank?' And then it's 'I'm gonna get evicted if I don't come up with the rent! Can you lend me $500?' And finally, it's 'Well, I got evicted. Can I come live with you?' Screw that. I have no patience with troubled relationships. I never let my friends complain to me about their relationships because they never *do* anything about them! If it's bad, bail and cut your losses. Either it's going to work or it's not. I'm not at all sentimental about relationships.

"I spent my whole childhood convinced that the world was going to be blown up someday, so I studied music like a maniac because I wanted to take it as far as I could before they dropped the big one. Now, it looks like they're not going to do it for a while at least, but I'm still bugged by that feeling. I can't waste my time on things that aren't working.

"Musicians always want something better. They're never satisfied with what they have, and they'll do anything to get a better gig. *Anything.*"

Un-Ghosting the Cardinal Ghost

In the midst of the strange and exciting goings on at Talkbass.com and elsewhere, I decided to take another chance. There were still some things I wanted to say to Carmen after all. I e-mailed her and unburdened myself to her, too.

> Hi, Carmen:
>
> I'm doing what they call taking stock, and it's actually pretty amazing. I can't play bass anymore, and I also have an incurable affliction called Meniere's disease, an autoimmune disorder that causes "rotational vertigo" attacks, where the world spins until you projectile vomit. It eventually causes hearing loss. You can manage it with medication and a super-restrictive diet (paper, water, and dirt, mostly), and it often goes into spontaneous remission after a few years. But in the meantime I'm pretty much housebound, 'cause I can't drive far. But you know what? I'm happier than I've been in years. I'm shedding all the bullshit, and I'm finally seeing things clearly.
>
> We had a black feral cat adopt us a year ago. He looked and acted exactly like my brother Tim's cat Syd, who died in 1998. This cat was so feral he hated all people and cars, but he came right into Tim's back yard and climbed up into my lap. When we opened the back door for him, he went into the house and jumped up on the sofa to take a nap. He had the same breathy meow as Syd the First and the same giant fangs, and he liked to have you sing to him while he ate. He also loved my mother and her house, which Syd the First did, too.
>
> He came to us with feline leukemia, so we had him only for a year. He was a little black shooting star that whooshed into our lives and then disappeared. But when it came time to send him back home, Tim told him as the drugs took hold that he can return any time he wants. Tim was devastated by the death of Syd the First, but now he talks about having another cat. And now he believes in an afterlife, which he didn't before. Syd the Second showed us what we'd already begun to suspect. I've attached a picture of Syd the Second in the Angry Chair

outside my back door, where he sharpened his claws. You can see the claw marks all over the wood. He was a moody bastard when he first showed up, but by the time he died was his old self again.

So even though I'm housebound, I'm doing better than I've ever done. There's no bullshit in my life anymore. Only the important things count. In honor of my hermitude, my wisdom (giggle), and my upcoming 50th, I finally did something I always wanted to do: *[Photo of me with my new gray full beard.]* I think I make a pretty decent old man.

So what's the damage on your end? Have you grown a big gray beard, too? Wanna let me see what you look like these days? It's a cliché, but it took me losing so much to finally get to where I always should've been. So I'm actually grateful. Did I ever tell you I was grateful for the time we had together? I hope you don't think it's inappropriate for me to say that. What can it hurt, really? I haven't seen you in 20 years, and I'm trying to let people know what they meant to me. I don't think that happens enough. If it bothers you, I'm sorry. That wasn't my intention. I want to honor you more than anything else, the way I'm trying to honor everyone who had a positive impact on me.

I've begun talking about my failed career as a music journalist. People seem to like it. If you're still interested in music, give it a peek. *[Link to Talkbass. com thread.]* Okay, then. That's what's happening. I hope all is well with you and yours, and if this is too much to deal with, give it a pass. I'll completely understand.

Take care,
Tom

She responded.

Hey, Tom.

I'm sorry to hear about your Meniere's diagnosis, but happy that you're finding happiness. Your Arthritic Tom stories are highly entertaining, but it's also frustrating not knowing the identity of your subjects.

I love the Syd the First and Second stories. Didn't Syd the First chirp like a bird when he was given turkey meat? You were the one who taught me about cats. I remember I thought [my cat] was very ill when I found her curled up in my closet drawer and you said, "She's just being a cat." I've been missing her tenderly since she left us in Sept. 2008. I didn't think she could be replaced, but two months ago I spontaneously rescued a snowshoe cat and gave him the name [withheld]. He's a delightful soul - full of spunk and thoughtful curiosity.

You've asked to see what my half-century-plus-one self looks like these days. For the past decade or so I've rarely been seen without a hat, so I don't know why I'm sending you these two hatless photos of me - I HATE any photo of me (with or without a hat), but since you already know me... why try to hide....... the second photo is with my daughter [withheld] ..... and the third is [my cat].

I don't understand why your facial hair is so white and the hair on your head is NOT.

Carmen

The photos of her had a massive impact on me. In the first one she looked fine. I was glad to see that she hadn't jacked up her face like every woman her age in Los Angeles. She was just the Carmen I knew and loved so long ago, a beautiful, mature woman with a pleasant expression, not quite a smile but close. There was more than a hint of the campiness I'd found so attractive in her. It was – I thought – a satire of someone who's trying to look serious for a portrait. I may have seen what I wanted to see, or she may have done precisely what I perceived her as doing. There's no way for me to know without asking, and it's not my place to do so.

In the second photo, she looked exactly like the woman in my Leslie Ditto painting *Deep Thoughts of a Pilot*. The pose and expression were nearly identical; both women even wore scarves. I printed out the second Carmen photo and took it into to my closet to compare it to my painting, which I haven't hung on the wall because I don't want it to get dusty. Carmen could've been the inspiration for it. She looked absolutely miserable and shell shocked, making no attempt to hide her pain.

For years I'd told myself that it was silly to think Carmen and I were destined to be together. I must've imagined already knowing her the first time we met. Now, I entered a state of indescribably intense emotions. It seemed that – like the year with Syd the Second and the way this book came to be – there was major significance in Carmen's photo matching a painting I'd been compelled to own the second I saw it over two years earlier. It couldn't be just a coincidence, but what did it mean? What, if anything, was I supposed to do about it?

First I wrote Carmen a quick message.

> Yes, Syd the First chirped like a bird when he ate turkey meat. It was hilarious.
>
> As for our culture's stupid-ass taboo on growing old, fuck that. I literally don't give the tiniest shit possible. You told me that you were sending me photos of your "half-century-plus-one-year-old self," but I think you're absolutely gorgeous, as you always were to me. I know the pressures that women face in this superficial society. It's all a load. I've opted out of most of our popular culture.
>
> T.

After a day or so of thought, I decided to push my luck with Carmen. Everything had taken such surprising turns that I thought it was now or never. I sent her a message.

> May I tell you something? It's about the photos you sent me. If you'd rather not get into it, I perfectly understand, and it won't upset me at all. What I want to tell you is an attempt to make amends and maybe to offer you something in exchange for still trusting me enough to send your photos.
>
> As I said, if you'd prefer not to, it's absolutely all right. I think you'll understand what I want to say to you, even if at first it may be a bit jarring and may not sit well. I think you'll understand my intent. It has to do with me being in a place in life where it's important that I thank people who had a positive impact on me. What I want to say to you is only about how I reacted to seeing you again.
>
> Up to you. No hurry, and no pressure. In fact, you don't even have to respond. I won't be upset. I promise. I'm putting you on the spot, so forgive me if I'm overstepping.
>
> Tom

She replied.

> Hi,
>
> I'm confused by your message. It seems like one long disclaimer....... a preface to what you're trying to say.
>
> WHAT do you want to say? WHAT was your reaction to the photos I sent? You thanked me for sending them because you said it was important for you to "see" me. You made a comment that you're in favor of how I look (and always looked) - THAT'S always nice to hear.

You haven't overstepped anything nor have I found anything that you've written to be inappropriate. So there's NO need to apologize in advance or after-the-fact for anything you express.

JUST SAY WHAT YOU WANT TO SAY.

Thank you.

C.

This was it. I plunged in.

Okay. Here goes. I don't know if you intended it or not, but in the photo you sent with [your daughter], I thought you looked very sad.

Since we broke up, I never cried. Not once since 1994. After I got your photos, I can't stop crying. Not because I'm sad, but because you confirmed to me that it was all real and not a hallucination. You said that you hated to be photographed and you always wear a hat when you are, but you said that since I knew you, there was no point in hiding your face.

My time with you was the most fulfilling period of my life. When that period was over, the doubts began to creep in. I wasn't sure anymore. I'm an obsessive writer, and I save everything I write. I went back and reread everything I'd written about the end of our relationship, and I thought that maybe I'd just fooled myself and had projected all these fantasies onto you. I was really angry at myself for a long time for thinking I'd fooled myself and been fooled, and it was all a waste of time, etc., etc.

I found a description I wrote about how I felt when I first met you. I won't include it here because it would be even more inappropriate than what I've already written. I started to think I must've imagined that whole scene, and my relationship with you must've been unreal. I now know it was real. In that endless Talkbass thread I keep blathering on about clarity. It really is the most important thing to me now. As long as I can see things clearly, I don't care if my hands or body or anything else craps out. If I die tomorrow, I'll die happy because I can finally see. It's amazing.

You gave me the best time in my life, and it wasn't supposed to happen. I'm not overstating it by saying you saved me. And for that, I'll always love you. I hope that's something that can give you strength when you need it and not upset you. I think you understand where I'm coming from. When I found out Steiv Dixon had died, I regretted never telling him how much he really meant to me. I felt terrible until he visited me in a dream and told me he was happier where he is, and I should stop worrying about him. He ordered me to stop, actually, in that bossy way he had. I didn't want to make the same mistake with you, even though by doing so I'm violating conventions. So if this upsets you, please forgive me.

Thank you for the opportunity to get it off my chest. I'm almost done being haunted by the past. All the pieces are slipping into place, and I see now that I'm actually incredibly lucky to have had our time together. There's nothing for me to be sad about. It was very rare, and I'm eternally grateful to you. I hope knowing that you have an undying fan will help you when you need it.

Take care,

Tom

Her response.

My, oh, my. Thank you for opening up your heart to me. I always knew that you struggled with your history. I didn't know that I represented a break from that mold.

I'm very curious to know how you felt when you first met me.

I'll tell you what I thought: you represented strength, intelligence, and humor to me. And then I tested all that by [withheld]. Clearly that was an unfair challenge to put you through. I'm sorry.

Very sad about Steiv. I didn't realize how much he meant to you.

How interesting that you detected sadness in the photo of me with [my daughter]. What most people consider a sad expression, I see as REAL. Perhaps you can tell me when the crossover happened between olden day photographs when the subjects merely WERE and the days when subjects were told to say 1 - 2 - 3 cheese. I utterly loathe smiley pictures.

Thank you for partaking in these exchanges. Your timing is uncanny. I'm currently on a three day retreat by myself.... so I have the luxury to be on my own schedule and I'm enjoying our electronic tête-à-têtes.

C.

I wrote back.

Here's what I thought when I first met you:

"I would never have gone for her, that flirty beautiful type, except for the fact that the second I saw her, I fell instantly in love. *Kaboom.* I saw her, and I said to myself, 'Oh. *There* you are. I've been looking for you. Where the hell have you *been?*' It was like we'd known each other many, many times before, and had been waiting to reconnect again in this life. There was an instant recognition; I even recognized her scent, which was all her own because she never wore perfume. As soon as I saw her, that first time, I remembered what her body felt like. She had the most amazing flared-out hips, and as I looked her over in her faded jeans, I knew exactly what it was like to sit on the edge of a chair as she stood in front of me, leaning into me, her arms around my shoulders, my arms around her pelvis and my cheek resting against the warmth of her stomach. This was a memory, not a fantasy. As I was being introduced to her, the nerves in my face and forearms began tingling as they recalled what it felt like to touch her. It was as though I were waking up. When we went to bed a couple weeks later, it was all familiar. I was my usual awkward self in the sack, but she still made me complete. She told me later that as soon as she saw me, she felt the same thing, that we were meant to be together. That has *never* happened to me before. She's the only woman who ever pursued me."

Don't get me wrong: I remember our problems. But my point is that you gave me the opportunity to experience something that shouldn't have happened. So for that I felt the need to thank you. All our problems – to me – were worth what you gave me. I don't think I ever told you that. I didn't really realize myself until recently.

I'm sorry for misinterpreting the photo of you and [your daughter]. In all the photos I have of you and me together, you're smiling, sometimes broadly. You have a gorgeous smile. I always felt guilty about how we left Japan. I feel I pressured you into it, and maybe you would've been happier if you'd stayed there in your DJ job that you loved so much.

My ghosts are releasing me, and I feel wonderful.

T.

She answered.

Tom.

You've described in depth the thoroughly sucky hand you've been dealt. You've also explained how you have been and are trying to navigate through this life in the healthiest way possible with as little damage to those around you.

Please understand that I've never blamed you for any of the choices I made. I admit that I've often wondered what would've happened if I stayed longer at the radio station, but Tokyo life for expats was a slippery slope and it makes me shiver to think that I could've easily grown very old there.

Even though we had some very tumultuous time together, I will only remember your essence which is an intelligent and good person..... I also hope your humor is intact.

I'm always here for you to talk about anything.

C.

P.S. It's funny that I thought about you just a few days before you emailed me the first time in this thread. I was listening to NPR's "This American Life" which featured Mike Daisey doing his monologue on Apple in China. (The podcast aired 1.8.12 and the show has since dedicated another episode to all the falsities of Daisey's "theatre journalism.") But I exclaimed to my kids HOW much Mike Daisey's humor and observations reminded me so much of YOU. Have a listen and be well.

And then I did push her for what would be the last time. I pushed harder than I'd ever pushed since we broke up. Without comment, I e-mailed my favorite picture of us. It was taken in a photo booth in Tokyo in January of 1988. She sat on my lap; it was winter, so we wore heavy coats. I loved her in heavy coats, gloves, jeans, and boots. The contrast of the heavy, masculine clothing with her rare, fragile beauty was intoxicating. In the photo I'm smiling with a sort of poleaxed expression, delirious with happiness, and I look as though I'm uttering a wordless noise of rhapsodic befuddlement: "*Ihhhh!*" She's radiant, with her best smile, beaming with magical, eternal, eye-squinting, uncontainable bliss, showing all her teeth, completely at ease and seemingly ready to burst, not just a goddess of beauty but one of mirth and elation, too. And it was because of *me*.

Her reply to this photo.

GAG. I look so goofy. I remember that very early happy time.

C.

I loved her goofiness. It was what made her special to me. I still miss it, and I know I'll never see it again, in this or any other life.

Her reaction hurt. I was the only one who'd ever gotten her to smile that way for the camera, and now it made her gag. But I could blame only myself for forcing open the door. After brooding for a few days, I described this series of exchanges to a friend. His response took me a while to decipher.

Cute! I love her even more.

You know why? Because it doesn't sound like she was angry with you. She merely explained herself. I like that, a lot. Kudos to her for being smart and kind to you.

Also, and I'm sure you know exactly what I'm talking about, I FUCKING LOATHE automatic smiling in photos. I always give the instruction to not smile. Sometimes it turns out well, other times, the subject takes this as an excuse to FROWN, which is the exact opposite of not-smiling. Not-smiling is one layer deeper than not-mugging. Don't fucking mug in my photo or I'll fucking take it over again.

So, yeah, you were right to love her. She's giving it right back, which is nice.

Now no more subtexting!

I gradually agreed with all of that, since it was true. One of my worst character defects is reading subtexts into things when they don't exist. My friend had once again zeroed in on the real problem. Carmen hadn't said anything wrong; what did I expect, that she'd tell me she wished she could be back with the one man capable of producing that smile in her? She's a completely different person now, who'd forgotten how we both felt when we met in Tokyo. In fact she'd forgotten almost everything about our relationship. As she said, I still know her, but her destiny has long since broken with mine. I'd put us both in an untenable position by e-mailing her the picture.

The ache I felt over her words faded, though I was still concerned about the sadness in the second photo she sent me and how the image perfectly matched my Leslie Ditto painting. However, I'm fully aware of boundaries, the delicacy of the subject, the suffering I caused, and areas that are not my business. I have no desire to disrupt, which is why I lard up my e-mails and letters to everybody with so many annoying disclaimers. Carmen had heard what I wanted to tell her. My message had been delivered. After another week or so, following a lot of research into owl symbolism and deciding what *Deep Thoughts of a Pilot* meant, why I was led to it, and what I was supposed to do about it, I made my decision. I let go.

In doing so, I drew on a conversation Carmen and I had in Tokyo about a song by the short-lived Duran Duran spinoff band Arcadia. The tune always made me choke up. Carmen liked it but said my emotional reaction was caused simply by the melodies and vocal harmonies in the chorus, which were third intervals. The music is moving by design. It's manipulative. I now accept that Carmen is in the same camp as the First Ghost, Brigitte, who told me, "I *do* care about people; I really do. But it's just not that big a deal for me to leave them if I have to. It's painful, but I can do it. I don't agonize over it." And that's fine. We're all individuals, each with our own methods of navigation.

The title of that Arcadia song that still chokes me up: "Goodbye is Forever."

Yet even after clearing the air with Carmen, fully acquiescing to our outcome, and jettisoning all the pain, anger, and sadness I'd felt about her for nearly 40 percent of my existence in this particular cycle, I still asked the question that'd stumped me since 1993: How do you live – now and however many more lifetimes – without the person you recognized and remembered the first time you saw her?

And then at long last I found the answer, by picking up the book that has brought me peace of mind like no other. The answer is, you don't have to.

> *I looked here;*
> *I looked there;*
> *Nowhere could I see my love.*
> *And – this time –*
> *She was in my heart.*
> *Truly then, I have no complaint,*
> *For though she be fair and fairer,*
> *She is none so fair as she*
> *In my heart.*

Finally, I could say in all honesty that I had no complaint.

Endnotes

[1] "Interviewing Bassist Stories," (accessed April 28, 2012).

[2] Wictor, *German Flamethrower Pioneers of World War I* (Atglen, Pennsylvania: Schiffer Publishing, Ltd, 2007), pp. 211-212.

[3] "Interviewing Bassist Stories," (accessed May 2, 2012).

[4] David Vincent, interview with the author, January 27, 2000.

Lessons Learned

Now let me crunch you
With full weight of affrighted love.
I doubted you
– I doubted you –
And in this short doubting
My love grew like a genie
For my further undoing.

Try not to think of this as preaching. I believe I've kept the preachiness to a minimum. It's more like your drunken uncle babbling away at a family reunion because he's on a roll and can't stop. If there's any point to this memoir, besides allowing me to get a few things off my chest and entertain you, it's to try and help people avoid making the same mistakes I did. So take these tidbits for what they're worth. Feel free to ignore them because one man's lesson is another man's... appendectomy? Catamaran? Fried rice? Beats me. I'm not trying to tell you how to run your life. Rather, I'm explaining that the way I ran mine won't work for anybody. Trust me. Still, these are only *my* lessons learned.

First a non sequitur: You may have noticed that an astonishing number of the most profoundly important events of my life happened in August, including my birth and the deadline for turning in the manuscript for this memoir. I have no clue what it means. Maybe something to do with this?

> An "august" man was one filled with the spirit of the Goddess... Probing ancient views of the Goddess is instructive. It shows a female figure is almost always more powerful than the male.[1]

It's confusing. My emotional reactions are more female than male and I'm attracted to butch women, which makes me august and therefore more powerful than the average man? I don't feel powerful; I just feel odd. But odd isn't all that bad, I suppose. Since I don't have a choice.

On to the lessons.

Recognize the Pig

Scott Thunes warned me about this in 1996 and 1997, but I didn't listen. As he says, I was a cute little muffin-cucumber with mush in my heart. He was the grizzled veteran of North Africa, Anzio, Normandy, and the Battle of the Bulge trying to tell the apple-cheeked replacement what war is really like. Impossible.

What happens is that people adopt a lifestyle first, and then they grow into it. Tim describes it as people moving into a house where everything is already laid out for them: clothes, furniture, car, even spouses and future children. It's a turnkey life. In the recovery industry, they have a saying: "Fake it until you can make it," meaning you should act as though you're sober and functional, and soon you will be. I never accepted this advice because the opposite is also true: "If you fake it, it can take you." A lifestyle will alter your values. You can't exist in a milieu without it changing you, like in the movie *Shock*

Corridor, about a journalist who poses as a mental patient in an asylum to get a story, and eventually he goes genuinely insane.

When the lifestyle takes over, there's no return. As the joke goes, "For breakfast, the chicken makes a contribution, but the pig makes a commitment." What I didn't accept until virtually yesterday is once the commitment is made, that's it. People can't undo their commitment any more than that slice of bacon can become a living pig again.

During my year of psychotherapy, I learned why I've always reacted with rage to being misunderstood and denigrated. I interpreted it as a negation of the self, which is what the primal experiences of my past did. They obliterated my identity. Most of us don't or won't accept that everybody reacts to the same circumstances differently. For some there's recovery. For others the damage is so great that only a semblance of life is possible. It depends on innate temperament. For those condemned to that twilight existence, there may be brief periods – say, three years, for example – of fulfillment if the stars align. These short intervals can't last, however. That's why every second of them must be seen as a gift. When they end, the bearer of the gift must be honored for creating that which would otherwise have never been. The bearer of the gift is a conjurer, magicking out of thin air something unfractured and clean. Something defensible.

In my twilight world, clarity and communication are paramount. When my attempts to communicate didn't get through, it made – note the past tense – me lose my marbles. Understanding that about myself was only half the battle. The second half was accepting that there are people with whom I will never, under any circumstances, be able to communicate.

That was what ended up costing me nearly everything, my refusal to accept that no matter how hard I tried, some people will simply never be open to what I say. If I'd recognized that in 1999, when I finished my therapy, I wouldn't have lost so much. On the other hand, I also wouldn't have written this memoir, and I wouldn't have the hard-fought appreciation for life that I have now. Even so, my advice to anyone reading this is to not take the route I took. Losing almost everything you love is an incredibly steep price to pay for clarity. For me there was no other way, but don't use me as a role model. Really.

People can and do throw away their minds and souls, and there's nothing you can do or say to reach them. Nothing. They're as committed as the pig, and as dead as fried-up bacon. They'll continue along the same path, forever. All you can do is disengage. Often it's a God-awful tragedy, painful beyond belief, but once you accept that they're committed, it's time to say goodbye.

Lost Lemurs Should Keep Moving

I was always tortured by my seemingly insurmountable talent for not fitting in anywhere and being able to kill conversations with anybody, whether millionaire musicians, managers, publicist, editors, military historians, tow-truck drivers, or homeless crazies. Then I saw a TV documentary about lemurs that explained everything.

The documentary was filmed on Madagascar or some other locale teeming with lemurs. There were so many lemurs that they'd evolved into entirely different species, each with its own distinct culture. There was one segment of this show that explained my life in about twenty-five seconds: A lemur from one species got separated from his tribe or clan and wandered into the territory of another species of lemur. Terrified, the lost lemur tried to interact with these stranger lemurs, using all the gestures and vocalizations of his own species, but the different lemurs had no idea what this lunatic was doing. They just stared blankly until the lost lemur gave up and huddled on the ground in total confusion and despair.

The mistake I made my entire life was trying to fit in with the wrong species of lemur. Unlike the lost lemur in that documentary, though, I'm no longer huddled in confused despair, devastated by the reactions of others.

I may never find my species. But that's no reason to give up and become consumed by impotent rage. It isn't the fault of the different lemurs; they're only doing what they were programmed to do. Alien gestures and incomprehensible sounds are just upsetting to them. A lost lemur needs to recognize that he's wasting his time and get the hell out, the faster the better for everyone.

If You Don't Like the New Cheeseburger, Stop Eating It

If Wendy's redoes its cheeseburger recipe and you don't like it, you have a choice of either continuing to eat there or stopping. How stupid would it be to keep going there every day to buy the new cheeseburger that you hate, getting angrier and angrier as you eat it day after day? The recipe has changed. Go somewhere else.

I do regret not being able to try Wendy's new cheeseburger and decide if I liked it or not. Meniere's disease makes it impossible to eat any fast food, ever. On the other hand, I'm thinner than I've ever been in my adult life. Most men really start packing on the weight at my age, but I'm still slimming down. Despite the benefits, I'm not a fan of this particular dieting regimen. My niece used to spin in circles until she was so dizzy she fell over. She's the only person I've ever met who loved being dizzy. I wish I'd inherited whatever mutated gene she has because I could then travel again and eat whatever I wanted and not care that the world spun like a centrifuge. I could even enjoy it.

So far I haven't met anybody who loves projectile vomiting. There are *National Geographic* photos of drug addicts undergoing some kind of cleansing treatment in a Tibetan monastery or somewhere, and they've been given a super-ipecac that makes them instantly projectile vomit. The photos show the addicts kneeling with what looks like jets of soapy water or white ectoplasm eight feet long coming out of their mouths, and they seem unbothered, their eyes closed and their hands spread loosely on their thighs. It's a meditative pose, kind of relaxed. But nobody appears to be actually enjoying it. There aren't any smiles, zany expressions, or peace signs flashed at the camera. It's businesslike projectile vomiting.

The comedian Dane Cook says that when you throw up, there's a tiny part of your brain that's having a good time because you imagine yourself as a vomit-breathing dragon flying over people, puking and crying. I see myself more as a vomiting phoenix careening up from the ashes.

Luckily my treatment has kept the rotational vertigo at bay for months now, except for two attacks that occurred because I was under incredible stress. During the first attack I had to call Tim to come take over for me. He arrived, loping along in his grim, apelike gait, read the riot act to my stressor, and the issue was resolved. Someday, instead of calling my brother, I might just projectile vomit into the face of the person causing me stress. I promise that you'd rather have me throw up like a fire hose on you than deal with Tim when he's in his II Samuel 22: 38-43 mode.

The point is, if it's a bad fit, you need to stop, a lesson I learned only after it was too late.

Know When You're Dead

After years of telling myself I was haunted, I discovered *I* was the ghost. I haunted the offices of *Bass Player,* the streets of Los Angeles, and the fog-shrouded Bay Area, long after my physical presence was gone and the people whose lives I'd touched had moved on. One of the theories behind the existence of ghosts is that they're the spirits of people who don't know they're dead, or who refuse to accept their circumstances, or who can't relinquish. All described me perfectly.

Luckily I was a minor-league, introverted ghost who haunted himself instead of others. I'm grateful that I didn't spend the last twenty years being an insufferable pain in the ass for anyone except myself. The past two decades weren't wasted, because I learned how to write and I became the planet's greatest expert on World War I flamethrowers, whose work has captivated untold smidgens of people. But being an angry ghost took a near-fatal toll on my emotional and physical well-being. If you can avoid it, don't become a self-haunting rager. Look instead to the examples set by John Taylor, Andy West, Curt Smith, Scott Thunes, and, of course, Ray Shulman. Your immune system will thank you.

Be Ready for Anything

This memoir was utterly unplanned. It turned out to be the best writing I've ever done. I owe it all to the readers of Talkbass.com.

In honor of them, I deleted my YouTube account, deep-sixing all the ridiculously belligerent comments I made over the past five years. Then I opened a new account under my real name and re-uploaded my "Mobile" video. Anyone who watched it could now do so without being annoyed by the stupid, self-indulgent things I said when I was anonymous and such a slave to anger that I went looking for online fights with even angrier people not worth a scintilla of my time or emotion.

I thought I'd never overcome my compulsion to have pointless arguments with strangers about things over which neither of us had control. Giving up all that self-generated conflict is one of my few inarguable successes.

Laugh at Yourself; Everybody Else Does

During the worst of my time with Carmen, the period in San Francisco when she regarded me as her mortal enemy, I saw an episode of *The Mary Tyler Moore Show* titled "Edie Gets Married." It made me laugh even though it was a dagger in my chest.

Lou Grant's ex-wife Edie told him she was about to remarry. He cheerily announced it to the newsroom and then immediately went off to a bar. Mary tracked him down and asked if he was all right. He answered that he was fine but just wanted to be alone for a while. When Mary suggested that he might still have feelings for his ex-wife, he said no, it was an entirely different issue: They'd been married twenty-three years, divorced for two years, and now she was about to marry someone else.

The problem was that they were drifting apart.

I still laugh at that scene, marveling at how writer Bob Ellison allowed me to find humor in my own agony. It's no longer a dagger in my chest. Instead, it's more like an emphatic tap with a finger, made by a close friend caught up in the heat of an argument. There's no reason for me to get upset. These things happen. What's important to remember is how much the friend tapping my chest means to me, despite the momentary twinge that finger causes.

God Only Guards the Tool Shed

When I sent the short story "Flashback: A Druid in Los Angeles" to Stephen Jay for his approval, he responded with one of the most remarkable messages I've ever received.

Reading your heartfelt words about the music I write was for me hitting the mother lode. I mean that in this way: Until you hit the mother lode, as a miner working on blind and sometimes delusional faith, you really have no way of knowing if there's "gold in them thar hills" or not. Your words convinced me that there is. I have now, as of this day, July 1, 2012, "seen" it. And I am forever changed.

This is really wonderful. Over the years many people have given me very positive feedback. But no one has ever expressed experiencing the transformative power as persuasively as you have. Your gift as a writer has enabled you to open my mind up to the most important truth there can be for me. That I should continue writing.

I came up to my studio this morning to work on a new song that really slips the bounds. It's called "God Only Guards The Tool Shed." It came to me in a literal flash, with no clue of why or what it meant. On reflection I realized that it could be a very nice way of saying we can have faith in our capabilities. Something in the universe appears to favor that idea.

I love writing music like a climber loves tackling Everest, because it's almost impossible and yet sometimes it feels like you can get there. It can be more painful and challenging than anything else I have experienced. As you know, the strength to jump off the cliff and become fully engaged to do that are always the issues.

Who knows where that strength comes from? Well, this morning I do. It comes directly from you! I am so energized and encouraged by what you said that this song is going to be fantastic. The essence of collaboration! Here we go. You will hear the new song very soon.

Thank you!

Steve

The song is indeed fantastic. It's beyond genre. The best way to describe it would be a kind of reggae-tango with completely unexpected rhythms, changes, melodies, and vocals that elicit powerful emotions. Stephen somehow managed the incredible feat of creating a song that's uplifting and mournful at the same time. It mysteriously, ingeniously articulates the gamut of the human condition, and it asks far more questions than it answers.

Here are some of the lyrics.

It feels like that's what it's for
God only guards the tool shed
Maybe a little more
Than before we started
Using the tools like instruments
Only way that matters now
Is if it all stays safe and sound

I hear what they're saying today
Better clean up the tool shed
Put all the stuff away
Spend the day finding each tool a proper place
All the saws and solder guns
And lock it all up once it's

Done and gone and put away
You-know-who's guarding it night and day
Over her shoulder

Those all-seeing eyes
Might envision a grander prize
Than I can disguise

Everybody's had déjà vu, the phenomenon of feeling you've experienced something before and you're reliving it. The French term means "already seen." You've also had presque vu, or "almost seen," the sensation of being on the brink of an epiphany. It's when a word, name, or memory is on the tip of your tongue.

Stephen Jay is the undisputed master of musical presque vu. He offers glimpses of meaning, and you almost grasp what he's saying. It can be maddening, but therein lies the potency of great art. I'm humbled to have played even a tiny part in the creation of this terrific song. It also helped me realize that what I've been doing recently is putting my tools in their proper places as I envision a grander prize. I believe that God does guard the tool shed, but it's entirely up to us to use our tools properly, keep them in working order, and clean them.

Thank you, Stephen, for both the gift of this song and a more poetic way for me to express one of my deeply held convictions.

Tune Out the Moon-promisers

For some reason when you achieve even the tiniest modicum of public exposure for anything, millions of strangers contact you and tell you all the wonderful things they're going to do for you. Don't believe any of them. I was promised ghostwriting gigs, consulting gigs, screenwriting gigs, columnist gigs, reviewing gigs, offers to write liner notes, offers to be interviewed for documentaries as an expert on flamethrowers, an interview with the BBC(!), offers to consult for documentaries on flamethrowers – none of it panned out. Not a single promise was kept. I agreed to them all and never heard from anybody again.

It made me furious, which was wrong. The world is full of those who pretend because it's fun. So when people you don't know offer you fantastic opportunities, thank them, accept, and then put it out of your mind. They're mental patients.

Watch for Patterns

To my long-ago archivist boss, who sang sea shanties and hissed, "Is there a pattern?" before firing me, I'd have to say yes, there are patterns everywhere. Not only did my actions comprise one big, self-destructive pattern, there also appear to have been all sorts of much nicer patterns at work. I may have been guided here every step of the way. In the introduction to this memoir I stated that I believe in both destiny – what I define as opportunities crafted for you specifically – and free will, the decisions you make when presented with those opportunities. After writing this book, my conviction has only been strengthened. Watch for the patterns. They might help you perceive your destiny, make the right decisions, dodge a lot of grief, and endure that which you thought you couldn't.

As I completed this book, I bought a photo postcard on eBay that really interested me for no apparent reason. It showed three young soldiers of the First Russian Special Brigade, Russian Expeditionary Force, serving in France. These men fought as assault troops with great bravery and distinction, taking massive casualties. Addressed to a woman named Frida and dated June 12, 1916, the postcard had a handwritten message that my friend Colonel Supotnitskiy transcribed for me so I could have it translated. It condensed everything I've expressed in this memoir into one incredible paragraph. Those of you who don't collect World War I postcards might not know that nearly all messages on them say things like, "Dear family: Everything is fine. How are things with you? Thanks for the pickled cabbage. Please send socks. Best regards, Hans." Finding something like this is unbelievably rare.

>Dear Frida!
>Here is direct proof that I am alive. But to what degree I am alive – this, apparently, should be of the most interest to you. I will respond to this only with silence; I do not wish to say anything because if you do not believe in me, then with what reasoning can I convince you, and why should I convince you and, for God's sake, for what? Each person approaches life from his own side, and something that one sees as the higher motion and progress of life, another would see without a doubt as a sign of death. In addition, not under the influence of external conditions of life but because of the inner workings of my mind I have changed my views so much that, if you have kept yours, it would make me their enemy. Thus speaks your friend who is now a devotee of pure thought, natural philosophy and, consequently, of occultism. Write about yourself. Address: Petrograd, Main Post Office, Secteur Postale 1-89 Française, Special Marching Battalion, 5th Company, 4th Platoon, F. Eger
>P.S. Enemy of your views because we saw lies and did not speak about it.

Writing my book has taught me one immutable fact: None of us are alone. Distance, circumstances, or even time may separate us from our kindred spirits, but that ought not diminish the power they have to sustain us. I hope F. Eger survived the war and he and Frida ironed out their differences. Their conversations must've been epic.

Be Grateful

When I spoke to so many formerly huge musicians who were in greatly diminished circumstances but weren't angry about it, I hadn't yet lost enough to appreciate what I had. It was only when I'd lost nearly everything I loved that I finally understood how important it is to cherish every nanosecond of happiness you're granted. Be grateful for all, because gratitude is what helps you accept loss.

On August 11, 2012, I terminated a relationship. As you may recall, the diagnosis of Dave, the Best Therapist in the World, was that the most I could hope for in life was to more quickly recognize that once again I'd gotten myself involved in a situation that would cause me harm. This faster recognition would allow me to extricate myself sooner if I were honest enough to admit the truth to myself. In this case, I was able to see the truth in only six months.

As a believer that our soul survives the death of our jalopy bodies, I used to worry that in the eternal afterlife I'd be just as messed up as I was in the physical sphere. I'm now convinced that we get several chances. There's been a definite upward trajectory in my understanding, so maybe after four million cycles I'll be whole. On the other hand, my cat Syd the Second shook off his dysfunction in only eight months, even though his brain was the size of a walnut. And *his* problems included uncontrollable biting and a deep terror of rugs. He really puts me to shame.

Ending this relationship overwhelmed me with a level of sadness I hadn't experienced since October of 2011, when the sorrow and rage that had defined me fell away. The grief of my loss triggered a severe rotational vertigo attack – the first in eight months – and the irregular heartbeat that had plagued me for most of my life. For a few hours I thought I'd die. Yet when I recovered physically, I found myself thinking only of the good memories she'd left me. My gratitude for those memories sustained me during my period of mourning, a process that for the first time didn't include anger.

I'd done an art installation for her as a birthday present. If you've read this far, you'll know that I always give women art. This was the first art project I'd attempted in twelve years; it was also to be the first art I'd given to her. She told me she didn't understand birthday presents. Why reward someone simply for being born? The truth is that the day you're born is when you as a named individual come into being. All cultures recognize the power one can have over someone by knowing their name, so the tradition of giving you gifts on the day you're born is to protect you. The intention is to ward off evil. Giving birthday gifts is human behavior that's unambiguously altruistic. It unites us in a desire to help each other overcome our shared vulnerability.

The installation was based on a battered antique seashell box with twenty cubbyholes. Though this woman hates being photographed – of course, and naturally she's also a small, dark-haired musician – I glued into the cubbyholes fifteen of my best images of her with and without her instruments, a shot of her cat, three reproductions of her painted self-portraits, and a picture I'd been lucky enough to take during one of the most uplifting moments we'd shared. It was a real challenge fitting the photos because each cubbyhole was of a slightly different size; the person who constructed the box was sloppy, so some of the cubbyholes were wider at the bottom than at the top. The only way to fit the pictures tightly was endless trial and error, slicing away narrow strips with a razor blade and steel ruler. Because of my eyesight, it took a long time.

I sprayed the box and photos with a clear matte acrylic coating designed to protect against moisture and UV damage, then I had the whole thing finished with a professionally made frame and a sheet of UV-resistant glass. It epitomizes the intended recipient's aesthetic of "crude elegance": a gray-painted wooden box a hundred years old – roughly nailed together and covered with unexplained spatters of green and red, white flecks of ancient sea salt, and the pencil marks of the long-ago craftsman who made it – married to a simple walnut frame and a sheet of glass. The sturdy, splintered, seasoned housing protects my musician, her creativity, and her cherished cat, hopefully for all time. My plan was to present it to her in person as a surprise. To do so I would've had to drive quite a distance, taxing all my endurance and probably endangering myself. It was a risk I would gladly have taken.

Since I wasn't able to give it to her, I kept it for myself. Though it's painful to look at it, I don't mind. Pain doesn't scare me anymore, and the images also represent happiness that outweighs whatever else I feel. The installation was to be my gift to her for what she'd given me. She was never able to receive it, but she knows what she meant to me. It's one of my best pieces. She would've loved it.

Someday, when I'm ready, I'll hang it next to *Deep Thoughts of a Pilot*.

Being Single, Middle Aged, and Housebound is More Hygienic

I still experience fitful little putt-putts of anger when I interpret something as a negation of the self. Since I rely on my computer for communicating with the outside world, it hurts when I get no response to my messages. To help me through these stormlings of petulance, I remind myself that most people have incredibly busy lives, full of spouses, children, jobs, and endless social commitments. I must be understanding of that, and more often than not, I am.

Several years ago, in West Hollywood, I saw a beautiful woman seated on a bench outside a store. I stopped and dawdled because she was truly breathtaking: about forty, with straight red hair to her shoulders, high cheekbones, sexy calf-length zip-up boots with high heels, faded jeans, a black leather jacket, and little round sunglasses. As I discreetly ogled her, two other women arrived and greeted her. This beautiful woman leaped to her feet and shouted as she hugged them, "I been so busy I haven't even had time to *wipe* my *ass!*"

People are busy, my fellow shut-ins. Show some empathy, for crissake.

Ignore Every Dietician and Exercise Guru

The secret to permanent weight loss and a state of perpetual physical fitness is Meniere's disease. Of course, you can't travel or go out to dinner with your friends, but that's what imaginary friends are for.

Let Them Run

The hardest lesson I had to learn was to identify the runners and not go chasing after them. All my life I entered relationships – romances, friendships, close acquaintanceships, collaborations – characterized by someone confiding in me, or giving me what I felt was an unmistakable signal, or coming right out and pleading for my help. When I responded, suddenly I was left in the dust as the person took off with the cartoon bongo-feet sound that ends with the *pcheew* of the high-speed exit. The confusion and despair this engendered in me are extremely difficult to get across. It genuinely caused me physical pain.

Yes, I know that there's a psychological syndrome called the "savior complex," which compels you to help others in order to both bask in the love and gratitude of those receiving the aid and garner the admiration of observers. Saviors can be quite narcissistic, controlling, and codependent. They can be angry, bitter, and manipulative, seeking out people with terrible problems so that the saviors can avoid addressing their own deficits and failures. Often saviors are self-pitying, histrionic martyrs who depend on validation from others, and they're generally impossible to reach, always knowing better and refusing to listen.

All true. But, as the famous – and probably apocryphal – quote from Sigmund Freud goes, "Sometimes a cigar is just a cigar." Sometimes we simply want to help because we hate to see others in torment. Besides, plenty of the people I tried to help were utterly disgusting specimens of humanity whose love would've sent *me* running for the hills. I haven't been able to find a syndrome that best describes my urge: helping on the condition that nobody acknowledge it to me or anybody else. I'm sure there's some twisted motivation there, but I'll let someone else figure it out. I've hit the wall when it comes to second-guessing myself.

It took me decades to break my habit of chasing runners. Like a retired foxhound, I still dream of the chase, of course. A certain turn of phrase, expression, or image, and I have the urge to bolt, disregarding the knowledge I acquired at such great cost, hoping that this time I'll catch up.

The bongo feet and *pcheew* take many forms. Sometimes they're manifested as nothingness. You relay a heartfelt response to what you perceive as pain, trouble, or an appeal, and the answer is dead silence or a complete changing of the subject. Other times you're told something like, "That's so amusing! What do you mean? I simply don't understand why you'd think that!" Usually, however, what runners give you in return for your offer to help is hostility.

It's both a game – a form of hide and seek – and a survival tactic. The running keeps the house of cards from collapsing in on itself. And therein lies the anguish for me because in an echo of the dualism word game Carmen and I played in a different era, the runner is like Schrödinger's cat, dead *and* alive simultaneously, fleeing you *and* reaching out, rejecting *and* embracing his or her circumstances, hellishly aware *and* in total denial.

Your mere words can destroy a life. The irony is, it's the runner who gives you such power. The faster they run, the more powerful they make you. And if you chase them, you'll grow in strength and destructiveness. Without meaning to, you'll become a tornado, earthquake, tsunami, hurricane, wildfire, and plague all rolled into one. By trying to help, you'll lay total waste.

So be merciful. Call off the chase and just let them run.

Don't Hate Yourself *When* You Backslide

I'm no angel. The last thing I want is for readers of this book to think I'm all cured and now I give off radiant beams of well-adjusted good cheer, like Nick Nolte after his single crying jag in *The Prince of Tides*. No matter how hard I try, I'll always have anger issues. Don't forget that the Best Therapist in the World recognized that there was a limit to how much I could improve myself this time around. On May 10, 2012, my computer hard drive crashed. Let's skip over the surreal farce it was dealing with indifferent, incompetent, dishonest pricks in order to get a new hard drive and restore my data, which I'd had the rare good sense to back up. I was without my computer for a week, in the middle of working on the greatest piece of writing I'd ever produced. There was no choice but to write in longhand, which was tough because of the arthritis. I couldn't sleep at all, seething at this latest blow.

On May 14, I looked out my window at 7:30 A.M. and saw one of Tim's large aloes strolling past on two tiny, pink-clad legs. What in the name of unholy, thermonuclear thunderation *now,* I thought. I snuck out my back door and discovered it was a miniature Asian woman, stealing a tree-aloe worth several hundred dollars. Tim had cut it off and left it in the back yard behind my house to dry out before he replanted it. This woman – with her bright orange hair and pink sweatpants – had come onto my property, down a 100-foot driveway, and taken the aloe, which was not visible from the street.

She wore a black fanny pack that could've contained anything, so I decided I'd better not confront her. Instead, I followed her up the street, hiding behind cars and the edges of buildings. We traveled one block south and approached a gated community. When she unlocked the gate and had trouble holding it open as she tottered under the weight of the fifty-pound aloe, I ran up and served as doorman. She staggered ahead without acknowledging me; I therefore followed her into the enclave, tagging along twenty feet behind until she arrived at her apartment and went inside. After noting the number and the street name, I came home, let myself into my parents' house to make sure they were okay, and then called the cops. While I waited, I wrote a detailed description of the woman, including the fact that she had a monkey face.

When the squad car arrived, the deputy laughed at the monkey-face line, told me to sit tight, and roared off. My mother came out and we inspected our properties; the tree-aloe was the only thing missing. In about twenty minutes, the cop returned with the Asian woman and Tim's aloe in the back seat of his car. I identified her through the window as she bowed, grinned, and clasped her hands in supplication. When asked, the deputy advised us to not press charges because it was a misdemeanor and he wouldn't be allowed to testify for us.

The woman allegedly spoke no English, and her adult daughter had said to the cop on the phone that it was all a misunderstanding. Her mother was a *Viridiplantae* Good Samaritan who wandered the streets, rescuing abandoned photoautotrophs. She thought the tree-aloe was going to be thrown away and had to save it. The cop said the thief had already potted it in her back yard and proudly showed him. I asked him if I didn't press charges, would he think I'd wasted his time? He assured me that I hadn't, because he'd recovered the valuable aloe. If we pressed charges, the woman's lawyer would be guaranteed to sue us for false arrest, and we'd have to pay legal fees and make multiple court appearances, while the low-income thief would certainly get a public defender.

I agreed to not press charges. The cop called the thief's daughter on his cell phone and brusquely ordered her to tell her sniveling mother to never come on our property again, because he now knew where she lived. If anything happened to us, he'd go right to the thief's house first. As I took the aloe from the back seat of the squad car, the thief bowed, smiled, clasped her hands, and sucked air past her teeth. "I soddy, sah," she said. "I soddy."

And right there in front of my eighty-four-year-old mother, I said, "Yeah, you're sorry you got caught, you fucking cunt."

Mom just gazed into the sky, watching the clouds. She didn't approve, but I think she understood.

Although angry, I didn't indulge in the volcanic rage I would've unleashed a few months ago, and within an hour I felt nothing at all for the thief except tired disgust. I even called the sheriff's station and spoke to the watch commander, commending the deputy for his professionalism. The lieutenant wrote down all my comments and told me it would go into the deputy's file.

The thief was very fortunate: When I later told Tim what'd happened while he slept, he calmly described to me what he would've done if he'd caught her and how he would've gotten away with it. The frightening thing is given her diminutive size, it would've worked perfectly.

Stay out of my yard, everybody. For your own sake. In fact, if you ever visit my hometown and see a skinny jogger with a red-and-white beard and abnormally long, sinewy arms, give him a wide berth. He really doesn't want to talk to you. I'm privileged to be one of the few people whose company he often enjoys, but it took us years to get there. The rest of you have no chance. Don't push your luck.

Confront Your Demons

Watch *Bad Day at Black Rock*. It has the best fight scene in the history of cinema.

Although I don't belong to any church, I was raised a Catholic. My parents remain devout Catholics who attend Mass every Sunday. Over the course of writing this memoir, I had lots of discussions with my mother about the themes I covered, including my lifelong struggle to confront and banish my demons. One evening I mentioned to her that I always had a weakness for the Catholic archangel Saint Michael because he's an armed and armored warrior, not some namby-pamby, languid, New Age androgyne with luscious lips. I love the term "archangel." It implies the sort of untainted, resolute, unapologetic purpose I always wished I had. Michael the Archangel destroys his opponents without a second thought.

The next day, Mom gave me a laminated copy of *The Raccolta* 447, "Prayer to Saint Michael the Archangel," an invocation of exorcism written by Pope Leo XIII in 1888.

> *Saint Michael the Archangel,*
> *Defend us in battle;*
> *Be our protection against the wickedness and snares of the devil.*
> *May God rebuke him, we humbly pray:*
> *And do thou, O Prince of the heavenly host,*
> *By the power of God,*
> *Thrust into hell Satan and all evil spirits*
> *Who wander throughout the world seeking the ruin of souls.*
> *Amen.*

Having experienced more than my fair share of wandering, evil spirits who sought the ruin of my soul, I gladly welcome Saint Michael the Archangel to my side. He's doubly welcome if he looks like the ferocious entity rendered in bronze by August Vogel, which stands over a defeated devil at the main gate of the Sankt Michaelis Church in Hamburg.

Develop an On-Off Switch

For people. It sounds heartless, but it really isn't. To survive, you must be able to instantly write off those who transgress. When they do or say certain things, they show you that it's no longer necessary to consider their desires or feelings. The truth is, you're not writing them off; they're writing themselves off.

Save your concern for the deserving. Like faeries, they'll reveal themselves if you're patient and kind. Keep in mind that they've had to develop on-off switches, too, due to their own experiences. They don't like having to flip that switch any more than you do, so they're careful. Caution is always warranted.

Before I wrote this book, I was unable to adopt Tim's policy of having an on-obliterated switch. It came in quite handy on occasion to have someone in my life who has such a switch. But I recently discovered that *in extremis* I have an on-obliterated switch myself. So far I've used it only once. I don't want to get into the habit of obliterating people who implacably try to impose their will on me for selfish, petty, vindictive reasons.

Scott Thunes told me that he'd love to see me just once thoroughly kick someone's ass. Well, I did, Scott. I did such a good job that the ass in question will never be un-kicked. It'll have footprints on it forever, like the surface of the moon. The thing is, I took no pleasure from it, and I didn't feel better afterward.

However, I have very little remorse for flipping my on-obliterated switch that one time. I can't decide if not being conflicted over what I did is a loss or a gain. Regardless, it's not something I ever want to do again, so my request to everyone – my non-negotiable demand – is to let me live out the rest of my life without being subjected to any more games, head trips, power plays, gaslighting, or stalking, all right? I still bleed when I'm cut, but I've learned to cut back – twice as deeply.

Thank you for your cooperation, and you've been warned.

If it Looks Like a Hole, It Probably is

In the early summer of 2011, I went into Tim's back yard on my way to his house for one of our afternoon conversations. I saw what I thought was our cat Syd the Second lying on the flagstone path to my left, but he looked weirdly flat. On closer examination, it turned out to be a black hole in the path. I carefully sidled up to it and discovered that it was several feet deep, with a second hole at the bottom. A semicircular wall of bricks was visible through the second hole. I went and got Tim, and we examined both holes with a flashlight. We determined that this was an abandoned septic tank we hadn't known about. My mother confirmed that the house had its own septic tank until the mid 1930s, when a municipal sewer system was put in. The tank had not been filled in, and now the brick roof had collapsed.

With our flashlight we could see that the septic tank was full of water, the surface of which was over six feet down. A fall into the tank would've been fatal if nobody had been around to pull you out. Being underground, the water was cold; hypothermia would set in, and you'd drown. Or you might've drowned immediately because you could've been knocked unconscious dropping through the second hole, hitting your chin on the rim or having bricks rain down on your head as the rest of the curved roof caved in. Even worse, a ton of earth could've fallen on you, ramming you far down into the blackness of eighty-year-old sewage.

We tied a rock to a length of twine and dropped it into the water to measure the depth of the tank: thirty feet. Judging by the curvature of the wall of bricks, it was five feet in diameter, which made it 590 cubic feet in volume. To fill the tank, we had to use sand, because rubble would leave too many voids. We therefore had pallets of paver sand in fifty-pound bags delivered to my house. A total of 1180 bags of sand were needed. Tim and I took bags of sand from the pallets; carried them thirty feet, including up two steep concrete stairs into his back yard; set them next to the hole; slit them open with a box cutter; and dumped them into the septic tank. All day, morning to night, what we did was walk, lift, carry, set down, slice, and dump. We repeated that process 1180 times, in the process carrying twenty-nine and a half tons of sand. By the end of the third day, the tank was filled.

To recapitulate: A mortal danger appeared at the heart of the circumstances in which I'd existed for over twenty years, and I didn't recognize it. I'd been within inches of total disaster for two decades without even knowing it. To rectify the problem required unbelievably hard, tedious, exhausting, depressing labor that had to be done because there was no alternative. When the work was finished, the problem was permanently solved, and I was grateful that Tim and I had been spared.

It was the most allegorical experience of my entire life.

Allow Yourself Time

In my pre-Meniere's life, I was a fanatical lover of Chinese food. Some of my best memories revolve around it. In college my floor mates and I went to an all-you-can-eat Cantonese buffet every Sunday, where in the course of a grand debate a kid named Mike dubbed me a "convictionless amoeba," one of the greatest insults ever uttered; Carmen was as devoted to Chinese cuisine as I was; and the best time I had with Roger and Dolores was a massive Szechuan orgy we had at the apartment of a hilarious actress who parlayed her deep, raspy voice and unusual appearance into a respectable career.

I didn't think much about the fortunes that came in the cookies. Then I had a visceral reaction to one: It nearly made me bawl. I got it on an August evening in 2010. Though I felt weak and fatuous believing it – a drowning man trying to save himself by grasping at a floating marshmallow – this little slip of paper was emblematic of compassion and support I'd encountered only a handful of times. It was *positive*. So what if thousands of copies had been printed up? The Golden Gate Fortune Cookie Factory in San Francisco produced it. For me, anything good associated with San Francisco is to be treasured. I mounted the fortune on a piece of acid-free paper and framed it so I could look at it every day. Here's what it says.

Allow yourself time – you will reach success.

As far as I'm concerned, I'm there, because I was able to banish the worst of the anger, bitterness, sadness, and self-hatred that crippled me. Everything else is gravy. The goal has been achieved. Hopefully, there's still time for whatever else I want to try in the earthly realm. If it happens, fine. If not, that's okay, too. Another sentiment expressed by Gore Vidal and shared by many: "It is not enough to succeed. Others must fail."[2]

Actually, that's not true anymore. I've failed enough for every single member of the human race, so now we're all free to succeed.

You're welcome.

On August 4, 2012, my friend Colonel Supotnitskiy sent me a birthday message.

We, the Supotnitskiy family, congratulate you on your birthday. We hope that in the next fifty years of your life you will realize all your creative plans and will preserve many of your youthful ideals. Your contribution to the study of the history of World War I will be more appropriately evaluated, as there is currently no other quality work on those historical events that you have studied. For the true scientist there are only books, not titles and ranks. Continue to operate in the same direction, to act constructively and creatively. As a historian, you're trying to find the truth and not reduce historical events to the usual clichés; this will ensure the longevity of your books.

We take this opportunity to congratulate you. Give my best congratulations to your parents. In the words of Vladimir Mayakovsky: "Make nails of these people..."

You, too, will be a nail in thirty years and beyond.

With sincere respect and appreciation for your work,

Your M.S.

Who would've thought?

Don't *Follow* Your Dreams; *Believe* Them

Though falling asleep has always been a challenge, my dreams are like films that stay with me. I often write them down. Most of my dreams are nightmares, the worst of which came during the period I was apart from Carmen in 1989 and recurred in cycles after I lost her. The nightmare clusters were sometimes triggered by contact with her; other times they began for no apparent reason. They usually involved me unsuccessfully trying to find her or else reuniting with her only to face her hatred, ridicule, or indifference. Some of these nightmares were so painful that they were like previews of what I imagine hell is, an eternal state of aloneness, hopelessness, sorrow, and horror.

Yet some of my dreams are overwhelmingly beautiful. Recently, I've had several in which Carmen and I are friends, having lunch at sidewalk cafés or driving along the coast somewhere, talking and laughing the way we used to. Banal to you but rapturous to me.

The first dream I ever wrote down dates from 1968, when I was six years old. Though I finally put it on paper at the age of thirty-three, recording it wasn't necessary because I still recall every second of it perfectly, as though I had it last night. It took place somewhere up in very high mountains with lots of jagged peaks and vertical faces, like the Alps or Himalayas. The mountains were covered with pillars shaped like giant bowling pins standing upside down. They were narrow at the base and flared out into a rounded bulb flattened at the top. There were thousands of them, each about 100 feet high, covering the peaks like a dense forest. On the top of each pillar was a bald monk in an orange robe, sitting cross-legged in the lotus position.

I shinnied up the nearest pillar, and as I got to the top I realized it was made of rubber. It swayed gently on its narrow stalk, forcing me to hold on tightly. I was terrified. The monk sitting on the top of the pillar smiled at me and told me not to be afraid. He said I had to jump off with him. With that, he began bouncing up and down, still in his sitting position, and then he leapt off. With the speed of a rocket, he careened all the way down into the valley thousands of feet below, his legs still crossed. He somehow maintained an erect posture, his hands folded casually in his lap as he sent rocks and dust flying in all directions.

An overwhelming sense of liberation and great fun hit me. There was no way I could get hurt. I jumped off after the monk, bouncing down the rocky side of the mountain, which was actually as soft and resilient as the mattress on my bed. Though I wasn't able to stay in a sitting position and rolled around violently, sliding first on my stomach, then on my back, then in a tightly curled ball, it didn't matter. As I went over the edge and plummeted into the abyss, all the other monks jumped off their own pillars in an avalanche of orange. We fell into the valley and became fireflies, glowing with our own light, and then we all rose together and flew into the dusk, side by side, in our millions. I felt incredibly happy and excited, as if nothing bad could happen to me, ever.

Things Just Might Turn Out All Right

When I was sixteen, I died. It was an attack of irregular heartbeat, the primary cause of death from cardiac arrest. Medications have kept my episodes under control since 2007, except for the one I experienced on August 11, 2012.

The night I died, my heart skipped beats, raced, and thudded so heavily I could feel it in my neck and fingertips. It was an extremely hard time for my family: I'd had two separate fist fights with two different brothers that evening, and now, as I tried to sleep on a rollaway bed in my grandmother's living room, hating everyone and everything, wanting to exterminate the world, I felt my heart stop. It was exactly like a power outage. I had time to think, "Uh-oh."

Suddenly, I shot up off my cot, passed through the ceiling of my grandmother's house, and zoomed into the sky. The night was cool and quiet, with patches of stars showing through the clouds. I accelerated violently, but it didn't bother me because I didn't have a body; I was light and diffuse, like a gas. My emotions were lighter, too, the fear, anger, and hate fizzing off into a kind of mild surprise. Ahead was a dark tunnel. As I entered it and streaked toward a dot of light in the distance, a sensation of absolute peace swept through me, from my vaporous toes to the top of my vaporous head. I felt a presence beside me, inside me, all around me, something that was both male and female, yet neither. It radiated an indescribable love, compassion, and understanding, far beyond a human's capacity. It was a being of metahuman perfection, the ideal balance of intelligence and emotion. And it was good. It was so good that I felt shabby and primitive in comparison, like a Neanderthal.

"Don't worry," the presence said. "Everything will be all right." Its voice was soft, musical, and stupefyingly, inconceivably powerful. I wanted to laugh and cry with relief because this being had absolute knowledge; it knew my worst thoughts and deeds but didn't turn away in disgust. It stayed with me, guiding me toward the approaching light that somehow didn't hurt my eyes even though it was brighter than the sun. At the end of the tunnel, a vista opened up. It encompassed all of creation, universes within universes, everything that had ever been and ever would be. The nearest I can come to describing it is that it was vaguely like an endless city in the Mediterranean, layers of whitewashed houses built up upon more and more layers of houses, rising up forever into a cobalt blue sky. There was the impression of a beautiful sea nearby, and a cool breeze wafted over my non-body.

For a nanosecond, it made sense. There was a click as all the pieces fell into place, a moment in which I understood everything. I thought, "So *that's* it! I get it!" Then, with a violent jolt – a kind of crash landing – I was back on the bed in my grandmother's living room. My heart had started again and beat in a steady rhythm.

I still remember understanding how everything fit together and meant something, but I can't summon the plan itself. The only thing I can say about it is that it was familiar. I already knew about it and was simply being reminded.

Though I forgot for a long, long time, I won't need reminding again.

Endnotes
[1] Barbara G. Walker, *The Women's Encyclopedia of Myths and Secrets* (Edison, New Jersey: Castle Books, 1996), pp. 79, 346.
[2] "Gore Vidal Quotes on Life and Sex," *The Gore Vidal Pages,* (accessed August 3, 2012).

Codas

There was a man and a woman
Who sinned.
And the man stood with her.
As upon her head, so upon his,
Fell blow and blow,
And all people screaming, "Fool!"
He was a brave heart.

The day my editor told me that this book would be sent to the printing presses at warp speed, it confirmed what the readers of Talkbass.com, Stephen Jay, Bryan Beller, Mike Keneally, Andy West, John Taylor, Gene Simmons, Scott Thunes, and so many others had told me: I was a good music journalist. Having my memoir published was the final affirmation that my three greatest accomplishments – my relationship with Carmen, my career in music journalism, and my ability to play the bass – were genuine, not fantasies of a fevered imagination. They were brief spans in which the twilight lifted and I walked with Saint Michael the Archangel.

My losses being verified as real allowed me to give the departed a proper sendoff at last. Though I miss them, I now feel only contentment that they were once in my life, not grief and anger that they're gone.

I contacted Scott Thunes and asked if he'd like to be included in my memoir; he agreed without hesitation. Then I offered to give him the manuscript to look over before I submitted it, exactly as I'd done when I was a music journalist. He was reluctant, saying he didn't want to interfere with how I told my story, but I informed him that it was my vision as the creator of this particular art project that he provide input. He eventually agreed that it would be a good idea for him to check what I wrote.

And now, Scott's comment on my video of me playing Gentle Giant's "Mobile."

> Well, I certainly am glad I saw that, finally, after all these years. I remember us learning it to play it. I, taking my time, looked at it two days before our talk and went "uh, no." You, on the other hand, spent your time shredding the hell out of it and making it talk. I apologize for not allowing you to fulfill your public duties as ripping this one out in front of our audience, but they wouldn't have appreciated it anyway, amirite? So, job very well done, and thank you for posting!

Some people will understand why I needed to hear that, and they'll fully appreciate the gift of freedom Thunes gave me. If you could comprehend how hard it is for me to accept both praise and criticism, you'd immediately grasp the reason I demanded he tell me his opinion publicly. I'll confess now that I knew he wouldn't tell me I sucked. Anyone who can play Ray Shulman doesn't suck. Besides, Scott isn't a cruel man. He told me the key to understanding him in 1997. It's right here in this book, as I'm sure most of you have already discovered.

On September 7, 2012, I got together with Scott for the first time in twelve years. We met at a restaurant in Hermosa Beach, before the Mother Hips played at Saint Rocke. When Scott saw me, he leapt to his feet, said, "Oh, you smart, thoughtful *angel!*" and hugged me tightly. A week earlier he'd told me that he appeared on page 90 of the October 2012 issue of *Bass Player*. It was an article about the taking of the exceptional photo of him that accompanied my piece "Requiem for a Heavyweight?" Since Bryan Beller is also on the cover of that issue, I did something for the first time in over a decade: I bought a copy of the magazine.

The conversation in Hermosa Beach mirrored the one Scott and I had on October 6, 1996, the day he entered my life. We fell right into discussing our favorite topics of music, movies, art, and weirdness. It was as though we'd never been apart. In many ways, we hadn't. The only change was that this time he briefly quizzed me about my illness, smiled and laughed a lot, and no longer had the edge of anger he'd displayed when I knew him before. He said he'd become the "indispensable man" in putting people at ease and making them feel better. It was true. He went out of his way to interact with the wait staff and manager, introducing himself and complimenting them on their service. The entire time we talked, he didn't scowl once. He showed me photos of his beautiful children and gorgeous wife on his iPad, and he told... *stories*. Great ones that I won't repeat because he needs to put them in his own book, which he *will* write before I die, or I swear I'll become an honest-to-God ghost – a macabre phantasm – and haunt him with moans and clanking chains.

"*Oooooooooooooo, Scott Thuuuunes! Youuuu shouuuuld've wriiiitten that booooooook! Looooooook what youuuu did to meeeeeeee!*"

After dinner we took our conversation outside as we walked the great distance back to the club, another echo of our first meeting. I told him I'd always thought I was a failure at everything, but I recently concluded that I was successful at surviving. Scott vehemently disagreed.

"You are a giant, huge-ass, explosively world-destroying success because you're *happy!*" he shouted as he reached out and gently rested his hand on my back for a moment. I remembered who else used to do that: Syd the Second. It's a complex gesture that serves several functions for both parties. Like Syd, Scott seems to have prevailed.

The show was great. It was, in fact, the first time I saw Scott perform in person. I was about ten feet away, so I was able to study his technique closely. He'd told me his biggest influence is Jimmy Page, which is clearly the case in that Scott's fingering is identical. It's a sort of flapping motion, the fret hand doing hammer-ons for every note. Some bassists keep their fingers as close as possible to the fretboard, barely moving them. Scott's approach resembles impatient tapping on a tabletop.

He alternated between pizzicato and a plectrum, sometimes within the same measure, accomplishing the switch by palming the pick in his right hand or tucking it in his mouth so quickly that I didn't notice when he'd made the change. He generated a massive variety of sounds and dynamics by simply adjusting his attack. Often he swung his pick hand in an arc over a foot wide, but he still hit the strings exactly where he wanted. He didn't play a single sour note even though he improvised all night as he took cues from his band mates.

Within the parameters of the bass line, he adds ornamentation that makes each performance unique. He never plays a song the same way twice. I saw a legendary bassist do a solo in 1988; to this day, he still presents audiences with the identical piece, note for note. Thunes is in a different dimension. He dwells entirely in the present, expressing what he feels at that moment. His entire body of live work is one endless solo. He's without question the most creative, elemental, and emotional bassist I've ever seen. What I found amazing is that while he played all over the neck, he rarely looked down at the fretboard. Stylistically, he has no peers. He's his own invention. If I had to describe his artistry in one word, it'd be "intimate": He has absolute connection with music, his bass, and people, one of the reasons he haunted me for so long. In all the important ways, he's achieved that which has eluded me.

I hope to see him perform again someday because it was truly extraordinary. It's not lost on me that I experienced Scott Thunes playing the bass only after I'd junked my toxic worldview. Whether the opportunity was happenstance, consequence, or reward, I'm grateful.

The ninety-minute trip to Hermosa Beach had wiped me out, proving that I'm now officially disabled. It was the longest drive I'd undertaken in a year, and it was simply too much. The photos of the evening show me trying desperately to not throw up even though I enjoyed every second with my former Collateral Ghost. When Scott and I had arrived at Saint Rocke after our long walk from the restaurant, I lost my balance and nearly fell on my face.

Quick as a ninja, Scott caught me and said to the doorman, "He's all right. He's with me."

• • •

In asking Carmen for permission to write about her, I offered the same deal I had to Scott. I'd show her the finished manuscript before I submitted it, and she'd have complete kill rights. In her case, though, I'd write only about our time together, not about her life before or after I knew her unless it was to quote her own words. She could also choose her pseudonym if she wanted. It was to be a narrative, not an exposé. We'd leave out much more than we included. Even so, it would take a lot of courage for her to give me her blessings and participate. I'd ask her to approve passages that would be extremely hard for her to read, but they were part of our history. Despite the moments of darkness and total misery I'd relate, the book would ultimately be an homage. It might not seem that way at first; she'd have to trust me one last time.

She responded immediately.

Hey, Tom.

You have my full permission to freely use in your memoir what I said, did, symbolized, etc., to you. Memoirs have been my favorite reading material these past few years.

This all sounds amazing. I'd love to read any excerpts containing my ghost ANYTIME. Thank you for offering. I promise not to interfere too much.

I'm still thinking about what struck you so powerfully about my comments on smiling (or rather, NOT smiling). I never said smiling was prohibited. I just HATE when people POSE for pictures and think they have to bare their teeth! I fully believe in catching people in natural action. In fact, when I take pictures of groups of people, I pretend to take the picture and then I actually start taking shots after my fake click.

Here I am showing teeth while playing out late last year. I joined a songwriting circle in 2001 and have been writing a lot and performing occasionally since then. A friend asked if I would share a gig with her so I hired a drummer and we did a 17 original song set – bold and satisfying.

BRAVO on the book deal!!!!

C.

"BRAVO" was written in letters over an inch high.

Attached to this message was a photo of her playing acoustic guitar and singing at a microphone in public. Smiling. I had no idea that she'd gotten back into making her own music; as far as I knew, she'd stopped in 1994. The image evoked in me a single, pure, uncomplicated emotion, which I hadn't associated with her in over twenty years.

Joy.

Bibliography

Books

Blunden, Edmund. *Undertones of War.* New York: Harcourt, Brace, and World, Inc., 1928.

Walker, Barbara G. *The Women's Encyclopedia of Myths and Secrets.* Edison, New Jersey: Castle Books, 1996.

White, E. B. *Charlotte's Web.* New York: HarperCollins, 1952.

Wictor, Thomas. *German Flamethrower Pioneers of World War I.* Atglen, Pennsylvania: Schiffer Publishing, Ltd., 2007.

— *In Cold Sweat: Interviews with Really Scary Musicians.* New York: Limelight Editions, 2001.

Articles

Wictor, Thomas. "Andy West: How Not to Sell Out in One Easy Step." *Bass Player* January 1996: 48.

— "Unsung Bass Stylists: John Taylor with Duran Duran." *Bass Player* April 1994: 12.

Reviews

Watson, Ben. Review of *In Cold Sweat: Interviews with Really Scary Musicians,* by Thomas Wictor. *The Wire* September 2001: 83

Wictor, Thomas. Review of *Carnival of Souls: The Final Sessions,* by Kiss. *Bass Player* May 1998: 72.

Letters

Resnicoff, Matt. Letter. *Bass Player* September 1996: 6.

Wyzard, Michael. Letter. *Bass Player* May 1997: 6.

Online Sources

www.gorevidalpages.com
www.leslieditto.com
www.oneloveforchi.com
www.stephenjay.com
www.supotnitskiy.ru
www.talkbass.com

Communications with the Author

Beller, Bryan. Interview with author. March 28, 1995.

Cheng, Chi. Interview with author. November 6, 1996.

Kadrovich, Anne. Interview with author. November 20, 1997.

Smith, Curt. Interview with author. June 10, 1998.

Shulman, Ray. Interview with author. July 14, 1997.

Thunes, Scott. Interview with author. May 4, 1997.

Vincent, David. Interview with author. January 27, 2000.

Zlozower, Neil. Interview with author. October 23, 1997.

Discography

Jay, Stephen. *Presque Vu.* © 2012 by Ayarou Music (BMI). To be released. Compact Disc.

— *Sea Never Dry.* © 1997 by Ayarou Music (BMI). Ayarou 15126. Compact disc.

Index

Thomas Wictor is the author of five books. A failed music journalist, failed military historian, failed novelist, failed ghostwriter, failed biographer, failed poet, failed essayist, failed rock musician, failed miniaturist, failed photographer, failed field representative for a document-retrieval service, failed delivery driver, failed temp worker, failed voiceover actor, failed copyeditor, failed technical writer, failed editor of the world's first online newspaper, failed bartender, failed archivist, failed longshoreman, failed ladies' man, and failed ally, he is the planet's only expert on World War I flamethrowers. He lives happily by himself in Southern California.